THE
UNDISCOVERED
OCEAN
From Marco Polo to Francis Drake

The sea is a boundless expanse, whereon great ships look tiny specks; naught but the heavens above and the waters beneath; when calm the sailors heart is broken; when tempestuous, his senses reel. Trust it little, fear it much. Man at sea is an insert on a splinter, now engulfed, now scared to death.

A'mriban-al-As, general to the Caliph Omar I (581-644)

As for naval skills, they [the Spartans] will not find them easy to acquire. You yourselves have scarcely mastered them, having worked at them ever since the Persian war... Seamanship is an art like any other; it is not something which can be picked up in one's spare time, indeed, it leaves no leisure for anything else.

Pericles addresses the Athenians
Thucydides, *History of the War between Athens and Sparta I*, 142BC

THE

UNDISCOVERED
OCEAN
From Marco Polo to Francis Drake

ANTHONY DEANE

TEMPUS

In memory of Jean Mary,
with my love, as always.

First published 2005

Tempus Publishing Limited
The Mill, Brimscombe Port,
Stroud, Gloucestershire, GL5 2QG
www.tempus-publishing.com

British Library Cataloguing in Publication Data.
A catalogue record for this book is available from the British Library.

ISBN 0 7524 3561 2

Typesetting and origination by Tempus Publishing Limited
Printed in Great Britain

CONTENTS

ACKNOWLEDGEMENTS

Undertaking this book has been greatly facilitated by the generous cooperation of many persons. I wish to express my heartfelt thanks to the officers and staff of the Argentine Navy. In particular, Contraalmirante Héctor Agustín Tebaldi, secretary general of the Argentine Navy, for his invaluable assistance; Contraalmirante Jorge Duhalde, director of the Educational Department of the Argentine Navy for information regarding Patagonia and Antartica; Capitán de Fragata Guillermo Andrés Oyarzábal, head of the Historical Branch of the Argentine navy, for pointing me in the right direction during my investigations of Vespucci, Magellan, and Drake; and Capitán de Navío Valladares, head of the Argentine Center of Naval Hydrographic Studies in Buenos Aires. I also wish to thank members of the Chilean Navy for their help and kindness.

I am grateful also to Elsie Krasting de Rivero Haedo, prominent Argentine author and historian, better known to the reading public by her pen name, Virginia Carreño, for accepting with grace my invitation to write the Foreword to this book. To Isabel Cáceres, cartographer of the Argentine Naval Hydrographic Center, for the excellent charts and maps she drew for this book, as well as Waldemar Cáseres, draftsman from Maldonado, Uruguay, for his fine drawings and illustrations. To Soledad Hernández Montañés, a dear colleague and friend, for her support throughout and her superb translation of the text of this book into Spanish – a repeat performance, after having translated my earlier work, *Nelson's Favourite: HMS Agamemnon at War 1781–1809*. And to Mercedes Christopherson for her help throughout, and Jennifer Feeley of San Francisco, who with her superb command of the language, her thoughtful comments, and much appreciated encouragement, helped me construct the manuscript. She has my most profound gratitude. To Irma Criseo, my secretary of thirty-five years, and Emmanuel Beraldi, for their steady, silent help and support, as well as many others who have read these pages, commented on them, and contributed in their own special ways. To all, I express my deepest gratitude.

FOREWORD

Anthony Deane, a writer born in London and brought up in Argentina, delights in anything to do with the sea. He might have followed a career in naval architecture, like his sixteenth-century ancestor, Sir Anthony Deane, the first scientific naval architect on record and designer of ships for Charles II, but circumstances intervened that drew him to the life of an 'estanciero' of the Pampas. Nevertheless, alongside this working attachment to the land, his hobby since boyhood has been to sail. He defied the treacherous waters of the Rio de la Plata and Southern Atlantic and became, I have heard, an exemplary Commodore of the Yacht Club of Punta del Este, a peninsula that over the centuries beakoned a refuge to navigators from Spain, Portugal, Italy, Holland, and England. Many of these bold adventurers have left their bones strewn on the bottom of the sea, together with their ships, lost to the soft sands that extend the length of the Banda Oriental and dance with the winds and tides, forming secret mountains on the sea bed, entrapping even the most astute navigators. Old salts that fish that coastline for a living occasionally bring up pieces of the wrecks of those ships: shards of crockery, cordage, pieces of glass, beams, bronzes.

When he writes, Deane does not dramatise events; he documents. He travels, studies, sails, delves into ancient documents, compares them to others, and spends hours in archives gathering the material he needs. He discovers not only the details of the battles of a given ship, but also the reasons and context that caused them. In his first book, *Nelson's Favorite: HMS Agamemnon at War 1781–1809*, he compiles an exhaustive historical study of the British Navy, while following the spirit of the ship from her day of launching until she foundered in Maldonado Bay in June 1809. To launch the book, two admirals of the Royal Navy honoured him with a banquet, held in the great stern cabin of the HMS *Victory*, Nelson's flagship at Trafalgar.

An avid pursuer of knowledge and born traveller, Deane straddles divergent worlds, in life and in prose: nautical and agricultural, British and Argentine, the Rio de la Plata viewed and inhabited from both sides. He brings to life real people from history with singular poetic vision, illuminating their great historic moments. In the book you are about to read, Deane widens his scope geographically, researching the early navigators of the New World: Italians, Spaniards, Portuguese, and English. To measure them in their true dimensions, he salvages each small incident and weaves them together. It is the work of a miniaturist, a calligrapher working on some great heroic canvas.

Undiscovered Ocean is made up of nineteen chapters of well-documented history, but so intensely interesting that one reads each like a separate novel. It opens by telling us of the early voyages to the Far East, in search of the source of herbs that had become staples to cooks and apothecaries as well as a valuable currency for many cultures of the time. Further on, he tells us of the travels of Marco Polo and the commercial route from the Mediterranean to China, preparing the reader for the great adventure of the discovery of America. Deane steps into the boots of these early navigators, conveying to us men made of bone, muscle, and sinew, whose complex humanity we can feel and understand. They endured lengthy voyages, lived under miserable conditions, suffered privations and hunger, faced winds, storms and muti-nies, improvised and made mistakes, and sometimes behaved unjustly. But above all, they were capable of great deeds. The merit of this book is in chronicling and bringing to life the spirit of these extraordinary men. Five centuries after the discovery of the New World, we share the experience of Columbus, Vespucci, Vasco da Gama, D'Alburquerque, Balboa, Magellan, Elcano, Francis Drake and many others, who with infinite genius and courage opened up the Occident and founded our Americas.

Virginia Carreño★
Buenos Aires

★Virginia Carreño is well known throughout South America and abroad as an historian, author and lecturer.

PROLOGUE

When Juan Sebastián Elcano led his little band of eighteen Christians and three natives, barefoot, emaciated, and carrying lighted candles, through the streets of Seville to the great cathedral of Santa Maria in 1522, the astonished and disbelieving inhabitants could not have grasped the full import of their incredible journey – that the earth is a sphere, and that this little bunch of ruffians travelled around it. Only a small elite of radical scholars understood the Ptolemaic concept of the spherical earth at that time. Yet this dilapidated crew, survivors of the expedition started by Magellan and completed by Elcano, turned that Ptolemaic concept into experiential fact. They also proved that the world's wild oceans, which threatened a thousand monsters and terrors for navigators in their diminutive ships, were navigable after all, and were a path to glory for those with the courage to conquer them.

You will read here some of the first intrepid voyages which initiated the era of discovery, an era that lasted five centuries and only came to an end in the mid-nineteenth. It was a magnificent era, one of the most exciting and demanding in history, pitting man not only against the bitter elements but also the constant challenge of survival. For instance, the limitations of space in ships' holds for storing victuals and water were always of critical concern, especially when sailing into the unknown. The line, 'Water, water everywhere, nor any drop to drink', as Samuel Taylor Coleridge put it, was never more true. The range of a sailing ship depended on variable factors: the compliment of officers and seamen, how climate affected the consumption of water and victuals, the speed of the ship, and the distance to the next port of call, if it were known at all, which was not always the case. Add to this the most essential ingredient of human prowess, without which they were doomed from the start: superb mastery of the winds and the stars and experienced knowledge of deep-water sailing.

During those 500 years when man possessed himself of his own planet – to which we could add 200 more if we reach back to Marco Polo – these great discoverers 'put a girdle round about the earth'. Some, like Magellan, perished in the attempt. Most contributed to mapping the world's remoter regions. Almost all of them left a record of their experiences, though sadly not all of those records survive. Their stories are fascinating, not only for their battles with the sea and encounters with strange peoples and places, but because their narratives reveal so much about themselves – what inspired them, be it spices or gold – and how they prepared, how they raised the money, how they handled subordinates, how they stood up to those who threatened their command and the many other crises that arose. Men living in cramped conditions and exposed at close quarters to the relentless elements for long periods of time build up tensions almost insurmountable for commanders to handle. It is always instructive to learn the various ways the human spirit reacts when pressed to the limits, for it is a spirit we all share.

Among the countless courageous navigators who opened up the world for us, Columbus, Vespucci, Vasco da Gama, and Magellan were the most renowned.

When we bring these early discoverers into focus, they emerge larger than life and as varied, determined, and valiant as ever history conjured, the stories of their personal hopes and dreams providing a poignant human backdrop to their momentous discoveries. They were not interested in exploration for its own sake. Their main interest, and the task entrusted them by the rulers and investors who sent them out, was to link Europe with other areas believed to be of economic importance. And not always sterling of character in terms of Christian virtues, most were urged on by visions of personal profit, long before the commercial exploitation of oil or drugs seen in their counterparts of today.

I have included the story of the Polos – and their twenty-four years of travel, ending with Marco's return in 1292 by sea from China to Persia – because it is the earliest recorded major seagoing voyage in history. I have also asked some unfamiliar questions: Why didn't the Chinese 'discover' Europe or America? Or did they? Why didn't the Arabs circumnavigate Africa and the world? Why was the discovery process of civilisation so slow in coming? And why did it take so long for people to learn that the earth goes around the sun? This is a story without an end. There is much that is still *terra incognita*, unknown territory. My focus remains on humankind's need to know – to know what is out there. There is so much more to bring to light.

I have striven to combine the knowledge revealed by the research of many scholars. In recent years, new material has been discovered in every field, and the effect has been to recast and revolutionise some parts of the story, modifying considerably our view of the whole. I have indicated in footnotes my debt to those whose labours have rendered possible the writing of these events, which I hope find a new immediacy and a new audience through this account.

Anthony N Deane
Estancia 'El Patacón'
Ameghino, Argentina

1

PATHS TO THE
ENCHANTED ORCHARD

Over the Eastern Oceans cast your eyes,
To see where islands numberless are spread:
Tidore, Ternate, view mountains whence arise
Flames undulating round the burning head:
Trees of hot clove thou shall behold, likewise,
With blood of Portugal e'en purchased;
Here are the golden birds, who ne'er descend
On earth, while living, but when life doth end.

Luis de Camões, Os Lucsiadas (1572)

Long ago and far to the east, beyond Baghdad and Calicut, beyond even Malacca and Peking, lay the fabulous isles, unknown to the great cartographers, where no vessel from the Christian world had ever arrived. Winged serpents, fierce gryphons and legendary monsters guarded their coasts and in the middle of an impenetrable forest reposed an enchanted orchard. The garden of the spices.

Camphor and cardamom, incense, myrrh and cinnamon, cloves, mace, ginger and nutmeg grew in fertile profusion in this garden, cultivated by celestial gardeners. Such were the Spice Islands, as fruit of the imagination of a medieval traveller.

The magic words which spoke of distant lands, of great voyages to the ends of the world, of unknown perils, and of fabulous monsters, went straight to the hearts of the men of that age and made them forget, far more than any economic argument could, the exorbitant prices that were charged for the spices from such a distant paradise. It was no wonder that the consumers remained content and the merchants were honest in their dealings. It only required a little imagination, and a portion of mystery and oriental enchantment to invest nutmeg and cloves, cinnamon and mace, with magic powers over body and mind.[1]

Even the most ignorant of servants in the castle kitchens knew the value of spices. Scarcely any food or drink was served without first being generously spiked, sifted, sprinkled, stuffed or larded with aromatic herbs. The apothecaries in their round, or sugar-loaf hats, made their fortunes through the spice-merchants. In addition to the bloodlettings and the purgatives, a few grains of hot pepper helped the sick to regain consciousness. Those who recovered fell on their knees in thanksgiving. Their gratitude echoed back, over the Red and Yellow Sea, to the Spice Islands whence the remedies had come. How could one ever think of hesitating to pay a little more for these exotic fruits, berries and barks, whose effects were so stimulating, relaxing and erotic? There were also other good reasons for this. Food was often so stale as to be almost rotten; it needed to be pounded and then disguised by strong spices or cheered up with colouring. The golden yellow of saffron and turmeric were the favourites, but medieval cooks also brightened their drab purées with sandalwood (for red), herbs (for green), and mulberries (for blue). Also, then as now, there was food snobbery. A pound of saffron cost as much as a horse and nutmeg was worth seven fat oxen per pound.[2] Encouraged by gourmets and doctors, the merchants did not lag behind in meeting the demand. At Venice, Marseilles, Barcelona, Bruges, London, Lubeck, Bergen and Novgorod, the spices were imported and marketed. From markets held during Venetian fairs, German merchants – the famous 'Tedeschi' – carried the goods across the Brenner and Saint Gotthard passes to ensure their distribution to the great commercial cities of Northern Europe.

Doctors of the seventeenth century made extravagant claims to the efficacy of nutmeg. They attributed that it could cure everything from the plague to the 'blody flux', a virulent and dangerous strain of dysentery. Others claimed it to be a powerful aphrodisiac, to the extent that Charles Sackville, styled Lord Buckhurst, jokingly, was known to say that Julius Caesar's libido was so poor that Cleopatra, even with the aid of 'nutmeg, mace and ginger' upon her 'Roman lover' would have failed to stir his loins.

In the case of His Lordship, however, his love of similar ingredients had the opposite effect for he knew that a spoonful of nutmeg before bedtime caused him to have a whole cluster 'of sweet, if troublesome dreams'. Buckhurst's addiction to nutmeg was to prove his ruin, however. His neighbour, Samuel Pepys, recorded how he was imprisoned for indecent exposure after running up and down all night almost naked through the street: 'This day Pierce doth tell me, among other news, the late frolic and Debauchery of Sir Ch. Sidly and Buckhurst, running up and down all the night with their arses bare through the streets, and at last fighting and being beat by the watch and clapped up all night.'[3]

On the other hand, Andrew Borde's *Dyetary of Helth*, an extremely popular book at the time, declared that nutmeg dampened sexual desire. However, it had failed to work on him, for this celibate former monk died in disgrace. 'Under the colour of virginitie and of wearing a shirt of hair, [he kept] three whores at once in his chamber... to serve not only himself but also help the virgin priests about the country.' Borde of all people should have stuck to taking nutmeg to subdue his sexual appetite but, as he wearily admitted, 'it is hard to get out of the flesh what is bred in the bone'.[4]

Nutmeg functioned as both an aphrodisiac and a hallucinogen as well as a condiment, while ginger, cinnamon, and pepper were especially prized as preservatives. Tacitus informs us that after murdering his wife, Poppaea, in AD65, Nero used a year's supply of Rome's cinnamon to bury her. A pound of ginger was worth a sheep in the middle ages, while a similar weight of mace could buy three sheep or half a cow. Pepper was counted out berry by berry by the merchants and was almost priceless. It could be used to pay taxes, rents, and dowries. Nor did these attributes lessen over the years before the invention of artificial refrigeration in the mid-nineteenth century.[5]

Nutmeg, the seed of the tree, was the most coveted luxury in seventeenth-century Europe; a spice that held such powerful medicinal properties that men would risk their lives to acquire it. Always costly, it rocketed in price when the physicians of Elizabethan London claimed that their nutmeg pomanders were the only certain cure for the plague, that 'pestiferous pestilence that started with a sneeze and ended in death'. Overnight it became as sought after as gold.[6] Perhaps, though it may not be specifically comparable, we can find some similarity with the drug traffic of today, when enormous sums of money are generated every trip, if successful. In a comparative way, it serves to illustrate the driving force behind the motivation of the early navigators to launch their ships into an unknown sea full of storms and monsters, regardless of the risks they knew it could entail.

The plague was the most serious threat to human life in the middle ages, periodically banished but not vanquished until much later. Its worst outbreak, from 1346 through 1349, claimed 25 million lives, or roughly one third of the population of Europe, North Africa, and the Middle East, with the dreadful habit of returning to one region or another every few years. It presented itself as a swelling of the lymph nodes under the arms or between the thighs. These large, painful, puss filled lumps, known as buboes, gave this pestilence its name, 'bubonic plague'. Ranging in size from almonds to oranges, they were the focus of treatment by doctors, whose pet remedies ranged from burning the buboes with incandescent gold or iron, then covering the wound with cabbage leaves, when not by a quartered pigeon or a plucked rooster. Left alone, the buboes enlarged each day only to burst on their own, causing such agony as to rouse the nearly dead to frenzy. Clutching at any suggestion of remedy, it is no wonder that the price of nutmeg rose to the heavens when it was said to be the certain cure.

It took until the seventeenth century for Europeans to have gained sufficient experience with the pestilence to recognise that the accumulation of dead rats in

Nutmeg traders to the Banda Islands, 1559.

Left and right: The nutmeg tree only grew in the Banda Islands in Elizabethan times. Its fruit was belived to cure the 'sweating sickness'.

Cameline, a French sauce from the Middle Ages, was a mixture of cinnamon, ginger, cloves, grains of paradise, mace, pepper and bread soaked in vinegar.

the streets and houses might be the cause of the disease. However, the fact remained elusive as people preferred to blame the plague on miasmas of swampy air, the full moon, conjunctions of the planets, famine and fate, beggars and prostitutes, even Jews. It would be 200 years until Alexandre Yersin, a French bacteriologist of the Pasteur Institute, identified the germ theory of the disease in 1894. No one realised then that microbes living in and upon the ubiquitous rats caused it. Rats that lived and travelled with impunity on land and aboard ship, exporting the plague as far as rats could run.[7]

To supply the western markets, whole fleets plied back and forth between Aden, Muscat, Ormuz and the Far East. At the same time the great overland caravans, numbering sometimes as many as 4,000 camels, crossed the vast Asian wastes along several routes that are known collectively as the Silk Road, laden with cloves, pepper, cinnamon, silks and gold. These priceless commodities of long-distance trade found markets from China, all the way to Europe via Babylon, Carthage, Alexandria and Rome.

From port to port, and town to town, the merchandise rose in price as it was taxed in succession by emirs, caliphs, and sheiks. A conservative estimate is that they rose in value 100 per cent each time they changed hands. At last, having crossed Anatolia or the Red Sea, the spices were delivered by Muslim merchants to such ports as Constantinople or Alexandria, from whence Genoese or Venetian ships carried it on the last leg of the journey to Western Europe.

The Arabs' monopoly had strengthened during Europe's Dark Ages. After the fall of Rome had left much of Europe to languish in darkness, a young camel driver named Mohammed, from Mecca, on the eastern shore of the Red Sea, had been fortunate enough to marry the widow of a wealthy spice merchant. He was a religious visionary of a new faith known as Islam (literally, 'submission'). Mohammed realised that faith and trade were not exclusive one of the other. While Europe languished in idleness until the tenth century, and Venice emerged under new winds of trade, Mohammed and his followers spread Islam to the East, reaching the Malay Archipelago in the thirteenth century.

As Venetian galleys sailed laden with sacks of spices, Europe remained ignorant of their origins, while Muslims knew them only too well.[8]

Christendom felt certain bitterness at having to submit to the frontier tolls and charges exacted by paganism, neither religious faith nor the dictates of trade could make any headway against the problem.[9] Only the Venetian republic was able to profit from all these transactions. On the one hand it kept control of the monopoly upon the distribution of goods from Islam; on the other, it derived great benefit from the contracts negotiated with the crusaders to bring them to the Holy Land, between 1096 and 1291. Their miserable fate is well known. Their vast armies eight times defeated, decimated, fighting in the desolation and the heat of the desert, to the final tragedy of the capture of Constantinople, the last bastion of Christianity in the Middle East, by the Turks in 1453.[10]

By the time Marco Polo made his first voyage to China in 1271, Venice's monopoly on spices was complete; however, no one from the West had ever visited the countries from which these spices originated. Marco was the first European to describe the clove tree, 'a little tree with leaves like laurel', but his claim to have seen one in mainland China owes more to his imagination than to reality, for unbeknown to the Venetians the tree could only be found on a handful of islands in the Indonesian archipelago.

These islands, over 100 of them, known as 'Spiceries', or the Moluccas, were scattered over an area of ocean more than half the size of Europe. Although these days they form a single province of Indonesia called Maluku, they fall into three distinct groups. To the north lie the volcanic islands of Tidore, Ternate, Moti, Makian, and Bacan, where clove trees – *Eugenia aromatica* – are native. Then some 400 miles to the south are the islands of Amboyna and Ceram, craggy and harsh, whose sweet smelling cloves had also been appreciated since antiquity.

The clove tree is an evergreen that grows to between 6m–12m tall, with small and simple leaves. Flowering begins about the fifth year and may yield up to 34kg of dried buds. These are handpicked twice a year and then sun-dried. As early as 200BC, envoys from Java to the Han-dynasty court of China, brought cloves with them that were customarily held in the mouth to perfume the breath during audiences with the emperor. During the late middle ages, cloves were used in Europe to preserve, flavour, and garnish food. At a much later date the Dutch eradicated cloves on all islands except Amboyna and Ternate in order to create scarcity and sustain high prices but in the latter half of the eighteenth century the French smuggled clove plants from the East Indies to Indian Ocean islands and the New World, breaking the Dutch monopoly.

Further south, almost in the crook of the arm of Ceram, though not affording them any protection from the monsoons, lie the richest and least accessible of them all, the Banda Islands. To get there needed a knowledgeable and courageous pilot at the tiller to steer a vessel through the treacherous waters that surround them. One of these islands is now the forgotten island of Run. In fact, it is of such insignificance today that it fails to be mentioned, or even figure, on the map of

The National Geographic Atlas of the world. It was not always ignored, however, as on maps of the seventeenth century it figures so large as to be quite out of proportion with those surrounding it. In those days, Run was the most talked about island in the world, a place that produced such fabulous wealth that the gold of South America seemed paltry by comparison.[11]

Nature bestowed upon the cliffs of Run a forest of natural trees surrounding its towering mountainous backbone; trees that gave off an exquisite fragrance that could be sensed from miles away. These trees grow up to 20m tall, are willowy in appearance, and have foliage like a laurel. They yield fruit when they are eight years old and carry on for sixty more or longer. They produce bell-shaped flowers that mature into fleshy lemon-yellow fruit, similar in appearance to an apricot. When fully mature the fruit splits in two, exposing a crimson-coloured aril, the mace, the cover skin surrounding a single shiny brown seed, which is the nutmeg – to the plain speaking – or *Myristica Fragrans*, to the botanist. The pulp of the fruit is eaten locally and after collection, the aril-enveloped nutmegs are conveyed to curing areas where the outer coating of Mace is removed, flattened out, and dried. The nutmegs are also dried gradually in the sun and turned twice daily over a period of six to eight weeks. During this time the nut shrinks away from its hard seed coat until the kernels rattle in their shells when shaken. The shell is then broken with a wooden mallet and the nutmegs are picked out. When dried, they are grayish-brown ovals with furrowed surfaces.[12] The Romans used it as incense. Later, the Dutch plotted to keep prices high and both the English and French counterplotted to obtain seeds to plant in other parts. This brought about the Dutch dipping the nutmegs in lime to prevent them sprouting.

It was the remoteness of the Banda Archipelago that protected the nutmeg from depletion. In the East Indies where spices grew like weeds, nutmeg was very rare; a tree that needed such a precise micro-climate to grow that it had found it's requirements only on the tiny cluster of the Banda Islands. It was further protected by rumours circulated by the Arabs of a monster that preyed on passing ships, a creature of 'devilish possession that lurked in hidden reefs'; by stories of cannibals; bloodthirsty savages that lived in palm-tree shacks adorned by human heads. There were stories of hungry crocodiles lurking in rivers; of hidden shoals, and 'such mighty storms and extreme gusts of wind, that even the sturdiest of vessels were placed in grave risk'. In fact, had these difficulties relating to reaching the source of the nutmeg been known in Western Europe, perhaps the explorers might have thought twice about setting sail for the islands?[13]

An English knight who claimed to have served the Great Khan of Cathay and the Sultan of Egypt during his travels between 1322 and 1356 wrote a best seller of medieval times, *The Travels of Sir John Mandeville*. In his book he perpetuated the views of the wondrous East with the teachings of the Bible in mind. The narrative, a mixture of thoughts of everyday life and grotesque accounts of monster races, became very influential among those who read it as with mapmakers of the time, because it was widely read. Atlases that relied upon the

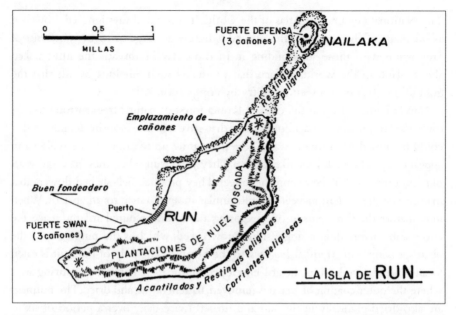

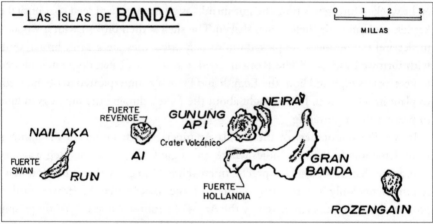

information brought back by Marco Polo and Oderic of Portenone incorporated both the mythical and the real peoples, and of course geography, which is illustrated in the drawings surrounding maps of the time.

There also existed another obsession, deeply rooted in the Christian tradition: on the eve of the age of discovery there was an accepted belief in Europe that the Garden of Eden was truly a place that lay in Asia. Handed down from the Middle Ages, it impelled Columbus, who wrote to the sovereigns of Spain after his third voyage to the New World, saying 'There are great indications of this being the terrestrial paradise, for its site coincides with the opinion of the holy and wise theologians… all of whom agree that the earthly paradise is in the East.' This image, like those of the Holy Grail, became a driving force for many an early navigator.

The association of Eden with the East was strong enough to be embraced by the Church as an ecclesiastical certainty and by the common people as well, in what

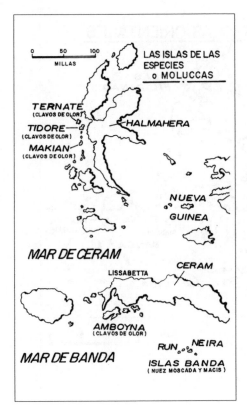

Previous page, this page and overleaf: A selection of maps showing the exotic destinations of the early explorers: the island of Run, the Banda islands and the islands of the Philipines, New Guinea, Sumatra, Timor, Java and Borneo.

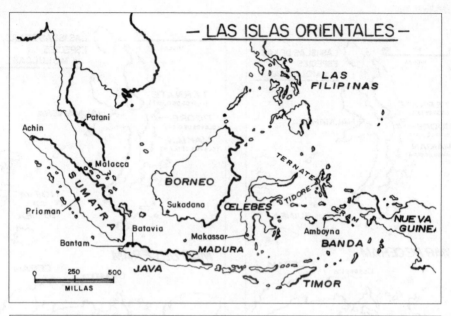

became known the Prester John legend. In 1144 a bishop claimed to have met a man known as Prester John who claimed to be the Christian king of an astonishingly wealthy land in Asia. The claim was substantiated around 1165 in a letter (later found to be a forgery) from this alleged ruler. Addressed to Immanuel I, emperor of Byzantium, it read in part: 'I Prester John, who reign supreme, surpass in virtue, riches, and power all creatures under heaven. Seventy kings are our tributaries... For gold, silver, precious stones, ani-mals of every kind, and the number of our people, we believe there is not our equal under heaven.... Every month we are served in rotation by seven kings, sixty-two dukes, and 265 counts and marquises... And if we have chosen to be called by a lower name and inferior rank, it springs from humility. If indeed you can number the stars of heaven and sands of the sea, then you may calculate the extent of our dominion and power.'

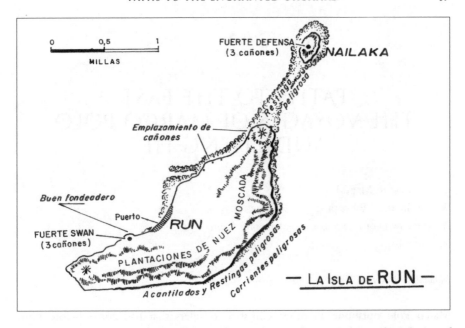

Thus inspired, several travellers, among them Marco Polo and Oderic of Pordenone, searched for this ruler. A few claimed to have found him among Christian Turkish tribes in central Asia. Though it seemed doubtful, the legend seized the European fantasy and no effort was spared to discover this land of wealthy Christendom among a territory of Muslims. By the fourteenth century, Prester John's kingdom was thought to be in Ethiopia. The Portuguese king, determined to seek him out, dispatched an envoy but though he found a Christian ruler, he was not the almighty one self-described in the famous letter. Some cartographers went as far as depicting the cleric on their charts. One, by Diogo Homem, dating from 1558, has among its pictorial details one of Prester John enthroned. This shows us how Europe's compulsion to reach the source of spices for the purpose of wealth was also driven by a strong compulsion of faith, a fearful mixture, as merchants, geographers, and seafarers pushed back the limits of the unknown.

In the two centuries that followed Marco Polo's return, in 1295, spices had become so popular that demand had far outstripped supply. Sufficiently adept in the art of making money, Venice's merchants knew that shortage meant high prices, and how to control the trade routes to retain their grip. Nevertheless, in 1499 a startling and unwelcome piece of news reached them: a small fleet of Portuguese ships commanded by Vasco da Gama had returned to Lisbon with a cargo of spices that had paid his expedition's costs sixty times over. Finally, the Portuguese reached the Spice Islands themselves during the closing days of 1511. After more than four centuries the Venetian monopoly had been broken and the spice race had begun. A trade that brought with it a tide of wealth that swept through a largely barbaric Europe. Cloves, nutmeg, mace, cinnamon, ginger and pepper gave birth to a new age of economics based on credit, to a new elementary banking system, and ultimately free enterprise.[14]

2
PATHS TO THE EAST
THE VOYAGES OF MARCO POLO
AND ZHENG-HE

On the road to Mandalay,
Where the flyin' fishes play,
An' the dawn comes up like thunder outer China
'crost the bay.

Mandalay, Rudyard Kipling (1865–1936)

Marco Polo outshone all other Christian travelers that had come before him. Franciscans friars had gone to Mongolia and back in under three years as missionary diplomats, but Marco Polo's journey lasted twenty-four years reaching beyond Mongolia to the very heart of Cathay. He crossed the whole of China all the way to the ocean to become the confidant of Kublai Khan, as well as governor of a Chinese city. Fluent, as he became, in the Tartar tongue, which he mastered in the course of his journeys, as well as a part of the daily life and culture of Cathay, his copious, vivid, and factual account of life, chronicled in his boldly titled *Description of the World*, became the most important source of knowledge of Asia to generations of Europeans, for over 200 years. It was, however, his return via Sumatra and India by sea from China to Persia, covering some 10,000 kilometres, to deliver a beautiful maiden of seventeen promised in marriage to Arghun Khan of Persia, that has the significance of being the earliest recorded major seagoing voyage in history – though the Norsemen of Norway were the earliest of the true explorers, little of their exploits were known to contemporaries and that little soon forgotten.[1]

Marco Polo was just fifteen years of age in 1269 when his father, Niccolò, and his uncle Maffeo, merchants of Venice, returned from their nine-year journey to the East. Another of Marco's uncles, also named Marco Polo, had trading operations in Constantinople and at Soldaia in the Crimea, where Niccolò and Maffeo had joined with him in his ventures. Young Marco Polo commences his own book with an account of his father's and uncle's travels, in which he took no part. In it he tells that Niccolò and Maffeo laid in a stock of jewels at Constantinople which they took by sea to Soldaia and from there north east along the Volga to the magnificent court of Barka Khan, the son of Genghis Khan, who not only treated them courteously and with honour, but bought their whole stock of jewels as well, as in the words of Marco 'causing the Brothers to receive at least twice its value'.[2]

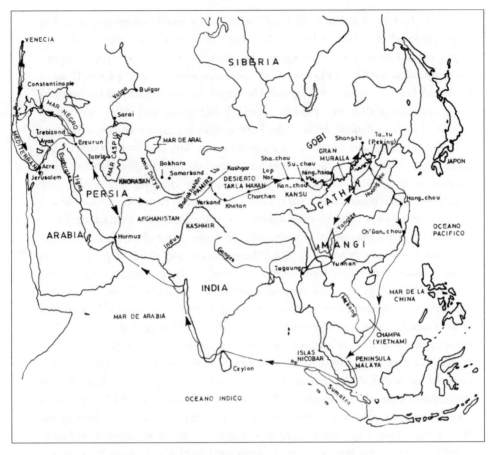

Marco Polo's route throughout Asia between the years 1271–1295.

A war broke out between Barka Khan and a rival Tartar prince that cancelled the Polo brothers return to Constantinople, causing them to take their trading ventures further eastward. Crossing the desert for seventeen days took them to Bokhara, where they fell in with some Tarter envoys that were on a mission to the court of the Great Khan, Kublai Khan. The envoys persuaded the Polos that 'Kublai Khan would be very desirous to meet them, and would treat them with great honour and courtesy', as he had never seen any Europeans before. With the promise that the envoys would guard them on the way, the brothers accepted the invitation. After a full year's journey, 'seeing many marvels of diverse and sundry kinds', they arrived at the court of Kublai Khan. The Great Khan proved every bit as friendly as promised and turned out to be an intelligent man of wide ranging curiosity, eager to learn everything about the West.[3]

Delighted by the Venetian brothers, he sent them back as ambassadors with gifts and letters to the pope, requesting he send him 100 missionaries educated in all the Seven Arts to teach his people about Christianity and western science. He also asked for some oil from the lamp burning at the Holy Sepulcher in Jerusalem. On arriving at Acre, in the Holy Land, in April 1269, the brothers learned that no new pope had been appointed after Pope Clement IV's death in 1268, so they went to see the Legate of the Roman Church in Egypt who resided in Acre – a wise priest of great authority called Tedaldo of Piacenza. They explained to him why the Great Khan of the Tartars had sent them to the Pontiff. The Legate listened intently to the brother's story, concluding that the mission would bring good and great honour to Christendom. 'Gentlemen', he said, 'the Pope is dead, but once a successor has been elected you will be able to take your mission to him.' The two brothers agreed and replied that while awaiting the election they would go and visit their families. They left Acre for Negropont where they boarded a ship and sailed for Venice.[4]

In Venice, Niccolò found that his wife had died, leaving their fifteen-year-old son Marco. After two years, the brothers resolved to start again for the East, taking young Marco with them, who was now seventeen and destined to make their trip historic. They went first to Acre to see the Papal Legate again, and asked his permission to go to Jerusalem to collect some of the oil from the lamp burning over Christ's sepulcher. When they returned, they went to the cardinal and said, 'We can see that the election of the new Pope is continually being delayed so we would like to return to the Great Khan, as we are beginning to feel that we have waited too long.'[5] The Papal Legate, who was one of the most important members of the Church of Rome replied that they should leave as soon as they were prepared for the trip. He then prepared letters to Kublai and references for Niccolò and Matteo. They had only just reached Ayas when they learned that their friend, Cardinal Visconti, had been elected Pontiff. Upon hearing this momentous news, they returned again to Acre in the Holy Land, where they went straight to visit him and prostrated themselves before him. Their friend, now Pope Gregory X, welcomed them with honour, blessed them and fêted their arrival. He prepared further letters for the Great Khan and sent him many gifts 'including objects made of crystal'. (Nice, handy items, to carry on a long horse and camel ride!)[6]

Pope Gregory X did not agree to sending the requested 100 missionaries but he did assign two Dominican friars, all the church could spare, to accompany the Polos who soon headed to Ayas once again,[7] where they discovered that the Sultan of Egypt, Bundukdari, had invaded Armenia, wreaking havoc with a huge army of 20,000 men. The Dominican friars took fright, and decided not to continue the journey. In Marco's account this seems not to have mattered much – suggesting that the Polos were more interested in profit and adventure than in propagating the faith. The friars handed all the Papal letters to Niccolò and Mateo and abandoning the Polos, turned back with the Grand Master of the Templars.[8] Now alone, the three Polos proceeded through Erzurum, towards the sunrise – as Marco called the east – to Tabriz, in the north-western corner of Iran. Tabriz was well known to contemporary Italian merchants, who coveted the 'goods that come there from strange lands', including 'precious stones ...found there in great abundance', probably imported from India and Sri Lanka. From Tabriz the Polos continued south, bound for the Persian Gulf, thinking they might find ships and arrange to sail to China.

Soon they reached the small city of Saveh, where Marco must have practiced his Persian. He says he had conversations about the three Magi, the wise men Balthazar, Gaspar, and Melchior, who went to Bethlehem to worship the infant Jesus. 'They repose in Saveh in three sepulchers very great and beautiful', he wrote, 'and the bodies, as if mummified, are still all whole and have hair and beards.' Though one doubts the story, perhaps Marco's collaborator, Rustichello, added the intact bodies in Saveh to make the text more vivid. In Marco's account, the wise men journeyed to Bethlehem with gifts – gold, incense, myrrh – where the baby Jesus gave them a stone. It signified that their faith should be strong, but they misunderstood and tossed it in a well. Then 'a burning fire came down from heaven straight to the well' and the Magi, realising that fire is holy, took it home to be kept eternally. And so, Marco concludes, 'is how fire came to be venerated in Persia.'

Later they joined a caravan as they started for Yazd, 310 miles to the south-east, crossing inhospitable deserts in Persia where there were 'many cruel people and murderers'. There were few towns, little water, and the landscape as monotonous as it is now – just high desert prickly with thorn bush. They must have been glad to see Yazd rising over the horizon. It was an oasis thanks to 'qanats', tunnels that brought water from the mountains miles away.

The Polos probably decided to go to China by sea after meeting Persian traders who had made the trip. The route was well established. It went to India, then to Zaiton or Quinsai in China. It seemed be quicker than the overland journey. But would it be safer? They discovered upon reaching Hormuz, at the mouth of the Persian Gulf, that 'their ships are very bad, and many of them are lost because they are not nailed with iron pins', Marco wrote. Rather, ship's planks were sewn in place with 'thread, which is made of the husks of nuts of Indie.' Of coconut fiber, in other words. After considering the dangers, instead they chose to go north and east overland, probably with another caravan, and traded their horses for camels, better suited to the arduous journey,[9] through deserts of surprising aridity toward the Khorasan region, what is now eastern Iran – I can imagine them loading their pack animals with bread, dried fruit, salted meat, and hard cheese to face the trip ahead. Turning gradually to the north-east they reached more hospitable lands in Afghanistan that pleased the travellers. There they came across the rubble of Balkh, which had once been numbered among the world's greatest cities, until Genghis Khan slaughtered the inhabitants during his Central Asian rampage in the 1220s.

'Ruined' describes Afghanistan today, after more than twenty years of war. Today most of Afghanistan is in the hands of the Taliban, or 'religious students', dominated by ultraconservative leaders, who effectively forbid education for women and sanction death by stoning for adulterers, while allowing their country to become the world's biggest supplier of opium. Their enemy, a more temperate regime whose military, called the northern alliance, clings to the northern part of Afghanistan. It is mostly an amalgamation of warriors who have survived Taliban onslaughts year after year.

The Polos continued into the frigid mountains of Badakhshân, noted for its rubies, lapis lazuli, 'the finest azure…in the world', and its fine horses. Marco tells us, 'there used to be horses here, which were directly descended from Alexander's horse Bucephalus, out of mares that had conceived from him and they were all born like him with a horn on their forehead.'[10] They stayed there a year to allow Marco to recover from a long illness, possibly malaria – that was cured by the benign climate of the district.

They continued up still higher, across the land of glaciers, ascending the upper Oxus with its many peaks over twenty thousand feet, through Wakhan to the plateau of Pamir, 'which the natives accurately called The Roof of the World. Wild game of every sort abounds. There are great quantities of wild sheep of huge size', Ovis Ammon Polli, the Marco Polo sheep. 'Their horns grow as much as six palms in length and are never less than three or four. From these horns the shepherds make big bowls from which they feed, and also fences to keep in their flocks. No birds fly here because of the height and the cold. And I assure you that, because of this great cold, fire is not so bright there nor of the same colour as elsewhere, and food does not cook well.' As the Polos ascended the Pamirs, they were not only physically on the roof of the world but in spirit as well. Beyond the Pamirs lay the desert, and beyond that awaited China – and seventeen years of adventure.

Descending from the cold Pamir flank, the Polos took the old caravan route through northern Kashmere, descending upon Kashgar, Yarkand and Khotan, regions that no European would see again until after 1860.[11]

They passed on to the vicinity of Lop-Nor and east to the edge of the desert that the Chinese call Gobi. They rested at Lop, a tiny town at the western edge of the desert, where travellers usually took on supplies and braced themselves against the terror of the crossing. They probably hired a couple of cameleers to help with their pack strings, and joined a caravan of traders who knew the location of the water holes.

> Beasts and birds there are none, because they find nothing to eat. But I assure you the one thing is found here, and that a very strange one, which I will relate to you.
>
> The truth is this. When a man is riding by night through this desert and something happens to make him loiter and lose touch with his companions, by dropping asleep or for some other reason, and afterwards he wants to rejoin them, then he hears spirits talking in such a way that they seem to be his companions. Sometimes indeed, they even hail him by name. Often these voices make him stray from the path, so that he never finds it again and in this way many travelers have been lost and have perished.[12]

A traveler half-crazed by thirst could go fatally astray while pursuing such a vision as Marco describes. The eerie sounds are said to be produced by moving sand or wind in the dunes.

They crossed the Gobi desert to the province of Tangut, in extreme north-western China, traversing the Mongolian steppes.[13] In his account of the Gobi, or the desert of Lop, as he calls it, Marco describes the barren waste, strikingly reproducing the description of the superstitious terrors of Suan Tsang, who crossed the desert 600 years before.

Marco seems most comfortable in writing about material things, such as fireproof cloth. 'I saw them myself', he said of the fibres, which were asbestos. Europeans believed the fibres came from an animal – a salamander – that lived in fire. Marco learned they were a mineral, mined in China. Another subject that called Marco's attention was sex. In a province near his route, he said, 'if when a man of this country sees that a stranger is coming to his house… he immediately walks out telling his wife to let the stranger have his will without reservation. Then he goes his way to his fields or vineyards and does not return so long as the stranger remains in his house. And I assure you that he often stays three days and lies in bed with this wittol's wife and does all he likes with her in bed.' He added that the women are 'fair, and gay and wanton'.[14] Marco does not say how he learned this but historians say the report rings true. Minority peoples had this custom. They thought outsiders were distinguished and would bring their family new blood and a better future.[15]

Early in 1275, after a trek of three and a half years, Kublai Khan cordially received the Venetians at the Mongol summer capital at Shang-tu, or Shangdu. It stood in a wide, shallow valley in what is now Inner Monglolia. The Polos had journeyed from Venice, 'Quite three years and a half: to kneel before Kublai.' He was, Marco told Europeans later, 'the most powerful man in people, in lands, and in treasure that ever was in the world. The greatest lord of lords of all the Tartars, the right noble Great Khan whose name is Kubilai' before whom they knelt and presented the sacred oil from Jerusalem and the letters from the pope. The twenty-one-year-old Marco made such a good impression on him that the Khan at once enlisted him in his service.[16]

About the time the Polos arrived in Shangdu, Kublai was finishing his new capital 200 miles south-east at Daidu, in the central part of what is now Beijing. Homes were heated with 'black stones… which burn like logs'. Marco says, 'Coal was so plentiful

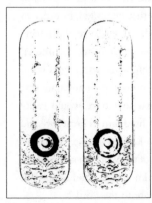

Mongol tablets with Uighur inscriptions found near the River Dnieper in 1845.

A fourteenth-century miniature showing the Great Khan giving a golden tablet of authority to the Polo brothers.

that everyone had a bath three times a week.' The large number of prostitutes – Marco mentions some 20,000 – could give one an estimate of Daidu's population.

He learned the languages of the Khan's subjects and was sent by him on a mission to a country six months away. During that expedition he travelled through the Shansi, Shensi and Szechuen provinces, and the wild country on the border of Tibet, to the province of Yunnan, called by the Mongols Karajang, as well as northern Burma. It is not so surprising to find the Polos in such favour with the Khan, as many foreigners were in the employ of the Mongol state that favoured them over the native Chinese, whom they mistrusted.

Marco observed the Khan's interest in strange countries, and his disgust at the stupidity of envoys and commissioners who could tell of nothing but their official business:[17]

> Now he had taken note on several occasions that when the Prince's ambassadors returned from different parts of the world, they were able to tell him nothing except the business on which they had gone, and that the Prince in consequence held them for no better than fools and dolts, and would say: I had far hearken about the strange things, and manners of the different countries you have seen, than hearing of the affairs of strange countries. Marco therefore, as he went and returned, took great pains to learn about all kinds of different matters in the countries that he visited, in order to tell about them to the Great Khan. Thereafter Messer Marco abode in the Khan's employment some seventeen years, continually going and coming, hither and thither, on the missions that were entrusted to him ... And, as he knew the sovereign's ways, like a sensible man, he always took much pains to gather knowledge of anything that would be likely to interest him, and then on his return to Court would relate everything in regular order, and thus the Emperor came to hold him in great love and favour .... And thus it came about that Messer Marco Polo had knowledge of, or had actually visited, a greater number of the different countries of the World than any other man; the more that he was always giving his mind to get knowledge, and to spy out and enquire into everything in order to have matter to relate to the Lord.[18]

The Great Khan was heard to say that only Marco Polo had learned to use his eyes. For three years, it is thought, Marco was named governor of Yang-chow, on another occasion he visited Kang-chow, the capital of Tangut, and perhaps Karakorum on the north of the Gobi, the former residence of the Great Khans. He was also present at Ciampa, or southern Cochin China, now Vietnam. Marco travelled the south-western Silk Road, as the Chinese now call that ancient route, known to the British and Americans as the famous Burma Road, the supply line for the allied and Chinese forces fighting the Japanese in World War II.

The Polos had become rich, and they began to dread what might follow Kublai's death. Their patron, now in his seventies, had become a gouty, alcoholic old man and Chinese resentment of the Mongol regime was growing. It was time to go home.

The Khan, however, was deaf to suggestions of their departure and the opportunity only came by chance. Arghun Khan of Persia, Lord of the Levant, and grandnephew of Kublai, in 1286 lost his favourite wife Queen Bulagan. Her dying request was that only a girl of her own Mongol tribe should fill her place. Arghun sent three emissaries, Ulatai, Abushka and Koja, with a large retinue to the Great Khan begging him to send a lady of the same lineage as Queen Bulagan. The Great Khan welcomed the three envoys with much festivity and then summoned a girl called Kokachin, a beautiful maiden of seventeen. However, the envoys could not escort her to Persia by land as fighting had broken out in Mongol fiefdoms along the way. They told Kublai that a sea voyage would be quicker and safer for the princess, than travelling by land.

At that time, Marco had just returned from an assignment to India and the Persian envoys, knowing the seafaring reputation of the Venetians, persuaded Kublai to allow the Polos to shepherd them across the sea. Kublai reluctantly acceded.

Top: The Khan's fleet sailing through the East Indies.

Middle: Medieval Tartar transportable wooden tents covered in felt.

Left: An ancient Chinese ship.

The Khan had fourteen ships outfitted out for the voyage with an entourage of 600 courtiers, 250 seamen, and supplies for two years. He gave the Polos friendly messages to the potentates of Christendom, including the pope, the kings of France, Spain, and England, as well as passports made from tablets of gold, that were granted to the Khan's emissaries known as tablets of authority, proclaiming in writing that they could travel freely throughout his domains and receive provisions for themselves and their attendants.

The fleet sailed from the port of Quanzhou (Zaiton). Many wonderful things lay ahead, not only 'all the doings of India…' but Sumatra and Siri Lanka as well. The homeward journey was going to be very terrible.

They sailed southward for three months, propelled towards the Equator by the north-east monsoon. The clumsy flotilla of fourteen junks, large ships for their time, 100ft long or more, with four masts and oars that took forty men to pull, crawled past Vietnam then Singapore. It took them three months to reach Sumatra. There they stayed five months as the north-east monsoon had died. 'The weather … did not let us go our way.' Since they were stuck there until the wind blew again from the north-east, Marco often visited the princess named Kokejin, the Blue Princess, because her name meant she was like the sky. After all, she had played a significant role in their liberation, inasmuch as Kublai finally had allowed the Polos to leave so as they could escort her to Persia.

Marco wrote he was much impressed by the fact that upon reaching Samudra – from which Sumatra derives – the North Star appeared to have dipped below the horizon. It was a matter that intrigued him. Sumatra was an insalubrious place. 'Rain comes down in buckets, up to eight feet of it per year and old Chinese records warn of malarious fevers.' Here may lie the clue to why only eighteen of the original 600 companions at the outset survived the two-year voyage. As well, the great Moroccan traveller Ibn Battuta, half a century later, says that while making his way from India to Sumatra, he saw two junks founder with great loss of life and he himself had to be rescued from his ship that also ran aground in a storm.

The fleet sailed on through the Strait of Malacca, passing the Nicobar Islands and touching land again at Ceylon, now Siri Lanka, before turning north up the west coast of India to the southern reaches of Persia. Finally, in 1293 or early 1294, the Polos at last reached Hormuz, where the Persian Gulf meets the Gulf of Oman.

On the long disastrous voyage, the Polos had 'saved and protected' the Mongol princess, while nearly all the royal attendants perished. However, in Hormuz they learned that Arghun, the ruler the princess was promised to, had died. She was given instead to his son Mahmüd Ghäzän, who at the time was with his army defending certain passes on the borders of Persia against enemy raids.

Of approximately 800 persons that had boarded the ships in China, Marco tells us that only eighteen survived. Of the three envoys, only Koja was saved, and out of the 100 women, there are conflicting reports, one version saying that only one died, another that only one survived – presumably the princess – at the end of

Left: Portrait of Kublai Khan, from a Chinese engraving.

Below: Medallions of Marco Polo and Kublai Khan.

the voyage. Sadly, there is no happy ending to the princess's odyssey; she was dead after less than three years in Persia, aged about twenty-two.

In his narrative, Marco gives an interesting account of the construction, and the sailing, of the Chinese ships. He tells us that:[19]

> They are built of the wood called spruce and fir. They have one deck; and above this deck, in most ships, are at least sixty cabins, each of which can comfortably accommodate one merchant. They have one steering-oar and four masts. Often they add another two, which are hoisted and lowered at pleasure. The entire hull is double thickness: that is to say, one plank is fastened over the top of another, and this double planking extends all the way round. It is caulked outside and in and the fastening is done with iron nails. Some of the ships, that is the bigger ones, have also thirteen bulkheads or partitions made of stout planks dovetailed into one another. This is useful in case the ships hull should chance to be damaged in some place by striking on a reef or being rammed by a whale in search of food – a not infrequent occurrence, for if a whale happens to pass a ship while she is sailing in the night and churning water to foam, he may infer from the white gleam in the water that there is food for him there and so charge full tilt against the ship and ram her, often breaching the hull at

some point. In that event the water coming in through the breach will run into the bilge, which is never permanently occupied. The sailors promptly find out where the breach is. Cargo is shifted from the damaged compartment into the neighboring ones; for the bulkheads are so stoutly built that the compartments are watertight. The damage is then repaired and the cargo shifted back.

The crew needed to man a ship ranges from 150 to 300 according to her size. They carry a much bigger cargo than ours. One ship will take as much as five or six thousand baskets of pepper. At one time their ships were even larger than those now in use; but in many places islands have been so washed away by the force of the sea that there is no longer sufficient depth of water in the harbours to take the larger ships, so they are built with a smaller draught. They are propelled by sweeps, that is to say oars, each manned by four seamen. These ships are tended by two or three smaller craft, some manned by sixty seamen, some by eighty, some by a

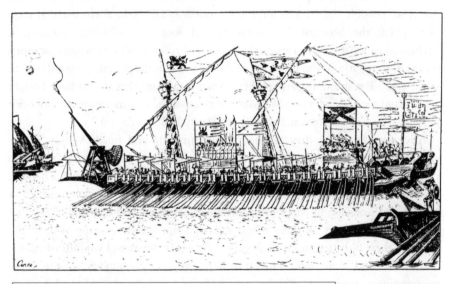

Above: Marco Polo's galley going into action at Curzola before he was taken prisoner.

Left: Medieval sailing ship sailing in the Java Sea, from a bas-relief at Boro Bordor.

hundred; which also carry substantial cargoes, some of them fully 1,000 baskets of pepper. These are propelled by oars and often serve to tow the bigger vessels with ropes and hawsers, not only when they are being rowed but also when they are under sail, so long that is, as the wind is more or less abeam, because then the smaller craft, precede the larger and help it along by means of tow-ropes. The big ships also take with them as many as ten small boats lashed to their sides outboard for use in anchoring and catching fish and supplying their other needs. The tender ships also carry boats. When a ship is in need of refitment, that is, of repair, after she has seen years of service, they refit her as follows. They nail on another layer of planks all round, over the top of the original two, so that now there are three layers. Then they caulk her afresh. This process is repeated yearly till there are as many as six layers, after which the vessel is rejected as no longer seaworthy.

The Polos eventually departed for Europe, but their movements at this point are not clear; possibly they stayed for a few months at Tabriz. Unfortunately, as soon as they left the Mongol dominions and set foot in a Christian country, at Trebizond in what is now Turkey, the Trebizond ruler, to whom golden passports meant nothing, forced the Polos to hand over some of their wealth – goods worth some 4,000 Byzantine hyperpyra. That was a huge sum that would have bought a thousand pounds of raw silk. Marco's book does not mention the robbery. Perhaps it was too belittling a subject for Rustichello to record.

After further delays they reached Constantinople and finally Venice, in the winter of 1295, after an absence of twenty-four years and having long since been given up for dead. A believable story surrounding their arrival says that when the shabby strangers appeared, exuding a 'certain indescribable smack of the Tartar both in air and accent' their noble relatives shunned and scorned them, but rapidly changed their attitudes when the unkempt wanderers ripped open the seams of their filthy garments to display their secret treasures. Handfuls of rubies, diamonds, and emeralds. The travellers, as often happens under these circumstances, 'were then affectionately embraced, and entertained at a luxurious banquet, where music and jollity were mixed with exotic reminiscence'.

Those were years of bitter rivalry between Venice and Genoa for the Mediterranean trade. On 6 September 1298, the Genoese under Lamba Doria struck their rivals in a climatic sea battle at Curzola, off the Dalmacian coast of the Adriatic, the larger Venetian fleet being under the command of Andrea Dandolo. The crew of a Venetian galley at this time amounted to 250 men under a comito or master. Marco Polo, an experienced seaman, served on one of the Venetian galleys as sopracomito or gentleman commander. The battle left the Genoese victors, with 7,000 prisoners. Among these was the gentleman commander.

Brought back in chains to a prison cell in Genoa, Marco befriended a fellow prisoner, relic of another Genoese victory, this time over the Pisans. This fellow, Rustichello of Pisa, (or perhaps Rusticiano), who was a fairly well-known writer of romances and a specialist in chivalry and its lore, then a fashionable subject, had considerable reputation for re-writing the tales of King Arthur and his Round Table.

Up to this time Marco had related his experiences among his friends, and from these stories he had acquired the nickname of Marco Millioni. Yet he had written nothing. When Rustichello listened to Marco Polo he saw the raw material for a new kind of romance and he persuaded the Venetian to cooperate. Marco in his turn sent to Venice for his notes. Taking advantage of their enforced leisure, Marco dictated a copious account of his travels to Rustichello, who wrote it all down in French with a heavy Italian accent – French was the literary language in Italy – and page by page, the great book *Description of the World* (*Divisament dou Monde*) was compiled for posterity. It is now generally agreed that his words are best preserved in a Paris manuscript written in the early fourteenth century in the same curious Italianate French that is found in his other writings. The book that was introduced to the reading public at the end of the thirteenth century entitled *Divisament dou Monde* was a description of a surprisingly large part of the world – from the Polar Sea to Java, from Zanzibar to Japan – and surprisingly enough most of it from first-hand observation. The world he revealed was almost wholly unknown and no other European foot had trodden some stretches of the trail he blazed for over 600 years.

Fortunately Marco was soon freed and returned to Venice. His subsequent life can be reconstructed in part, through the testimony of some legal documents that have reached us. Marco bought a property that may have included several houses close to Venice's Rialto district, described as a mansion. Here Marco spent

Marco Polo in prison at Genoa.

Pope Gregory X.

The Piazzetta in Venice in
Marco Polo's day.

the last twenty-five years of his life. He married soon after being freed from prison, aged about forty-five, and fathered three daughters. He seems to have led a somewhat retired life, managing a not too conspicuous fortune, and died at the age of seventy.

A famous story relates how as Marco lay dying in 1324, friends begged him to recant before he met his God. He replied, 'I did not write half of what I saw.' It is known that in his will he set free a Tartar slave who might have possibly followed him from East Asia.

Several other great medieval travelers – Friar Odoric of Pordenone, Niccolò de Conti, and Ibn Batuta, the traveler from Tangier, as well as the noted French chronicler and biographer of Saint Louis, Jean de Joinville, (1224?–1317?) – also dictated their books. The jingle of money, or the reward of celebrity, were not dangled before writers as incentive in those days, nor was literacy required to get hold of political power. The opening sentence to the prologue of Marco Polo's book exhorts: 'Emperors and kings, dukes and marquises, counts, knights, and townsfolk, and all people who wish to know the various races of men and the peculiarities of the various regions of the world, take this book and have it read to you.'

Rustichello wrote Marco Polo's book in French, which was current in Western Europe among the laity in those days, as Latin was among the clergy. Before long it was translated into most European languages, and numerous manuscripts survive. Never has a single book brought so much authentic information before the audience of the known world.

Sometimes called the Mongol dynasty (1279-1368), the Mongols later discovered that the empire that they had conquered on horseback could not be governed on horseback. They needed a proper administration to hold their vast empire together and that was precisely what they did not have.

Within China, where they were aliens and invaders, the Mongols always had difficulty maintaining control. Distrusting the conquered, they either employed their own people or foreigners like Marco Polo, to cover high government positions. They ruled China as conquerors and their ways, and not the least their tolerance of foreign religions, irritated traditional Confucians. The Chinese, with ancient literary tradition, a developed technology, and fastidious ceremonialism, found many reasons to condemn their barbarian conquerors.

Stemming from the dry grasslands of the north, the Mongols had never taken to the habit of bathing. 'They smell so heavily that one cannot approach them.' A Chinese traveler reported that 'they wash themselves in urine'. However, Marco Polo was awed by the ruthlessness and hardiness of the Mongol soldiers who drank mare's milk, carried barely any baggage, and were of all men in the world the best able to endure exertion and hardship and the least costly to maintain and therefore the best adapted for conquering territory and overthrowing kingdoms. Marco observed in his travels around the country that the Mongols had become degenerate and dissolute and were despised by the Chinese population.

Famine in the south and disastrous flooding of the Yellow River multiplied problems for the ruling Mongols. Coupled with their ruthless exploitation of the Chinese, the hardships brought about by the climatic disasters fostered widespread resentment of the Mongol rule. What followed were outbreaks of rebellion all over the country.

Toghon Temür Khan (1333-1370), the last of the Mongol emperors, of dissoluteness only comparable to Caligula, took ten close friends into the Palace of Deep Clarity in Peking where in a sacrilegious series of encounters they adapted the secret exercises of Tibetan Buddhist Tantra[20] ceremonial sexual orgies. History tells how the Khan lying on his couch after choosing from a bevy of naked girls would signal one with his finger and would pinion her upon him like some forest creature on a huntsman's spear. Girls were summoned from all over the empire to join in functions that would prolong life by strengthening men with women's powers. All that found most pleasure in intercourse with men were chosen and taken to the palace. After a few days they were let out. The families of the common people were glad to receive gold and silver. The nobles were secretly pleased and said: how can one resist, if the ruler wishes to choose them?

The people did resist, however, and the rebellion came to a head when Chu-Yüan-chang, 1328-1398, better known by his reign title, Hung-Wu, unified the country and established his capital at Nanking, a populous and strategically located city on the Yangtze River. He was the founder of the Ming dynasty. Hung Wu was a self-made man of great talents who had organised the rebellion under the very noses of the Mongols. Folk history recalls that during the last years of the Mongol rule, the nervous Khans placed an informer in nearly every family, forbidding people to gather in groups. The Chinese were prohibited from carrying arms, meaning that only one family in ten were allowed to possess a carving knife. But somehow the Mongols had forgotten to suppress the Chinese custom, at the coming of the full moon, of giving each other little round full moon cakes, decorated with pictures of the full moon hare and which, like fortune cookies, had a piece of paper inside. The crafty rebels, we are told, used these innocent looking cakes as means of spreading the word. Inside were the instructions for the Chinese to rise and massacre the Mongols at the time of the full moon in August 1368.

The dissolute Toghon Temür Khan fled with his empress and concubines, first to the fabled summer palace at Shangtu, the famed Xanadu, and later to Karakorum, the original Mongol capital, where he met his death. At the same time Mongol princes and generals were fighting among themselves, and the Mongol Empire was falling apart. During that first year of the Peking uprising the great Tamerlane, with his headquarters far westward in Samarkand, was constructing the first stage of his own plan for world conquest. His empire, however, huge by any standard, was only a quarter of the size of that of Genghis Khan.

Dismemberment of the Mongol Empire and the strong nationalism of the Ming dynasty doomed the Catholic missions of the fourteenth century. It interrupted the paths of safe passage described only a few decades before. Tamerlane did keep the passage open within his realm where Europeans could go as far as Tabriz in Persia. Samarkand where Tamerlane's power stopped briefly became the Athens of Asia. But soon after his death in 1405, Samarkand, the once busy way station on the Silk Road, lay in ruins, an Asian ghost town. Tamerlane's empire was only a memory.

———✺———

ADMIRAL ZHENG-HE

Early in the 1400s Admiral Zheng-He (pronounced jung huh) sailed from China to conquer the lands to the south and west. He was a young Muslim from a rebel family who had been seized during the uprisings against the Mongols by the Chinese army when he was just a boy. As was common practice with young male prisoners, he was castrated but survived when most of the others died. He was extremely intelligent and became a physically imposing figure who also had the qualities of a natural leader. Furthermore, he was lucky enough to become houseboy to the prince of Yen, Zhu Di.

In time both the prince and the houseboy became close and conspired against the prince's uncle, the emperor of China. Their revolt succeeded and the prince of Yen took the throne as the Yung-lo emperor – who reigned between 1402 and 1424 – and proved to be a vigorous, though aggressive ruler. After torturing to death those that had opposed him, he subjugated Viet Nam. He personally campaigned against the reorganising of the Mongols in the north and rewarded Zheng-He with the command of a great fleet to demand tribute from rulers overseas and assert for China a conspicuous position in the world. He also returned the empire's capital to Peking, giving that city its modern name.

From 1405 to 1433 Zheng-He led seven major expeditions with the largest armada the world would see for several centuries consisting of 300 junks manned by 28,000 seamen. His greatest vessels were known as the treasure ships, the largest measuring 140m overall and 55m of beam, with up to nine masts that in calm weather hoisted red silk sails. These ships had several decks as well as luxury cabins, and galleries that wrapped around the sterns. Also there were supply ships, carrying horses and troops, as well as some twenty tankers with fresh water and all escorted by armed warships and patrol boats.

The fleet also had a compliment of interpreters for Arabic, Persian and many dialects; astrologers to forecast the weather; astronomers to guide the ships by the stars; pharmacologists, to collect medicinal plants and prescribe cures; and two protocol officers to organise official receptions, as well as carpenters, riggers, sailmakers, cooks and servants.

Zheng-He's ships had watertight bulwarks and balanced sternpost rudders attached to their flat sterns, advanced elements of design that would be copied by the Arabs and which, due to their contacts with the west, were soon adopted throughout Europe. The sophistication of Zheng-He's fleet shows how far ahead of the West in technology the Far East had become. The Chinese certainly possessed the technical resources to have anticipated the Portuguese in the Indian Ocean, wrote William McNeill in *The Rise of the West*. Clearly they would have been up to the task of rounding the Cape of Good Hope on the way to Lisbon, or even the Horn to raise the coast of California and then circumnavigate the world.[21]

More than half a century before Columbus, Zheng-He had reached India and East Africa. He learned about Europe from the Arab traders and could have sailed there but seemingly was not enticed by the idea. The Chinese had no interest in wine, wool or other European manufactures. It was Africa and India that drew them with their ivory, medicinal plants, spices, exotic woods, elephants and other specimens of wildlife. One account tells of the excitement caused by the arrival of a couple of giraffes at the court in Peking, brought back by Zheng-He. They caused an enormous stir in China because they were thought to be the mythical qilin, or Chinese unicorn.

Recent findings by British researcher Gavin Menzies, based on his discovery of a Chinese map in Venice penned in 1459, indicate Zheng-He rounded the Cape of Good Hope, crossed the Atlantic to the Caribbean and went on to circumnavigate the globe, guided by the star Canopus. Menzies tells us that nine of Zheng-He's colossal junks were lost in a hurricane in the Caribbean during December 1421. If Menzies' theory proves true, it indicates that Zheng-He discovered the New World seventy-two years before Columbus. Menzies maintains that a Venetian traveller, Nicolo da Conti, acquired many of Zheng-He's maps after he died. In his memoirs published in 1434, da Conti mentions having travelled to China from Europe touching at Australia on the way. Consider that this is 350 years before Captain Cook arrived there.

Various museums and libraries around the world have maps in their collections that conflict with history as we know it. For instance, the British Library has one dated 1507 depicting the full coastline of North America (Columbus' fourth and final voyage left Spain in April 1503 but he never touched the coast of North America, while John Cabot had in June 1497); the museum of Topkapi Saray in Istanbul has a chart depicting what looks like the coast of Patagonia dated 1513 (Magellan's expedition sailed from Spain in August of 1519, returning under Elcano's command in September 1522); the Library of Congress has a map of Australia dated 1542 (probably the first European to have reached Australia was the Dutchman Willem Jansz in 1605); and The Biblioteca Estense, in Modena, has a chart of 1502, depicting the entire outline of the African Continent (Batholomeu Dias had only rounded its southern tip in 1488).

Menzies says that during a visit to Venice in 1428, the eldest son of the king of Portugal acquired some Chinese charts that he thinks might have been the basis for maps used by Columbus, Magellan, Da Gama, and Cook. All mention in their logbooks the use of charts, without telling us who the cartographers were. It now seems likely that the results of Chinese cartography had reached Europe before the era of the Great Discoveries and that these maps guided European cartographers of the time to drawing what we thought were rather fanciful oceans and continents. Though we will have to wait for the proofs of Menzies' theory, it is tempting to consider that it might have been a Chinese map, or its influence on a cartographer of the time, that convinced Magellan to press on and find the Strait against all odds. Antonio Pigafetta, the chronicler of his voyage, wrote in his journal: 'If it were not for Magellan we would never have found the Strait… But the Captain General… knew where to sail to find a well hidden strait… he saw [it] depicted on a map… in the treasury of the king of Portugal, made by that excellent man, Martin de Boemia.' Though pressed to do so, Magellan never gave away the details of the map he said he saw in the secret archives in Lisbon (beyond what he mentioned to Pigafetta, and the cartographer he mentioned never existed) but the map apparently convinced him he would find the Strait, and he did. The mere fact of the existence of a map showing the coast of Patagonia and the famous Strait points to some expedition having sailed those waters to gain the information.[22]

Emperor Yung-lo died in 1424, and after a period of peace and prosperity, China endured a series of power struggles and exploitive domination of weak emperors by favoured eunuchs who, by conniving and intrigue, gained access to government office. Nevertheless, those emperors, by and large, were conscientious rulers, though in the ultra-conservative Confucian mode.

The only serious disruption of the peace occurred in 1449 when the eunuch Wang-Chen led the Cheng-tung emperor into a disastrous military campaign against the Oyrat's western Mongols. The Oyrat leader Esen Taiji ambushed the Imperial army, captured the emperor, and besieged Peking. The Ming defense minister, Yü Chien, forced Esen to withdraw and for eight years dominated the Chinese government with emergency powers. When he fell ill in 1457, the Cheng-tung emperor, having been released from prison by the Mongols, resumed the throne and Chien was executed as a traitor. The conservatives emerged triumphant from the struggle after all.

Admiral Zheng-He died on a return journey to China and, it is thought, was buried at sea. The Confucians ended the voyages of his successors, halting the construction of other vessels and, with the backing of the new emperor, set about dismantling the Chinese navy. It was as if the fruits of the Chinese endeavour would contaminate rather than enrich their society.

A centralised decision, made in Beijing, stopped any Chinese initiative from venturing and exploring and sadly set the agenda for the whole nation. However, practical considerations also played their part: the Mings were preoccupied with the danger of new incursions along China's lengthy border that gave on to the lands of the Mongols to the north and west. Horsemen were the threat, ships they thought were a needless diversion. China was big, and rich enough to survive without International trade. So its rulers decided it was better to protect what was their own rather than roam the seas in pursuit of greater wealth. Thus when the Portuguese finally arrived in the Indian Ocean they found a world dominated not by the Chinese but by the Arabs instead.

By 1500 the Chinese government had made it a capital offence to build ships with more than two masts and, in 1525, it delivered its *coup de grace* by ordering the destruction of all its ocean-going ships. The greatest navy in history, which a century earlier counted 3,500 vessels, was wiped out in a few days along with Zheng-He's sailing records. It is evident that due to the folly of China's Ming rulers China had set a course that would lead it to poverty, decline, and isolation. It can also be said that the catastrophe of looking inwards instead of sharing their knowledge with other cultures opened the doors for the rise of Europe and eventually America.[23]

An afterthought: a Spanish nobleman, Ruy Gonzáles de Clavijo, and two companions, were sent as envoys, in 1403, by King Henry III of Castile to solicit the alliance of Tamerlane against the Turks. They went by ship to Trebisond on the far corner of the Black Sea, then overland as far as Samarkand. They witnessed the splendor of Tamerlane's capital with its communities of captive craftsmen, silk weavers, potters, armorers, and silversmiths, all captured from the cities he conquered. Clavijo was told that it was a six-month journey to Cambaluc (Peking), but decided against the attempt. Before Clavijo and his party could return from Samarkand, Tamerlane had died, the princes were in revolt, and anarchy once again descended on the overland routes to the East. The Spaniards had to thread their way homeward avoiding robbers, and escaping countless battlefields strewn all across the remnants of Tamerlane's realm.

Clavijo's tribulations confirmed the end of the heroic age of overland travel. Instead of eyewitness accounts of life in the capital of Cathay by Europeans honoured by the great Khan, Europeans now had to depend on rumour, on occasional reports of captives and slaves, for word from the fabled East. It became apparent that from then on the only way to the Far East and its spices would be by sea, but how? The quest was about to begin.

3

THE ROAD FROM ALEXANDRIA

I felt once more the strange equivocal power of the city,
its flat alluvial landscape and exhausted airs...
Alexandria; which is neither Greek, Syrian nor Egyptian,
but a hybrid...

Justine, Laurence Durrell (1965)

From earliest times the world's greatest trading route had run from the eastern Mediterranean down to the Red Sea, and across towards India and China. There is evidence of the Egyptians and Babylonians going as far south as Somalia in the second millennium BC and east into India. During the life of Alexander the Great this trade route was developed and maintained, as much as anything, by his use of coinage. Coins with Alexander's face were accepted from India to the Lebanon, from south Russia to the upper reaches of the Nile. In 1331BC Alexander decided to found a city at the most suitable point to handle the quantities of commodities going and coming across his empire. The city was to be built in stone at a place where two natural harbours, facing east and west, would permit the arrival of vessels whichever way the wind was blowing at the time.

Situated at the mouth of the Nile, Alexandria became the greatest trading capital of the world. From Somalia in the south came spices. From the Sudan came elephants, iron and gold. From France, Germany and Russia came furs and amber. From England, sadly only tin. Alexandria received goods from all over the world and redirected them to their destinations. In the first century, Dio Chrysostom, the Greek sophist and rhetorician (*c.*AD40–115), said, 'The city has a monopoly of the shipping of the entire Mediterranean... situated as it is at the crossroads of the whole world.'

For 600 years Alexandria prospered, both as a trading community and an intellectual center, thanks to the great library, founded not long after the city was built. Here the greatest teachers of the time gathered to write and give lectures in one of its ten halls devoted to each of the subjects taught. There were rooms for research, for study, and quarters for teachers in residence. After the death of Alexander the city was ruled in turn by Persians, Greeks, Carthaginians and finally Romans.

The library was a treasure trove of all that was virtually known. There were over half a million manuscripts in 235BC and by the time of Julius Caesar (102–44BC)

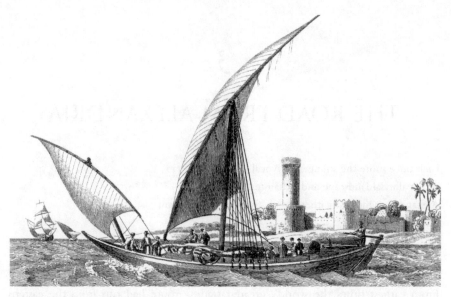

A Turkish djerme off Alexandria.

the figure had risen to 700,000. The collection was further enlarged by a law which required a visitor to lend any manuscript in his possession to the library for copying, and ordered the search for books in any vessel entering its port.

The subjects taught covered most fields of contemporary learning: mathematics, geometry, astronomy, philosophy, medicine, astrology, theology and geography. It is not surprising, therefore, that Alexandria being a seaport, special attention was given to geography and its associated field of astronomy. At some point between AD127 and 151 one of the greatest scholars who ever taught in Alexandria, Claudius Ptolemy, wrote thirteen volumes titled Mathematike Syntaxis ('The system of Mathematics'), bringing together what was known at the time about astronomy.

Astronomy had been a field for study since very early times, first by the Babylonians and to a lesser extent by the Egyptians. It started as an interest in the stars, the moon and the sun, as a means to perfect a calendar by believing that the observation of the sky would enable them to record the seasons with greater accuracy. Gradually the study took on the myth and magic of the astrologers. Predicting eclipses, or the behavior of disappearing constellations at different times throughout the year gave power to the priest-kings. By the time the Persian King Cyrus was called upon to save the country from civil war in 539BC, brushing aside the hocus-pocus of superstition his astronomers divided the sky into twelve constellations, 30 degrees apart, in a circle of 360 degrees, which laid the basis of the zodiac. From 300BC the Chaldean Tables were developed, which became the basis for Ptolemy's work.

The accuracy demanded in measuring degrees of position and minutes of time demanded the use of astronomical instruments. Ptolemy produced a star table, as part of the System (erroneously placing the world at the center of the universe, known as the 'Geocentric,' or 'Ptolemaic' scheme. It was later advanced to Copernicus' heliocentric system, which placed the sun in the center of the universe instead) listing 1,022 stars and giving their positions in the sky as he saw them from Alexandria. He also designed an instrument, in his laboratory, for measuring these positions: the astrolabe, which was to become the basic tool for observers of the heavens for the next thousand years.

Though Ptolemy's star tables were a great advance for navigators, few sailors took advantage of them – although Greek and Roman sailors did use stars to keep on course – but little more. As the Roman writer Lucan said in 63BC, 'We follow the never setting axis that guides the ships. When the Lesser Bear rises and stands high above me in the yards, we are looking towards the Bosphorus.' Meaning that with The Bear to the north – to port – the ship was heading east.

Three hundred years after Ptolemy, Rome fell and much of the work that had taken place in Alexandria was lost in the confusion and the anarchy of Europe when the Romans withdrew, and although teaching at Alexandria continued under the Byzantine emperors, the importance attached to the library declined. No one knows when the burning of the books occurred. There are several opinions: accidental fires during the time of Roman domination; destruction at the hands of fanatical Christian mobs in the fourth century AD; or, perhaps, in AD646 when the Muslims finally took Alexandria and, according to Arab writers, burned the books in the hearths of the city. Regardless of whoever was responsible, most of the texts were lost.

A lateen rigged privateer running to anchor.

We know today of Ptolemy's system only because of the strange route taken by a single surviving copy that had reached the library of a monastery during the middle of the eighth century, at Jundi Shapur, in south-western Iran. The Arabs, shortly after founding Baghdad, in AD765, made contact with the monastery only a few miles away and discovered in its library a collection of manuscripts containing large amounts of Greek scientific material. Becoming aware of its importance, they sent scribes to copy and translate the texts into Arabic and thus, the Syntaxis was one of the first to be translated. As the work of the translators grew, the Caliphs acquired or took from the Byzantines more and more Greek texts, especially those dealing with medicine and astronomy.

In AD911, Islam spread westward into Spain, conquering it all except Asturias and Navarre. The caliphate of Córdova linked to the kingdom of Granada – lasting up to 1492 when Boabdil was forced to surrender the besieged Granada without resistance – marked a golden age for Spain.¹ Arab translators and writers like Averroes, Albumazen and Al-Kwarizmi brought the ancient texts, and their own analysis of them, to the awareness of Western Europe. Thus it happened that Alfonso X, El Sabio – the wise – king of Castile from 1221 to 1284, and one of the first Christian kings of what had long been Muslim Spain, set up a school in Toledo during the mid-thirteenth century, to translate the Arab texts into Latin. It was thanks to these translations that the star tables finally came to the West, and to the hands of the navigators who would ultimately use them.

In the thirteenth century, contact was being established between the Mediterranean and the North Sea. However, master mariners still sailed their ships as the Romans had, only between May and September, as from November to March the skies were uncertain and merchants preferred not to risk capital that could easily be lost in foul weather.

During the sailing season navigation was aided by the old Roman lighthouses around the Mediterranean as well as by landmarks. Vessels would approach harbour with a weighted lead at the end of a line that had a hollow bottom filled with sticky tallow to tell them the depth and the composition of the seabed, which by experience would tell them where they were.

Sailing, however, was hampered by design. The old Roman square sail still dominated the seas off Europe but it was useful only to run before the wind, a fact that would force masters to wait for the wind to turn favorable before setting out. The delay diminished the amount of ships at sea in an already short sailing season. The square sail, therefore, restricted the manoeuvrability essential to the contrary winds of Europe.

The sail design that changed these adverse conditions had been in use in the Mediterranean since, perhaps, the eighth century. It stemmed from the Arab dhows that in turn took it from the Chinese junks. Its name, lateen, meaning Latin sail, derives from the European misconception that it came with the East Romans from Constantinople. Triangular in shape, it is bent on to a yard that is then attached, somewhere near its middle, to the mast. By enabling it to swing in

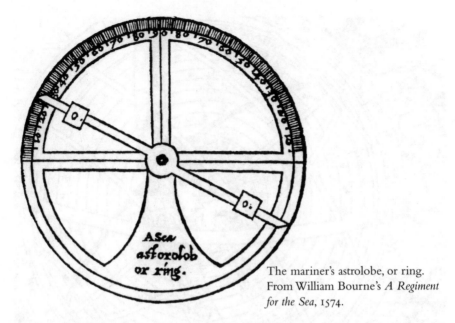

The mariner's astrolobe, or ring.
From William Bourne's *A Regiment for the Sea*, 1574.

any direction it can catch the wind even when the ship is heading almost directly into it. The adoption of the lateen sail increased the number of voyages, since masters no longer had to wait for a favorable wind before leaving port. Because of it, the pace of trade quickened, and consequently the size of the ships increased and more cargo left port.

It made sense to make one ship do the work of two, thus saving money and boosting profits. However, as the European grain fields boosted their output, the larger ships, even with lateen sails, were extremely difficult to handle. They were the wrong shape to run up onto a beach or manoeuvre alongside a quay, except in anything but ideal conditions.

Steering had always been by the use of stern oars, but there comes a point when the size of the ship makes steering oars cumbersome and impractical. The design of the rudder, as we know it, came from China. Adapted by the Arabs, it was gradually introduced into the Mediterranean and the northern European countries. Known as the sternpost rudder because it projects from a post attached almost vertically to the center of the stern, a stern that has to be flat to house the post with its metal rudder fittings, it gave the captains of these larger ships the necessary control of their vessels. With the change in design of these things, the vessels themselves took on a different look: pointed bows with square sterns, a shape that provided more cargo space, which in turn encouraged the merchants.

Warriors returning from the Crusades brought back luxury goods like spices, silks, precious woods and dyestuffs that could not be bought in Europe. This created a demand for them and consequently became the driving force behind the early Italian maritime republics of Venice, Genoa, and Amalfi, to set up trading posts in Arab and Turkish lands. These Italian states, however, were setting the

Above: Ptolemy's view of the universe, consisting of concentric crystal spheres each carrying one of the seven known planets (including the sun and moon) and the outermost, the stars. In this scheme, the earth is at the centre of everything.

Opposite: Compass card with both points and degrees. From John Davies' *The Seaman's Secrets*, 1594.

prices and keeping the profits. Matters became even worse in 1453, with the fall of Constantinople to the Turks and the consequent loss of contact with the Eastern markets, so prices rose still higher. It was in reaction to this, prompted by the desire to find a route of their own to the spice islands, that Prince Henry of Portugal, known as 'The Navigator,' sent his fleets of exploration down the coast of Africa in search of supplies. With those first African expeditions the serious problems of oceanic navigation began to appear.

Prince Henry's expeditions were made possible by a device that probably came from China and was brought to Europe by the ubiquitous Arabs. There are occasional references to it, the first by a traveling English monk by the name of Alexander Neckham who returned from Paris with news of a mysterious needle that always pointed in the same direction. Another friar, Peter of Maricourt, wrote of experiments he had conducted when he was with the Duke of Anjou at the siege of Lucera in Italy, with something he called a 'dry pointer'. Alfonso the Wise, of Toledan Star Table fame, decreed that all sailors should carry the needle and by the end of the thirteenth century it had come into general use throughout the Mediterranean. It was common for it to be stuck on a straw and floated in a bowl

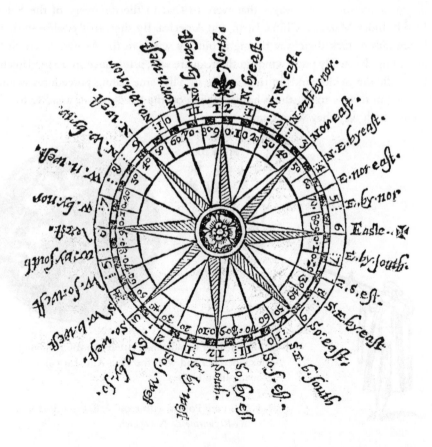

of water, but history tells us that in Amalfi a card had been attached showing all the points of the compass, derived from the directions of the major and minor winds. Also a frame had been added to protect the device: the compass was now 'boxed'. At last the navigator could plot his course accurately to within one thirty-second of a circle, the wind directions having been subdivided into eight major winds, eight half-winds and sixteen quarter winds. The standardisation was taken from experience in the Mediterranean Sea, where for the most part the winds blow constantly and reliably in the same way.

The economic effects of the compass on world trade can hardly be exaggerated. Together with the combined use of the lateen and square sail, and the sternpost rudder, the compass altered sailing habits completely and almost immediately. Whereas at the beginning of the thirteenth century the seas had been closed in winter (sailing was actually forbidden by law in Italian maritime cities during winter months), with the advent of the compass, ships could sail under cloudy skies, by day, or by night. Consequently the number of voyages doubled, crews were kept in regular employment and the investors were encouraged to keep working and extend their trade.

So it was that the fall of Constantinople, by cutting trade with the East, sparked the great transoceanic voyages that were to lead to the discovery of the Spice Islands, India, Malaysia, China, Japan and America. By ships that could use their lateen sails to tack their way through contrary winds to the Azores, where they picked up the steady trade winds in their square sails, using once more the lateens to handle the fickle winds in the Caribbean. The same sailing procedures would be used in reverse to get them home, relying on the needle in all weather to tell them which way they were going.

Above: A silver tetradrachm, dated *c.*290BC, showing Alexander as a god with the Zeus Ammon ram's horn growing from his head.

Left: Shooting Polaris with cross-staff. From Pedro de Medina *Regimento de Navigacion.*

4
PRINCE HENRY
THE HERMIT OF SAGRES

An age will come after many years when the Ocean will loose
the chain of things, and a huge land lie revealed; when Tiphys
will disclose new worlds and Thule no longer be the ultimate.

Seneca, Medea

During the Renaissance, countries in the West concluded that they should do
something to break the Arabian monopoly. To open a parallel route would be
illogical as the Arab's ability and knowledge to drive camel trains through the
desert was a specialty acquired over centuries that they dared not emulate.

The Mogreb, the Mauritania of old that gave rise to the word Moore, was a
melting pot of African and Semitic races from the Mediterranean. It received the
Asian spices from Egypt, by land and by sea by means of the Arab intermediaries.
These commodities arrived in Tunisia, Constantine, Oran and Arzila after having
crossed the Sahara from Timbuktu, Walata and Wada. Ships flocked to Mauritania
from Venice, Pisa, Genoa, Sicily and Cataluña to buy gold, ivory, ebony, pepper and
slaves, selling in turn clothes, textiles, glass beads, perfumes, oats and wheat. Although
purchasing these goods in Timbuktu shortened distances and were therefore cheaper
to buy than in Mediterranean ports, it did not solve the basic problem of eliminating
the Arab intermediary. Then, as now, it boiled down to the matter of cutting costs.

Emerging from the maritime obscurity of the Middle Ages, Renaissance men
felt capable of responding to the enormous challenge of finding an alternative
route and the only logical one appeared to be by sea. With courage that astounds
and a blind trust in their nautical ability, the two superpowers, Portugal and Spain,
designed and built ships capable of facing the feared sea, its storms and legendary
monsters. To a large extent, this transformation was due to an obsessive mystic
who history has nicknamed 'The Hermit of Sagres'.

For 569 years, the Atlantic boundary of the Roman Empire was Lucitania,
situated in the western extremity of the Iberian Peninsula. Occupied alternatively
by the barbarians and by the Arabs, it had been wrested from Islam by Alfonso II
of Castile. Later, King John I of Portugal, whose alternative sobriquets were either
the Bastard, or the Great, founder of the Aviz dynasty, had seized the Portuguese
throne in 1385. He defeated the king of Castile in the decisive battle of
Aljubarrota with the aid of English archers, thus securing the independence and
unity of Portugal.

King John I cemented his English alliance by marrying the devout and strong-willed Philippa of Lancaster, daughter of John of Gaunt of England, although he still kept his mistress in the palace even after his marriage. Philippa bore the king six sons, the third of whom, Henry, was born at Oporto on 4 March 1394. He and his older brothers, the princes Duarte and Pedro, were educated under the supervision of their parents; and were taught soldiering, statecraft and the appreciation of literature.

Twenty-six years after the battle of Aljubarrota, King John came to terms with the king of Castile and with him signed a treaty of friendship in 1411. To celebrate the occasion King John I followed the chivalric custom of the times by organising a tournament to last a whole year. Knights were to be invited from all over Europe to take part in this mock warfare, and the jousts would give the king's three eldest sons, who had just reached manhood, the opportunity to earn their knightly spurs by public acts of chivalry. However, the three young men backed by the king's treasurer and other advisors dissuaded the king from his expensive plan. Instead, they suggested he offer them an opportunity for deeds of Christian valour by launching a Crusade against the Muslim bastion and trading post of Ceuta, on the north-western tip of Africa, across the strait from Gibraltar. It was suggested that by attempting to conquer the city he could also atone for his earlier deeds of Christian bloodshed by washing his hands in the blood of the infidel.[2]

Prince Henry, still only nineteen, helped to plan the attack that in many ways shaped his future. He was given the task of building a fleet in Oporto, to the north of the country. After two years of preparation, the Crusade was launched with a fanfare of religious fervour. A monk in Oporto had a vision of the Virgin Mary presenting a gleaming sword to King John. There was an eclipse of the sun, a good omen, but Queen Philippa fell desperately ill of the plague that had swept Portugal. Assembling the king and her three eldest sons to her bedside, she gave each a fragment of the true cross to wear in holy battle. To each prince she also presented a knightly sword and with her expiring breath she gave her blessing to the expedition. In addition a papal bull, solicited for the occasion, gave the participants all the spiritual benefits of a Crusade to those who died in the effort.

The Portuguese stormed Ceuta from the sea on 24 August 1415. Well armed and supported by a contingent of English archers, their army reduced the Muslims in a one-sided battle within very few hours. Only eight Portuguese Crusaders were killed while the streets of the citadel were strewn with the blood and bodies of the Muslims. That Henry distinguished himself in battle is indicated by his immediate appointment as governor of Ceuta, which did not require he reside there permanently but obliged him to see that it was adequately defended.

The sacking of the city that followed gave Prince Henry a glimpse of the huge wealth that lay hidden in Africa and beyond, as the loot was precisely the cargo that had been delivered by the caravans arriving from southern Saharan Africa and from the Indies in the east. Beyond the straightforward necessities of life such as rice, wheat and salt, the invaders found stores of exotic cinnamon, cloves, peppers, ginger, nutmeg and other spices. Furthermore, the houses of the inhabitants were hung with tapestries and carpeted with rich oriental rugs quite beyond the usual booty of gold, silver, and jewels. To preserve order, the victors left a small garrison while the rest went home. However, on advice of a renewed Muslim attack, when the rulers of Fez (Fés) in Morocco and the kingdom of Granada in Spain joined in an attempt to retake the city, Prince Henry hastened to relieve Ceuta with reinforcements. On arrival he found that the Portuguese garrison had beaten off the assailants and held the city. This time Henry committed himself to learn as much as he could about the African caravan trade during the several months he was there.[3]

Over the years Ceuta had been a Muslim enclave, it had bristled with some 24,000 shops selling gold and silver, copper, brass, silks and spices, all brought in by caravan. However, since the city had become Christian, the caravans ceased to arrive, business dried up, and the citadel had become a ghost town. It left the Portuguese with two options: either they made peace with the surrounding Muslim tribes or they must conquer the hinterland.

Prince Henry collected information about the places in the interior from where the treasures had come. He learned about a curious 'silent trade' designed for those that did not know each other's language and about the Muslim caravans that upon leaving Morocco went southwards across the Atlas Mountains arriving after a long trek of twenty days at the banks of the Senegal River.

Unloading their camels, the Moroccan traders laid out separate piles of salt, beads made from Ceutan coral, and cheap manufactured goods. They then retreated out of sight. The local tribesmen, who worked the mines where they dug for gold, came to the bank of the river and put a pile of gold beside each heap of Moroccan goods. Then they in turn retreated out of view, leaving it to the Muslim traders to either take the gold offered for each pile or reduce the pile of their merchandise. Once again the Moroccan traders withdrew to their tents, and the process continued. By this system of commercially accepted manners the Muslims collected their gold and returned to Morocco. When Prince Henry heard about this strange process it interested him.

Always the Crusader at heart, Henry declared his intention to capture Granada from the infidels as retaliation for their intention to recapture Ceuta. The expedition was already underway when King John forbade it, as it would antagonise the kingdom of Castile, on whose threshold Granada lay. King John, who had spent years fighting the attempts of the Castilians to annex Portugal, wanted no part of it and gave orders to Henry to return home. The Prince turned back and instead of returning to the court in Lisbon, he went through the Algarve, the southernmost province of Portugal. There on the rocky promontory of Sagres, near Cape St Vincent 'where endeth land and where beginith sea' as the great Portuguese poet Camoëns described it, 'there, a natural place for ships on all northsouth routes to anchor' the Prince founded a small court of his own.[4] In 1419, at the age of twenty-

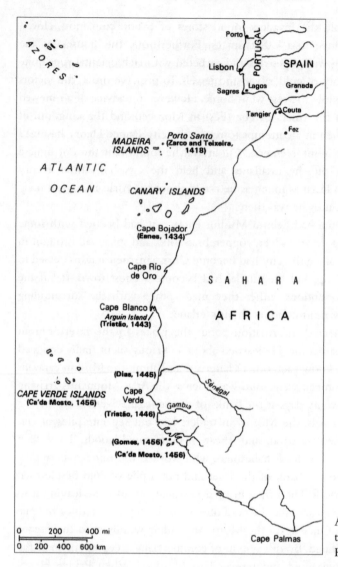

AZORES

Porto

Lisbon

PORTUGAL

SPAIN

Sagres

Lagos

Granada

Tangier

Ceuta

Fez

MADEIRA
ISLANDS

Porto Santo
(Zarco and Teixeira,
1418)

ATLANTIC

OCEAN

CANARY ISLANDS

Cape Bojador
(Eanes, 1434)

Cape Río
de Oro

S A H A R A

Cape Blanco
Arguin Island
(Tristão, 1443)

A F R I C A

(Dias, 1445)

Sénégal

CAPE VERDE ISLANDS
(Ca'da Mosto, 1456)

Cape
Verde

Gambia

(Tristão, 1446)

(Gomes, 1456)

(Ca'da Mosto, 1456)

0   200   400 mi

0   200   400   600 km

Cape Palmas

Areas reached under
the sponsorship of
Henry the Navigator.

five, Henry was created governor of the kingdom of Algarve. The next year he was
made grand master of the Order of Christ, the supreme order sponsored by the
pope, which had replaced the crusading order of the Templars in Portugal. While this
did not oblige him to take religious vows, it did oblige him to dedicate himself to a
chaste and ascetic life. However, he had not always refrained from worldly pleasures;
indeed, as a young man he had fathered an illegitimate daughter. Little is known of
the prince's private life during the 1420s. Duarte and Pedro both married, but Henry
remained single to the end of his life.

The funds made available through the Order of Christ largely financed his
great enterprise of discovery, which also had as its object the conversion of the
pagans to Christianity and because of this all of Henry's ships bore a red cross on
their sails.

In antiquity, geographers like Marinus and Ptolemy had given the south-west tip of Portugal the name of Promontorium Sacrum, the Sacred Promontory. Later, the Portuguese shortened it into Sagres and gave the name 'Infante's town' (Villa do Iffante) to the town where the Prince took up residence. There is a lighthouse there today built on the ruins of the building that Prince Henry made his headquarters for forty years. Standing on the harsh cliffs of Sagres today, one can capture the appeal that inhospitable place must have had for an ascetic like Prince Henry who wished to put as much distance as possible between himself and the court formalities in Lisbon.

According to Henry's enthusiastic biographer, Gomes Eanes de Zurara, Prince Henry was not an engaging person. Though he tended to compare himself to Saint Louis, a gentle figure, Henry had the zeal and energy of a fanatic Crusader. He lived like a monk and, as a matter of fact, at his death he was found to be wearing a hair shirt.[5]

The surname Navigator, applied by the English to the Prince, though seldom by Portuguese writers, is a misnomer as he himself never embarked on voyages of discovery. He took to the sea only once to invade Ceuta. Nevertheless, his intelligence, imagination and patronage were so bountiful that he attracted to Sagres all who were interested in navigation and geography, professors, cartographers and navigators. His court grew into both a research centre as well as a laboratory of evolution where he applied his zeal, inventiveness, and his crusading energy to the exploring enterprise. In the Crusading world he had left behind, the known was dogma and the unknown was unknowable, while in the explorer's world the unknown was simply the undiscovered.

Step by step Prince Henry made Sagres a centre for cartography, for navigation and for shipbuilding. He knew that the unknown could be discovered and charted by clearly marking the boundaries of the known, which meant replacing the old maps with carefully made new ones, piece by piece. To achieve it he brought to Sagres a Catalan Jew from Majorca, Jehuda Cresques, son of the well known cartographer Abraham Cresques, who supervised the piecing together of the facts brought back by Prince Henry's explorers. Certain Arab and Jewish mathematicians aided them.

He required his captains to keep logbooks and record accurately on charts all the many details they saw of the coast to be brought back to Sagres. By this means cartography at Sagres become a cumulative science.

To Sagres came sailors and travellers from every corner, each adding a new fragment of fact to be carefully noted down and set in place like pieces of a jigsaw puzzle. Besides Jews, there were Muslims and Arabs, Italians from Genoa and Venice, Germans and Scandinavians.

At Sagres were also kept the manuscript records of the great travellers that had been collected by Prince Henry's brother Pedro during his long tour of Europe on which he visited England, Flanders, Germany, Hungary, and the principalities of Moldavia and Walachia (now Romania) before returning home through Italy,

Aragon and Castile. From Italy Pedro brought back to Sagres, in 1428, a copy of Marco Polo's travels that he had translated for Prince Henry's benefit, as well as a map of Marco's itinerary.

The perfecting of navigational instruments were studied and carried out. New models were constructed and tested, as well as new navigational techniques. The mariner's compass was already well known, though in other places astrologers who talked of occult powers akin to necromancy had contested its use. (Tricks performed with the lodestone had got Roger Bacon into trouble a century before.) At Sagres, however, the compass was looked upon as an invaluable instrument and many other instruments of navigation were either perfected or invented to enable mariners to reach out further and, above all, to return home with the facts and information of their discoveries.

As Prince Henry's navigators sailed further south than any Europeans had gone before, they ran into the problem of defining latitude. Since the best means was by measuring the altitude of the sun at noon, Prince Henry's technicians devised a simple cross-staff instead of the costly and complicated astrolabe. It consisted of a graduated stick with a moving crosspiece which could be aligned with the horizon as well as the sun to measure the angle of the sun's elevation. The congregation of cosmopolitan scientists at Sagres also helped to invent the quadrant and other instruments for navigation, as well as new mathematical tables to complement them.

Ships were designed at Sagres and built to their architect's specifications at the nearby port of Lagos, a Tercena Nabal or naval arsenal. Oak for keels came from Alentejo on the edge of the Algarve. Pine for the hulls grew along the coastal areas of Portugal, where law protected it. With its resin they waterproofed the rigging and caulked the seams of the hulls. Lagos prospered to the sounds of saws and adzes while around the dockyards flourished the skills of the blacksmiths and the crafts of the sail and rope makers.

The back staff, used to measure the height of the sun, did not require the user to look directly at the sun.

The astrolabe, also used to measure
the height of the sun, was less
accurate than the cross staff.

Experiments on the drawing boards at Sagres produced a completely new type
of vessel without which Prince Henry's exploring expeditions and the great
seafaring adventures of the next century would not have been possible. It was
specially designed to bring seafarers there and back. The familiar square-rigged,
heavy barca or the larger Venetian carrack were cargo vessels appropriate for
sailing with the wind and well suited to Mediterranean waters, where the size of
a trading ship was a measure of its profit. But a ship designed for discovery was
not a cargo vessel. It had its own special problems but was conceived to go long
distances in unfamiliar waters and to be able to sail as close to the wind as
possible. An exploring ship was useless unless it could get there and return to its
port of origin complete with its cargo of news and information that could be
carried in a small packet, or even in the mind of a person. This was the clear
objective given by Prince Henry to his designers.

The vessels he had in mind did not need to be big but they had to be highly
manoeuvrable as seafarers were always tempted to sail out with the wind, which
usually meant having to return against it. It is therefore understandable that the
profitable trading vessels of the enclosed Mediterranean were not what the
explorers needed in the unknown open ocean.

The ships designed at Sagres were specially conceived with the explorers' needs
in mind. Prince Henry found some clues for the design in the Arabian caravos
used since antiquity off the Tunisian and Egyptian coasts, modelled on the still
more ancient vessels that the Greeks had made from rushes and hides known as
dhows. They were rigged with lateen sails, slanting and triangular, bent to a yard,
more or less fore and aft with the peak, or fore end, very much higher then the
nock, or after end. On these vessels the Arabs often carried crews of up to thirty,
in addition to a cargo of, perhaps, fifty to 100 horses, or cattle. A smaller but
similar and more manoeuvrable vessel, the caravela (meaning diminutive), had
been in use on the Douro River in Portugal for 100 years. Combining some of
the cargo-carrying features of the caravos with the manoeuvrability of the
caravelas of the Douro River as well as further additions, Prince Henry's
shipbuilders designed the famous caravel.

These extraordinary little vessels, displacing some fifty tons, were about 70ft in length and 20ft in beam. They usually carried a crew of some twenty, who slept on deck, except in foul weather, when they went below. 'The best ships that sailed the seas' was the opinion of the Venetian mariner Alvise de Cadamosto after his African voyage inspired by Prince Henry in 1456. Columbus' three ships, the *Santa Maria*, the *Pinta* and the *Niña* were all of caravel design; however, it is well to mention, all things being comparative, that the *Santa Maria* was only one fifth the size of the Venetian square-riggers of her day, which proves that bigger is not necessarily always better.[6]

For over twenty-five years Don Enrique kept his gaze fixed on that invisible rudder, which he handled from Sagres and Lagos. A silent conqueror of space, he was able to provide the Portuguese navigators with the necessary science to dominate it. He is the origin of the European maritime expansionist policy and is relevant, not only for his importance in the history of ideas, but also in the universal evolution of nautical science.[7]

Prince Henry died on 13 November 1460, and was buried in the church of St Mary in Lagos, but a year later his body was removed to the superb monastery of Batalha. His great-nephew, King Dom Manuel, had a statue of him placed over the centre column of the side gate of the church of Belem, and in 1840 a monument was erected to him at Sagres, in recognition to the Navigator who never went to sea.

In his inimitable way, José Saramago, Portugal's Nobel laureate, tells us in a reflexive tone, in his *Voyage to Portugal*, to visit the church at San Antonio de Lagos. 'From the outside it is not worth a thing', he says. 'Hewn stone, empty niches, windows surrounded by shells, an ugly shield. But inside, and after so many, and in reality, tiring gold-carved altar pieces, after so much wood carved into volutes, palms, leaves, bunches of grapes and vine tendrils, after so many cherubs with double chins and more rolls of fat than decency admits, after so many illusions and masks, it was fair for the traveler to find all this again, summed up and hyperbolised on four walls. The master carvers lost their heads in the church at San Antonio de Lagos. This is the kingdom of the craftsman of make-believe. Who painted the roof? Nobody knows...'

5

SEA PATHS
BEYOND THE THREATENING CAPE

All hope abandon, ye who enter here!

The Divine Comedy, Dante Alighieri (*c.*1310–1321), Inferno, canto III, 1. 9

Upon an old Majorcan world chart, dated 1375, can be seen today, where the cartographer has written opposite Cape Bojador, 'here is the end of the world'. At that exact point, Henry the Navigator believed the route to the Indies began. Prince Henry's admiring chronicler Gomes Eanes de Zurara, wrote that:

> The noble spirit of this Prince, was ever urging him both to begin and to carry out very great deeds, he had also wished to know the land that lay beyond the isles of Canary and that Cape called Bojador, for that up to his time, neither by writings, nor by the memory of man, was known with any certainty the nature of the land beyond that Cape... it seemed to him that if he or some other lord did not endeavour to gain that knowledge, no mariners or merchants would ever dare to attempt it, for it is clear that none of them ever trouble themselves to sail to a place where there is not a sure and certain hope of profit.

It's unlikely we will ever know if Prince Henry's original idea was to find a sea-route around Africa to India. It seems likely, however, that at first he was driven by an impulse to venture south-west into the sea of darkness and even further along the uncharted coast of Africa. Certainly, it was the unknown that beckoned Prince Henry.

Genoese sailors had discovered the Madeiras, and the Canaries, as well as the Azores in the mid-fourteenth century. However, it was Prince Henry's people whom in 1420, after disembarking on Madeira (its name means wood in Portuguese) set a fire to clear the forest that by mistake burned on for seven years. Due to the forest fire, the potash incorporated from it into the soil lightened its components, which suggests it might have been the perfect stabiliser for the Malmsey vine stock imported from Crete. Its justly famous Madeira wine is today the proven and lasting product of this transformation.

Looking at a modern map of Africa it is difficult, without a magnifying glass, to find Cape Bojador, situated on the west coast of Africa just south of the Canary Islands and some thousand miles north of the continent's great westward bulge. Through the glass, we see it as a tiny bump on the coastal outline, so slight as being almost imperceptible. The Cape consists of a rocky coastline with treacherous reefs that cause dangerous currents, surrounded by a sandy barrier. The cape is difficult to perceive from seaward until close to shore, but in the early fifteenth century Cape Bojador was a fearful barrier beyond which no seafarer in his right mind would dare to venture. Rumours said that, beyond it, further south, the heat was so intense that ships foundered and seamen were rendered down to death in the boiling sea. However, when we compare Bojador to other risky promontories such as the Capes of Good Hope and the Horn, we realise that Cape Bojador was merely a barrier of the mind, an example of many superstitions common to explorers that held them back through fear. The expressive Gomes Eanes de Zurara, Prince Henry's contemporary chronicler, tells us why ships had hitherto not dared to pass beyond Cape Bojador:

> And to say the truth this was not from cowardice or want of good will, but from the novelty of the thing and the wide-spread and ancient rumour about this cape, that had been cherished by the mariners of Spain from generation to generation... For certainly it cannot be presumed that among so many noble men that did such great and lofty deeds for the glory of their memory, there had not been one to dare this deed. But being satisfied of the peril, and seeing no hope of honour or profit, they left off the attempt. For, said the mariners, this much is clear, that beyond this Cape there is no race of men nor place of inhabitants... and the sea so shallow that a whole league from land it is only a fathom deep, while the currents are so terrible that no ship having once passed the Cape, will ever be able to return... these mariners of ours... [were] threatened not only by fear but by its shadow, whose great deceit was the cause of very great expenses.

At Sagres, Prince Henry knew he would never overcome the geographical barrier unless he first defeated the barrier of fear. Between 1424 and 1434 he sent out fifteen expeditions to attempt to round the Cape and all returned with excuses for not being able to do so. Superstition triumphed every time. One mariner told the prince that upon arriving off the legendary Cape the waves became a fearful red from sand of that colour that crumbled from the overhanging cliffs of the shore; that the sea abounded with millions of sardines swimming in the shallows; of whirlpools and rocks beneath the surface, and no sign of life at all along the desert coast. If this was not the very image of the end of the world, what else could it be?

Gil Eannes reported back to his master, in 1433, that Cape Bojador was insurmountable. But Henry did not take that for an answer and the following year sent him back with the promise of a larger reward if he made a second attempt. Eannes set sail and as he approached the Cape he turned westward for two days after which he came about and sailed south to discover that the Cape was already behind him. When he anchored at last and landed on shore he found it barren but by no means the gates of hell. Zurara informs us he doubled the Cape, despising all danger, and found the lands beyond quite contrary to what he, like others, had expected. And although the matter was a small one in itself, yet, on account of its daring, it was reckoned a very great achievement.

Prince Henry had broken the barrier of fear. The threatening Cape had been defeated and a different world had opened up. In 1435, he sent Gil Eannes out again with the royal cupbearer, Alfonso Baldaya. This time they reached another fifty leagues down the coast, and though they did not encounter any people they found footprints of men and of camels. Baldaya went out again in 1436, with orders to bring back a native from those parts. When he reached a large inlet that he hoped might be the mouth of the Senegal River of the silent trade in gold fame, he found no river, though they named the inlet the Rio de Ouro anyway. The Senegal, they would learn later, was actually 500 miles further south.

Step by step and year by year, the exploration of the west coast of Africa proceeded with no commercial rewards to show for the efforts. In 1441 Numo Tristão and Antão Gonçalves reached Cape Branco, and then the island of Arguim, which they immediately fortified. There they were able to capture two natives. From the same area, three years later, Eannes brought back the first human cargo of 200 Africans to be sold as slaves in Lagos.

Zurara's eyewitness account of the first sale of human merchandise in Europe is pathetic in the extreme, a painful vision of the cruelty, anguish and despair to come. Mothers would clasp their infants in their arms, and throw themselves on the ground to cover them with their bodies so that they could prevent their children from being separated from them. Though Zurara insisted that they were treated with kindness, and no difference was made between them and the freeborn servants of Portugal, these poor wretches had been wrenched from their homeland and had lost their freedom. They were taught trades, he said, were converted to Christianity, and eventually some intermarried with the Portuguese.

The turn around in the public attitude due to the arrival of this human merchandise was notable. Many, from the king down, had criticised the prince for wasting funds that could be better spent than on his obsessive pastime of exploration. When Henry's elder brother Duarte succeeded King John in 1433, he had not hesitated to lecture and reprove his brother for such shortcomings as extravagance and lack of scruples in the raising of money. But now the public feeling was different. Those who had been foremost in complaint grew quiet, and with soft voices praised what they had so loudly and publicly decried. 'And so they were forced to turn their blame into public praise; for they said it was plain the Infante was another Alexander; and their covetousness now began to wax greater.' The general feeling was a fair and just vindication of Prince Henry's extraordinary efforts and now, to cap it, everyone wanted to share in his successful Guinea trade.

Between 1444 and 1446 there was a burst of exploring activity. One of Prince Henry's immediate aims was to find an African gold supply – the existence of which he is thought to have learned from the Moors of Ceuta – to strengthen the Portuguese economy and to try and make the voyages pay for themselves. In 1445 one of the Henry's captains, Denis Dias, at last reached the entrance to the Senegal River – taking it for a branch of the Nile – and a year later Numo Tristão, who with Antão Gonçalves had discovered Cape Branco, sighted the Gambier River.

When Denis Dias rounded Cape Verde, the most western tip of the bulge of Africa, in 1445, the most barren coastline had been passed and the Portuguese trade with West Africa now demanded up to twenty-five caravels per year.

Alvise da Cadamosto (Cada Mosto), a Venetian – who anticipated other Italian sea captains like Cristoforo Colombo, Amerigo Vespucci, and the Gabotos who served foreign courts – sailing south along the West African coast for Prince Henry, accidentally discovered the Cape Verde Islands and turning east towards the continent, he explored the Senegal and Gambia Rivers 60 miles inland from the sea. An articulate man, his engaging accounts of curious tribal customs, of elephants, hippopotami, and of tropical vegetation, beckoned others to follow in his steps.

Cadamosto offers a typical example of the extensive way in which Dom Enrique accepted foreign assistance: if the interested parties funded the caravels and loaded them with goods, on their return they would hand over 25 per cent of the goods they brought back with them to the crown, and the rest would be for them; if it was the prince providing the funding they would receive 50 per cent, and if no profit was made the crown would bear the eventual losses. The conditions suited Cadamosto, a twenty-two-year-old youth full of resolve enthusiasm, so the deal was struck. The result was a succession of trips with other companions in search of business and adventure, besides an exact and instructive chronicle of the islands, coasts and inland tribes obtained after nine years of dangerous journeys. Cadamosto got to know the Cape Verde islands and saw those of Madeira, Funchal and the Canaries. He penetrated the Senegal, delving into the customs and beliefs of the Africans and discovering the fauna and the flora. Navigating in the south he met up with the Genoan, Usodimare, and carried on with him christening rivers, capes and islands. His tale was published in Vicenza in 1507, in *Paesi novamente ritrovato*. He returned to Venice in 1463.[1]

By the time of his death at Sagres in 1460, Prince Henry had set in motion the discovery of the West African coast. His explorers were still about 800 miles short of the equator but the great barrier of fear had been overcome and the first continuous organised exploration of the unknown had begun.

Henry's death caused only a momentary halt in the endeavour of exploration. In 1469 his nephew, Alfonso V, in financial difficulty, discovered a way to make exploring into a profitable business. Dom Alfonso struck an unusual agreement with a vassal of his court, Fernão Gomes. Gomes was a wealthy citizen of Lisbon who, after lengthy discussions with the king's advisors, committed himself to discover at least 100 leagues – 500km – of the African coast each year for the next five years. In return, he would receive the monopoly of the Guinea trade from which he would pay the crown its share. The rest is the story of a steadily rising curtain, as well as a tribute to private enterprise.

The series of annual discoveries on the West African coast made by the Gomes contract was impressive. It commenced by rounding Cape Palmas at the continent's south-western tip, into the Bight of Benin, the island of Fernando Po at the eastern tip of the Guinea coast and then southward beyond the equator. Prince Henry's ships had taken thirty years to cover a length of coast that Gomes under his contract covered in five. When his contract expired, the king, Don Alfonso, gave the trading rights to his son John, who at his father's death in 1481 became King John II of Portugal. The launching of this agreement initiated the next great age of seafaring and discovery.

As imports from the West African coast arrived in Portugal they enriched the treasury and provided King John II with the needed capital to pursue his ventures. Cargoes of pepper, ivory, gold and slaves became so rewarding that they gave their names to those parts of the continent on the Gulf of Guinea where they had originated. The Grain Coast was named after Guinea pepper known as the 'Grains of Paradise'. The Ivory Coast, The Gold Coast and the Slave Coast were also named for obvious reasons. King John II with his sharp sense of the national interest founded a fortress and trading post in the heart of the Gold Coast at Elmina (São Jorge da Mina) in 1481–1482. There is a story attached to this event as told by Ruy de Pina:[2]

Those buildings were raised on his land, because of the friendship he had shown them. The Mine had already produced gold when Don Juan considered it convenient to build a strategic fort there from where to explore, exert political control in the neighbourhood, manage the spread of trade and set up a slave trade that the Infante Don Enrique, due to moral scruples, had not wanted to encourage.

Diego de Azambuja, a confidant of the king, was appointed to head the armada, which was composed of ten caravels and two urcas. The caravels were fast but could only ship 50 to 60 men. However, the urcas, heavier vessels, could carry over 600. At the beginning of January 1482 the first talks were held with Caramanza, the black king in the region.

On meeting the black king and his companions, Azambuja said that King Don Juan had sent him because on previous trips the Portuguese had noticed Caramanza's desire to serve them and the speed with which he loaded the ships. 'And because those things arose from love, the king wanted to pay them back with love that would be more advantageous than his, because it was love for saving of his soul, man's most valuable asset.'

This edifying speech over, he then spoke of God, sin and baptism. But that love for the good black man and the saving of his soul – Azambuja continued to say in all seriousness – was not the only thing; the whites wanted to, if he accepted baptism, show him even more love by setting up, preferably in other spots where kings had requested it as a great honour, a fortress with houses and a warehouse. This would be to defend him. Thus, he would be powerful in the land and would be master of his neighbours as 'nobody would dare to perturb him once the fortress and the power of its King was there to protect him'.

The houses were for the members of the enterprise, and the warehouse to store the merchandise they brought with them and that which Caramanza would send regularly. For them, Don Diego ended, it was a pleasure that Caramanza must have got emotional over such an overflow of love; but it was in fact simple 'without being honey-tongued or perfidious'. He said he was moved by the King of Portugal's concerns for his soul and well-being, which in fact he deserved for the correctness of his previous conduct with them. He weighed up Azambuja and his companions and armed men and referring to the residences that they wanted to raise in his land, he pointed out that men of such quality would not feel at home in that savage land of Guinea, and that consequently, as this could be followed by fights, he requested them 'to have the decency to leave and allow the ships to return in the future as they had before so that there would always be peace and understanding between them. Friends that meet from time to time continue to be the best of friends, which if they were to be neighbours because of the nature of the human heart, and so, at peace with each other, his people would be better disposed to hear of that God which he wanted him to know of.' The refusal was wise and courteous but was superfluous.

Azambuja replied in the same way as in his previous speech, and on his insistence, without referring to baptism, which at the beginning had been a condition sine qua non but not now, the black king gave in. Although, like before, he did not believe in the white man's love.

Azambuja was bringing with him from Portugal a large part of the stones required to build the fort so that it was raised in a very short time. He had misunderstandings with the black men in the neighbourhood. He killed a few and imprisoned those from the neighbouring village. And so the La Mina citadel with its chapel and Christian layout was left isolated and easily defendable. In it he left 60 men and sent ships back loaded with gold, ivory, pepper and slaves.

Another factory was erected shortly after in a Benin port, from where a vast land-based slave traffic was begun as the natives that came to sell them gold and ivory did not have horses or camels, so that the Portuguese used them as slaves after their arrival at the coast with their goods and having loaded their ships.

After Azambuja's ships returned to Lisbon, Diogo Cão was sent out and discovered the mouth of the Congo in 1482 and began the custom of setting up engraved stone markers surmounted by a cross as tokens of Christian faith and proof of first discovery.[3]

When the mariners sailed below the equator they could no longer see the North Star, which made them look for another way to determine their latitude. Striving to solve this problem King John, like Prince Henry before him, collected experts from everywhere and he set up a commission headed by two learned astrologer mathematicians, a Portuguese dividend from the persecutions in Spain, across the border. As in 1492, when the Spanish inquisitor-general Torquemada gave Jews three months either to leave the country or convert to Christianity, the brilliant Abraham Zacuto left the university of Salamanca and was welcomed to Portugal by

Dom João II. Zacuto's disciple, Joseph Vizinho, had accepted the king's invitation ten years earlier and, in 1485, had been sent on a voyage to develop the technique of determining latitude by the height of the sun at midday. His theory was to record the declination of the sun along the whole Guinea coast.

The Almanach Perpetuum that Zacuto had written in Hebrew nearly twenty years before was the most advanced work for finding position at sea by means of the declination of the sun when navigating below the equator. When translated into Latin by Vizinho, it became the most valuable assistance to Portuguese navigators for half a century.

Dom João II carefully planned an expedition he had in mind for a long time. It was a carefully organised undertaking with a large capital investment and a numerous crew. For commander he chose Bartholomeu Dias, who had superintended the royal warehouses in Lisbon and had sailed a caravel down the African coast. Dias' expedition comprised two caravels of fifty tons each and a store ship never before added to a discovery trip and which would enable the caravels to reach out further to sea. Dias had with him six Africans who knew the coast and had been on previous voyages. Well fed and dressed in European clothes, the Africans were dropped off at different places down the coast with samples of gold, silver, spices and other products so they could show the natives, in the style of the silent trade, what goods the Portuguese wanted.

After landing the last of these Africans, Dias' ships ran into a storm that developed into a gale. Running before the strong northerly wind, with close-reefed sails in very rough seas, they were driven far off shore for the space of two weeks and southwards into the open sea. Blown south, the air got steadily colder. 'And as the ships were tiny, and the seas colder, and not such as in the land of Guinea... they gave themselves up for dead.' As soon as it was possible Dias came about and steering east for several days he sighted no land. In despair he turned north for 150 leagues, and on 3 February 1488, he suddenly sighted high mountains. He came to anchor in Mosel Bay some 230 miles north-east of what is now Cape Town.

The storm they had run into had accomplished what no amount of planning could have achieved as it drove them around the southern tip of the African continent. When the sailors eventually put their feet on shore, the natives tried to drive them away by pelting them with stones. Dias stood his ground, took aim with his crossbow and killed one with an arrow, which ended the encounter. He then followed the coastline north-east for another 300 miles to the mouth of the Great Fish River, that he named 'Infante', and then into Algoa Bay.

Dias was keen to continue into the Indian Ocean, and so fulfill the hope of many centuries, but the crew had no intention of carrying on. Weary, and terrified by the great seas and boisterous winds that they had encountered, all the crew, with one voice, demanded they proceed no further. Supplies were low and could only be replenished by hastening back to the supply ship. Dias consulted with his captains, all of whom signed a sworn document declaring their decision to turn back. Dias reluctantly agreed. As the ships sailed back, he passed the stone marker they had placed to signify their arrival 'with as much sorrow and feeling as though he were taking leave of a son condemned to exile'. Recalling the dangers faced on his outward journey, he was reluctant to end it without completion. On his return voyage he named the cape they had rounded at the southern tip of Africa 'Cape Stormy', Cabo Tormentoso. However, once back in Lisbon, Dom João II changed its title to the more prophetic name of Cape of Good Hope.

When they at last arrived back at the supply ship they found that only three men were alive out of the nine they had left behind. One of them was so overcome at seeing his companions that he died of a sudden heart attack, being very frail due to illness. The worm-eaten supply ship was unloaded and burned and the two caravels made their way back to Lisbon, from where they had left sixteen months and seventeen days before.

At the dockside at Lisbon harbour, looking closely at the weather-beaten caravels as they came into view, stood the still unknown Cristóforo Colombo. Everything about the ships and Dias' extraordinary voyage of discovery was of great personal interest to him. Columbus had come to Lisbon intending to make a second effort to persuade Dom João II to support his expedition to the Indies by sailing westward across the Atlantic but, disappointingly, the king's commission of experts had turned him down.

Dom João did not reject Columbus' proposals outright as he considered it more diplomatic to submit them to his scientific advisors. Whatever the true reasons were for turning Columbus down, the excuses he provided deprived him of hope. Perhaps the king might have selfishly wanted to keep the route to the orient solely for Portugal. However, whatever the reason was, he would regret it bitterly ten years later.

The prominent Argentine historian, Roberto Levillier, gave us his thoughts on the matter thus:

> Dom João looked at Columbus without seeing him. It is very common for men of state not to look at the other during a dialogue; they listen intensely with eyelids lowered, comparing foreign thoughts with their own in silence. And they let themselves be carried along by their greater faith in the council of their advisors. In this case Dom João II said no, because neither he nor his councillors considered the project reasonable, or Columbus capable of carrying it out. And Queen Isabella said yes, driven by her instinct and her immediate rapport and sympathy for Columbus, who made her see as he saw and believe what he believed. It is probable that if from the first visit yes had been her sole responsibility, Columbus would not have had to endure six years of setbacks.[4]

Dias' moment of triumph was a season of disappointment for Columbus. It showed that the eastward sea route to the Indies was now feasible, to the point,

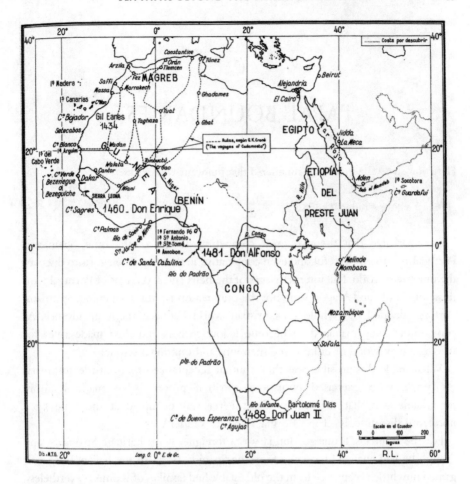

Progress of the Portuguese Discoveries as from 1434–1488.

perhaps, of making Columbus' project superfluous. Columbus noted in the margin of his copy of Pierre d'Ailly´s *Imago mundi* that he was present when Dias handed Dom João his epoch-making report and that it quickly had become apparent to him that he would now have to seek backing for his enterprise from a nation that had not yet found its own way round Africa.

Dias was never properly rewarded by his sovereign and, sadly enough, became the forgotten man of Portugal's age of discovery. He later supervised the building of ships for Vasco da Gama, but he was not included in Da Gama's crucial voyage to India. Only his death, in 1500, while commanding one of Cabral's thirteen-ship fleet off the coast of Brazil, was somewhat appropriate. A hurricane sank four of the ships, one of which was Dias's, 'casting them into the abyss of that great ocean sea... human bodies as food for the fish of those waters, which bodies we can believe were the first, since they were navigating in unknown regions... '.

6

PAPAL BOUNDARIES

Have you always deceived and conquered that innocent with tricks?

Argonautica, Appolonius Rhodius

It is remarkable that the two great competing powers of the time, Spain and Portugal, remained peaceful, and even cooperative in their separate efforts to discover the unknown world. The intermarriages of the heirs and sovereigns of Portugal with those of Castile and Aragon were not the only reason for this happening. Spain and Portugal divided the whole un-Christian world between them in advance. As competitors, they managed to become fellow seekers and they made rules for sharing a new world of unknown dimensions and unknown resources.

What made this possible was their mutual acceptance of an outside authority, the pope, who exercised enormous spiritual power. What made it more remarkable was that the seat of Saint Peter was occupied at the time by a notorious dissolute, Rodrigo Borgia, Pope Alexander VI.[1]

For the Romans, Rodrigo Borgia was a foreigner – his heritage Spanish – and though he had changed his name from the Spanish 'Borja' to the Italian 'Borgia', it gained him little acceptance from the old established families of Rome. Nevertheless, he was lucky in that his uncle had become pope as Calixtus III[2] and immediately flooded Rome with members of his Spanish kinsmen and friends, Rodrigo included. 'Catalans' the Romans called them contemptuously and watched in fury as the lucrative offices of the Church and of Rome found their way into Spanish hands. Callixtus III was generous to his compatriots but fatherly to his kinsmen. He adopted the two sons of his sister – Rodrigo and Don Pedro Luis – and showered the greatest possible honours upon them. Rodrigo, in 1456 already the bishop of Valencia, was created cardinal at the age of twenty-six. The following year he was named to the powerful and lucrative post of vice-chancellor of the Church, a position where it would have been difficult to avoid making money, and Rodrigo made the best of it.

By the time he reached his early forties, Cardinal Rodrigo Borgia was reckoned to be the second richest man in the collage of cardinals, a group that included some of the richest men in Europe. Although he owed his initial advancement to nepotism, it required considerable knowledge and cunning, not only to maintain but also to expand his wealth and power. 'Intellectually, he is capable of everything', a contemporary wrote:

He is a fluent speaker, writes well – though not in literary style, is extremely astute and very energetic and skillful in business matters. He is enormously wealthy, and through his connections with kings and princes, commands great influence. He has built a beautiful and comfortable palace for himself between the Bridge of Sant' Angelo and the Campo di Fiore. His revenues from his papal offices, his abbeys in Italy and Spain, his three bishoprics of Valencia, Portus and Cartagena, are vast. His office of Vice-Chancellor alone yields him 8000 gold ducats annually. His plate, his pearls, his stuffs embroidered with silk and gold, his books are all of such quality as would befit a king or pope. I need hardly mention the sumptuous bed-hangings, trappings for his horses and similar things of gold, silver and silk, or the vast quantity of gold coin, which he possesses. Altogether, it is believed that he possessed more gold and riches of every sort than all the cardinals put together excepting Estouteville.[3]

That vast hoard of wealth was required for other purposes besides simply vulgar display. Gone were the days when papal elections could be decided by force of arms. Matters were now much more orderly since the issue was decided by gold, not steel, by bribery, not force. With that purpose in mind Rodrigo Borgia devoted himself to amassing bullion as well as benefices, an activity that his office of vice-chancellor provided to advantage over his colleagues. When someone protested at his indiscriminate distribution of pardons for the most outrageous crimes – one of which included the murder of a daughter by the father – he responded flippantly, 'It is not God's wish that a sinner should die, but that he should live – and pay.'[4]

However, Rodrigo Borgia led a scandalous life, fathering at least seven children whose names are known, including four with Vannozza de' Catanei, mother of Cesare, Juan (Giovanni), Lucrezia and Joffré. He also fathered Rodrigo and another Giovanni, with the beautiful Giulia Farnese – La Bella Giulia – sister to the future Pope Paul III (nicknamed the Petticoat Cardinal). At least it can be said that Borgia lavished provision for them, especially on Vannozza's children, who became his principal interest in life.[5]

His private debaucheries were openly displayed to public amazement with a cynical indifference to scandal. (Among his many and lurid crimes Rodrigo Borgia did not include hypocrisy, which left him wide open to his enemies.) In June of 1460, the sober Pius II wrote to the young Rodrigo Borgia, cardinal and vice-chancellor of the Roman Church, the following letter:

Beloved Son,
We have heard that, four days ago, several ladies of Siena – women entirely given to worldly frivolities – were assembled in the gardens of Giovanni di Bichis and that you, quite forgetful of the high office with which you were invested, were with them from the seventeenth to the twenty-second hour. With you was one of your colleagues whose age alone, if not the dignity of his office, ought to have recalled him to his duty.

We have heard that the most licentious dances were indulged in, none of the allurements of love were lacking and you conducted yourself in a wholly worldly manner. Shame forbids mention of all that took place – not only the acts themselves but their very names are unworthy of your position. In order that your lusts might be given free rein the husbands, fathers, brothers and kinsmen of the young women were not admitted... All Siena is talking about the orgy... Our displeasure is beyond words... A cardinal should be beyond reproach...[6]

In 1492, at the comparatively early age of sixty, Pope Innocent VIII died. Consequently, during the last week of July the conclave was called to elect a new pope and it met on 6 August. Even before it congregated the trafficking in votes had risen to impressive proportions. It became known that the king of France had paid into a bank 200,000 gold ducats to ensure the election of Giuliano della Rovere and the Republic of Genoa had followed up with another 100,000 for the same cardinal, their favourite son. The French endeavour was fatal to della Rovere's chances. While his fellow cardinals were quite prepared to sell him their votes, they balked at the French interference. This reaction cleared the field for the next bidders.

During the first week of the conclave, no one dominated the scene. The Florentine envoy reported to his masters that the situation was turbulent, due to the undeclared motives and allegiances. According to an observer from Ferrara, among the most likely candidates Rodrigo Borgia was last among a list of the top four. However, this shrewd observer thought that Borgia's vast wealth might yet bring about his election. Had he not boasted that he had sacks of gold enough to fill the Sistine Chapel? Regardless of the bitter memories of his Spanish uncle, Callixtus III, the conclave was now reasonably free from outside interference.

By the evening of 10 August, Rodrigo Borgia, well aware of the enormous benefits the election would ultimately shower upon him, had bought the votes of thirteen cardinals. They included members of the noblest Roman families. But once assured their price would be paid, none hesitated to sell his vote to the despised foreigner.

With impressive stealth and persuasion he deployed his vast wealth. Later, a bitter epigraph circulated that said, 'Alexander sells the keys, the altar, Christ himself – he has the right to for he bought them.'[7] It was an accurate enough statement as during the first four days of the conclave Rodrigo bargained and obtained the support he wanted. That is to say, except for Ascanio Sforza who remained his sole rival. He too was enormously wealthy and, as an added plus, he could count on the wide-ranging support of his family, the ruling dynasty of the powerful duchy of Milan. During the evening of the tenth of August, Borgia took Sforza aside for a private discussion. Realising the moment had come to see who could outbid the other, Rodrigo opened with a dazzling array of bribes: Hard cash? An archbishopric? An abbacy? The vice-chancellorship itself? Sforza was an able bargainer and closed for the office of vice-chancellor and a settlement in cash as well, which Borgia immediately honored. Before dawn next day four mule-loads of bullion – gold according to some reports, silver according to others – were on their way to Sforza's palace.

Eight cardinals held to their principals of not accepting bribes but Borgia needed only one more vote to gain his nomination. That one vote was the most debased of them all for its seller was the ninety-six-year-old cardinal of Venice. The gold fever had struck even this old man, who could hardly expect to enjoy the price of his simony for very long. Ultimately, as it turned out, he received the shamefully small price of five thousand ducats, but his vote gave Borgia the necessary majority. The college went through the motions of election, praying to the Holy Ghost for guidance – to the vexation of Cardinal Giuliano della Rovere who protested that the whole thing was a farce – and shortly after daybreak on the morning of 11 August 1492 the name of Cardinal Rodrigo Borgia was taken from the urn.

'I am pope, I am pope' he cried excitedly and hastened to robe himself in the gorgeous vestments of his new rank. He made none of the modest disclaimers demanded by tradition. Instead, Johannes Burchard, the papal master of ceremonies, was immediately ordered to prepare slips of paper bearing the legend, 'We have for pope Alexander VI, Rodrigo Borgia of Valencia', to scatter among the population congregated outside. Once again, Borgia showed no hypocritical modesty. Not for him were the Piuses or the Innocents or the Clements. He chose for his name that of the greatest pagan conqueror of them all, Alexander. In the same month of August 1492 that saw Rodrigo Borgia seated on the throne of Peter, Christopher Columbus set sail across the Atlantic on his first voyage of discovery.

To resolve the territorial disputes between Spain and Portugal, Rodrigo Borgia named a committee to study the situation, though he ruled over it from above, steering the resolution in favour of his mother country within the appearance of neutrality. The pope very quickly issued three papal bulls or decrees on 3–4 May 1493, just a few days after Isabella and Ferdinand had received Columbus on his return from his first voyage. In the first of them, the pope gave Spain dominion over the lands discovered by Columbus, with the same privileges that previous popes had granted to the Portuguese in Guinea. Neither power was to occupy any territory already in the hands of a Christian ruler, while both powers agreed to evangelise any territory that they occupied. It is worth noting that none of the other European powers facing the Atlantic ever accepted this disposition or the subsequent agreement deriving from it.

In matters of state such as this, the pontiff was usually advised by a council of learned bishops and cardinals who debated the case, with or without the pope present. After their usually long-drawn out deliberations, their decisions became decrees, some of which then became church doctrine. If, as in this arbitration case, the parties involved embraced the church as their official religion, it would oblige them to adhere to the papal decision. The decrees were known as papal bulls, so named for the bulla, a round fixed leaden seal, affixed to pronouncements from the pope himself.

While the papal bull of Alexander VI, of May 1493, had defined the geographical boundaries of the unknown world between Spaniards and Portuguese for future possessions, King John II of Portugal, who had the advantage of a superior navy, would not stand by while the pope gave away his empire to Spain. With his navy behind him, he first negotiated with Ferdinand and Isabella to avoid the consequences of the pope's declarations. Then, a third bull − Inter Coetera − established a line − La Raya − that Columbus himself had proposed for dividing the world. This line lay along a meridian 100 leagues (483km) west of the Azores and the Cape Verde Islands. Everything west of this line belonged to Spain, and everything to the east belonged to Portugal. João II protested this decision, but his protests to Rome only made the situation worse. On 25 September 1493 − the same day Columbus sailed from Cadiz on his second voyage − the pope gave the rulers of Castille and Aragon dominion over all territories discovered in the Orient and over the 'Indies' in particular

This was altogether too much for King João II, who decided to negotiate the matter directly with his close relatives Isabella and Ferdinand. After much hard bargaining, the Spanish agreed to a modification of Pope Alexander's edict. This agreement was ratified at the palace of Tordesillas in northern Spain, on 7 June 1494. There, in the royal palace of the same name, Spanish and Portuguese ambassadors reaffirmed the papal division, and the line was again moved, this time 370 leagues (1,110 miles or 1.786km) west of the Cape Verde Islands or at 46° 37' west of Greenwich.[8] The king of Portugal promised not to send any expeditions west of the line and Spain agreed not to trespass beyond it to the east. However, the line was so imprecise as to cause as much trouble as it solved.

In 1448 the cartographer Andrea Bianco put his signature to a map on which he drew the outline of part the coast of Africa and further to the west the northern coast of Brazil. Bianco's map brought forth what the king of Portugal would prefer to have suppressed, that the Portuguese had crisscrossed the Atlantic, discovering the New World in the process, long before Columbus had arrived. This was the reason for King John II's insistence on pressing for the line of demarcation to be moved further west. Though his insistence seemed fussy and ridiculous at the time, he achieved by this means Portugal's legal rights to Brazil six years before Pedro Alvarez Cabral made the discovery official.[9]

After the treaty was signed, questions arose almost immediately. For instance, from which of the several islands was the distance to be drawn? The interpretation depended on the convenience of the party. The new boundary enabled Portugal to claim the coast of Brazil but it caused inescapable problems. To give only one example: in South America, according to an erroneous Portuguese interpretation at the time, the line gave them possession of the northern bank of the Rio de La Plata, where they arrived in 1573 and later built a citadel they named Colonia del Santísimo Sacramento in 1680. Regardless of the political fuss it caused, they managed to hold onto their stronghold for 98 years, until it was finally ceded to Spain by the signing of yet another treaty, this time of San Idelfonso, in 1778.

The Treaty of Tordesillas evaded war at that moment, and it remains one of the most celebrated treaties in European history, but it was so plagued with ambiguities that nobody knows whether it really ever went into effect. For instance: from which Cape Verde Island should the line be measured? Precisely how long was a league? How would you measure it at sea? It would take centuries before technology existed to draw the precise line of longitude. In any event it did affirm Portugal's right to part of Brazil as well as its eastward sea path to the Indies. Regardless of assuring peace between the parties, it is left for one to surmise what contribution the Spanish monarchs might have disbursed to Rodrigo Borgia's coffers for his intervention.

To those Christians who were concerned about the occupant of the throne of Saint Peter, Alexander gave them immediate hope. On the morning after the conclave he addressed the consistory, admonishing solemn warning that he intended to reform the college and purge it of its sins – above all of simony. The fourteen cardinals, who were at that same moment assessing their gains from the simoniacal election of this pontiff, must have been rendered mute and deep in thought.

For the ordinary Roman who throughout the centuries delighted in circuses, Alexander planned the most elaborate of coronation ceremonies. Even as cardinal his theatrical displays for the feast of Corpus Christy processions had outshone every other, now as pope he lavished the Vatican horded wealth of centuries to display with splendour the advent of the Borgia dynasty. The Borgia arms, the great Spanish bull passant, appeared at every street corner. Near the Palace of Saint Mark a huge figure of a bull was erected from whose head gushed wine in a non ending stream. Gilded naked bodies of pubescent boys and girls posed as living statues; flowers overflowed from balconies of every house along the processional route while triumphant arches added their blaze of colour to the summer streets.

Rome was great under Caesar – but greater far under Alexander.
The first was only a mortal man – the second is a God.

So the triumphal arches proclaimed and the blasphemy went unnoticed.

As Alexander displayed his true nature, contemporaries began to perceive him as a man little removed from a monster. Perhaps the nature of Renaissance man inevitably exaggerated, but against the chorus of shrill invectives remain the judgments of sufficiently sober men to give solid ground to the accusations.

Alexander VI.

Francesco Guicciardini, a major Florentine scholar who later served Alexander's successors, granted him his eloquence, his industry, his administrative skill.

> But these virtues were bound up with far greater faults. His manner of living was dissolute. He knew neither shame nor sincerity, neither faith nor religion. Moreover, he was possessed by an insatiable greed, an overwhelming ambition and a burning passion for the advancement of his many children who, in order to carry out his iniquitous decrees, did not scruple to employ the most heinous means.[10]

There had been many excesses committed previously by the papacy but the Borgia clan hungered after power, and in grasping for it, nearly destroyed the papacy in the process.

Borgia had at least three other children before the four that Vannozza de' Catanei had bore him. For his eldest son Pedro, he obtained the dukedom of Gandia in Spain. The young man was destined for a high secular career, but he died before his father became pope, so his title – as well as his father's ambitions for him – were transmitted to the next in line, Giovanni, fourteen years old at the time. He and Cesare, with their sister Lucrezia, were removed from Vannozza's care and placed in the care of Borgia's cousin and lifelong confidante, Madonna Adriana. And it was there, three years later, that Borgia met the beautiful Giulia Farnese – to whom the wags in Rome accorded the title of 'Christ's Bride', after the pope had taken her to his bed. She was perhaps sixteen at the time and had married Adriana's only son in the papal palace.

Lorenzo Pucci, a cousin to Julia, visited the house that sheltered the three women, which Pope Alexander loved above all others. Pucci, it seems, wandered into a domestic and friendly scene.

Madonna Giulia had just finished washing her hair when I entered. She was sitting by the fire with Madonna Lucrezia, the daughter of our master, and Madonna Adriana and they received me with great cordiality.

The conversation turned to family affairs. Pucci thanked Giulia for her favours, had the compliments gracefully returned and then was taken to see the new baby, Giulia's first born.

She is now well grown and, it seems to me, resembles the pope. Madonna Giulia has grown a little stouter and is a most beautiful creature. She let down her hair before me and had it dressed. It reached to her feet – never have I seen anything like it. She has the most beautiful hair. She wore a headdress of fine linen, and over it a sort of net, light as air, with gold threads interwoven in it. In truth it shone like the sun. She wore a lined robe in the Neapolitan fashion, as did Madonna Lucrezia, who after a little while went out to remove it. She returned shortly in a gown almost entirely of violet velvet.[11]

Lucrezia, in her thirteenth year, had been married for six months already. Legally speaking it was her third marriage, since marriage contracts had been exchanged on her behalf twice before. But that had been when Rodrigo had been a mere cardinal of the church – glad enough to obtain even a minor member of Spanish nobility for his illegitimate daughter. However, after becoming pope her value increased astronomically. The two contracts were repudiated and Alexander looked for a politically more lucrative husband. He cast his eye on Giovanni Sforza, kinsman to whom Alexander owed the tiara.

Giovanni Sforza eagerly accepted the invitation. Lucrezia had not yet acquired the appalling reputation that her father and brother's ambitions had thrust upon her. Judging by her early years before she was moved like a pawn, and her later years when she became removed from the family atmosphere, her true character became visible, at least to those that cared to record it. She was generous, like her father, easily influenced and led, and not particularly intelligent. Her physical attributes could not compare with Giulia's but still she was attractive. 'She is of middle height and graceful in form. Her face is rather long, the nose well cut, hair golden – eyes no special colour. Her mouth is rather large, with brilliantly white teeth, her neck is slender and fair, her bust admirably proportioned.' Indeed, young Giovanni Sforza might count himself fortunate. On 12 June 1493, the marriage was celebrated in the Vatican. The reception that followed took place in the great Sala Reale and all the adjoining apartments. The walls covered in tapestries and upon a dais was placed the Chair of Peter, decorated with brocade. Other lesser chairs were placed on either side of it and over the marble floor were scattered velvet cushions in brilliant colours.

Johannes Burchard, the German born papal master of ceremonies, faithfully recorded the event:

Don Juan Borgia, Duke of Gandia, the pope's son and Donna Lucrezia's elder brother, was commanded by His Holiness to escort Lucrezia. He brought her in as far as the last room, a Negro girl carrying her train, and she was followed by Donna Battistina – the granddaughter of pope Inocent VIII of blessed memory – and her train too was born by a Negress. Donna Giulia Farnese, the pope's concubine, and many other Roman ladies, numbering in all about one hundred and fifty, followed Lucrezia and Battistina

   The festivities lasted all night. All Rome that counted were there, including the ambassador from Ferrara who wrote to his prince:

   When the banquet was over the ladies danced and, as an interlude, we had an excellent play with much singing and music. The pope and all the others were there. What more can I say? My letter would never end were I to describe it all. Thus we spent the whole night, whether for good or ill I will leave it to your Highness to determine.[12]

At the party the elder brother, Giovanni, overshadowed Cesare in the magnificence of his attire. But Cesare had benefited from the golden shower, for his father had given him a cardinal's hat at the first consistory in August the previous year. He was destined for the church even as a boy. The reigning Sixtus IV obligingly dispensed Cesare, as a four-year-old boy, from his canonical impediment – 'being born of a cardinal and a married woman' – that cleared his path. Now eighteen, Cesare was a cardinal, bishop of Pampeluna, archbishop of his father's old diocese of Valencia, as well as numerous lesser benefices, all of which was simply a by-product of being a Borgia. Giovanni was already Duke of Gandia. He had delayed his departure to Spain and marriage to a Spanish princess to be present at Lucrezia's wedding. Alexander married off his last son, Joffré, to Sancia, daughter of the ruling house of Naples. Within a year of becoming pope he linked his family to three of the most out-standing houses of Italy and Spain. Only France remained to be brought into the net.

   A week after Giovanni Borgia had been given the title of Duke of Gandia, on 14 June 1497; his mother Vannozza gave a dinner party in his honour in the vineyard of her home outside Rome. The guests enjoyed the evening and towards dusk Giovanni and his brother Cesare, together with their servants and friends, rode back to the papal palace. At some distance from it Giovanni bade his friends good night, and with his groom and another man in a festive mask, rode away into the darkness.

   When Giovanni was not found next morning, 'His Holiness became very anxious, but continued to hope for the Duke's return during the rest of the day, having persuaded himself that his son had spent the night with some girl and did not want to be seen leaving her house in daylight.'[13] A sensible assumption knowing Giovanni's habits. However, at nightfall the groom was found, very badly wounded and unable to talk. Alexander, now terribly alarmed, ordered a massive search to be conducted.

   The searchers questioned a wood dealer who said he had seen two men walking on either side of a horse keeping a body slung over it from falling. He

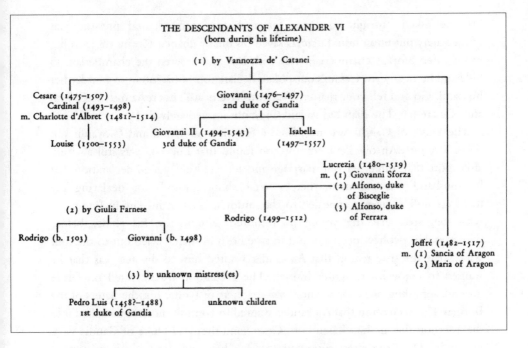

THE DESCENDANTS OF ALEXANDER VI
(born during his lifetime)

(1) by Vannozza de' Catanei

Cesare (1475–1507)
Cardinal (1493–1498)
m. Charlotte d'Albret (1481?–1514)

Giovanni (1476–1497)
2nd duke of Gandia

Louise (1500–1553)

Giovanni II (1494–1543)
3rd duke of Gandia

Isabella
(1497–1557)

Lucrezia (1480–1519)
m. (1) Giovanni Sforza
(2) Alfonso, duke
of Bisceglie
(3) Alfonso, duke
of Ferrara

(2) by Giulia Farnese

Rodrigo (1499–1512)

Rodrigo (b. 1503)   Giovanni (b. 1498)

Joffré (1482–1517)
m. (1) Sancia of Aragon
(2) Maria of Aragon

(3) by unknown mistress(es)

Pedro Luis (1458?–1488)   unknown children
1st duke of Gandia

said that keeping his head down in his boat, he had seen them back the horse up to the river Tiber and picking up the corpse, throw it into the water. As the cloak floated, they threw stones at it until it sank.

Three hundred watermen were soon assembled and the river dredged. 'Truly, now, was Alexander VI a fisher of men', the wags of the town mocked. At about midday the body of Giovanni, Duke of Gandia, was recovered from the filthy water. He was dressed in all his finery, down to a pair of gloves under his belt that contained thirty ducats. His throat had been slit and nine other knife wounds stabbed in his body.

The murderer was never found, though suspicion rested on many people: the Orsinis, who had been dispossessed to give Giovanni their estates; the Sforzas, particularly young Giovanni; a number of personal enemies, including a likely cuckold; and finally the dead man's brother Cesare. This was not brought up until a year after the murder, when Cesare threw off his priestly robes to appear as a prince. Nevertheless, once the rumour was out it grew out of proportion until it overshadowed all the other accusations and was accepted as a fact. It was supposed to be due to jealousy of his brother's secular glory and a desire to obtain his titles and honours for himself. There appeared to be no particular animosity among the brothers and Cesare seemingly had nothing to gain from the murder. As cardinal Sforza speculated, it was most likely 'something to do with a love affair'.

On 21 July 1498, Alexander's daughter Lucrezia was married for the second time, the first of a complex plot to put her brother Cesare upon the throne of Naples. There was an impediment, however; she was still legally married to Giovanni Sforza. The Borgias had decided upon a plan and Sforza was in the way.

He was asked outright to agree for a divorce, refused, and pressure was immediately put upon him. Lucrezia saved his life by chance. Cesare came to her room when Sforza's chamberlain was with her. She ordered the chamberlain to hide and he overheard Cesare's outspoken declaration of his intent to murder her husband. 'Go and tell your master what you have heard', Lucrezia instructed him after Cesare left. The man did so and Giovanni immediately fled.

The Duke of Gandia was murdered a few days afterward and Giovanni was given a respite. An obedient commission found that Lucrezia was still a virgin after more than three years of marriage and accepted her signed declaration that her husband was impotent, thereby establishing grounds for declaring the marriage null. Giovanni appealed to the sardonic head of his family, Ludovico, who suggested that the young man should demonstrate his ability before witnesses. His nephew declined, and in rage born of shame cried out to the four winds that the true reason that Alexander wanted him to divorce was that he wanted to enjoy his daughter himself. The accusation instantly fell on fertile ground, appealing not only to the pornographers of Rome but the haters of the Borgias. The accusation that Alexander wanted to commit incest snowballed into the assertion that he had. Then both Cesare and the dead Duke of Gandia were drawn in. They too were supposed to have been involved in an incestuous relationship with Lucrezia. Added to the charge already in circulation that Cesare had murdered his brother, this was to taint all the males in the family with a colour that was never wholly to be washed away.

On July 14 Lucrezia was married, very quietly, to Alfonso Duke of Bisceglie, son of the king of Naples. She brought with her a huge dowry, but part of it was intended to persuade the king to give his daughter Carlotta to Cesare. Carlotta, however, would have nothing to do with the proposed husband, and nothing would move her from her resolve.

Alexander had received Cesare's request to relinquish his cardinalate with great displeasure, but in the end he had given in. It was a victory over his father although it meant he would be stripped of his lucrative benefices. But the wealthy and generous king of France, Louis XII, stepped in prepared to dispense honours to him after the pope agreed to dissolve Louis' existing marriage to his ailing and misshapen wife, Jeanne of France, leaving him free to marry the beautiful and wealthy heiress Anne of Brittany. In gratitude, he agreed to the marriage of Cesare to Charlotte d'Albret, a princess in her own right – her married life proved happy as it lasted precisely four months. Charlotte, already pregnant, never saw him again.

Determined to regain the Papal States for the Vatican that over the years had been taken over by different warlords – papal barons they called themselves – Cesare put himself at the head of the papal troops. In combination with his newly found ally, Louis XII, Cesare attacked Milan. It went smoothly enough. Ludovico Sforza fled, and the Milanese welcomed Louis, who declared himself Duke of Milan by right of inheritance. With the aid of King Louis, Cesare attacked the northern section of the

Papal States, the Romagna, onto the Adriatic Sea. Each of the Romagnol cities was the personal stronghold of some warlord who, with reluctance recognised the authority of his overlord, the pope. The campaign was not an impressive performance except for the cities of Imola and Forli ruled by the viraginous Caterina Sforza. Abandoned by her people she fought on with immense courage, spurred on with as much personal loathing for Cesare as by any political considerations. She knew she had reason to fear, when she inevitably surrendered to a French captain, who later that night over a card game ransomed her to Cesare for 30,000 ducats. She now belonged to Cesare Borgia , and he could do with her what he wished. To prove it, he raped her successively in her cell over the next few days.

On 26 February 1500, Cesare entered Rome in triumph, dressed in black and surrounded by bodyguards also clothed in black for dramatic effect. Caterina Sforza, the late Lady of Imola and Forli was dragged behind him in golden chains and, after being displayed to the mob, was imprisoned in Sant' Angelo. She would never again have seen the light of day had it not been for the French. They had greatly admired the gallantry of her defense, and under pressure Alexander was forced to release her.[14]

It was from here onward that the reign of Rodrigo Borgia, Alexander VI, took on its most ignominious colours. Up to then the Vatican had been the scene of scandalous enough behaviour; now, the pope and his immediate entourage became actively criminal as well as deliberately perverted. It was no longer just the gossip mongering enemies of the Borgias who carried the stories, exaggerating them as they spread them, but even the pedantic Johannes Burchard coldly described the scenes that not even the pornographers of the day could have improved on. Lucrezia, with her fatal compliancy, was involved. Burchard, as was his way, merely recorded the fact that she was present when fifty Roman harlots were brought into the palace to couple with fifty palace servants for prizes presented by Alexander. It is true that outsiders embroidered the tales of the event, making her into a promoter rather than an observer.

It is also true that she stood with her father at a window in the Vatican palace while Cesare with a crossbow picked off a number of unarmed criminals turned loose in a courtyard for the occasion. Cesare had taken over as undisputed lord of Rome outside the Vatican and he imposed a terror upon it that the city had never experienced under Alexander. While Alexander killed for political reasons, Cesare killed for any reason. A drunken masquerader had his hand cut off and tongue cut out for mocking him. A Venetian, accused of circulating an insulting pamphlet, was condemned to be put in a bag and drowned in the Tiber. The Venetian ambassador came to plead with Alexander but the pope only shrugged his shoulders. 'The Duke is a good natured man – but he can not tolerate insults. I have often told him that Rome is a free city, and that everyone may write and speak as he pleases. Evil is often spoken of me but I let it pass.' The Duke's reply was: 'Rome is accustomed to write and speak – maybe – but I will teach such people to take care.'[15]

Cesare had come to Rome not only to display his military achievements but for money to continue his conquests. It was a superb stage to display his triumph, for the year 1500 was a year of the church's jubilee and Rome was crowded with pilgrims from every nation in Europe. The jubilee gifts of tens of thousands of pilgrims meant huge amounts of money for the Borgia coffers. Also, in September, nine new cardinals were created. 'Most are men of doubtful reputation. All have paid handsomely for their elevation – some of them have paid 20,000 ducats and more – so that between 120,000 and 130,000 ducats have been collected. Alexander VI is showing to the world that the amount of a pope's income is exactly what he chooses.'[16]

Apparantly Cesare was jealous of Alexander's generosity toward Lucrezia, not because she was competing with him for her father's personal affection but because he felt that the fat revenues she was provided should be devoted to his own campaigns. Lucrezia's husband Prince Alfonso Bisceglie had lost his value. The Spanish and French had temporarily united to topple Bisceglie's family in Naples. Alexander had coolly agreed to provide the victors with his son-in-law's inheritance, so the duke found himself in exactly the same position as Giovanni Sforza had been three years before. He fled but foolishly returned at Alexander's bidding. He now lived in fear and watched for the first hostile sign from his wife's atrocious family.

In the evening of 15 July 1500, as he was crossing the Piazza San Pietro, several masked men rushed towards him from the shadows of the surrounding buildings. He tried to turn back but they grabbed him and throwing him to the ground they beat him senseless as well as knifing him with a stiletto from his chin to his naval. As a papal guard ran to the scene, the attackers, startled, ran toward the street that led out of the square. The guard, while shouting for help, carried Alfonso into the papal chambers where he was nursed by his wife and sister, who now alarmed, cooked his food in the room for fear of poison. Though badly wounded he had narrowly escaped. Convinced that Cesare was behind the attempt, as soon as he had partially recovered, Alfonso, supported by two Neapolitan guards, stood on the balcony of his room overlooking the papal gardens and recognised Cesare strolling there alone. Taking a crossbow from one of his guards, Alfonso shot a bolt at the walking figure in the garden. It narrowly missed its mark thus condemning him to death.

There is considerable mystery as to how Alfonso was killed. A Venetian report states that after the episode of the failed attempt he returned to his invalid bed where in the evening he was visited by Cesare with one of his assassins. After forcing the women to leave, Alfonso was strangled. This time there was no question. Everyone knew Cesare was responsible for the killing.

In September Cesare left Rome at the head of 10,000 men to reduce Rimini, Faenza and Pesaro, all under the protection of the Venetians. He had only one dangerous enemy and that was time itself for strong as his father might look, he was nevertheless an old man. 'He [Cesare] had good reason to fear that a new pope would be hostile to him', Niccoló Machiavelli considered:

and seek to deprive him of what had been bestowed on him by his predecessor. He therefore made four distinct provisions, in the first place by utterly destroying the families of all those nobles whom he had deprived of their states so that no future pope could reestablish them. Secondly, by attaching to his interests all the gentry of Rome in order to control the power of the pope. Thirdly, by securing a majority in the College of Cardinals. Fourthly and lastly, by acquiring so much power in the lifetime of his father that he might be able to resist the first attack of the enemy. Three of these designs he had effected before the death of Alexander.[17]

Alexander's strategy was twofold: to maintain the flow of gold into his coffers and to confuse the enemy. He handled both tasks with the greatest skill. First he agreed to invest both the kings of Spain and France with the dismembered kingdom of Naples, causing the French and Spaniards to quarrel over the spoils. But Louis needed Cesare in his struggle with the Spaniards, which enabled Cesare to shake off his dependency on the French, a condition that had served to check his more outrageous activities. Now at the head of his troops he took Faenza, Cesena, Sengaglia, Urbino and Camerino. Upon receiving the news of the fall of Camerino, the pope happened to be with the Venetian ambassador Antonio Giustiniani who reported: 'He could so little contain himself that, to give some relief to his feelings and mark the importance of the news, he got up from his chair and went to the window and there he listened as the letter of his Duke was read aloud.'[18]

The murder of Alfonso Bisceglie brought its dividends, as Lucrezia, now free to marry again, was offered to the son of Ercole d'Este the present Duke of Ferrara, whose dominions bordered Cesare's to the north and formed a buffer between the Romagna and the often hostile Venetians. The twenty-four-year-old Alfonso d'Este was very hesitant to be added to the long list of Lucrezia's ill-fated husbands but the colossal bribes that were offered made him overcome his initial reluctance. On the positive side was the fact that he gained a pius and virtuous wife, for Lucrezia, as adaptable as usual conformed to the respectability of the Ferrarese court in the same way she had joined in the licentious celebrations in Rome. Her father considerately granted Ferrara a dispensation to postpone the start of lent, 'so that the people there could lawfully eat meat and have festivals and thanksgiving when Donna Lucrezia arrived'.

The late summer of 1503 was unusually hot and sultry in pestilential Rome. The stench emanating from the streets gave a clear warning of the dangers of remaining in the city. The area around Vatican hill was a fetid marsh, malarial in summer, and normally Alexander would have sought the coolness of one of his country villas. But August began badly for him. His cousin, Cardinal Giovanni Borgia, had fallen victim to the Roman summer and his funeral took place on the first day of August. As Alexander solemnly watched the procession from his favourite window in the Vatican Palace, he remarked, 'This is a bad month for stout people' and barely had he said it an owl flopped through the window and fell at his feet. He was terrified by the significance of this bad omen.[19]

The affairs of Cesare were reaching a climax – a massive expedition was being planned against Naples.[20] The pope therefore felt obliged to remain in the center of affairs.

The eleventh anniversary of Alexander's accession fell ten days after his episode with the owl. There were no particular celebrations to mark it, and observers remarked that the pope was melancholy and downcast, not his usual jovial self at all. On the following day he fell ill – desperately ill – and so did Cesare and a certain Cardinal Adrian Corneto at whose villa Alexander and Cesare had dined two days earlier. Gossip had it that Corneto had been marked down by father and son as their next victim. According to the Venetian ambassador Antonio Giustiniani, the Borgias' practice – father and son – was to fatten their victims before slaughter with ever richer benefits for which the victims received colossal sums, before dispatching them with a certain 'white powder'.

It was no difficult matter in those days to write off the murder of a person to natural causes, especially cardinals who tended to be elderly men. But the hatred in which the Borgia were held made any accusation of death seem highly probable. More so as Italians were morbidly obsessed with the concept of poison as a political weapon – Machiavelli even enshrined it as an accepted political philosophy. It conformed to the national taste for coldly planned vengeance and any death not obviously attributable to violence or the plague was simply accounted for by the theory of poison. However, poison was notoriously difficult to administer to a man on his guard – Cesare personally preferred the more direct method of open murder – but the Borgia as arch criminals had perfected the skills of the arch poisoner. The 'white powder' of the Borgia – a crude preparation of arsenic that was not easy to disguise and was unpredictable in its effects – became a magic potion employed by all members of the family. They could strike down an enemy a hundred kilometers away and at any time they chose within reason, since they had agents spread around the country. It was too much to expect that the gossips of Rome would accept Alexander's fatal illness as the result of the fetid summer humours of the city of Rome. Adrian Corneto thought that he himself had been poisoned, and true to form a whole story was weaved around this suspicion. Cesare was supposed to have prepared the potion but the poisoned cup had been switched so the unsuspecting Alexander and Cesare had drunk freely of it.

Cesare, though very ill, started to recover after a few days; Alexander, however, was doomed. For a week, the seventy-year-old man battled with pains and a burning fever that also laid prostrate his tough young son. On the very same Friday that Cesare took a turn for the better, Alexander, now ghostly pale, entered his death agonies. An hour later Alexander's confessor was summoned and the last rites administered.

Rumors of supernatural happenings made their rounds. Servants swore they overheard the dying man pleading with some invisible being for a little more time – he had sold his soul to the devil who had promised him a pontificate of exactly eleven years and one week. 'The devil was seen to leap out of the bedroom in the shape of an ape. And a cardinal ran to seize it, and, having caught it, would have given it to the pope. But the pope said, "Let him go, let him go. It is the Devil." And that night he fell ill and died.'[21] And long after his death water boiled in his mouth and steam poured out of the apertures of his body.

The pragmatic Burchard mentions nothing of demonic visitations. The story he had to tell was, stated plainly, definitely squalid: on 18 August 1503, Alexander was still in extremis when Cesare's men forced their way into the Vatican and collected all portable treasure. When the pope died, his valets immediately plundered his bedroom unhindered, for no person of rank came near the corpse until Burchard, as part of his duties, came to dress it. It lay all that night unattended, and when in the morning the Office for the Dead was recited over it, the palace guards attacked the handful of priests praying around the bed. The priests fled, leaving their ruler's corpse unguarded.

Fearing that the Roman people might break in and desecrate the body in their hatred, Burchard had it moved to a chapel where it remained throughout Sunday. When he came back to prepare the body for burial, he found that the changes wrought by death had made it too large for the coffin. Coldly pragmatic he described meticulously in his diary the appearance of what had been Alexander VI. 'The face was mulberry-coloured and thickly covered with blue-black spots: the nose swollen, the mouth distorted, the tongue doubled over, the lips puffed out so that they seemed to cover the whole face.' The attendants from the mortuary joked obscenely as they tried to stuff the corpse into its coffin. They eventually succeeded but only by taking the miter off, rolling the body in a carpet, and then pounding it into the coffin with their fists. 'No candles were lit, and no priest or other person of dignity attended the corpse.'

> So died pope Alexander, at the height of glory and prosperity about whom it must be known that he was a man of the utmost power and of great judgment and spirit, as his actions and behaviour showed. But as his first accession to the papacy was foul and shameful – for he bought with gold so high an office – so similarly his government was in agreement with its vile foundation. There was in him, and in full measure, all the vices both of flesh and spirit... There was in him no religion, no keeping of his word. He promised all things liberally, but bound himself to nothing that was not useful to him. He had no care for justice, since in his days Rome was a den of thieves and murderers. His ambition was boundless, and such that it grew in the same measure that his state increased. Nevertheless, his sins meeting with no punishment in this world, he was to the last of his days most prosperous. In one word, he was more evil and more lucky than, perhaps, any other pope for many ages before.[22]

This judgment by Francisco Guicciardini, the great Florentine scholar, was written over a generation after Alexander had gone to his grave. But Guicciardini's charge that Alexander had been 'the most evil' pope for ages has a ring to it that does not take into account the incompetence and moral treachery

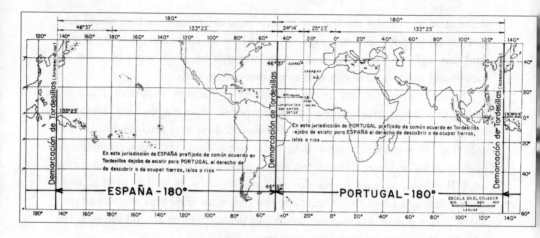

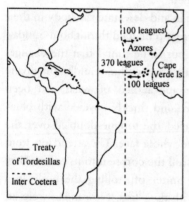

Maps showing the division of the conquered world between Spain and Portugal in 1494.

of his enemies. The judgment was based on opinions of contemporaries coloured by the hatred of men who had been despoiled or threatened by the pope but who remained indifferent to the grotesque corruption of the papacy except as it benefited them politically. The Renaissance Papacy had a cluster of more popes that could aspire to the title of 'the most evil'.

Cesare himself attributed to bad luck the total collapse of his empire upon his father's death. 'He told me himself', Machiavelli remarked, 'the very day that Julius II was elected, that he had foreseen every obstacle which would arise on the death of his father – except that, at the precise critical period, his own life would be in imminent danger.' Cesare, after his father died, woke up to the reality he had lost when he found the great enemy of the Borgia, Cardinal Giulano della Rovere, was elected pope as Julius II. The Awesome Pope (Il papa terribile) the Italians called him, who by preference lived in armour but yet had diplomatic skills to outmatch Cesare's.

Lucrezia alone remained loyal to her brother, but there was little she could do. The Borgia reign, based on total power, had now lost any semblance of it. Ceasare, encircled by resurgent enemies, fled to Spain, and there, three years after Alexander's death, he died fighting bravely enough, but as a common mercenary.[23]

7

ADMIRAL OF THE OCEAN SEA

And if there had been more of the world,
They would have reached it.

Luiz Vaz de Camões, The Luciadas, VII, 14

It was the year 1486, and after Columbus' failure of persuading King John II of Portugal to back his idea of sailing west to the Spice Islands, he sought out the court of the Catholic Kings at a propitious moment. The sovereigns were going from triumph to triumph, submitting the nobles, beating foreign enemies and consolidating national unity. Despite the queen's favourable disposition and her faith in Columbus, his haughty manners, as if he were God's chosen, antagonised the royal advisors. The recent commencement of the Inquisition added to the war in Andalusia against the Moors, imposed serious responsibilities on the king and queen distracting them from new adventures. However, Columbus by believing firmly in his role as God's Ambassador while attributing his inspiration to the Holy Trinity, went ahead and submitted his proposal to King Ferdinand and Queen Isabella in writing.[1]

The marriage in 1469 of Ferdinand of Aragon and Isabella of Castile united several Christian kingdoms. As their court moved from city to city around the land, the monarchs gained control over local nobles and authorities and built an army that would one day become the most powerful of Europe. Both these kingdoms were on a religious crusade against Islam. The 700-year battle, the *Reconquista,* as it was named, had shaped warrior people, created a dominant language – Castilian-and fostered ardent Catholicism. The Christian rulers had pushed the Moors south-eastward until they only occupied the kingdom of Granada.

After submitting his petition, Columbus began a seven-year struggle for approval. He appeared repeatedly before Isabella and Ferdinand, making presentations to the royal council and before learned commissions. Offering the monarchs what he believed was the key to the riches of the Indies, Columbus was met with skepticism, even ridicule. The *letrados*, the advisers, disputed his belief in a relatively short Atlantic crossing, just as the Portuguese had done. Finally, in 1487, Columbus was dismissed.

Although he was given hope of future support, he felt a personal rejection. With the bitterness of humbled pride, he swore that he would seek out authorities to confound his enemies. One of his enduring traits was persistence. 'I plough ahead' he said, 'no matter how the winds might lash me'.

Columbus was born in 1451, probably between 26 August and 31 October, the son of Doménico Colombo, a weaver, living then in the port city of Genoa and later at Savona, and of Suzanna Fontanarossa. The evidence concerning his early life is sparse and admits different interpretations. One is that at first he followed his father's business from one town to the other, while another account tells us that he went to sea at fourteen. In any event he became a pirate in the service of René d'Anjou early in the 1470s, and a few years later he went to live on the Greek island of Chios.

Serving under his namesake and probable relative Guillaume de Casenove-Coullon aboard a Flemish ship (as part of a convoy escorting merchant vessels to Northern Europe by means of the Straits of Gibraltar), on 13 August 1476, his ship attacked by a French squadron caught fire and sank. Fortunately the event took place off the coast of Portugal near Lagos, only a few miles from where Prince Henry the Navigator had set up his headquarters. The twenty-five-year-old Columbus in the water clutching to a floating oar, propelled himself ashore. There could not have been a more fortuitous landing for an ambitious young navigator. The friendly people of Lagos revived him and sent him off to look for his younger brother Bartholomew in Lisbon.

Prince Henry had converted Portugal into the exploring nation of Europe. By the year 1476, its trade with Africa had brought it worthy dividends in cargos of slaves, malagueta pepper (almost as fiery as the East Indian variety), ivory and gold dust. Prosperity in Lisbon was there for all to see. Christopher and Bartholomew Columbus opened a shop where they drew and sold nautical charts. By gleaning information from the returning Portuguese captains they would update their existing charts by adding to them the latest information.

Portugal was the westernmost end of the known world so Lisbon, and Sagres, were the natural meeting places for mariners bent on discovery. In Lisbon future exploits were talked about, prepared, financed, and manned. The city had always been a busy center for the arts, now it added to its qualifications the sciences of cosmography and astronomy. By then, the Portuguese discoverers were inching down the west coast of Africa and had reached the Gulf of Guinea. But the full shape of Africa, which Ptolemy had drawn in his imagination, had not yet been navigated so no one knew what lay beyond.

In 1484, when Columbus offered what he called his 'Enterprise of the Indies' to King John II of Portugal, it seemed worth considering that a western sea passage to the Indies might not only be the shorter but the only maritime route to reach them. He also felt he had been divinely selected for a mission, an assurance that he often set forth in his writings. His was a life rich in dramatic scenes. His very arrival in Portugal, being miraculously saved from the wreck of his ship, and then landing so close to the rock of Sagres where Prince Henry the Navigator had established his academy, seemed to justify his sense of having been chosen. This self-assurance was reflected in the arrogant manner he projected, a prideful attitude that made him few friends.

A full decade earlier a westward sea route to the Indies was proposed to King John's predecessor, Alfonso V who had gone as far as to inquire the opinion of a famous Florentine astrologer-cosmographer, Paolo dal Pozzo Toscanelli.[2] Toscanelli had proposed to Alfonso V, in a letter dated 25 June 1474, 'a shorter way of going by sea to the lands of spices, than which you are making by Guinea'. Toscanelli, one of the more advanced cartographers of his age, had actually drawn a map of the Atlantic Ocean, a copy of which he included with his letter to the king in Lisbon.

When Columbus heard of this letter he wrote to Toscanelli in great excitement asking for more information. By return messenger he received an encouraging letter enclosing another chart, one that he eventually took on his voyage. The chart convinced Columbus, turning his belief into passion for Toscanelli's great-untested theory. But he yet had to convince investors to loosen their purse strings and those that could finance him were hard to persuade.

Genoese, the tongue to which Columbus was born, was a spoken dialect, not a written language, so it was no help to him in documenting his ideas to do with his enterprise of the Indies. On the other hand, Italian was a written language that might have helped him had he mastered it, but it was a language that he could neither speak nor write. He learned Castilian by his own efforts, which was the preferred language of the educated classes on the Iberian Peninsula, including Portugal. However, when he wrote Castilian he used Portuguese spelling, which suggests he might have learned Portuguese first. Somehow he taught himself to read and write in the Latin lingua franca that was essential to communicate with the community of scholars, and persuade the learned.

Christopher Columbus signed himself successively, Colombo, Colomo, Colom, and Colón. The last was the form he preferred and wished to be used. His brothers, both in Spain and in the Indies, called themselves Colón and Hispanicised their Christian names as well. One explanation is that Columbus came from a Spanish-Jewish family in Genoa that spoke only a Genoese dialect that few understood. This, it is said, made him practically illiterate upon leaving home and therefore pushed him to adopt Spanish as his language.

Soon after landing in Portugal, Columbus sailed to Iceland and it seems that during his journey, he already was thinking of his voyage west to Cathay. In 1478 he married Felipa Perestrello e Moniz, a member of a noble family of Portugal with whom he had a son, Diego, born in 1479 or 1480. He then settled for a time on Porto Santo, one of the Madeira Islands, where his brother-in-law had inherited the captaincy. It is possible that while on the island, a man who was considered the finest mathematician, astronomer and scholar of nautical sciences, the eccentric Rodrigo Faleira, had advised Columbus that a New World existed to the west.

Columbus made a couple of voyages from there to the trading post of La Mina on the Gold Coast of Africa, the southernmost extremity of the then known world. When on the high seas during these voyages, he also received a number of hints of the probable existence of lands beyond the western horizon: big canes, tree-trunks of different species to those in Europe and Africa, pieces of carved wood, and other floating objects that were unfamiliar to him.

Back in Lisbon, he read assiduously in Cardinal Pierre d'Ailly's collection of geographic tracts called *Imago Mundi*, a book he seems to have kept by him for years, and Marco Polo's account of the East. But although he studied Ptolemy, whose misconception of the extent of Asia further strengthened his belief that it could be reached by traveling westward, added to Toscanelli's theory he elaborated his own and many erroneous conclusions. Columbus had spent years collecting evidence and expert witnesses for the likelihood of a westward voyage to reach the Indies. The project was at least speculative, yet its feasibility depended on two simple premises that were not at all exotic. Among the more learned it had become axiomatic that the surface of our planet was six-sevenths dry land and only one-seventh water. The rationale for this seemed obvious at the time, since God had set man above all the rest of Creation. Nature, therefore, could not have made so disorderly a composition of the globe, as to give the element of water preponderance over the land, destined for life and the creation of souls as affirmed João de Barros, the Portuguese historian, who gives us our best account of Columbus' efforts to convince the king of Portugal of his project. If the earth was a sphere and the total surface of the oceans amounted to only one-seventh of it's surface, then there was not much sea available to separate Spain from the westward of the Indies. Thus he believed that the Western Ocean could not be extensive, and his enterprise was feasible.

Success always seemed to be around the corner, but in 1489 Columbus had still three years to wait. We do not know how he passed his time except that he sold charts and books and read many himself that he found in the libraries of monasteries where he received hospitality. Some have been preserved in his son Fernando's 'Biblioteca Colombina' at the Cathedral of Seville. The books Columbus scoured, he covered with more than 2,500 notes in the margins, underlining many passages, and often drawing a pointing hand for emphasis. All but two of the marginalia are written in Latin or Castilian. Some are cryptic, and a few, like his signature, appear in code; this secretive aspect of his nature has struck many scholars. Columbus' marginal notes, especially in Pierre d'Ailly's *Imago Mundi*[3] and Pius II's *Historia Rerum Ubique Gesstarum* (1477), are most revealing. Let's look at the following ones from Pierre d'Ailly:

> The end of the habitable earth toward the Orient and the end of the habitable earth toward the Occident are near enough, and between them is a small sea.

> Between the end of Spain and the beginning of India is no great width.

> An arm of the sea extends between India and Spain.
> India is near Spain.

Aristotle [says] between the end of Spain and the beginning of India is a small sea navigable in a few days... Esdras [says] Six parts [of the globe] are habitable and the seventh is covered with water. Observe that the blessed Ambrose and Austin and many others considered Esdras a prophet.

The end of Spain and the beginning of India are not far distant but close, and it is evident *that this sea is navigable in a few days with a fair wind*.

To sum up his thinking, Columbus concluded: first, that the world was indeed round as Ptolemy said; second, that the distance *by land* between the edge of Spain to the edge of India is very long; third, the distance *by sea* between Spain and India is therefore very short; fourth, the length of a degree is 56⅔ miles. These miles were not Arabic (1,9755m), which would have made the figure remarkably accurate, but Italian (1,477.5), which made his Equator about one-quarter too small. Columbus calculated that the land distance between Spain and India was 282°; this left him with only 78° for the sea distance, which he further reduced by his method of reckoning the degree of longitude by one quarter, a colossal error. The outcome of all these errors was that India would be about 6,275km (3,900 miles) from the Canaries, more or less where America happens to be. However, being unaware of his errors, the conclusions he had come to set his imagination afire and although vague about his plan, he was clear about what he wanted in exchange: honour and wealth, definitely in that order.[4]

At first Dom Joao II of Portugal, was much taken by the enthusiasm of the engaging young Genoese. Columbus, having read a good deal in Marco Polo... reached the conception that over this Western Ocean Sea one could sail to this Isle of Cypango [Japan] and other unknown lands, and for this purpose he asked the king to man and equip three caravels. But the king gave him small credit, finding Columbus to be a big talker and boastful in setting forth his accomplishments, and full of fancy and imagination with his Isle Cypango. The king finally rejected his proposal in 1484.

1485 proved a bad year for Columbus in more ways than one. His wife died and, with his five-year-old son Diego, he left the country where he had spent years of his life and moved to Spain hoping for better luck in promoting his project. In Spain Columbus applied for help to the powerful Duque de Medina Sidonia who said he was not really interested, then to the Conde (later Duque) de Medina Celi who housed and sheltered him from 1484 to 1486. The Duke was enthusiastic until he realised that the project was too much for him and, in 1486, sent Columbus on to the court of King Ferdinand and Queen Isabella in Córdoba where he was eventually granted an audience.

Not entirely persuaded by the fast talking Columbus, the Spanish monarchs decided to set up a special commission of learned men and mariners to study the young man's proposals. This commission chaired by the Queen's confessor, Hernando de Talavera, bishop of Avila, and two Jewish mathematicians respected for their knowledge of celestial navigation, made him wait four years. Contrary to common legend, their rejection was not based on any disagreement about the shape of the earth. Educated Europeans by this time had little doubt about planet earth being spherical. Nor was it because the commission was either incompetent or backward in its views. The committee seems to have been troubled by Columbus' secretive and incoherent attitude, especially about his underestimating the distance westward to Asia. In the end their misgivings proved better founded than Columbus' hopes. However, one must admit that most of the commission's arguments were sound. Suppose that no America existed, no ship of that era, however competent and resolute her commander, or frugal in provisions and water, could have made the 10,000-mile non-stop voyage from Spain to Japan, as Magellan's voyage would prove later.

During those four years that Columbus awaited the special commission's final decision, he went from city to city following the court. At Salamanca he befriended Diego de Deza, a professor at the university, who became tutor to Don Juan, the heir to the throne and his friend throughout. During this period, when he made Córdoba his home, Beatriz Enriquez de Arana, the orphaned daughter of a farming family, caught the widower's eye. They became lovers and, in 1488 Beatriz bore him a son. Columbus named him Ferdinand, after the king. But it seems his ambitions, would not compromise his advancement by marrying a commoner, although it weighed on his conscience, he would never give her his name.[5]

Columbus now underwent trying times due to the bureaucratic palaver of the commission that sat on the fence, neither approving nor rejecting the project. The members learnedly debated the width of the Western Ocean, which kept Columbus frustrated while twiddling his fingers.

Sensing that his Spanish quest was at an end, Columbus went to La Rábida, near Huelva, where, by chance, he met two men that were to restore his faith: the friar-astronomer Antonio de Marchena, and the pilot and ship owner from Palos, Martín Alonso Pinzón. Pinzón told him that a year earlier, in Rome, he had been informed by a papal cosmographer of those lands which were still undiscovered. Columbus sounded him out and then, gaining confidence in Pinzón, asked him to become his partner. Pinzón accepted.

A turning point came early in 1492 when Bobadil, the last of the Moorish rulers, surrendered the keys of Granada. Columbus was an eyewitness: 'On the second day of January... in the great city of Granada, I saw the royal banners of Your Highnesses placed by force of arms on the towers of the Alhambra, the citadel of that city, and I saw the Moorish King come to the city gates and kiss the hands of your highnesses.' The long war against the Moors had ended; now the energies of the kingdom could be directed outward.[6]

At this critical juncture Columbus' repressed pride broke through; he made extravagant demands that almost destroyed his chances for a royal agreement. They were in every sense exorbitant, including being knighted, appointed grand admiral and viceroy, while insisting they be hereditary titles, and he requested a percentage of all revenues from these new territories. The king and queen were stunned by his pretentious audacity and were left vacillating. In disgust, Columbus was actually en route to take ship for France to help his brother persuade King Charles VIII to back his venture, when Queen Isabella, urged on by her keeper of the Privy Purse, Luis de Santangel, suddenly decided to back Columbus. Santangel had pointed out that support of Columbus' enterprise would boil down to no more then a week's entertainment of a royal visiting dignitary, which was true. Whether it was due to being unable to endure him offering his plan to her royal neighbor that brought about her change of mind we will never know. She would pledge her crown jewels if necessary, she said. Fortunately, this proved unnecessary. However, whatever the reason was it could be said that it took something as powerful as feminine intuition to break the deadlock.

Although the voyage was now decided upon in principle, there were many more *cosas de España* to be endured. It was not until April 1492 that the final contracts between Columbus and the Sovereigns, the *Capitulations* as they are called, were signed and sealed. Therein the Sovereigns, 'in consideration that Cristóbal Colón is setting forth to discover and acquire certain islands and mainlands in the Ocean Sea, promise him to be Admiral thereof, and Viceroy and Governor of lands that he may discover. He shall have ten per cent of all gold, gems, spices, or other merchandise produced or obtained by trade within those domains tax free; he shall have the right to invest in one-eighth of any ship going thither; and these offices and emoluments will be enjoyed by his heirs and successors forever.' The Sovereigns also issued him a brief passport in Latin, stating that they were sending him with three caravels toward the regions of India (*ad partes Indie*) and three identical letters of introduction, one to the Grand Khan (the emperor of China) and the other two with a blank space so that the proper title could be inserted. The years of persuasion and promoting were at last at an end. Now Columbus' element would be the sea, where personal charms would not help, for there were no friends at Neptune's court.

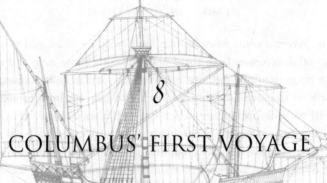

8

COLUMBUS' FIRST VOYAGE

The wind and the waves are always on the side of the ablest navigators.

Edward Gibbon (1737-1794)

It was a sensible decision to fit out the fleet and recruit the men at Palos de la Frontera, a sleepy little seaport called so because of its nearness to the Portuguese frontier. The port of Palos gave onto the Río Tinto, 2½ miles upstream from the famous old monastery of La Rábida. Around the middle of 1485, Columbus with his small son Diego had taken passage in a merchant ship for Spain and disembarked in Palos. Though he might have chosen that destination for no better reason than having been offered free passage by the skipper, it turned out as fortuitous as swimming ashore at Lagos nine years before.

When the ship rounded the Banco de Umbria, the mud bank at the entrance to the Rio Saltés, of which the Río Tinto was a tributary, Columbus must have made a silent genuflection towards the buildings of La Rábida, as they passed close to the monastic buildings that housed the Franciscan order. The Franciscans had taken more interest in discoveries throughout history than had any other arm of the church. It was a fact that Franciscan missionaries had been in China from 1320 and in many cases were anxious to return. So, it is not altogether surprising that once Columbus explained his thoughts of finding a New World they showed more than a mild enthusiasm.

As Columbus trudged about Spain looking for support he worried about what to do with little Diego. Remembering that the Franciscans often maintained boarding schools connected to their monasteries, Columbus and son made the dusty journey on foot from Palos to La Rábida. Upon their arrival, according to a physician who happened to be visiting the monastery, Columbus asked for bread and a cup of water for the boy, he arranged admission for Diego as a border in the monastery, and struck up a conversation with Antonio de Marchena, a studious and intelligent monk who was visiting the friary. Father Marchena wrote a letter on Columbus' behalf to Hernando de Talavera, the queen's confessor. He also gave Columbus a letter to the Duke of Medina Sidonia, which led him to Count Medina Celi and eventually to the court and to Queen Isabella of Castile. The letter to Talavera asked the right to petition the royal council, which made recommendations to the crown. The itinerant court was then at Córdova, more than 100 miles away. When

Columbus arrived there, he found it a crowded military camp, the advance base for the war against Granada.

As Pierre Chaunu in his compilation of voyages to the Indies mentions, Palos, a nursery of Spanish blue-water mariners, lay so close to the Portuguese frontier that an exchange of caravel designs was not only easy, it was obvious. Without La Rábida and Palos there would have been no Voyage of Discovery, at least not in 1492.

Columbus had made friends of the Pinzón family, leading ship-owners, and master mariners who had built ships like the caravels of Portugal, and who enjoyed the confidence of the local seamen. With his friend Fray Juan Perez, the prior of La Rábida, Columbus made a public appearance on 23 May 1492 at the church of San Jorge (Saint George), in Palos, where a notary read the royal order giving authority for the expedition. Outside, a *nave* from Galicia named *Marigalante*, owned and captained by Juan de la Cosa, lay in port. Columbus chartered her as his flagship and officially renamed her *Santa Maria*. As she later left her ribs on a reef off Hispañola, and no drawings or models of her survive except the several conjectural ones that have been made since – as well as the three full-size replicas that were constructed in Spain over the years – we can only surmise her particulars. She was probably of about 100 tuns burthen, meaning that her capacity of cargo was 100 tuns (double hogsheads of wine.)

Her rig consisted in a mainmast taller than her length; the main yard as long as her keel spread an immense square sail – the main course – that would provide most of the driving force. Above the main course a short yard spread a tiny main-top-sail. The foremast, much shorter than the main, carried one square sail. The mizzenmast, stepped on a high poop, carried a lateen sail, and under the bowsprit hung a square spritsail, which, rather inefficiently, performed the function of a modern jib. The other two ships that made up the fleet were caravels. Here are the details of Columbus' little fleet as far as we know them:

Santa Maria, nao of *c*.100 tuns burthen, *c*.26m overall.
Captain: Cristóbal Colon. Master and owner, Juan de la Cosa. Pilot, Peralonso Niño. Alguacil (marshal), Diego de Arana. Escribano (scribe, secretary, purser,) Rodrigo de Escobedo. Interpreter, Luis de Torres. Surgeon, Juan Sánchez. Seven petty officers, captain's steward and page. 11 able seamen, 10 grumetes. Total 40.[1]

Pinta, caravela redonda (square rigged caravel) of *c*.60 tuns, *c*.21m overall.
Captain; Martín Alonzo Pinzón. Owner and able seaman Cristóbal Quintero. Master, Francisco Martín Pinzón. Pilot, Cristóbal Garcia Sarmiento. Marshal, Juan Reynal. Surgeon, Maestro Diego. Two petty officers, 10 able seamen, 8 grumetes. Total, 27.

Niña, caravela of *c*.50 tuns, *c*.17m overall. Her true name being *Santa Clara*.
Captain: Vicente Yáñez Pinzón, brother to Martín Alonzo Pinzón, and later to prove one of the finest sailors of the era. Master and owner, Juan Niño. Pilot,

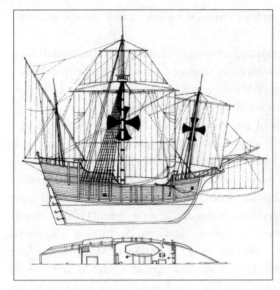

All illustrations on this page and opposite are taken from *The Story of Sail*, Veris Lazelo and Richard Woodman. Naval Institute press, Annapolis, Maryland, USA 1991 pp55, 59.

Left: Santa Maria in 1492. It is most likely that she bore upon her sails the crosses that marked the quasi-religious nature of her voyage.

Below: Santa Maria in 1492. A further interpretation, based on the hull of a *caravela redonda*, seems equally plausible given the scarcity of real knowledge.

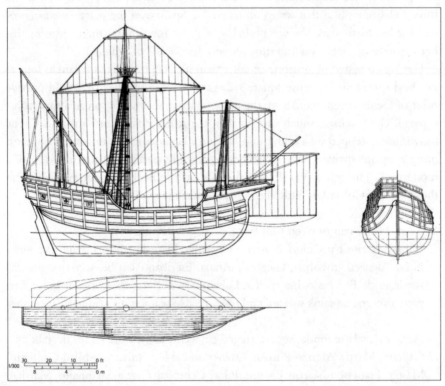

Sancho Ruiz de Gama. Surgeon, Maestre Alonso. Marshal, Diego Lorenzo. Two petty officers, 8 able seamen, 6 grumetes. Total 21.

On Spanish ships the order of precedence was: captain, pilot, *escribano* secretary, scribe, the equivalent of a purser, and master.

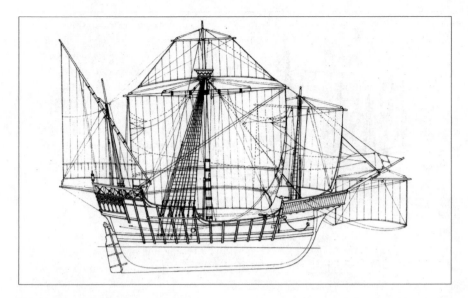

Top: Santa Maria in 1492 appeared to be a
sophistocated vessel.

Right and below: Santa Maria in 1492; an
analysis of the rectangular top-sail
handled from the large top.

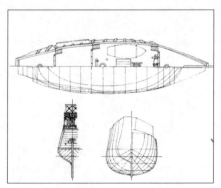

   The first two ships had castles fore and aft, the *Niña*, only aft. They were armed
with 4in (10cm) *Bombardas* for heavy granite balls and *espingardes* for smaller lead
projectiles. As Columbus did not know whether he was to come across new
savages or old civilizations, he loaded his ships with cheap merchandise to relieve
the aboriginals of their gold but also took on board one Luis de Torres – who had
been a Jew and knew Hebrew and Chaldeans and a little Arabic – in case he met
the Grand Khan.

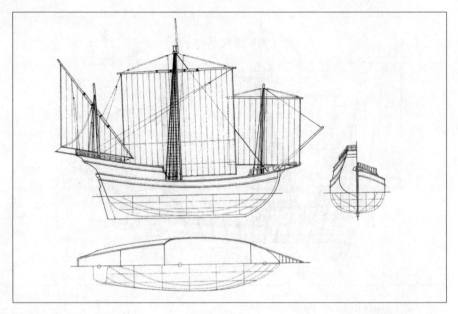

Pinta in 1492, a conjectural reconstruction.

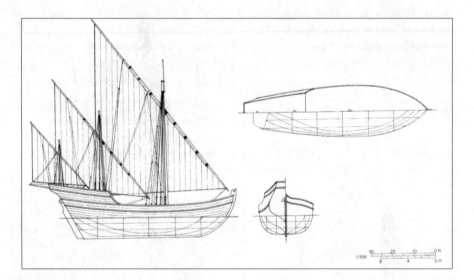

Niña in 1492. *Niña* was incontestably a standard lateen-rigged caravel. Columbus returned home in this vessel in 1493.

The story that the queen pawned her jewels to fund the expedition is quite untrue. More than 1,000,000 maravedis came from the funds of the Santa Hermandad (Holy Brotherhood), and the sum of 500,000 maravedis was supplied by Columbus himself (advanced by Pinzón).

Regarding the crew: the only foreigners on board were Columbus, one other Genoese, one Venetian, and one Portuguese. There were no priests and no idlers, as sailors used to call those who did no physical work. Each captain was allowed only one page or servant.

It was usual in those days for a Spanish ship to also have a nickname that the sailors preferred to use; theirs for *Santa Maria* was *La Gallega*, The Galician. *Santa Clara* was given the nickname *Niña*, because the Niño family of Palos owned her. *Pinta*'s nickname we do not know, though it was probably derived from a former owner named Pinto. *Niña* was always Columbus' favourite. She brought him safely back to Spain from his first voyage, carried him back home on his second, and still made another voyage later to Hispaniola. At the start she was rigged with lateen sails like a Portuguese caravel, but on reaching the Canaries Columbus had her rerigged square, better for sailing in the trades when running before the wind.

The planks of the three ships were fastened by treenails (trunnels, as they were called in English), consisting of wooden pegs made preferably from the same wood as the planks. Iron nails or bolts were used sparingly to avoid electrolytic action between the seawater and the iron fittings, otherwise the metal parts would rapidly decay. The ships carried stone ballast. Their sides were painted bright colours above the water line while below, it was payed with pitch made from pine-resin to discourage barnacles and teredos (that unfortunately had little effect on them). Crosses and heraldic emblems were emblazoned on the sails, and bright coloured flags were carried to be hoisted entering and leaving port. The royal ensign of Queen Isabella, quartered by the castles of Castille and Leon, were hoisted on the main truck, while the banner of the expedition with its green cross on a white background with a crown on each arm in honour of Aragon, flew from the foremast.

The majority of the enlisted men were from the province of Huelva, one of the eight provinces of Andalusia.[2] Quite a few of them came from the district of Niebla within the confines of Huelva. The seamen received as payment perhaps the equivalent of some us$ 8.00 in gold a month, the petty officers twice that amount and the grumetes about us$ 4.60.

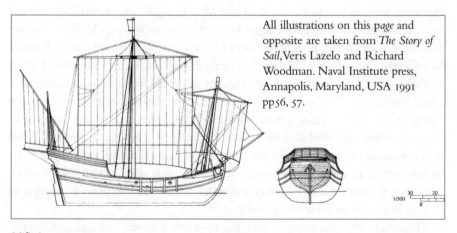

All illustrations on this page and opposite are taken from *The Story of Sail*, Veris Lazelo and Richard Woodman. Naval Institute press, Annapolis, Maryland, USA 1991 pp56, 57.

Niña in 1492.

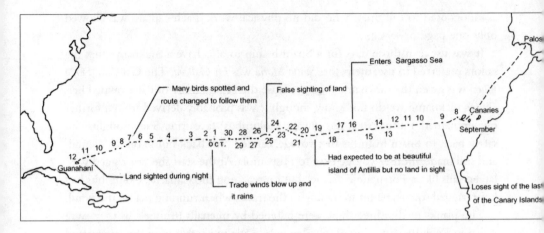

Columbus' first voyage.

Enlisting sailors was always a problem so the jailbird practice was no exception for Columbus. Three young fellows who had been imprisoned for helping a condemned murderer to flee were set free in exchange for shipping with the expedition. Though the eyes of the petty officers were upon them for most of the voyage, they proved to be trustworthy and sailed with Columbus on later voyages, as did several others. The Admiral picked his crews sensibly. They were sound, capable men from around and about the locality. Though mostly illiterate, and highly superstitious when sailing beyond sight of land, they managed to conquer their fear in the hope of winning adventure, gold and glory.

The expedition would have left from the port of Cádiz, Spain's major seaport onto the Atlantic, had it not been designated the main port of embarkation for the departing Jews on that particular day. Their Most Catholic Majesties, Ferdinand and Isabella, had determined that 2 August be the dateline for the expulsion of all of the Jews from Spain. It was decreed that any of them remaining beyond that date would be executed unless they embraced the Christian faith. Those that remained, known as *conversos,* would be assimilated into a society governed by the rules of the Spanish Holy Inquisition. They would, nevertheless, face the stigma of their race by not being able to prove racial purity, *limpieza de sangre*, an anacronism that would perpetuate unabated well into the nineteenth century. *Limpieza de Sangre* was still a requirement for entrance into the corps of officer cadets up until 1857.[3] Even St Teresa of Avila, venerated by kings and common folk alike, would never disclose the ignomy shown her grandfather, a *converso*, who had been publicly flogged in Toledo at an *auto da fé* for his apostasy.[4]

    Thousands of pitiful refugees, carrying their few pathetic belongings, filled the dockside, their only crime being faith in their religion and their God. They would be crammed into the holds of ships that crowded the port of Cádiz. Once in the open sea they were to be taken to the Netherlands, the only Christian country that would receive them, while others, perhaps the most fortunate, sailed to seek refuge in the more tolerant world of Islam.[5] Columbus' own journal recorded his trip was ordered only after the realm had been cleansed of Jews. His Catholic Majesties now sent him to the idolaters of India on another highly Christian mission: 'Their conversion to our Holy Faith, and ordained that I should not go by land to the Orient, but by route of the Occident, by which no one to this day has ever gone.'

Columbus' fleet was ready for sea on 2 August. Every man and boy confessed his sins, received absolution and communion at the church of San Jorge in Palos. The Captain General, as we can now call Columbus, went on board *Santa Maria*, in the small hours of Friday 3 August 1492, and made the signal for the fleet to get under weigh.

The very same tide that carried the hapless Jews from a country of discrimination and persecution carried Columbus' three vessels from Palos de la Frontera down the Río Tinto towards the open sea. As they passed close to the monastery of La Rábida, they must have heard the friars chanting the ancient hymn *Iam lucis orto sidere* with its haunting refrain, *Et nunc et in parpetuam*, 'evermore, and evermore'.[6]

It was Columbus' experience of navigation that ensured the success of the voyage. Instead of setting his course due west from Spain, he first sailed southward to the Canaries and so prudently avoided the strong headwinds and monstrous seas of the North Atlantic. At the Canaries, after their week-long inaugural cruise, he made, as it were, a right-angle turn to cut straight across the Atlantic.

On the first leg *Pinta* having broken one of the gudgeon pins of its rudder, the Captain General decided to send her in to Las Palmas for repairs, while *Santa Maria* and *Niña* went to Gomara, westernmost of the known Canary Islands. After anchoring he sent some men ashore to fill the water casks and purchase bread, cheese, and to salt down some native beef. He sailed back to oversee *Pinta*'s repairs.

By 2 September all three ships were anchored, once again, off the port of San Sebastián, at Gomara Island. The castle overlooking the beach was the home of Beatriz de Peraza y Bobadilla, under thirty years old and beautiful by all accounts. She was the widow of Gomara's governor, Hernan Peraza, who had been murdered because the Canary Islanders resented his overbearing and cruel rule. Seemingly Columbus became attracted to Doña Beatriz. Michele da Cuneo, a nobleman from Savona and friend of the Columbus family, uses the quaint expression 'tinged with love' to describe the Admiral's feelings, but that is all that is known for certain about this event.

Doña Beatriz had lived on Gomara since 1482. At the age of seventeen, this attractive looking noblewoman became the queen's maid of honour and then, as might be expected, the king's mistress. As punishment, Isabella forced her to marry Peraza. One of Peraza's vassals had recently murdered a Spanish nobleman and on account of this, Peraza in turn was murdered. Doña Beatriz, widowed after six years of marriage, was still young and attractive when Columbus anchored in Gomara bay. Further details of their relationship are unknown, but when Columbus and his fleet passed by Gomara a year later, Doña Beatriz greeted him with artillery salvos, public illuminations and fireworks. By the time of Columbus' third voyage, in 1498, their passion, if it ever existed, had died. Beatriz had become the mistress of the future ruler of the Grand Canary Island whom she married. She in turn was later murdered for reasons of state or revenge, after she had ordered two people hanged. One had accused her of immorality, the other was a political enemy. The Spanish sovereigns summoned her back to court to explain her actions. A few days later she was found dead in her room.[7]

Once the additional stores were hoisted in and stored aboard the ships, on 6 September 1492, the fleet weighed anchor and set sail. Columbus announced the course: 'West. Nothing to the north. Nothing to the south.' Having set it, Columbus found fair winds and the vessels scudded ahead.

Celestial navigation was in its infancy but reasonable estimates could be made from the height of the North Star above the horizon and its relation to two others: the Guards of the Little Bear, or Little Dipper, plus a meridian altitude of the sun. These coordinates, corrected by the sun's declination, for which tables had long been provided, also could produce latitude. However, the instruments available, the quadrants, and the astrolabe, were so primitive that most navigators took their sights while ashore. In Columbus' case, he relied entirely on 'dead reckoning', less a scientific technique than a practical skill, it consists in plotting one's course and position on a chart using three prime elements: direction, time and speed. He took his direction from the several compasses he had on board, common to the dry-card type used on small craft until fifteen years ago. He also had a circular card graduated to the 32 points, N, N by E, NNE, NE, by N, NE, and so on, with a piece of lodestone under the north point. It was mounted on a pin and enclosed in the compass box with gimbals so it could swing freely with the motion of the ship.

The compasses on Columbus' three ships were mounted on the poop deck under observation of the officer of the watch. The rudder was connected directly to the tiller with no pulleys in between so it was extremely heavy to steer. Furthermore, the helmsman had no view at all and kept the course steady only by the feel of the tiller and orders he received through a hatch called down by an officer from the deck above.

Columbus and his officers noted the passing of time by the use of a half-hour sandglass that was turned as it emptied to keep track of the seven 'canonical' hours. The glass was hung from a beam, so the sand could flow freely. When the sand ran down, a ship's boy turned the glass and the officer of the watch would record it by making a stroke on the slate. Eight glasses made a watch. The ships bells today are the modern version of marking the slate. However, sandglasses were ill adapted for daylong timekeeping, they had to be turned frequently at the precise moment when the last grain had dropped. This system would be corrected by watching the sun for local noon, a custom that Columbus would do nearly every week.

The Captain General's journal of his first voyage, tells us he overestimated his distance covered by 9 per cent. This did not prevent him from finding his way home because the mistake was constant, and the time and course were correct. What is really surprising is the speed of his vessels. In October 1492, for five consecutive days, the fleet averaged 142 miles a day, the best days run being 182 miles, averaging out at almost 8 knots. Niña and Pinta covered 198 miles in one day, and at times took off at 11 knots.

Once the three ships had finally lost sight of land, the greatness of Columbus' skills of navigation began to reveal themselves, for it was at this moment that he conquered by faith, willpower and persuasion the resistance of the unbelieving and faint-hearted members of his crew. Showing a shrewd mixture of determination and tactical caution he handed out an 'instruction' to the men that after 700 leagues they should not navigate at night because land would certainly be near. On 13 September he observed that the relation of the magnetic north pole to the true North Pole changes with the position of the observer.

The outward passage had its anxious moments. For instance on 21-23 September, when they entered the Sargasso Sea, that vast area of sargassum gulfweed, the crew, never having seen anything like it before, became alarmed. Fearing that the ships would become trapped in the weeds, they demanded that the captain change course to find open water. For a whole month the weather swung from good to bad, as did the men's moods. 'There will be no wind to come back' the unbelievers grumbled, just as a few gusts of favourable wind came to the rescue of their leader. If Columbus sailed on endlessly westward, the seamen feared they might never see their families again, so, they thought it might be best to toss him overboard, turn the ship around and head for home. Sensing what was on their minds, the Captain General reminded them of the dire consequences for them all if they returned to Spain without him. However, the outward journey was blessed with the precious ingredient of luck. The weather had been, in fact, so benign that, to use his own romantic words, 'the savour of the mornings was a great delight. The weather was like April in Andalucia, the only thing missing was to hear the nightingales singing'.

On 25 September Columbus became troubled by anxiety and sought the help of Pinzón, who that very evening declared he had sighted land. Columbus altered course in search of it but it vanished. This disappointment led to a conspiracy that might have degenerated into mutiny had not Pinzón intervened in time. On 6 October Pinzón suggested altering course towards the south-west, but Columbus was too proud to listen. However, the sight of birds flying towards the south-west made him change his mind and follow Pinzón's and the bird's advice, rather than his chart. He changed course accordingly.

Pinzón had become so discouraged that he wanted to turn back. However, Columbus persuaded him to sail on, with the promise that if land were not sighted within three days he would turn back with him. 'All the night they heard birds passing', and he saw in the water some logs and reeds that gave them hope. Next day the wind grew fresher that carried the little fleet along at 7 knots. As the sun set under a clear horizon the wind blew from the north-east at gale force and the ships picked up speed and scudded along at 9 knots. The Captain General refused to shorten sail and signaled for everyone to keep a watchful eye since the sovereigns had offered a reward of a year's extra pay to the man who sighted land first.

At 10.00 p.m. Columbus, with a seaman thought they saw a light 'like a little candle rising and falling'. But the light did not make him alter course. The ships sailed on, pitching and rolling, throwing up spray and white foam from their bows while their wakes reflected the moon as they ploughed on through the sea. Two hours after midnight, Juan Rodiguez de Bermejo, the lookout aboard *Pinta*, spied something like a white cliff shining in the moonlight and called the deck, *Tierra! Tierra!* Captain Pinzón confirming the landfall fired a gun as agreed and shortened sail to allow the flagship to catch up. As *Santa Maria* came abreast of *Pinta* Columbas shouted across the water, 'Señor Martín Alonzo, you *did* find land! Five thousand Maravedis for you as a bonus!'

Columbus cautiously ordered that the ships shorten sail and bear off until dawn. Daylight showed them a land of unbelievable beauty. The fresh green of the landscape was set off by a calm sea of aquamarine blue. The Spaniards could hardly believe their eyes. They laid on sail and sought an opening on the west coast through the barrier reef, which they came across before noon. Sailing into a shallow bay in the lee of the island they anchored in five fathoms. The Admiral went ashore in the flagship's longboat displaying the royal standard of Castile, together with both Captains Pinzón in their boats flying the standard of the expedition. 'And, all having rendered thanks to Our Lord, kneeling on the ground, embracing it with tears of joy for the immeasurable mercy of having reached it, the Admiral rose and gave this island the name San Salvador', Holy Saviour. The island was Guanahaní to the inhabitants, or Wattling Island today, one of the Bahama islands. But everything Columbas saw persuaded him that he was among 'the islands which are set down in the maps at the end of the Orient. Though he saw gold in the noses of some islanders, he left in a hurry to see 'whether I can come across the island of Cipango' (Japan).

Perhaps one of the most remarkable, though the least celebrated, of Columbus' achievements was his ability to later find the lands that he had accidentally discovered on his voyages. Remarkable, because his navigating techniques were so primitive and rudimentary. In Columbus' time, celestial navigation was in its infancy and he was unskilled in the use of the astrolabe. It is unlikely he ever used a cross-staff. He used the magnetic compass to fix direction, and then estimated the speed by guesswork, watching the bubbles, weeds, or some other object go by. But Columbus was above all a sailor, a man of the sail. For a skillful mariner

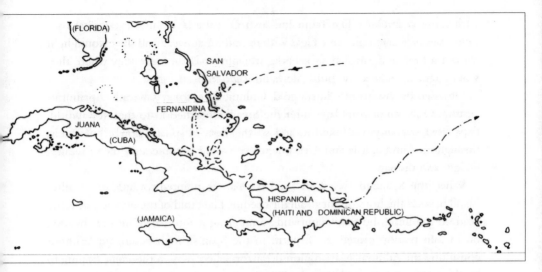

Columbus' route through the Caribbean during his first transatlantic voyage. He explored
the Bahamas, the north-east coast of Cuba, and the northern coast of Hispaniola.

like him, the winds were the mystery he had to master and, like any a seasoned
sailor, solid knowledge of the winds became an instinct. We could say, indeed, that
Columbus navigated by a heightened sense of intuition. Modern racing
yachtsmen agree that a sailing ship in today's world, after all that has been learned
over the last five centuries, could do no better than follow Columbus' route
outward, as well as homeward bound.

For a fortnight he wandered among lovely islands giving them graceful Spanish
names, and hoping the Lord would show him where gold is born. From San
Salvador to Santa Maria de la Concepción, which the English prosaically later
named Rum Cay. On to Fernandina, now Long Island, Isabela after the queen,
today Crooked Island, and on the morning of 28 October they entered Bahía
Bariay, a harbour in the Oriente province of Cuba, marked by a lovely mountain
today called La Teta de Bariay which Columbus said had on its top another peak
like a pretty little mosque. They sailed westward along the coast of Cubanacan,
(Cuba) and the Admiral, mistaking the name for El Gran Kan, sent an embassy
up country to present his letter of credence from their Catholic Majesties to the
Chinese emperor and a rich gift for the Khan, along with glass beads and trinkets
to buy food en route. Led on by visions of Cambaluc, which had been named by
Marco Polo as the Mongol capital of China where the Khan held his splendid
court, they hiked up the valley of the Cocayuguin River, arriving at a simple
village with some fifty thatched huts, although they were feasted by the local
casique as messengers from the sky and the people kissed their feet. But they got
no word of the Great Khan and so they turned back feeling badly let down. Yet,
on their way back, they encountered many people who were going to their
villages, both women and men, with a firebrand in their hand and herbs to drink
the smoke thereof, as they are accustomed. It was the first contact of Europeans

with tobacco smokers. The Taino Indians rolled the leaves into cigars that they called *tobacos*. Carrying a large cigar as they walked, at every halt they would light it from a firebrand, small boys keeping it alight until the next stop, where they would light up, take a few puffs and hand it around.

Obsessed by visions of China's gold, Columbus' embassy saw only a primitive custom. Only some years later, after the Spaniards settled in to the New World, they tried smoking and liked it, and so the custom spread, slowly but surely, throughout Europe, Asia and Africa, where it would become a source of wealth, delight and dismay.

When the Spaniards asked for gold the natives pointed towards some other island beyond the horizon they called Bebeque. They told of the people gathering gold on the beach by candlelight and hammering it into bars. This breathtaking bit of information caused the first rift in the Spanish high command. Without consulting the Admiral, Martín Alonso Pinzón sailed away in the *Pinta*, hoping to be the first to arrive at El Dorado. Needless to say, he never found Bebeque, or gold by candle or any other light.

Columbus sailed along the coast of Cuba in the company of *Niña*. At one point they entered a bay (Moustique Bay) where they were detained for five days due to winds from the east. Here the Admiral, seeing the grandeur and beauty of the island, and its resemblance to Spain, named it *La Isla Española* or Hispaniola, the Spanish Island. While dallying there some seamen captured a young and beautiful girl wearing only a golden nose plug. They brought her on board and though she indicated she would be pleased to stay with the lads, the Admiral sent her ashore very honorably, clad in slop-chest clothing and bedecked with bright jingling hawk's bells and Venetian glass beads. The girl turned out to be a casique's daughter. The following day nine of the Spaniards were conducted ashore to a big village of a thousand people or more and given everything they wanted, food, drink, girls and parrots.

On 15 December, *Santa Maria* and *Niña* entered the Tortuga Channel and anchored off the a beach close to a fresh water stream that flows down a valley that Columbus called The Valley of Paradise. The next day some 500 men accompanied by their youthful cacique came down to the beach to see the ships. Invited by the Admiral, the cacique boarded the *Santa Maria* bedecked in his gold finery. He dined alone with Columbus in the great stern cabin and is said to have behaved with royal poise and dignity. Afterwards, Columbus had him piped over the side, naval fashion, and given a twenty-one-gun salute. It crossed his mind that these people were ready to be exploited, very cowardly, and fit to be ordered about and made to work, to sow, and do aught else that may be needed. He thought of slavery. The sin of greed reared its head in an otherwise sanctimonious mind that struggled with the two different and antagonistic strains. Strains that curiously enough, appear also in his name: Christ bearer and Colonizer. Columbus raised crosses everywhere, but he also kept an eye on the material value of things even to seeing men as goods for sale.

During the night of 22–23 December and the following day more than a thousand canoes came out to visit *Santa Maria* as well as another 500 who swam out, regardless of the caravel being anchored more than 3 miles from shore. An envoy of Guacanagarí, the casique of Merien (in the north-west of Haiti), arrived with the gift from his master of a magnificent belt with a solid gold buckle, and invited him to call. Columbus needed no second invitation as everyone persuaded him that the gold mines were in that direction, the central part of the island called Cibao, which sounded to him very much like Cipango, Japan. Consequently, at sunrise on 24 December, *Santa Maria* and *Niña* raised anchors and departed with all hands planning to spend a merry Christmas at the court of the casique, who might turn out to be the emperor of Japan.

Fate decreed otherwise. With the wind against them, they were unable to reach their destination by daylight. At 23:00 hours they became becalmed inside the Limonade Pass to the barrier reef with barely a breath of wind and only a slight ground swell. Exhausted from the previous night's entertainment by the natives, they were overtaken by a feeling of complete security engulfed the flagship – the most dangerous delusion a seaman can entertain. Even the Admiral retired to bed for the first time in forty-eight hours and the helmsman gave the tiller to a young grumet to join the rest of the watch in slumber.

As midnight ushered in Christmas Day, 1492, *Santa Maria* settled on a coral reef so gently that it was not noticed for some time. The young boy at the helm, feeling the rudder ground called out. Columbus hurriedly came on deck followed by the Master, Juan de La Cosa, and all hands. At first, the Admiral saw a good chance of getting the ship off since only the bow had grounded. He gave orders to La Cosa to take the ship's boat and carry an anchor out astern to kedge her off. Instead of obeying orders, Cosa had himself rowed to *Niña* where Captain Pinzón refused to receive him and instead sent a boat from his ship to help in the rescue.

In the meantime the ground swell carried the *Santa Maria* higher and higher up on the reef driving the sharp spikes of coral through her hull and filling her with water. In the morning the crew, helped by the Indians, worked hard to float her off but there was nothing to be done. They salvaged the stores, equipment, and trading trinkets that, according to the Admiral's account, the Indians faithfully guarded without purloining so much as a lace point.

Assuming that God had willed that he should found a colony at that place, the Admiral erected a fortified camp ashore and named it *Villa de la Natividad* (Village of the Nativity) honoring the day of the disaster. It was quickly built, mainly from planks taken from the wreck on the northwestern side of *Hispaniola* (today's Haiti). Sixteen men from the flagship and five from the *Niña* volunteered to remain behind, under the command of the Aguacil (Marshal) of *Santa Maria*, Diego de Arana, a relative of his mistress Beatriz Enriquez. Columbus left them a large share of his provisions, most of the trading trinkets, plenty of ammunition, so the natives should obey with love and fear, and the flagship's boat. After a farewell party with Guacanagarí and his men, when a fine time was had by all,

Niña fired cannon balls through the remains of *Santa Maria's* hull to impress the natives. The next day at sunrise, on 4 January 1493, with the Admiral on board, *Niña* hoisted sails and sailed for Spain.

Two days later, the Admiral sighted *Pinta* sailing on an opposite tack and the two ships came along side each other after which, Columbus sailed back 40 miles (64km) to seek a safe anchorage for a meeting. Martin Alonzo Pinzón came aboard the flagship and gave an account of his doings over the last three weeks. Columbus rejected his explanations and threatened to have him hanged from the castle door, to which Pinzón answered, 'it is what I deserve for having raised you to the honour in which you stand'. Though the quarrel was patched up, the two men remained estranged. However, perhaps because Columbus was inwardly glad to have company on the long voyage home that he decided to overlook Pinzón's behaviour and let bygones be bygones.

Carrying the greatest discovery of all time in his breast, Columbus was well aware it would not be known unless he took good care to deliver proof of his exploits to the court in Spain. In the privacy of his stern cabin he settled down to compose his report to Fedinand and Isabella. In it he revealed he had no doubt that he had reached the Indies. He generalised with the all the confidence of a first-time tourist: the natives, he asserted:

> were so ingenious and free with all they have, that no one would believe it who has not seen it; of anything that they possess, if it be asked from them, they never say no; on the contrary, they invite you to share it and show as much love as if their hearts went with it, and they are content with whatever trifle be given them, whether it be a thing of value or of petty worth. In all these islands, I saw no great diversity in the appearance of the people or in their manners and language, but they all understand one another, which is a very singular thing, on account of which I hope that their Highnesses will determine upon their conversion to our holy faith, toward which they are much inclined.

On Wednesday 18 January 1493, three hours before daybreak, the ships sailed from Samana Bay on the eastern end of Hispaniola to return home. The west wind with which they started out soon dropped to a mere breeze and the caravels sailed as best they could, close hauled on the starboard tack. *Niña* and *Pinta* could sail as close to the wind as five points (56°) if they had a smooth sea, but under usual conditions they could do no better than 6 points (67°), added to these limitations, *Pinta* was slow on the wind due to a sprung mizzenmast. In practice, it meant that if it blew from the southeast, the ships could steer ENE; if the wind was from the east the best course toward Spain that they were capable of was NNE; and, as was quite usual, if the trade wind backed to the NE, they would have to come about on the port tack and steer ESE.

All through January 1493, they sailed further north and entered the northern limits of the trades. There the wind held and blew them across the horse latitudes as seamen named the calms between 30° and 33° N. Beneath a full moon, they sailed through the undulating meadow of gulfweed of the Sargasso Sea where boobies and fork-tailed frigate birds were flying about and the sea abounded in tunas.

On the last day of January the wind freshened from the west which gave the Admiral the opportunity to set a course due east. The weather turned cold and a fresh gale sprung up. The caravels made an average run of 150 miles per day over four days, attaining a speed of up to 11 knots at times. The westerlies died down on 7 February the caravels made little progress. The captains got together and discussed their position with the rest of the officers. They all thought, except the Admiral, that they were much further south then they actually were, but Columbus estimated correctly that they were almost due south of Flores Island, and decided to call in at one of the Azores, if he were able. They nearly did not make it, however, as without knowing it they were sailing straight into an area of very foul weather in one of the worst winters on record, a winter when hundreds of vessels were lost and scores more were wrecked on shore. Ships lay at their moorings at Lisbon for months, and the harbour of Genoa froze over. With winds of full gale strength from the south-west to west, the three caravels had to pass through three weather fronts.

Niña stripped down to bare poles scudded before the wind but labouring heavily in frightful seas that broke over her from stem to stern. With only her reefed main course set, and the yard slung low, the Admiral and Captain Pinzón took turns as officer of the deck, watching every wave to warn the helmsman below. One small mistake by either man and she would have broached-to, rolled over and sunk. It would have been useless for Pinta to try to rescue survivors in such a sea.

The following night both captains seem to have resigned themselves to let the wind do as it pleased and the two ships lost sight of each other never to see themselves again until reaching Spain. The wind blew harder still and Niña's crew vowed to go in procession in their shirts to the first shrine of the Virgin they encountered if they were spared. The wind started to die down. Desperate in case both ships and all hands perish, at the height of the gale Columbus wrote a condensed version of his journal on a parchment, wrapped it in waxed cloth, put it in a cask and hove it overboard. The cask was never found but sundry versions of the Admiral's 'Secrete Log Boke' until a few years ago were still being offered to collectors.

For four days the Admiral went without sleep, but on Monday 18 February he arrived at Santa Maria, the southernmost island of the Azores, where at last he anchored near the little village called Nossa Senhora dos Anjos (Our Lady of the Angels). He was so pleased that he admitted in his journal that he had kept secret the distances covered daily in order to put other sailors off the track of his Indies.

In the village there was a little chapel dedicated to the Virgin who had appeared to a local fisherman, surrounded by a halo of angels. There could not be a more appropriate place for the seamen to fulfill their vow pledged at the height of the storm.

What then took place was a scene that in retrospect one might expect today in a hilarious comic opera. There were the men in church overflowing with the greatest bit of news in centuries, kneeling on the flag-stones of the nave, dressed only in their shirts, as befitted penitents, heads bowed, to offer thanks to the Virgin Mary for having been spared, when they were set upon by the whole town, on horse and afoot, and thrown into jail. Later an armed party came out to the caravel but Columbus angrily refused to allow them aboard and threatened to conquer the island by force. The stalemate continued for some days until the local priest, acting as an intermediary, was able to study the Admiral's papers and convince the garrison captain that his apparently fantastic story of being an Admiral of Spain and of having come from the Indies was in fact true, and not on an illicit voyage to West Africa, trespassing on the rules agreed to in a papal bull of Pope Alexander VI. The captain had even gone out in a boat hoping to capture Columbus and the three men that had remained on board, who intended to make their pilgrimage later. Columbus had refused to let the Portuguese official on board and threatened to train his guns on the town and bring back the hostages if his men were not released instantly. However, before the captain could make up his mind, a fierce wind blew into the bay, *Niña*'s cables parted and she was blown off shore almost to *São Miguel*. On board were only the Admiral, the master, three seamen and the Indians they had brought with them. They struggled with the ropes, put the ship about and managed to return to the island to find that in their absence and prompted by the priest the Portuguese governor had cross-examined the prisoners and discovered he had been mistaken. Embarrassed, he surrendered them and provided Columbus with fresh water and new provisions.

Two days out from Santa Maria, having left the island on 24 February 1493, *Niña* was blown off course. On the night of 2 March a cold front overtook her with a violent squall, which split the main course and blew the furled foresail and mizzen to ribbons. Columbus did the only thing he could under such dreadful circumstances – forge ahead under bare poles. The following day after sunset, with lightening and thunder renting the sky and huge seas breaking aboard, the wind blew so strong that it seemed to raise the caravel into the air. Fortunately, it was a night of full moon that shed enough light through the clouds to enable them to see before dawn the dark shadow of the devastating Portuguese rocky coast dead ahead of them. The wind blew from the north-west and the coast ran north-south. Columbus wore ship, not without difficulty, and performed the daunting manoeuvre, known to all old-time seamen, of clawing off a lee shore. One little foresail had been saved intact. They bent it to the foremast and set a course south, parallel to the coast.

When it dawned on 4 March Columbus recognised the Cabo da Roca, a promontory of the mountains of Sintra that juts into the sea north of the entrance to the Tagus. With only one square sail left and the likelihood of foundering on the ironbound coast of Portugal, the Admiral elected to enter the Tagus and anchor at Lisbon to refit. His intention had been to continue south around Cape

St Vincent and enter Palos but in such foul weather the risk of attempting it was far too great. He well knew that by entering Portugal he was placing himself in the hands of Dom João II who had turned him down twice, but his first concern was to get the message of his discovery to Spain, so, with the earliest light of dawn and with the sun chasing the clouds, he turned the bow towards the cape, passed Casçais and the tiny fishing village of Estoril, to the amazement of the fishermen who, equating weather with the tiny caravel couldn't believe their eyes, crossed the bar at the river's mouth, sailed up the Tagus and anchored off Belem, the outer port of Lisbon, at nine o'clock.

Columbus had plenty to worry about. Would the Portuguese allow him to refit and provision before proceeding to Spain? And what had happened to *Pinta*? Anchored close to *Niña* was a Portuguese man-of-war whose captain sent an armed boat with an officer to order Columbus to report on board and give an account of himself. The Admiral refused but showed his credentials, which satisfied the officer and his captain. Columbus had previously sent a letter to Dom João asking permission to anchor at Lisbon and on 8 March a courtier brought the answer granting his request and invited Columbus to visit him while his ship was reprovisioned. The Portuguese king received him cordially and with full honours at the monastery of Santa Maria de las Virtudes where he was staying, though the court chronicler says he was really furious with the Admiral, suspecting the discoveries had been made on territories on which Portugal had prior rights. Some of his courtiers, it appears, would gladly have had him assassinated then and there but fortunately the king refused, while admitting that his Indian guests (for Columbus had brought a few of the healthier Indians with him) looked very different from any Africans he had ever seen. Two of these even made a map of the Antilles with beans, convincing the monarch that their origin was a very different one to what he suspected. As well, their pulled eyelids, the shiny black hair on their heads and the lack of it on their faces and chests, showed a rather different human to the slaves imported from Portugal's west African colonies. After the meeting Dom João cried out, 'Why did I let slip such a wonderful chance?' It is said that he despaired and called himself *hombre de mal conocimiento*, a man of bad understanding. During the conversation, Dom João apparently suggested that the new lands were within the latitudes granted to Portugal by papal decree, but Columbus refused to give ground.

Columbus and his group departed on 11 March 1493, escorted by a troop of cavaliers, to visit the queen at the Convent of Santo Antonio da Castanheira. The Admiral was so sore from his mule back ride when he got back that he chartered a boat, on reaching the Tagus, to take him down river to *Niña*. When he stepped on deck he was very pleased to find that during his absence she had been supplied with a new set of sails and running rigging, and had taken on fresh provisions, among them, wood, water and wine. With all her crew on board, the following morning, 13 March, the noble little caravel weighed anchor from Lisbon and sailed down the Tagus and entered the open sea.

Strangely, *Pinta* was not far behind. She had missed the Azores, and by so doing, the worst of the tempests. By the end of February she had arrived in Bayona in the Ria de Vigo, in north-west Spain. There, Martin Alonso Pinzón attempted to outwit Columbus by announcing his arrival, sending news of the discovery to Ferdinand and Isabella at Barcelona, and requesting an audience with the monarchs to tell them about the voyage. The sovereigns responded curtly that they would prefer to hear the details from the Admiral himself. Despondent, Pinzón weighed anchor and sailed *Pinta* from Bayona to Palos.

At daybreak on 14 March 1493, *Niña* wore ship and rounded Cape St Vincent passing the beach where Columbus had swum ashore seventeen years earlier. At midday of the fifteenth, she crossed the bar of the Saltés and anchored off Palos. *Pinta* arrived on the same tide. The sight of *Niña*, already berthed and neatly bedded down as if she had been there for a month, was too much for Martin Alonzo Pinzón. Ill from the trials and tribulations of the voyage, his age (he was older than Colmbus) and mortified at being snubbed by the sovereigns, he could stand no more. He left for his country home near Palos, took to his bed, and died within a month.

Thus ended, 224 days after it began, one of the greatest recorded navigation sagas in history.

FAME AND FORTUNE

When Columbus arrived in Lisbon aboard *Niña*, he sent a copy of his official report of the voyage to the Spanish sovereigns at Barcelona. Fearing Dom Joao II might intercept it, he also sent another by official courier, and a third to the municipality at Córdova. Before proceeding to Seville to await the reply he fulfilled his vows at the local church and took time to spend two weeks with his old friend and sponsor Fray Juan Pérez at La Rábida. On Palm Sunday he arrived in Seville with the six Indians who had survived the voyage, in time to attend the traditional ceremonies of Holy Week.

In Seville, on Easter Sunday, he received to his great joy a letter addressed to Don Cristobal Colon, Admiral of the Ocean Sea, Viceroy and Governor of the islands that he hath discovered in the Indies. These were the titles he had requested and had been granted – albeit reluctantly – if he found the Indies. The use of them now indicated they believed he had. The letter went on: 'It is our will that that which you have begun with the aid of God be continued and furthered, and we desire that you come here at once; therefore for our service make the best haste you can, so that you may be timely provided with everything you need... to go back to the land which you have discovered.'

Columbus at once drafted a report to the sovereigns on how the new colony should be colonised. He envisioned that some 2,000 settlers be recruited to build houses in three or four settlements in return for a license to trade for gold with the natives. Each of those licensed would be required to return to the town to hand over his gold to an official at stated intervals who would deduct the

Sovereigns' fifth, the Admiral's tenth, as well as another tax to support the church. However, gathering gold would be allowed during only part of the year in order that the settlers had time to grow crops. He stated that foreigners, Jews, infidels, and heretics must be kept out of the Indies while priests should be sent to convert the natives to the Catholic faith.

Columbus was aware that the Taino Indians could not be expected to come to the beach to sell their gold as the Africans did. Regardless of whatever means the Spaniards used to extract gold from the natives it would be subject to controls at the trading factory on the coast, and all transatlantic traffic must go through Cadiz.

The report was forwarded to the king and queen by courier, and Columbus set off on his long overland journey to Barcelona, taking samples of gold and many other things never before seen or heard of in Spain. The Admiral purchased suitable clothes for the occasion in accordance with his rank. Along with him, traveling on horseback or in wagons, went a few of his officers and servants and the six long-suffering Indians clad in loincloths, wearing their ornaments and carrying spears and tame parrots in cages. Along the route people turned out to see the hero and his entourage and made a great commotion cheering them on.

Upon arrival at Córdova, the municipality gave him a reception. There he met with his mistress Beatriz, whom he had not seen for eight long months and greeted his sons Diego and Ferdinand both of whom joined his entourage. They continued on through Valencia and Terragona arriving at Barcelona around 20 April 1493. As he approached the hall of the Alcazar where the sovereigns held court, it is recorded that his dignified presence, his gray hair, and his heroic countenance tanned by eight months at sea, made the nobles present compare him to a Roman Senator. Approaching the thrones ahead of his attendants and in the presence of the whole court, Ferdinand and Isabella rose to greet him, and when he knelt bowing his head to kiss their hands they bade him rise and seated him beside their son, the Infante Don Juan, on the dais. He was now to be titled Don. The weaver's boy had indeed come far; up, as Columbus wrote himself, from nothing.[8]

Columbus called forward his Indians, who he had taught to bow, they then stepped aside and he exhibited the rare artifacts he had brought with him: samples of gold, the alleged rare spices explaining their particular values, he gave a long account of his voyage and discoveries, and answered a multitude of questions while discussing plans for his return. Then all adjourned to the chapel where a *Te Deum laudamus* was solemnly sung in Latin by the officiating bishop and answered by the priests in attendance as well as the choir. It was observed that at the last line, *Oh Lord, in Thee I have trusted, let me never be confounded*; tears were streaming down the Admiral's face.

This was the culminating moment of his life (he was forty-one) and never would he know its equal. It was a moment when he could have had anything he desired, a castle, a pension, or an endowment. In retrospect, it seems that it might have been more sensible had he taken his profits and left to others the responsibility of colonization, but he was not that sort of man. Had he been, his great voyage of discovery would not have taken place. He had to return to the islands and see them settled by Christians, he had to organise the gold trade, he must reach an understanding with the natives, and he must meet the Grand Khan or some other Oriental Potentate of higher hierarchy than Guacanagarí.

He was full of energy, in the prime of life, and if the rights granted him, relevant to his offices of Admiral and Viceroy, had been respected by the crown he would have been far richer than by any gift he might have received in Spain. He also regarded the work for which God had appointed him to be just begun.

The sovereigns had received him in a scene of solemnity and honours that staggered the court, including the right to display the royal symbols of a castle and a lion on his arms. Wealth and honour was indeed his. He nevertheless insisted on being paid the prize of 10,000 maravedis promised to the first man of the crew to see land. The money never reached the humble sailor who actually had first sighted land. In disappointment born of indignation, he went over to Morocco and became a renegade. This episode sheds some light on a side of Columbus that was to bring him much unhappiness – the sin of avarice.

Columbus stayed on at the court in Barcelona, over Whitsuntide, Trinity Sunday, and Corpus Christy, lionised by courtiers who otherwise would have ignored his existence, and flattered by the same scholars and skeptics that had once dismissed him as an ignorant adventurer.

The King and Queen, as well as the Infante Don Juan, graciously accepted to act as godparents to the six Indians who were baptised. The first, a kinsman to Guacanagarí, they christened Ferdinand of Aragon; another Don Juan of Castile; while the cleaver interpreter was named Don Diego Colón. Don Juan was adopted by the royal household but died within two years; the other five returned with the Admiral to the New World.

These christenings expressed the good intentions of the sovereigns and Columbus towards the natives, but back in the Indies human greed had to be satisfied first. Forced labour exterminated almost the entire native population of Hispaniola within half a century; however, the natives unwittingly had their revenge on Europeans through *Treponema pálida*, the spirochete of syphilis, brought back to Spain by the conquerors after contracting it in the Indies. Though prudishness tends to hide the facts, we know full well that the Spanish conquerors had sex with the Indian females, and although the interest was often mutual, it did not exclude rape. Columbus' boyhood friend, Michele de Cuneo, writes of a very beautiful Carib girl whom he had captured in a fight and whom Columbus had presented to him as a slave. 'Having taken her into my cabin', Cuneo says, 'she being naked according to their custom, I conceived a desire to take pleasure. I wanted to put my desire into execution but she did not want it and treated me with her fingernails in such a manner that I wished I had never begun. But seeing that (to tell you the end of it all), I took a rope and thrashed

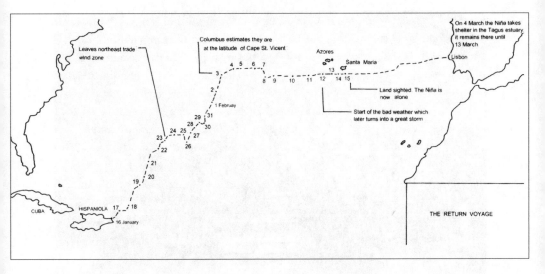

Columbus' return voyage.

her well, for which she raised such unheard of screams that you would not have believed your ears. Finally we came to an agreement in such a manner that I can tell you that she seemed to have been brought up in a school of harlots.'[9]

Whatever the conditions of the agreement, sexual contact was the principal way in which the diseases of both continents were brought together, and one disease in particular more than any other related to this contact: syphilis.

The first outbreak of the disease in Europe was in 1494 among the soldiers of a French army that marched to Naples and back. Bishop Las Casas, an admirer of Columbus, who loved the Indians and who spent a large part of his life in a vain effort to protect them, states in his *Apologetica Historia* of around 1530 that the disease was transmitted to the French soldiers by Spanish women who were infected by the Indians brought to Barcelona by Columbus. He goes on to say that after repeated questioning of the natives of Hispaniola, he believed the disease to be one of long standing in the New World; so long indeed that the natives did not suffer greatly from it. However, among the Europeans it exploded into the most hideous and malignant forms, with many fatalities, just as measles and smallpox affected the Indians when introduced by Europeans. It appears, therefore, that the Indians brought back by Columbus to Barcelona were so cheerfully entertained by the women of the town as to infect them, who then either infected Spanish volunteers in the army of Charles VIII or accompanied the army as camp followers. There is room for controversy about this, as we must take into account that the incubation period – the interval between contact and the appearance of the chancre – varies from ten to ninety days, with an average of twenty-one days. Therefore, *Niña*'s crew for the return voyage could not have contracted syphilis, as all were healthy and able to work the ship up to the moment of landing, after spending two months on board. Columbus mentions it

Theodore Goetz, 'Burning heretics'; eighteenth-century copper engraving.

with some amazement since on African voyages it was quite usual for sailors to contract other maladies and sicken and die before reaching port. As for those in *Pinta*, Ruy Diaz de Isla, a Spanish surgeon, wrote a treatise on syphilis published in Seville in 1539. In it he mentions that a spirochete infected a pilot of Palos named Pinzón, and implies that he attended him. Three Pinzóns shipped in *Pinta* and while it is true that the captain, Martín Alonzo, died shortly after the ship's arrival, it being said that it was due to other causes, it seems likely it was due to syphilis. However, Diaz de Isla admits the disease spread from Barcelona. It grew into plague proportions throughout Europe and among the Spanish colonists of Hispaniola who used an Indian remedy made from guiacum or lignum vitae that had no therapeutic value whatsoever, although both natives and Europeans valued it greatly thinking it to be the supreme cure.[10]

Columbus' confident assertion that he definitely had reached the Indies was accepted by the Spanish Sovereigns and the pope, but not by everyone. Pietro Martire d'Anghiera, an Italian humanist attached to the Spanish court, wrote in a letter that the size of the globe seemed to indicate that Columbus could not have reached Asia. In a letter written to Cardinal Sforza in November 1493, he described Columbus as *Novi Orbis Repertor*, Discoverer of a New World. To him, as to others at the time, New World did not mean necessarily a new continent as we define America today, but any undiscovered land unknown to Ptolemy; a group of islands adjacent to the Malay Peninsular would be a New World. Columbus came to that conclusion in 1498, and so did Amerigo Vespucci a little later. But Vespucci, more learned, more enlightened, with a better grasp of the science of navigation and navigation itself, got the credit. Was it unmerited? The jury is still out on that one, so let us each decide for ourselves.

9

THE SWORD AND THE CROSS – COLUMBUS' SECOND VOYAGE

America was discovered accidentally by a great seaman
who was looking for something else; when discovered
it was not wanted; and most of the exploration for the next
fifty years was done in the hope of getting through or around
it… History is like that, very chancy.

The Oxford History of the American People (1965), Samuel Eliot Morison (1887–1976)

We should not forget that Columbus made three more voyages to the New World, any one of which entitles him to figure amongst the finest navigators of all time. The Second Voyage, of 1493-94, employed a large fleet and also set up the first European colony in America that survived. It was also important for discovery of the Lesser Antilles, the Virgin Islands, Puerto Rico, the south coast of Cuba, and Jamaica.

On 20 May 1493 Columbus received his appointment as commander of the new fleet. There was every need for haste. It had been reported to the sovereigns that Dom João II of Portugal was outfitting a fleet of his own to sail westwards, and that only strong pressure persuaded him to postpone its departure while the matter of Spanish and Portuguese spheres of influence was thrashed out diplomatically. To hurry things along Ferdinand and Isabella entrusted the task of organizing the new expedition to a committee headed by Juan Rodriguez de Fonseca, Archdeacon of Seville, jointly responsible with Columbus for coordinating the second voyage. Fonseca, a shrewd businessman was soon able to finance the venture. He assembled a fleet of seventeen ships, and victualed them for a round voyage of six months, although the Admiral later blamed the committee for providing shoddy materials. The enterprise was accomplished with surprising speed as the Spanish threw themselves into the new adventure with passionate zeal.

The organisers recruited at least 1,200 sailors, soldiers, and colonists, and collected the necessary tools, implements, seeds, plants and domestic animals to start a colony. Local citizens of Jerez furnished wheat that was ground into flour and baked into ship biscuit – the famous hardtack – that has been the staple of a seaman's diet almost to our day. Cattle and swine were slaughtered and pickled in brine. Wine that should have been delivered in fine new casks came in second hand butts, or barrels put together with unseasoned oak that, upon reaching the tropics, leaked their contents into the bilge's, thus provoking the Spaniards in Hispaniola to endure the unusual hardship of drinking only water for several months. Then there was the matter of a cavalry troop of twenty lancers who sold their thoroughbred barbs in Cadiz, purchased some second rate nags, and lived high on the difference. However, there were to be no women on the voyage, and with an all-male complement of 1,200, and with no Spanish consorts available, the decision would have far-reaching consequences. The men would forcibly take native women, which would provoke bullying and violence against the Indians. This in turn, would initiate the process of racial mixing that would lead to the creation of Latin America's great mestizo populations.

Ferdinand and Isabella urged the Admiral to hasten to their court 'so that you may be timely provided with everything you need... you must not delay in going back there'. The king and queen also had clear ideas of how matters were to proceed in their new overseas dominion, which they passed on to Columbus in the form of instructions, issued on 29 May:

> Their highnesses charge and direct the said Admiral, viceroy and governor, to strive by all means to win over the inhabitants of said islands and mainland to our Holy Catholic Faith...to treat the said Indians very well and lovingly, and abstain from doing them any injury, and arrange that both people have much conversation and intimacy, each serving the others to the best of their ability. To see to the conversion of the Indians, they were sending six priests among the colonists.

Meanwhile, to satisfy material ambitions, Columbus was to establish centres for trade in gold and other valuables, much as he himself had suggested. Furthermore, he was not to forget his original purpose – to continue his explorations, and especially to make contact with the Grand Khan's mainland domain.

In June 1493, accompanied by five of the six baptised Indians and his younger brother Diego, Christopher Columbus set out by carriage, and on foot, from Barcelona. After passing through Madrid and Toledo he took the pilgrim's road to Guadalupe in Estremadura, where he prayed fervently to the famous Virgin of Guadalupe, and the monks asked him to name an island after her. On through Trujillo where a thirteen-year-old boy named Francisco Pizarro, the future conqueror of Peru, was caring for his father's herd of swine. En route to Seville he passed through the small town of Medellin where a small boy named Hernando Cortez must have seen him go by. Only twenty-eight weeks after *Niña* had returned from her first voyage, the fleet weighed anchor in the Bay of Cadiz. It was late September, somewhat later in the season than the first departure. In a festive atmosphere, the crews returned the salutes of the crowd assembled on land, and Venetian galleys ceremoniously escorted the flotilla to the open sea. As on the previous westward passage, he stopped at the Canary Islands. At San Sebastián de la Gomara, he was greeted by joyful cannonades by Beatriz de Bobadilla. Columbus tarried but a few days spending his time topping up the vessels with

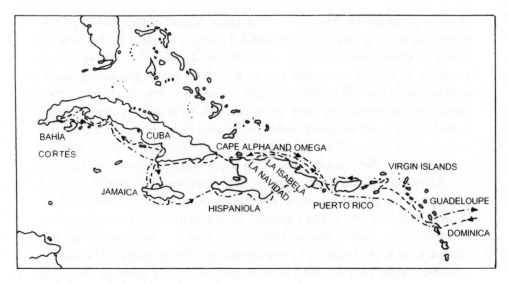

Columbus' second voyage; the route through the islands.

water, citrus fruit, and vegetables, seeds, mares, sheep, goats and pigs – the old world's contribution to the future New World colony.

Beyond the island of Ferro, on 13 October, the fleet picked up the trade wind. Columbus then set a course west by south, aiming for the unexplored islands of the Lesser Antilles, the nearest islands to Spain that he had been told about by the natives on Hispaniola. The fleet sped along, day after day, before the strong steady winds, settling down to the pleasant ritual, undisturbed by shifts of wind or changes of weather. Flecked with whitecaps the sea was a spectacular deep blue, schools of flying fish springing like flashes of silver from the bow wave, and with sixteen ships around her the view from the high-pooped flagship was one of white sails, all the way to the horizon.

By 2 November, after only twenty-one days at sea, they sighted land; Columbus christened the island of his landfall *Dominica*, it being his Sabbath day island. The following day, as the fleet sped westward, they sighted a round flat island which he named *Mariagalante*, as tribute to his flagship, and then a little group which he called *Todos los Santos*, after the recent feast of All Saints. (French since the seventeenth century, they are still known as Mariegalante and Les Saintes.) Columbus shaped his course towards a large kidney-shaped island that he named *Santa Maria de Guadalupe*, as he had promised the monks he would do and anchored his fleet under the southern slope of the island's 5,000ft volcano, where he remained for five days.

Columbus had intended to stay overnight but a shore party from the vessels got lost and he had to send out four shore parties to find them among the dense foliage of the tropical rain forest. Since the natives were none other than the dreaded man-eating Caribs, they were lucky to be found at all. In the course of their wanderings, the searching Spaniards learned a good deal about the Carib customs. Although the logbook of Columbus' second voyage has been lost, Alvarez Chanca, the surgeon to the fleet, left a record in which he describes the Caribs or Caniba, the tribe from which the word cannibal is derived, 'whose custom is bestial. These warlike people preyed on the neighbouring islands, travelling up to 600 miles (965km) in their canoes. They were armed with arrows tipped with tortoiseshell or fish bone and they took the women they succeeded in finding, especially the young and beautiful ones, and kept them for their own service, and as servants.' The Spaniards saw the cannibals on Guadalupe, or rather they saw one of their villages. Most of the Carib men had left on a raid and the few that remained fled, into the forest, with their women and children. They left behind some Arawakan prisoners. According to Chanca, these captives told us about incredible cruelties. 'The Caribs ate the children they had with them. They raised only those born to mothers of their own stock. The men that are captured alive are taken to the houses to be butchered when they are needed. The dead are eaten right away. They say that human flesh is better then anything else in the world.'

From Guadalupe the fleet continued north and west along the Leeward Islands. They were the first Europeans to follow this lovely ark, and the names the Admiral bestowed upon them are with us still. *Santa Maria de Monserrat*, after a Catalonian monastery, today's Montserrat; and further to the east, *Santa Maria la Antigua*, after a famous painting of the Virgin in Seville Cathedral. Nevis, now British, was named after *Nuestra Señora de las Nieves*, Our Lady of the Snows, although no snow ever falls there.

At St Croix, *Santa Cruz* to the Spanish, some thirty Spaniards landed to look for fresh water; there they freed (or captured) some Arawaks from a Carib village. While returning to the ships, they encountered a canoe full of Caribs. There were only four men and two women but they fought furiously with poisoned arrows, according to Pietro d'Anghiera. One Carib was killed and several were wounded. The Spaniards suffered two casualties, one of whom died a few days later. Possibly the first Carib in history ever to be subdued was one of the two girls in the canoe captured in the fight by Michele de Cuneo and presented to him by the Admiral as a slave. (The account of her subjugation is told in the previous chapter.) After the clash there were cannibals running onto the beach in great numbers, dark skinned, fierce and terrible, painted red and other colours to increase the horror of their appearance. This was the first real battle in the New World, and it came as a shock to the Europeans who assumed that all Indians were like the gentle, tame Arawaks – peaceful folk who could be moulded into faithful subjects and good Christians.[1]

Columbus did not stay on at St Croix lest the Caribs bring up reinforcements. Looking north he cast his eyes on a cluster of islands on the horizon and decided to investigate them. As the ships approached, more and more islands appeared. The Admiral appropriately named them *Las Once Mil Virgenes*, in honour of St Ursula and her 11,000 seagoing virgins who, according to Butler's *Lives of the Saints* 'these holy martyrs seem... to have met a glorious death [at Cologne] in defence of their virginity from the army of the Huns... They came originally from Britain, and Ursula was the conductor and encourager of the holy troop.'[2]

The Admiral used the smaller craft to explore these Virgin Islands, the caravels and Cantabrian barques. He dispatched them through the easterly passage to look at *Anegada* and ran before the wind down the channel later named after Sir Francis Drake. The larger vessels in deeper water sailed south of two larger islands, St Thomas and St John. The fleet united west of St Thomas and rounded the southwest point of Puerto Rico. From there they crossed the Mona Passage, and at eventide made a landfall on Cape Engaño, Hispaniola. The fleet continued to Caracol Bay, where on 27 November they anchored outside the pass, in view of what had happened on Christmas Eve the year before when the *Santa Maria* was lost. Anticipation was high as the seventeen ships, representing the might and glory of Spain, approached the settlement, but their flares of greeting were met by silence, by darkness. Late at night a canoe approached, manned by Indians calling *Almirante, Almirante!* and, when Columbus came on deck, they presented him with gifts from Guacanagarí, assuring him that the Spaniards at the settlement were well except for a few that had died. What an understatement! Diego Colón, the Indian interpreter, wrung the truth out of them, a tale so dreadful that Columbus at first refused to believe it.[3] Soon the truth trickled out. They would find no gold, no settlement, and no colonists. Columbus and his men found the ashes of Navidad, and the decomposed corpses that told the tale and a sadness and profound grief seized their hearts. Discipline had been absent in the outpost and greed unchecked. After fighting among themselves, the men had split into several groups. One led by Columbus' old friend, and cousin of his Córdoba mistress, Diego de Arana, remained at the fort. Several others led by the king's butler, Gutierrez, began bullying the natives of the hinterland while looking for more women and gold that Guacanagarí was able or willing to supply. They fell afoul of Caonabó, the casique of Maguana in the center of Hispaniola. Tough and vindictive, he killed the Gutierrez gang and marched on Navidad to wipe out and destroy the source of the trouble. This was an easy task, as Arana and his men were more occupied with their female slaves than with their defence. Only ten men were left under Diego de Arana to guard the fort. Caonabó disposed of them easily, hunting down and slaughtering every Spaniard who took to the bush.

Columbus' friend Guacanagarí, who had moved to a village further away, sent for the Spaniards saying he had been wounded in the defence of Navidad. Dr Chanca, the fleet's surgeon, examined him, but found no wounds or scars. The Spaniards decided he was faking. Guacanagarí was trying to avoid blame for the slaughter. In spite of his fake wounds there was no evidence that he was guilty of taking part in the colony's destruction. Nevertheless, the Benedictine monk Father Bernardo Buil urged Columbus to punish the chieftain, but the Admiral decided that this would be unwise and ordered the dead to be buried. Columbus had left thirty-nine men in the settlement at La Navidad when he left for Spain; now all of them were dead. The La Navidad debacle sowed seeds of distrust that were to plague Columbus' dealings with the Taino Indians and poison his attempts to govern the island he claimed for Spain. But he stuck stubbornly to his mission. He ordered a search for any gold his ill-fated sailors might have buried and then set sail again – this time in search of Cibao, a place he had heard about during his first voyage. The Tainos had told him that gold was plentiful in Cibao, so it seemed an ideal site for a new settlement – a much better place than Navidad, which had been chosen not by design but as a result of the wreck of the *Santa Maria*.

To reach Cibao, Columbus had to sail along the coastline of Hispaniola towards the east, a course that made the fleet beat against the eastern trades. It took them a month to travel the 30 miles (48km) to Monte Cristi. Then he set sail for Puerto Plata, now a city in the Dominican Republic. He described it in his logbook as 'a gulf, with the most beautiful and flourishing land in the world, protected by a mountain chain at the foot of which there is an excellent harbour.' The Admiral had thought that there ought to be an abundance of good rivers and gold there, but now on his second voyage, he was thwarted in his efforts to return to Puerto Plata. For twenty-five days his fleet battled the trades and westward-flowing current, tacking back and forth day in and day out, hove-to at night, in order to avoid the dangerous coral reefs, without making much headway. By the end of this time the fleet had only covered 37 miles (60km). The winds were so adverse, according to Chanca that the difficulties were greater than any we had encountered during the whole journey from Castile.[4] The frequent shifting of sail and constant wetting with salt spray wore sailors down, exasperated the colonists, and killed a large part of the livestock on board.

The Admiral was finally forced to anchor in a poorly protected harbour in the lee of a peninsula that afforded shelter from the east wind, 26 miles (42km) short of his goal. There on 2 January 1494, on a little hill about 16ft (5m) above sea level, Columbus founded a settlement which he named La Isabela after the Queen, some 35 miles (56km) from the present-day city of Santiago. The site of La Isabela like that of Navidad was forced upon Columbus by circumstances beyond his control – in this case the adverse winds.

Unfortunately, the selection of the site was a telling opening to Columbus' career as viceroy, a role he filled with nowhere near the competence he showed as Admiral of the Ocean Sea. Unlike Navidad, the new colony was relatively large. Michele da Cuneo, a native of Savona, whose report is an important source of information about the second voyage, says, 'we built a hundred houses as small as the huts we used at home for bird hunting, and they are covered with grass'.[5]

Isabela was founded as a trading post. Even as such the site was ill chosen, like so many of the first European colonies in America; for instance, Roanoke Island,

Virginia, and the early settlement of Buenos Aires, onto the Río de la Plata. Isabela had no proper harbour, only a roadstead open to the north and west, and no fresh water either. But Columbus was in a hurry to get his men on shore and send most of his ships home. He had already wasted a month looking for a site that the Navidad garrison should have found, and the gold nuggets, which they should have collected, were not there. He had to start trading quickly and produce something of value to please his sovereigns.[6]

Men were put to work felling trees, cutting coral stone, and digging a canal to bring water from the nearest river. But insufficient wine and provisions had been brought from Spain. Workers fell ill of malaria or from drinking water from contaminated wells and eating strange fish, although Dr Chanca tried every new species on a dog before he would let any Christian touch it. Columbus, impatient to get things done, drafted some of the gentleman volunteers for the hard labour, to their utmost indignation. They had come to fight and find gold, not to do menial work. If they refused they got no rations, and that they considered a contemptible way to treat a Castilian hidalgo.[7]

The Admiral organised two reconnoitring parties – one under Alonso de Ojeda,[8] the other under Ginés de Gorbalán – to find Cibao and its fabled goldmines. Ojeda had obtained three great gold nuggets. Within two weeks he was back at Isabela bringing the first good news for many weeks. 'All of us made merry', wrote Cuneo, 'not caring any longer about spicery, but only for this blessed gold.'

The Admiral feared what might happen if he ran out of provisions. The crews of seventeen ships were accumulating pay and eating up food, several hundred men were sick, Dr Chanca had run out of medicines, and there were barely enough basic provisions to see the ships home. He decided to retain only *Mariagalante*, *Gallega*, *Niña*, and two smaller caravels; the remaining twelve vessels he dispatched homeward under the command of flag captain Antonio de Torres. Torres's fleet completed the crossing from Isabela to Cadiz in thirty-five days, arriving on 7 March 1494, a record that stood for centuries.

Torres had access to the sovereigns being the brother to the governess of the Infante Don Juan, and so presented to them a verbal report that had been outlined to him by Columbus. This *Torres Memorandum*, as it is called, gives an account of Columbus' common sense views on colonization. He strived to say that if he failed it would not be because of his mistaken ideas but from inability to control lazy and churlish hidalgos who hated him as a foreigner. The Dominican Friar Bartolmé de las Casas[9] wrote 'that even the Archangel Gabriel would have been hard put to govern persons as greedy, selfish and egotistical as the early settlers of Hispaniola'. Columbus made the mistake of mentioning the idea of capturing Caribbean natives – specifically the Caribs, enemies of the Tainos – as slaves. For the good of the souls of the said cannibals, and even the inhabitants of the island [the Taino]. The Queen said no but Columbus – no doubt desperate to make up for the failure to deliver gold and spices – proceeded in direct defiance. Thus the process of Spanish enslavement of the Indians in the New World would begin.

About a month after dispatching the ships home under Torres, the Admiral, who wanted to be part of any further exploration, set off in person, on 12 March 1494, with 500 men on a reconnaissance of the interior. They travelled on foot and horseback, over the coastal mountains of Hispaniola.

It was a spectacle unlike any ever seen west of the Azores. Trumpet blasts sounded through the mountain valleys, drums echoed, the banners of Spain and of the church rippled above a helmeted, armoured parade of adventurers flanked by their beastly, fearful, mastiffs. But perhaps most terrifying of all were men on horses, half man, half beast to the eyes of the Taino Indians along their route. 'Columbus' impressive Grand March fairly astounded the natives and convinced them that the Europeans were mighty enough to attack and hurt them', wrote Friar Bartolomé de las Casas.[10]

They crossed a spacious valley so fresh, so green, of such colour and altogether so full of beauty, wrote Las Casas, that the Admiral, who was profoundly moved by all those things, gave great thanks to God and named it Vega Real, the Royal Plain. They marched up the northern slope of the cordillera guided by friendly Indians until they reached a ridge between the Bao and Janico rivers, where Columbus left fifty men under Mosén Margarit to construct a rough earthen fort that they named after Santo Thomas – today called Fortaleza. 'On that trip', wrote Cuneo, 'we spent twenty-nine days with terrible weather, bad food, and worse drink; nevertheless, out of covetousness for that gold, we all kept strong and lusty.'

That was not true of the folk in Isabela. They were by no means lusty or strong. Not even gold had they found to compensate for living and working in that unhealthy climate. Almost all of their provisions brought from Spain had been exhausted. Discontent was rife, mutiny was seething, several of the troublemakers were in irons, and Columbus, with his brother Diego in command, had removed to his flagship all firearms and munitions as a precaution. Columbus set out to return to Isabela. A couple of days after he arrived, a messenger from Margarit galloped in with a report that Caonabó was gathering his warriors to attack the new fort. In his response to a request for reinforcements, Columbus hastily sent off a party of about seventy soldiers. A week later he sent a much larger party of some 400 under Alonso de Ojeda with orders to relieve Margarit, and then explore the country. Columbus stressed to Ojeda not to harm the Indians, reminding him that the sovereigns desired their salvation even more than their gold, but the first thing Ojeda did was to cut off the ears of a native who stole some old clothes, and to send the casique who he thought responsible in chains to Isabela. Ojeda then relieved Margarit who with some 400 men roamed the Vega Real extorting gold from the natives, exhausting their food supplies, carrying off boys as slaves and young girls as concubines.

Before Columbus learned about these things, he had departed to explore Cuba, leaving his brother in charge of Isabela. Diego Colon, a virtuous person, discreet, peaceable and simple, was woefully incapable of reining in adventurers, or raising the morale, much less of controlling people like Ojeda and Margarit whose idea of the enterprise was to grab all the gold that they could and administrative orders be damned. But Columbus felt that there was no one else in the colony that he could trust.[11]

On 24 April, Columbus put to sea again with three caravels. *Niña* served as flagship while two smaller lateen-rigged caravels, the *San Juan* and *Cardera* accompanied her. These last are described as much smaller than *Niña* with crews of only fourteen to sixteen compared with *Niña's* twenty-eight to thirty. On board the *Niña* were Juan de la Cosa, the chart-maker (not the same man as the owner of the *Santa Maria* from the first voyage), who later drew what many believe to be the first map of the New World; fortunately for history, Columbus' gossipy friend Michele da Cuneo shipped as passenger, one of the priests joined the expedition, and Diego Colón, the best of the Indian converts who had learned to speak fluent Castilian, came along as interpreter. For officers, Columbus had one of the *Niños*, Pedro Terreros, as well as a few other veterans from his first voyage.

April is a good month to sail in the Greater Antilles, when the trades can be depended on by day and an offshore breeze by night. It is a season when it is also cooler and there is no fear of hurricanes. During the next five months Columbus explored the southern coast of Cuba, discovered and almost circumnavigated Jamaica, which he named *Santa Gloria*, and reconnoitred the southern coast of Hispaniola. Andrés Bernáldez, chaplain to the archbishop of Seville, who heard the Viceroy describe the voyage after his return to Spain, has left a vivid record of the natural splendours witnessed by Columbus during this part of his second voyage. 'On the Cuban coast', wrote Bernáldez, 'the sweetest perfume wafted from the land to the sea, and *Santa Gloria* – Jamaica – is the most beautiful land that human eyes have ever seen.'

At sunrise on 15 May 1494, while sailing from the Gulf of Guacanayabo on the southern coast of Cuba, they sighted an archipelago of small islands that Columbus named *El Jardin de la Reina*, the Queen's Garden. According to his description, these cays were then very beautiful, adorned with royal palms and calabash trees. They admired the flamingos, 'great birds like cranes, but bright red', and watched the natives hunting turtles in a unique way: the hunter would catch and train a pilot fish (which has suckers on its head) and let it loose on a line when in turtle waters. The fish would connect itself by its suckers to the turtle's shell, and the Indian had only to haul in the line to capture the turtle. The pilot fish was then rewarded with little bits of meat. Columbus would tell this story back in Spain and although many listeners found hard it to believe, sounding extravagant, it was true.

However, though Columbus was impressed by the natural splendour of his surroundings, this was not the object of his search. He was looking all the time for the doorway to China where according to Marco Polo 'there are so many merchants and so rich and in such great numbers that they can not be counted. And I also say to you that all the good men and women do nothing with their own hands, but they live as elegantly as if they were kings and the women as if they were angelic beings.' Bernaldez later wrote that Columbus still believed he was about to discover the Indies (*descubrir la tierra firme de las Indias*). He remained firmly convinced that he was on the edge of Asia. It was only a question of finding Cathay, proceeding through the Strait of Malacca, passing into the Bay of Bengal, and then reaching the Indian peninsular.

This obstinate belief seems to have motivated the Admiral, at least on one occasion to have ignored, or even falsified, the evidence. On 12 June an astonishing scene took place while the ships were anchored in the Cuban bay now known as Laguna de Cortés. Fernando Coumbus tells us what happened: 'Seeing that the coast of Cuba extended far to the west, and that sailing there was very difficult because of the countless multitude of little islands and shoals that were everywhere, and since by that time provisions were beginning to run low, the Admiral decided to head back to La Isabela. But he first ordered it to be formally declared – for which he had the notary Pérez de Luna put it in writing – that they were on the shore of the Asian continent. Whoever doubted it, Columbus would persuade. Whoever acknowledged it and then said the contrary would be fined almost a year's salary and have his tongue cut out. In the end, forty-two men – captains, pilots, and seamen – signed a declaration stating that they had reached mainland Asia.' It is possible that some may have believed it, as the Cuban coast was much vaster than a normal island, so perhaps it *was* the mainland after all. However, Columbus knew differently. The day before, he had obtained evidence from a native that Cuba was an island. So he either deliberately lied to his men, or really believed he was in Asia regardless of the evidence to the contrary. It could have been the latter. Back in Spain, having completed his second voyage, Columbus told Pietro Martire d'Anghiera, an Italian humanist at the Spanish court as well as the court historian, that he had gone almost as far as the *Chersoneso Aureo* (in ancient literature, the name for the Malay Peninsular, near present-day Singapore).[12]

Sailing westward along the southern coast of Cuba, the caravels came across shoals that they could only get across by the laborious process of kedging, which meant rowing an anchor ahead, dropping it and then hauling the ship up to it by the windlass while her keel scraped the bottom. They even passed the region of the Taino and entered the stronghold of the Siboney but Diego Colón, the interpreter, was not able to talk with them, as he was not familiar with their language.

The return voyage to Isabela started on 13 June 1494. It proved long and tedious, beating to windward against the trade winds and the westward-flowing current. 'If the ships in the Indies only sail with the wind abaft the beam', wrote Columbus, 'it is not from bad design or clumsiness; the great currents, which run there in the same direction as the wind, so make it that nobody attempts to struggle close-hauled, for in one day they would lose what they gained in seven; nor do I except the caravels, even Portuguese lateeners.' Columbus learned that to make progress in the Caribbean was to stay in smooth water, avoid the current and work the land breeze at night. It took him twenty-five days to make good some 200 miles. Fed up with that, he made for blue water and then it took him ten days to cover 180 miles.

Sailing around the western end of Jamaica, they edged along the southern coast, anchoring every night. The Indians were friendly, one casique startlingly so. He came out to the flagship at the fore of several canoes, his family and suite dressed in magnificent parrot-feather headdresses but little else. The chieftain wore a coronet of disks of gold and copper alloy interspaced with small polished stones. In the bow of his canoe stood a herald draped in a cloak of red feathers and carrying a white banner. His wife was also adorned with similar jewellery but nothing else that could be called clothing 'except for a little cotton thing no bigger than an orange peel'.

Their beautiful daughters, aged about fifteen and eighteen, were completely naked. When they drew alongside the Admiral was in his cabin so absorbed in reading in his prayer book the office of terce, that he did not notice them until they stepped on deck. The casique bowed ceremoniously and then proposed, through Diego Colón, the interpreter, that he and his family sail to Spain with the Admiral to visit the Catholic Sovereigns, and to see the wonders of Castile. Though tempted by the thought of the impression it would make at court, Columbus' humanity prevailed. He thought of the cold weather and hardships on the trip home, of the indignities the pretty daughters might suffer from the sailors, and of the effect of a complete change of climate on these innocent souls. So after receiving the casique's homage and fealty to Fernando and Isabella, the Admiral sent them off with gifts of trinkets.

Food was running short, his crews were restless, and his ships were leaking and in need of repair. Leaving Jamaica on 19 August, he crossed the Jamaica Channel, and sighted Cape Tiburón, Haiti. For the next five weeks they battled their way slowly eastward against headwinds along the south coast of Hispaniola. From a bay on the shore where eventually would rise the city of Santo Domingo, Columbus landed nine men with orders to cross the island on foot by way of the fort of Santo Tomás to advise his brother of his impending return. Before returning to Isabella, Columbus planned a slave raid on Puerto Rico, but after rounding the island of Saona and entering the Mona Passage between that island and the island of Mona, off Puerto Rico's western coast, he fell ill. He ran a high fever that, said Las Casas, led to a lethargy that deprived him of sense and memory and almost proved fatal. His symptoms today suggest a nervous breakdown due to a lack of sleep, perhaps inadequate food and frequent drenching from the elements. He probably had the start of arthritis, which was to trouble him gravely throughout the last ten years of his life. His officers held a council and decided after rounding Cabo Engaño, the eastern extremity of Hispaniola, to run before the wind to Isabela, where the three caravels arrived on 29 September 1494. The Admiral was unconscious, and had to be carried ashore in the arms of his seamen.[13]

From a navigational point of view Columbus' return from the western extremity of Cuba to La Isabela was a skilful element of seamanship. Although he had not found the empire of the Grand Khan, his had been a considerable accomplishment. Not only had he discovered Jamaica, but he had opened up the most valuable of Spain's insular possessions, while demonstrating that he was equally adept at coastal piloting as he was charting a course across the ocean. His shipmates of that voyage never tired of expressing their admiration for his feats of navigation and of his expressions of consideration and human kindness towards them.

When he recovered consciousness he found that he was ashore and in a bed and beside him, to his joy, was his brother Bartholomew. It will be recalled that Columbus had written to him in France asking him to join his second voyage, but that he had arrived in Spain too late to do so. In response to another request from Columbus he had taken his sons Diego and Fernando to court where the king and queen had promised them appointments as pages to their son, the Infante Don Juan. The sovereigns were so well impressed with Bartholomew that they decided to appoint him in charge of three caravels to take supplies to Hispaniola. He had, in fact, arrived in June, three months before Columbus' return to Isabela.

As soon as Columbus was fit enough, his first act was to appoint Bartholomew as Adelantado (lieutenant-governor), a move that further alienated the malcontents at Isabela.

During the Admiral's absence, his rather meek younger brother Diego, having heard about the cruelty and rapacity of Margarit and his men, protested his behaviour by letter threatening him to mend his ways, or else. This so enraged the Spaniard that he stormed into Isabela with part of his force, where he won over some of the anti-Columbus faction including Father Buil, who proved to be a leading troublemaker on Columbus' second voyage. He then seized the three caravels that Bartholomew had brought, and sailed with his supporters for Spain, where he circulated slanders against the Columbus brothers.

Meanwhile, Margarit's men had broken up into gangs and were still pillaging and terrorizing the countryside, until in sheer desperation the natives reacted, ambushing and killing several Spaniards.

Columbus completely misjudged the situation and instead of punishing the roving gangs of Spaniards, as they deserved, he sent strong parties inland with horses and mastiffs against the natives. After some brutal clashes some 1,500 unfortunate men, women and children, most of them quite innocent, were rounded up and brought to Isabela. By this time four more caravels, this time commanded by Antonio de Torres, had arrived with supplies; and as there was no gold or anything else of value to send home, Columbus filled their holds with some 500 of his Indian captives, men and women, to be sold in Spain as slaves. The settlers at Isabela were then authorised to help themselves to another 600, and the remainder, mostly women with young children, were turned loose.

Michele da Cuneo records how these wretched captives, when set free, fled in desperation, 'leaving their children to their fate on the ground'. The lot of those shipped home was terrible. Debilitated and ill, some 200 died at sea and were thrown overboard. The survivors were landed at Seville where Andrés Bernaldez, the clerical chronicler, saw them put up for sale in the slave market 'naked as they were born'. Adding 'they were not very profitable since almost all died, for the country did not agree with them'.

Meanwhile in Hispaniola, Columbus had provoked a state of open warfare. A casique named Guatiguaná, who had already once escaped execution, rallied a force of some thousands of natives in the Vega Real to march on Isabela. Columbus learned of this and appointing Bartholomew and Ojeda his lieutenants, led a force of 200 men, and twenty cavalry with twenty Spanish mastiffs against them. Near Puerto de los Hidalgos, where the northern range descends into Vega Real, the natives having walked into a well-planned ambush were routed in a brief but bloody battle. This, the first pitched battle between Europeans and Indians, took place at the end of March 1495. A couple of weeks later, Ojeda captured the dreaded Caonabó, toughest of the casiques, who had been responsible for exterminating the Navidad garrison. He was confined in irons to the jail at Isabela, 'fretting and gnashing his teeth like a captive lion'. Put on board a ship he died en route to Spain.

Columbus was not a merciful victor. He demanded gold tribute from the defeated Indians. The little hawk's bells that earlier had been given to the natives in friendship were transformed into instruments of oppression: every three months, decreed Columbus, each adult native was required to stuff enough gold to fill one of the bells. If the Indian was a chieftain he had to contribute a calabash full, and as receipt each was given a small brass medal to wear around his neck. Not surprisingly, the natives soon abandoned their villages and fled to the mountains, for there was so little gold in the island that men and woman had to work long hours washing and panning in the mountain streams to gather their quarterly tribute. Many that were unable to do so took their own lives.

Meanwhile in Spain the calumnies of Fray Buil, Margarit, and others against Columbus had reached the sovereigns, who decided to send Juan Aguado, a colonist who had returned with Torres, to investigate the matter and report to them. He arrived at Isabela with four provision ships in October 1495, and with great pomp, he and his notaries began by gathering complaints from the Spaniards in the town. While the rogues, bullies, and fortune seekers continued their raids on the surrounding countryside, and their atrocities against the natives.

Finally, naming his brother Bartholomew governor in his absence, Columbus sailed home on *Niña* on 10 March 1496, leaving behind a devastated and ravished Hispaniola. The pillage of the New World had begun; Hispaniola was an island paradise no more.

THE ADMIRAL'S THIRD VOYAGE – MAINLAND DISCOVERED 1498-1500

So Columbus said, somebody show me the sunset
and somebody did and he set sail for it.
And he discovered America and they put him in jail for it,
and the fetters gave him welts,
and they named America after somebody else.

The Face is Familiar, Ogden Nash (1940)

Columbus arrived back in Spain exhausted and ill. The ordeal of the voyage had taken its toll. Although only forty-five, his hair and beard were snow white and he was suffering from arthritis, opthalmia (a severe inflammation of the eyes), as well as gout, an affliction that was becoming more recurrent.

The court was at Valladolid in northern Spain and while he awaited a royal summons he stayed with a priest friend named Andrés Bernaldez, chaplain of the archbishop of Seville at Los Palacios, a small town near the city. He kept out of the public eye leading a quiet life, and the few times he ventured into the streets of Seville he wore the simple brown habit of a Minorite friar.

When the invitation from the sovereigns arrived in late July, Columbus organised another impressive cavalcade. Two members of the cacique Caonabo's family accompanied him on mule back. Servants rode ahead with cages of bright coloured parrots whose screeches heralded the arrival of the hero and his entourage. When entering an important town, Caonabo's brother wore a massive gold collar around his neck and on his head the cacique's crown, 'very big and tall, with wings on its sides like a shield and golden eyes as large as silver cups'. However, by now so many disillusioned colonists had returned from Hispaniola that the Spanish public had become sceptical, and for all of Columbus' brave show his progress inspired few cheers.

Arriving at Valladolid he learned that the court had moved to Burgos, some 80 miles away, where he hurried to find his sons Diego and Ferdinand, who were royal pages to the sovereign's son the Infante Don Juan.

The king and queen courteously received the Admiral, especially after he presented them with a purse of gold nuggets as big as pigeon's eggs.

Apparently, reports of Hispaniola's problems had not shaken their faith in Columbus. On 3 April 1497, at Burgos the Infante Don Juan married the

Archduchess Margarita of Austria, and three weeks later, with this momentous event off their minds, the king and queen authorised Columbus to go ahead with plans for his next voyage.

The Admiral promptly put in a plea for a fleet to be outfitted for him. Exploration, he argued, must not be interrupted. Five of the ships he asked be laden with provisions for Hispaniola and another three for his use, to seek out a continent, which, he cunningly said, the king of Portugal believed to be in the ocean south of the Antilles. Dom João of Portugal was dead, but the mere fact that he had believed of the existence of this continent stimulated Ferdinand and Isabella to strive to get there first. However, Columbus could get nothing from the sovereigns until news from Portugal indicated that D. João's successor, Dom Manuel I, was indeed fitting out a large overseas expedition under Vasco da Gama that was almost ready to depart, destination unknown. Might he not also be looking for this same part of the world?

The king and queen confirmed Columbus' rights, titles, and privileges and ordered him to recruit 300 colonists for Hispaniola at the royal expense. They also authorised him to find thirty women to join the expedition who would receive no pay but were expected to marry upon arrival. These were to be the first Christian women to go to the New World. All malefactors confined in jail, excepting traitors and heretics, were offered pardon if they sailed with the Admiral to the Indies and stay a year or two.

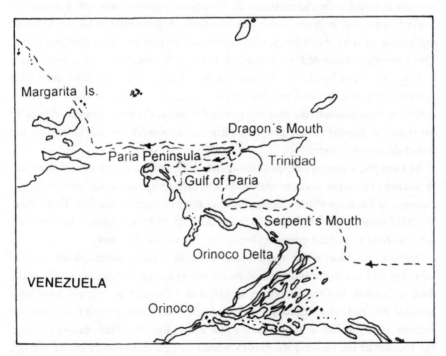

Columbus' third voyage.

Columbus sent these fellows directly to Hispaniola, a decision he was later to regret.

In January 1498 *Niña* and *India* sailed for Hispaniola; and three more caravels followed in short order with supplies. They were commanded by Alonso Sanchez de Carvajal, one of the Admiral's most faithful captains, a veteran of his second voyage; Pedro de Arana, brother to Columbus' mistress, and Giovanni Antonio Colombo, his first cousin.

The squadron assembled at Seville and dropped down the Guadalquivir to the roadstead at Sanlúcar de Barrameda. There the Admiral came on board and on 30 May 1498, the same day that Vasco da Gama arrived at Calicut, the third voyage to America began.

Three of the vessels had orders to head to the Canary Islands, and from there follow the now familiar route directly to Hispaniola. With his three ships – a carrack and two caravels – Columbus planned to cross the equator into the Southern Hemisphere, where according to Jaime Ferrer, a Catalan cosmographer and jeweler, he would find 'grand and valuable things, such as precious stones, gold, herbs and spices'. (In the end, however, Columbus remained north of the equator for the duration of the voyage.)

At Funchal in Madeira, where he had formerly resided, he was now received as a hero. From there it was only a three-day run to the roadstead of San Sebastian, Gomera. The romance with Doña Beatriz had apparently died – if ever there had been one – since all that was recorded was that 'we loaded cheeses'. It was just as well for the Admiral that his flirtation never ripened into marriage, as Doña Beatriz was as cruel as she was beautiful. A gentleman who she believed had spread rumors about her sexual capers was invited to visit her at the castle. This little *tête à tête* ended when the lady rang for her retainers and ordered them to hang her guest by the neck from a rafter of the castle hall until dead. Not content with that, she ordered his corpse strung up outside his own residence. After a second murder, this time for political reasons, she was summoned back to court by the Spanish sovereigns to explain her actions. A few days later she was found dead in her room.[1]

At Gomera, Carvajal's Hispaniola squadron of three caravels parted from the exploring expedition and cut across towards Dominica, while Columbus shaped a course to the Cape Verde Islands covering the 750 miles in six days. From there he sailed south-west for about 450 miles until he reckoned he was in about the same latitude as Sierra Leone, before setting his course due west.

Progress was slow, as the trade winds were light and soon faded into a dead calm. He had reached the doldrums. In his report to the sovereigns he tells of the 'heat so intense and the sun's rays so hot that I thought we should have been burned'. For eight days the ships wallowed in the sea drifting with the equatorial current until at last a favourable wind came up from the east-south-east. For the rest of the crossing the ships scudded along exhilaratingly under full sail, logging an average of 180 miles a day.

At noon on 31 July, land was sighted. It appeared at first to be three small hills, but was later found to be one large island, which the Admiral named *Trinidad*, having placed this voyage under the special protection of the Holy Trinity. Changing course to approach the land they sighted the south-eastern point of the island. Columbus named it *Cabo de la Galera*, because its peaked cliffs resembled a three-cornered hat. The ships continued to sail along its southern coast until a bay was sighted where a stream of cool sweet water crosses the beach at what is now called Erin Bay. Parties went ashore, washed their clothes, bathed to wash the caked salt and sweat from their bodies, and had a fine time yelling and kicking up a din in the hope of attracting some pretty Indian females from the jungle.

Columbus weighed anchor on 2 August and sailed through the narrow *Boca del Sierpe* into the great Gulf of Paria that lies between Trinidad and the mainland. One supposes that he sailed through the Boca at the turn of the tide, for he made no remark in his diary about the current that swirls around the mid-channel rock that he named *El Gallo* – the cock, as it looks like a cock's comb; it is now Soldado instead.

Two days later there was another landing and contact was made with the natives. They were certainly not Asians as Columbus had hoped. Nevertheless, he found them attractive and described them to the queen as 'very graceful in form, less dark than others in the Indies, and with long straight hair'. He thought them also, 'more shrewd and intelligent and less timid' than those of Hispaniola. The Admiral, hoping to be able to trade, ordered some brass chamber pots and other shining objects to be displayed over the bulwarks, but this did not impress the Trinidad Indians. Next he tried putting on a show for their benefit. He ordered a pipe and tambourine player to sound off and the ship's boys to dance but this caused the Indians to let fly a shower of arrows, none of which, fortunately, hit anyone on board.

Columbus now steered due north, attracted by the sight of mountains on the Paria peninsula across the gulf. Approaching the promontory, he enjoyed the gorgeous view that greets the sailor today: astern the placid Gulf; westward, beneath the setting sun, stretched a succession of mountains and rugged headlands; to the east lay the high broken islands in the *Boca del Dragon* and behind them the mountains of Trinidad. As it was a very clear evening, the Admiral could devise an island that might have been Tobago. He anchored for the night in *Bahía Celeste* towards the end of the Paria peninsula and the next day turned west to explore the shore along the continental side of the Gulf.

He probably had himself rowed ashore upon reaching a sandy cove where he had sighted a thatched hut and a fire burning. But the natives that had fled upon the sight of the ship had been replaced by swarms of monkeys who chattered incessantly at the Spaniards. This was the first place where the Admiral had set foot on mainland America; the first time, indeed, that any European had done so since the Vikings in the year 986. The date of Columbus' landing was Sunday, 5 August 1498. Two days later, following his usual custom, he had a great cross raised, and in the presence of uncomprehending natives he took possession of the area for Spain.

The Admiral resumed the exploration of the Gulf on 8 August. Some women from one of the villages on the shore came on board wearing necklaces of pearls that came from the other side of the peninsula. This event caused great excitement among the Spaniards who bartered with the women who were willing to sell their pearls for the usual trading trinkets.

Cruising further down the coast of the Gulf they discovered the mouth of the Rio Grande as well as the estury of the Orinoco that emptied into it. Stubborn as usual, Columbus would not admit that the rivers flowed from a great continent and giving up the search for an outlet that was not there he turned east again as the moon rose above the horizon.

The land breeze held and with the current in their favour they reached the Bocas that night and anchored in a pretty little port named *Puerto de Gatos* (Cat Harbour) on Chacachacare Island. At early dawn, the fleet weighed and stood into the *Boca del Dragón* (The Dragon's Mouth), the strait between Trinidad and the mainland of Venezuela. The name is still in use for all four channels that connect the Gulf of Paria with the Caribbean, and dangerous indeed they are for small craft. There the ships were caught in the turmoil between the fresh water from the rivers flowing out of the Gulf and the rush of the salt water coming in from the Caribbean. They 'thought to perish' when the wind dropped and caravels drifted towards the rocks, but the current of fresh water prevailed over the salt and slowly carried them out to safety.[2]

Once into the Caribbean Columbus sighted towards the north the island of Grenada some 60 miles distant. He named it *Asunción* as it was the vigil of the Feast of the Assumption. At dawn on 15 August, he sighted the island he named Margarita, after the charming and good-natured Infanta Margarita of Austria. Unfortunately the Admiral did not delay to look for the pearls that were there in abundance as he was in such a hurry to get to Santo Domingo. It was a mistake as matters in Hispaniola would have been no worse for the delay had he stayed a month collecting pearls by the bushel to carry home to Spain and bolstering his prestige by it into the bargain.

Worse was to come as in the meantime, news of Columbus' discoveries in the Gulf of Paria had reached Spain. Alonso de Ojeda managed to get hold of the Admiral's chart and surmising the priceless opportunity the Admiral had missed persuaded Archbishop Juan de Fonseca of Seville, empowered by the sovereigns to grant licenses, to grant one to him to further explore the area. In the autumn of 1498 with companions who included the mapmaker Juan de la Cosa and the Florentine, Amerigo Vespucci, he sailed from Spain. He found the rich pearl fisheries which Columbus had missed around Margarita Island and went on to discover the islands of Bonaire, Curaçao, Aruba and the Gulf of Maracaibo.

Leaving the mainland he turned north for Hispaniola, carefully avoiding Santo Domingo and sailed to the Bahamas. Having filled his holds with slaves, he returned to Spain.

On 17 August, bound for Hispaniola again, Columbus reflected on what he had seen. He wondered if the immense Venezuelan river, the Orinoco, might be the one that flows from the Earthly Paradise 'that everyone says is at the end of the Orient'. Even though Columbus had strived to transform European thinking as well as cosmography, part of him still believed, or wanted to believe, in the legends passed on by Ptolemaic and medieval geographers. Still the evidence was too much for him to overlook. He recorded in his journal: 'I believe that this is a very great continent, until today unknown. And reason aids me greatly because of that so great river and fresh-water sea, and next, the saying of Esdras... that the six parts of the world are of dry land, and one of water... And if this be a continent, it is a marvellous thing, and will be so among all the wise, since so great a river flows that it makes a fresh-water sea of 48 leagues'. This passage in his journal, 'his very words', Las Casas assures us, is typical of the workings of the Admiral's mind. For weeks he had been sailing long the coast of the continent he sought, though refusing to believe it was so because it did not match his idea of what it should look like. Finally, however, the vast volume of fresh water gushing into the Gulf and vague gestures of the natives flew together in his mind to prove it and change his mind.

From Margarita on 15 August he set a course NW by N for Saona Island off Hispaniola, as a good place from where to coast downwind to Santo Domingo. He ordered the caravels to heave-to every night and heave the lead frequently, and to sail only by day when the dangerous reefs could be detected by changes in the colour of the water. He made his landfall on Alta Vela 120 miles south-west of Santo Domingo. 'It weighed on him to have fallen off so much', wrote Las Casas but he correctly decided that his miscalculations were the result of the strong current. It is unlikely that a modern sailor could do better provided only with Columbus' knowledge and instruments. If not superb dead reckoning, he must have been provided with divine guidance; perhaps it might have been a combination of the two!

A few days later they sighted a small caravel approaching from the direction of Santo Domingo, the first vessel his fleet had seen since leaving Spain. The ship fired a gun and luffed up alongside the flagship and to the Admiral's delight on board was his brother Bartholomew. He had gone out to pursue the provision squadron under Carvajal, which had stupidly continued to sail westward instead of landing at Santo Domingo. After this happy reunion, the four caravels beat up against wind and current in eight days to the new capital, not bad going at all under the circumstances.

On the day he had reached furthest west in the Gulf of Paria he had written some prophetic words of this voyage in his journal:

And your Highnesses will gain these vast lands, which are an Other World, and where Christianity will have so much enjoyment, and our faith in time so great an increase. I say this with very honest intent and because I desire that your Highnesses may be the greatest lords in the world, lords of it all, I say; and that all may be with much service to and satisfaction of the Holy Trinity.

It showed superb faith and it was a remarkable prophecy! Columbus the zealot, however, was not unprepared for some grand new revelation about the shape of the planet. 'God made me the messenger of the new heaven and the new earth of which he spoke in the Apocalypse by St John, after having spoken of it by the mouth of Isaiah; and he showed me the spot where to find it.' This revelation required revision of the orthodox dogmas of the earth:

I have always read that the world comprising the land and the water was spherical, and the recorded experiences of Ptolemy and all others have proved this by the eclipses of the moon and other observations made from east to west, as well as by the elevation of the pole from north to south. But I have now seen so much irregularity that I have come to another conclusion respecting the earth, namely that it is not round as they describe, but in the form of a pear...or like a round ball, upon one part of which is a prominence like a woman's nipple, this protrusion being the highest and nearest the sky, situated under the equinoctial line, and at the eastern extremity of this sea where the land and the islands end... [The ancients] had no certain knowledge respecting this hemisphere, but merely vague suppositions, for no one has ever gone or been sent to investigate the matter until now that Your Highnesses have sent me to explore both the sea and the land.

Here, finally, was the actual earthly location of the Scriptural landscape, which medieval Christian cosmographers had so long featured at the top of their maps:

I am convinced that it is the spot of the earthly paradise whither no one can go but by God's permission... I do not suppose that the earthly paradise is in the form of a rugged mountain, as the descriptions of it have made it appear, but that it is on the summit of the spot which I have described... I think also that the water I have described [i.e. of the Orinoco] may proceed from it, though it be far off, and that stopping at the place which I have just left, it forms this lake [the Gulf of Paria]. There are great indications of this being the terrestrial paradise, for its site coincides with the opinion of holy and wise theologians, and, moreover, the older evidences agree with the supposition, for I have never either read or heard of fresh water coming in so large a quantity in close conjunction with the water of the sea. The idea is also corroborated by the blandness of the temperature; and if the water I speak does not proceed from the earthly paradise, it seems to be a still greater wonder, for I do not believe that there is any river in the world so large and so deep.

Columbus' geographical location of the Terrestrial Paradise on this unexpected mainland was no random fantasy but the only rational explanation to reconcile the existence of such a vast source of fresh water with his Christian doctrine, his Ptolemaic knowledge of geography, with his Asiatic identity of Cuba, and the certainty of a direct sea passage around the Golden Chersonese to the Indian Ocean.

Before returning to Spain in 1496, Columbus had given the job of constructing a new capital on Hispaniola. The following year, Bartholomew had carried out these instructions by founding Santo Domingo on the southern coast of the present day Dominican Republic, not far from the gold mines that the Spaniards had recently discovered. On 31 August 1498, Columbus arrived in Santo Domingo where according to Fernando, he hoped 'to rest from the troubles and stress of his third voyage and find peace among his people'. Instead he found himself in the middle of a crisis. Politically the island had been torn apart by a struggle between those loyal to the Admiral and his family who controlled the central and southern part of the island, and a party of rebels to the west who were loyal to Francisco Roldán, a man who the Admiral himself had made *Alcalde* (mayor and magistrate) of Hispaniola.

Roldán's revolt lasted two more years before Columbus was able to settle it. In the end he capitulated to the rebels' requests by granting each colonist a parcel of land with the natives on it. Las Casas says that 'the farmers who were paid to cultivate the land and the miners [the Spaniards that is] behaved like idlers and lived off the sweat of the Indians, each one usurping by force three, four, ten of them to keep as servants'.

Then came a further blow, this one from overseas. As Oviedo describes it, 'their Catholic Majesties, angered by the information they had about the way in which Don Christopher Columbus and his brother were governing this island, decided to send as governor a venerable knight, and familiar of the court, a very honest and religious man'. The venerable knight was Don Francisco de Bobadilla.

Bobadilla arrived in Santo Domingo on 24 August 1500. The first thing he saw upon landing was a gallows from which seven Spanish corpses were hanging, and Diego cheerfully remarked that five more were due to be hanged next day. These men had rebelled under Adrián de Moxica and had been captured with Roldan's assistance. Bobadilla, shocked by what he saw and heard, without waiting to hear the Columbus side of the argument, took over both fort and government, tossed Don Diego into the brig of his flagship, impounded all the Admiral's effects, won over the populace by granting them permission to gather gold anywhere, and when the Admiral appeared after being summoned, had him fettered and confined in the city jail. Bartholomew, who was in the interior with a loyal army, might have marched on the capital and released his brothers but the Admiral neither dared, nor cared, to defy the royal authority Bobadilla represented. On his advice, Bartholomew lay down his arms and was thrown into jail as well.

After compiling a file of anti-Columbus depositions from discontented and mutinous Spaniards, the royal commissioner decided to ship all three brothers home to Spain for trial. In early October of 1500, the Admiral and Diego, both chained, were placed on board caravel *La Gorda*, bound for Spain. Bartholomew sailed aboard another vessel. The captain of *La Gorda* 'would have knocked off the Admiral's irons', said his son Fernando but his father 'would not permit it, saying they had been put on him by regal authority and only the Sovereigns could order them struck off'.[3] The Admiral bitterly resolved, 'to save these shackles as relics and as a souvenir of the reward for his many services'.

It is not easy to consider this sad and humiliating episode objectively, but in the end it seems to have been motivated largely by politics and 'reasons of state'. A modern historian, Paolo Emilio Taviani, calls it a *coup d'etat*: the crown was undoing the curious partnership it had made with the Columbus family, having decided to manage the increasingly lucrative business in the 'Indies' on its own. In other respects the decision was an outgrowth of changes that were happening in Europe itself, where feudal relationships were beginning to give way to the bureaucratic functioning of the modern state.

Fair winds accompanied the homeward voyage of *La Gorda*, as if the Ocean Sea wished to alleviate the sufferings of her Admiral. Before the end of 1500 he landed at Cadiz still in chains. Accompanied by his jailer he lodged at the monastery of Las Cuevas in Seville. The spectacle of Columbus in chains is said to have left a lamentable impression on the populace. However, six weeks elapsed before the sovereigns ordered him released from his fetters and summoned him to court.

Isabella and Ferdinand at the Alhambra in Granada received Columbus and his two brothers on 17 December 1500. The sovereigns promised justice: they allowed Columbus to keep his now empty titles of Viceroy and Admiral, as well as permission to send a trusted envoy to Hispaniola to make Bobadilla disgorge the moneys Columbus was owed from the island's trading and gold mining profits.

Nothing less than total restoration of his rights, titles, properties and offices would satisfy Columbus. But it was futile for him to expect to get everything back – he and his brothers had made too much of a mess of things in Hispaniola to expect to be entrusted again with the overseas government. As the vast continent opened up, it was unrealistic for him to expect that the sovereigns would grant similar privileges as they had before in the expectation of him setting up a trading factory and discovering a few islands. Columbus would have been well advised to call it a day and settle for a castle, a pension and a new title but he was not a man to give up anything. Had he been, he might never have discovered the New World.

After waiting eight months, Columbus learned the worst: Don Nicolás de Ovando had been appointed the new governor and supreme justice of the islands and mainland though, he was not given the title of Viceroy. He left Cadiz on 13 February 1502 with a magnificent fleet of thirty ships carrying 2,500 sailors, colonists and soldiers, to supply the colony with new blood.

11
THE FINAL VOYAGE –
1502-1504

What if wise men as far back as Ptolemy
Judged that the earth like an orange was round,
None of them ever said, 'Come along, follow me,
Sail to the west and the East will be found.'

Anonymous

Eager to sail once more to the Indies, Columbus now asked for the means to make a fourth voyage, and a month after Ovando sailed for Hispaniola the sovereigns authorised the venture.

Columbus could round out his arguments, confirm his Christian faith, and fulfill his obsessive desire for reaching the Indies only by finding the sea passage around Marco Polo's Golden Chersonese. With this specific purpose in mind, the same for which ten years earlier he had undertaken his first voyage, Columbus commenced his fourth and last one.

With four caravels and 150 men, including his brother Bartholomew the ships set out from Seville on 3 April 1502. On the way down river they careened at Casa Vieja to clean the bottoms of the ship's hulls and paint them with pitch to discourage teredos.[1] From the river mouth the caravels proceeded to Cadiz, where Columbus and his fourteen-year-old son Fernando boarded ship and the tiny fleet put to sea on 11 May 1502.

Somewhere between Cuba, which he still believed to be China, and the Terrestrial Paradise to the south he determined to find the strait through which Marco Polo sailed from China into the Indian Ocean. This time he carried with him a courteous royal letter addressed to Vasco da Gama, just in case the two explorers met upon the way. Understandably the Pacific Ocean, still unknown to Europe and as yet without its name, did not figure in anyone's calculations.

Perhaps even more important to Columbus than the voyage itself was the Sovereigns' assurance that his privileges would be preserved, for himself and his heirs. While the ships were being fitted out Columbus made several copies of *The Book of Privileges*, which he had begun before his third voyage. Two he sent to a bank in Genoa, one he left with his son Diego, and one he handed in to the monastery of Las Cuevas for safekeeping. In addition he made a new will that ensured that if he died his mistress Beatriz de Arana would not be bereft. The sovereigns, however, had put restrictions on the venture. Columbus was not allowed to enter into private trading. He was to take an official accountant, Diego Porras, who was to have charge of all gold, silver, pearls and precious stones that might be found. He was prohibited to carry off natives as slaves, and he was forbidden to stop at Santo Domingo on the outward voyage, though he might do, if necessary, on his return.

A rapid Atlantic crossing brought the fleet in sight of the Caribbean island of Santa Lucia. On 29 June 1502, Columbus anchored off Santo Domingo, the capital of Hispaniola. Although forbidden to call there on the outward voyage he had good reasons to do so. Among other things, there were letters to send home. He hoped to be able to exchange the *Santiago*, one of the caravels that had proved a poor sailor, for another. But more urgently he sought shelter from a hurricane which instinct and experience warned him was in the making over the next two to three days.

Inside the harbour had gathered a great convoy of some thirty ships fitting out to carry Bobadilla and a considerable cargo of gold back to Spain. Columbus warned them not to sail because a hurricane was imminent. He himself sailed his own ships westward to a sheltered part of the island. However, as the weather seemed to be fine Bobadilla ignored the warning and his fleet departed. Having barely cleared the island and while crossing the Mona Passage, the violence of the hurricane struck them from the northeast. The chaos was indescribable. The majority of Bobadilla's fleet sank with all hands, a few were driven ashore and smashed to pieces and three or four limped back to Santo Domingo. Only a few ships managed to escape. Some 500 men were drowned, among them Columbus' old enemies Bobadilla and Roldán, his old friend Antonio de Torres, and the casique Guarionex, who was on his way to Spain as a captive. One caravel, the *Aguja*, proceeded to Spain after the hurricane blew over. Its cargo included 4,000 gold pesos earmarked for Columbus. This led to some of Columbus' detractors to add sorcery to their list of accusations, as how else could the Admiral's treasure survive when everything else perished? Of course, Columbus' luck had nothing to do with magic, it was just another demonstration of his superior seamanship, more precisely sea-sense. Columbus had accurately read the warning signs of impending bad weather.

The Europeans had never encountered storms of this intensity, even in the stormy North Atlantic or in their eastward forays to the Indian Ocean. The word hurricane itself is derived from a Caribbean word, *hurican*, the result of very low atmospheric pressure, a feature of all tropical climates, but particularly of the Caribbean.[2]

From Santo Domingo, Columbus, whose fleet had survived by anchoring close under the land (three of his vessels dragged their anchors but suffered little damage and no casualties) set a course south-west past Cuba. The fleet crossed the Caribbean, 360 miles wide at this point, in three days. When the wind moderated a lookout sighted a group of islands off the coast of Honduras.

At Bonacca or Guanaja, the largest of the lofty and spectacular Bay Islands, some 30 miles off the coast of what is now Honduras, they encountered the biggest native

Columbus' fourth voyage.

canoe they had ever seen. 'Long as a galley, and eight feet (2.9m) wide, made completely out of one piece of wood', with a canopy amidships made out of palm fronds. It carried twenty-five natives and was loaded with goods. These were Mayans from the Bay of Campeche, part of the Gulf of Mexico, visiting their southern trade centres. Columbus forcibly detained the skipper as guide and interpreter.

After crossing the 30-mile strait to the mainland, the fleet anchored off the site of Trujillo, later founded by Cortez. During the next four weeks Columbus coasted slowly east in appalling weather and against strong and persistent headwinds. He wrote to his sovereigns that he had never experienced a tempest so violent or that lasted so long. 'In all this time', he told them, 'the ships lay exposed, their sails rent, their rigging and other equipment destroyed, and my people broken in health, continually swearing to be good and vowing to go on pilgrimages and even hearing each others confessions.' Columbus himself became seriously ill, but what fortified him was the steadfast courage of young Ferdinand.

On 14 September the coast turned sharply south. The headwinds turned to following winds, and the long ordeal was over. On board hymns were sung and prayers of thanks were offered and the Admiral named the Cape separating present-day Honduras and Nicaragua, *Gracias a Dios* (Thanks be to God). Since the coast here tended southward, this marked the end of his long dead-beat to windward. Now they were able to relax and sail along on the port tack a safe distance from the shore.

During ten pleasant days spent at anchor behind Uvita Islet, off today's Puerto Limón, Columbus learned from the Indians that the name of the country was Veragua (Panama), that it was an isthmus and that in nine days' march he could reach another sea and a native province called Ciguare, where there was an immense quantity of gold. Columbus identified it with Chiamba, Marco Polo's name for Cochin China, today's Vietnam, so he concluded that India was only a ten-day sail away.

While anchored behind Uvita Islet, the natives sent on board two virgins, one about eight and the other about fourteen years old. 'They showed great fortitude', recorded Ferdinand (who was then about the same age as the elder), 'gave no signs of grief or fear but always looked cheerful and modest. The Admiral... had them clothed and fed and had them sent ashore.' The Spanish continence astonished the natives, and next day when Bartholomew went ashore to take possession of the place in the name of Spain, the natives thought his writing materials, quill, pen, paper and ink in a cow's horn to be magical instruments and tossed brown powder in the air to exorcise the place from the evil presence of the sexless Spanish sorcerers.[3]

If Columbus had pressed on over the mountains and through the jungle for 200 miles (320km), he would have found the Pacific Ocean and history's verdict of this fourth voyage would have been different. Instead he decided to establish a settlement in Panama prompted by having discovered gold on the coast of Veragua. The natives, according to Fernando, were 'as naked as when they left their mother's womb; all they wore was a gold mirror around their necks'. Sometimes the people gave these gold mirrors to the Spaniards as gifts, sometimes trading them for two or three little bells. Sniffing prosperity, shore parties went prospecting in a nearby river that the Admiral named the Belén (Bethlehem) and returned with so much gold that it was decided Bartholomew should remain with *La Gallega* and some eighty men to form a small mining colony, which he named *Santa María de Belén*. He had chosen the worst spot on the coast of Central America to establish a beachhead.

Columbus had anchored his caravels inside the sand bar for better protection from the elements. However, the Rio Belén now fell so low that the caravels could not cross the bar to the open sea. At this moment there came the inevitable change in attitude on the part of the Guaymi Indians. The crews of the caravels had been sneaking off by twos and threes to trade with guns in hand, and violate the native women. The cacique Quibián had put up with a good deal thinking his visitors would depart but since they showed every intention of making a permanent settlement, he decided that he had enough. He sent men in canoes to reconnoitre Belén. They acted so suspiciously that Diego Méndez, an 'hidalgo', one of the Admiral's gentleman volunteers, decided to row along the coast to spy them out. In a short while he came upon a camp of a thousand howling warriors. With the amazing courage of the Spaniard in the face of danger, befitting a man born in the bloody shadow of the bullring, he stepped ashore alone and confronted them. Then returning to his boat, kept out of arrow range all night observing the Indians' movements. After realising that surprise had been lost, the Indians retreated to Quibián's village. Méndez followed them and in the midst of a horrible uproar, coolly took out a barber's kit and had his hair cut by his servant Rodrigo de Escobar. This action not only stopped the yelling but also intrigued the cacique Quibián to such a point that he ordered his own hair to be trimmed Mendez style. Mendez presented him with the shears, mirror and comb, after which the Spaniards were allowed to leave in peace.

In the meantime Columbus was preparing to hurry back to Spain for additional resources. Dreams of treasure sent him across the Atlantic in 1492. Ironically, now, ten years later, the same dreams would keep him from discovering an even greater prize, the Pacific Ocean.

The local Indians and their cacique Quibián had been friendly enough, but on seeing huts and a storehouse being built, they realised that the strangers meant to stay and their attitude changed. Quibián decided to attack the Spanish ships and huts and massacre the inhabitants. His plans were discovered, and there followed a battle that ended with one Spaniard killed and several wounded. The Indians were driven off with great loss of life and a few of them were taken as hostages, who later committed suicide.

Columbus should have grasped the fact that his trading post could not survive surrounded as it was by thousands of hostile Indians. Instead he made another bad decision: to seize the cacique Quibián and hold him hostage to insure his people's good behaviour. The cacique and some thirty others were ambushed by an armed party of Spaniards, taken prisoner and placed on board the flagship. However, Quibián broke his bonds and managed to escape, rousing his people against the intruders.

The sailors, in the meantime, were towing the four caravels across the bar, leaving behind the *Gallega* for the use of Bartholomew and the Belén garrison. On 6 April, while the men were saying their farewells, and only twenty men and Columbus' Irish wolf hound were guarding the fort, the natives struck by the hundreds with bows, arrows and spears. They were beaten off mainly due to the fierceness of the wolfhound, but the Indians killed Captain Diego Tristán of the *Capitana* who upstream was filling the flagships water casks. Only one of the boat parties escaped, and ten were killed. Ferdinand, in his history of the voyage, states that in contrast to the Spaniard's stolid courage, an Italian member of the garrison, a certain Bastiano, was seen running away by Diego Méndez (who had succeeded Tristan as captain of *La Capitana*.) He shouted at him to 'About face!' to which the Italian replied, 'Let me go you devil! I am going to save myself!' and he did.[4]

In fear of another mass attack, Bartholomew withdrew his men to the beach behind a barricade of casks but the situation was untenable so it was decided that the settlement be abandoned. As *La Gallega* was unable to cross the shallow bar, everything of value in her was transferred by raft to the other caravels and she was then scuttled. No longer having hostages to assure good behaviour (since those aboard the flagship had either escaped or hanged themselves in the hold), Columbus decided the garrison be evacuated promptly. Diego Mendez built a raft upon which all the Spaniards ashore and most of their gear was lightered across the bar. Thus Santa Maria de Belén again reverted to the wilderness it had once been.

Columbus decided to sail eastward to a point south of Hispaniola from where he estimated he could fetch Santo Domingo on one long starboard tack. The three caravels were in appalling condition, their timbers rotten and so riddled by teredo worms that 'all the people with pumps, kettles and other vessels were unable to bail out the water'. Of the three, the *Vizcaina* was the worst, and she had to be abandoned at Porto Bello, which Columbus had discovered and named the year before.

On 1 May 1503, having navigated almost the entire Central American coast, the Admiral set sail once more towards the open sea. The northern trade wind was off the starboard bow and sailing close-hauled the two ships drifted with the wind for some 100 miles (160km) Then, writes Ferdinand Columbus, 'we came in sight of two small, low islands, full of turtles; the sea around there was filled with them, so they looked like little rocks'. These islands were two of the Cayman's, a final discovery. With great difficulty, the two ships, which could barely keep afloat, arrived in Puerto Santa Gloria, a harbour on the northern coast of Jamaica that Columbus had seen on another trip in 1494. Columbus and his men stayed there, having beached his lashed together ships, for an entire year.[5]

Diego Méndez, who reached a successful agreement with the local caciques to provide a regular and ample supply of food, solved the problem of supplies. In order to avoid provoking them the Admiral ordered that no one was to stray from the ships. Columbus then tried to send a message to Hispaniola asking for help. A first attempt by Diego Méndez failed when Indians captured his canoe with a native crew at the eastern tip of the island. However, he managed to escape and made his way back to the cove where the ships were. Soon afterwards he set out again, this time with two large canoes, the second commanded by the Genoese Bartholomew Fieschi. Both canoes, with six Spaniards and six Indians each, succeeded in traveling the 108 miles (175km) to Hispaniola, with a stop at Navasa after the first 78 miles (126km).

On Jamaica, Columbus' men tired of waiting and hoping, mutinied and escaped in stolen Indian canoes. The Porras brothers, Francisco and Diego, who had been forced upon Columbus by the Treasurer of Castile, the lover of their sister, led the mutineers. The rebels failed in their attempt and turned back. They kept to themselves and, no longer obeying Columbus, took to roaming about the island, pillaging the Indian villages. For this reason the Indians ceased bringing food to the settlement.

Faced with an imminent threat of starvation Columbus countered with typical ingenuity. Among the books he carried on board was the *Ephemerides astronomicae ab anno 1475 ad annum 1506* by Johann Müller, otherwise known as *Regiomontanus*. These astronomical charts predicted an eclipse of the moon for the night of 29 February 1504. Columbus sent a messenger to invite the caciques and leading Indians to a conference that day. When they had gathered he made a threatening speech about the power of God, their wickedness, the punishment that would follow and the warning sign – a lunar eclipse – that they would receive. He told them to watch the moon. The eclipse came on schedule, exactly as predicted in the *Ephemerides*. According to Ferdinand Columbus, 'their fear was so great that, with great weeping and screaming all around, they came running to the ships loaded with provisions'.

Columbus used the eclipse as an opportunity to measure the time difference between Cadiz and Puerto Santa Gloria. He also tried to calculate the latitude of his position, and came to within 31 miles (50km) of fixing his exact location, a virtual bull's-eye by the standards of the time.

A small caravel arrived from Hispaniola but excitement turned to bitter disappointment when they learned that she had not come to rescue them but merely to deliver two casks of wine and some salt pork. They also brought a message from Ovando telling them to be patient. Help, it said, would soon arrive.

Columbus tried to settle the dispute with the mutineers and magnanimously offered them a general pardon, but instead it came down to a fight and in a pitched battle, as the natives looked on in astonishment, Bartholomew Columbus and his loyalists defeated the mutineers. Several rebels were killed; several others including Francisco Porras were captured, and a few were hanged.

Late in June a caravel chartered by Diego Méndez arrived. After just over a year at Jamaica Columbus and his men were taken aboard. The journey back to Santo Domingo was tedious in the extreme, due to adverse winds and currents. The capital was reached on 13 August 1504, where Columbus was welcomed warmly with a great show of friendship by Ovando, who had done nothing to help him. However, the governor showed his true colours when he freed and showered favour on the Porras brothers.

After another month, on 12 September, Columbus, with his brother Bartholomew, his son Ferdinand, and about twenty others, sailed for home. The passage of fifty-six days was long and tempestuous, and although the mainmast broke and the crew contrived a jury mast out of a spare, they finally arrived at Sanlúcar de Barrameda on 7 November 1504. Sick and prematurely aged, the Admiral disembarked but in such ill health that he had to be carried to Seville.

The High Voyage was over, after two and a half years at sea, including the year marooned in Jamaica. If the most adventurous, it was the most disappointing of the four. He had not discovered the Strait, as there was none in that region . The isthmus he discovered was of no importance to the sovereigns, nor was the gold-bearing Veragua in any way exploitable. Nevertheless, he had done his best, as he wrote to his son Diego shortly after his arrival: 'I have served their Highnesses with as great diligence and love as I might have employed to win Paradise and more; and if in somewhat I have been wanting, that was impossible, or much beyond my knowledge and strength. Our Lord God in such cases asketh nothing more of men than good will.'

By the time the Admiral reached Seville, the sovereigns were holding court at Segovia and the queen was suffering from an illness that turned out to be her last. She died on 26 November 1504, less than three weeks after Columbus returned from his fourth and final voyage. 'The world has lost its noblest ornament', wrote the courtier Pietro Martire d'Anghiera about the discerning, strong-willed queen who had continued to govern from her sickbed until the day she died.

'The Admiral made no small show of sorrow', wrote Ferdinand Columbus in the final pages of his father's biography, 'since it was she who had supported him and favoured him; and he had always found the king to be rather cold and opposed to his affairs.' This comment might be unfair to King Ferdinand of Aragon, after all Columbus' voyages were undertaken with the support and patronage of both Isabella *and* Ferdinand. But it is important to remember that the 'Indies' belonged to the Crown of Castile and were technically speaking part of Isabella's domain.

Queen Isabella understood what Columbus was trying to do, respected and protected him from his detractors. She never sneered at him and respected his rights. Ferdinand had also supported him, but the Indies was, after all, the queen's overseas kingdom. At the time of her death, Columbus was fifty-three years old and in bad health. He was also bitter about the way he had been treated by the sovereigns. He believed they had failed to honour the payments and privileges to which he was entitled. He rented a house in Seville and presented his case through his son Diego, now an officer of King Ferdinand's guard to whom he wrote a series of letters outlining his various claims and giving detailed instructions how they should be pressed. Diego made little progress, and in the end Columbus decided to seek a royal audience directly with King Ferdinand. He felt he was well enough to travel, provided he could ride a mule; a horse's gait was too rough for him. The crown, under pressure from the horse breeders of Andalusia, had forbidden the use of mules for riding, so the Admiral had to beg for a special permit. The king granted it and in May 1505 Columbus started out on his long journey to the court at Segovia, north of Madrid.

The king received Columbus cordially, but refused to acknowledge the validity of the Admiral's claims. However, Ferdinand did allow an arbitrator to be named. At Columbus' request, the arbitrator was Father Deza, the Franciscan who had supported him in that final crisis in 1492 and who was now archbishop of Seville.

As the court moved to Salamanca and on to Valladolid, the Admiral painfully followed. As the days went by his arthritis grew worse, and he became bedridden. Nevertheless, he felt so certain of justice being done that he made a will providing legacies out of his expected revenues. Almost at the last moment of his life, his hopes were raised by the arrival of the Infanta Doña Juana to claim her mother's throne of Castile. She had been at court when Columbus first returned from the Indies and had been fascinated by the wonderful stories of the New World and the artefacts and Indians he had shown them. Now he saw a glimmer of hope in that she might confirm the favours granted him by her mother. But he was far too ill to move so he sent his brother Bartholomew to kiss the young sovereign's hand and plead his cause.

With Bartholomew away Columbus' failed rapidly. On 19 May 1505, realising that the end was not far off, he dictated and signed a long codicil to his will in which he confirmed his son Diego as sole heir to all his property and privileges. He added substantial legacies for his two brothers and son Ferdinand, while Diego was entrusted to provide adequately for Beatriz de Arana, Ferdinand's mother.

Next day he grew worse. Both son Diego and a few faithful friends and followers, such as Diego Méndez and Bartolomeo Fieschi, gathered at his bedside. A priest was quickly summoned and said mass, during which all received Holy Communion. After the concluding prayer, the Admiral, remembering the last words of his Lord and Saviour, murmured them as his own, 'In manus tuas, Domine, commendo spiritum meum' – 'Into Thy hands, O Lord, I commend my spirit'. It is said he sent for the chains, which symbolised the degradation he had suffered under Bobadilla, and that he was clutching these in his hands when he died.

A very modest funeral followed. The court sent no representative, no bishop, no royal dignitary attended and the official chronicle did not mention either his death or his funeral.

After temporary burial at Valladolid Columbus' body was transferred to the monastery of Las Cuevas at Seville, where it remained for thirty years. In 1536 it was removed again, this time across the Atlantic to Hispaniola where it was reburied beside the grand altar of the cathedral of Santo Domingo. It remained there for more than 250 years. When Hispaniola was ceded to France in 1795 the relics, now reduced to dust and a few bones, were again exhumed and transferred to the cathedral of Havana. From whence once more they were returned to Seville after Spain had lost Cuba to the United States in the war of 1899-1902.

The huge sums claimed by Columbus were never paid. Nevertheless, King Ferdinand approved Diego's right to the title of Admiral. Soon after his marriage in 1509, to Doña Maria de Toledo, a lady of the court, he was appointed governor of Hispaniola. He stayed there long enough to prove himself to be an able administrator, unlike his father. He built a massive castle, the ruins of which still stand, and died in 1526 aged forty-six, leaving a son Luis who proved to be a bitter disappointment. The present heir and representative of Christopher Columbus belongs to the Lareatagui family, descendants from the distaff side. He still retains the hereditary title of Admiral and Duke of Veragua.

It is one of those ironies of history that the Admiral himself died ignorant of what he had really accomplished, still insisting that he had discovered a large number of islands, a province of China, and an 'Other World'. But of that vast extent of the ocean that lay between that Other World and Asia, he had neither knowledge nor suspicion. If only he had gone far enough southward along the continental coast or crossed the Isthmus of Panama, he would eventually have found his way into the Indian Ocean.

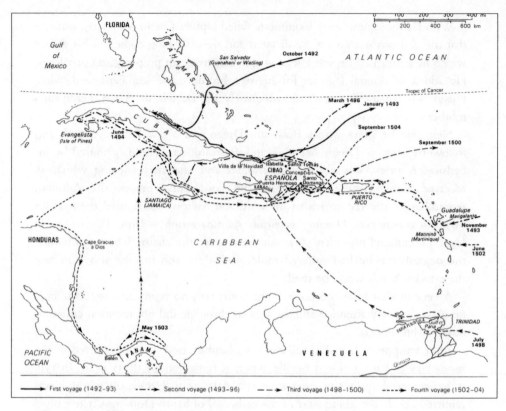

The voyages of Christopher Columbus.

Columbus had his faults, but they were also the defects of qualities that made him great: his unbreakable faith in God, an indomitable will and his stubborn persistence despite neglect, poverty and ridicule. Regardless of the efforts of armchair navigators to denigrate him, the essential of all his qualities was his seamanship. He was in essence a master mariner and navigator. Never was a title more justly bestowed than the one he so jealously guarded – *Almirante del Mar Océano* – Admiral of the Ocean Sea.

12

THE ROAD TO MALACCA

Enough for us that the hidden half of the globe is brought to
light, and the Portuguese daily go farther and farther beyond
the equator. Thus shores unknown will soon become accessible;
for one in emulation of another sets forth in labours and mighty perils.

Pietro Martire d'Anghiera (Peter Martyr), 1493

The bold twenty-six-year-old King Manuel I, who succeeded Dom João II on the
Portuguese throne, was nicknamed 'The Fortunate' because he inherited so many
grand enterprises. He set in motion a scheme to follow up on Bartholomeu Dias'
rounding of the southern tip of Africa on 3 February 1488. The new enterprise was
to be another grand voyage that this time would take the sea route all the way to
India, to open up a new way for trade and quite possibly of conquest. The king's
advisers cautioned him against the venture. Would it not cause the annoyance of all
the great powers, the Spanish, the Genoese, the Venetians, and naturally the Muslim
states, whose commercial interests would be threatened? But Dom Manuel did not
falter and overruled their objections. To lead the expedition he chose a member of
his household, Vasco da Gama (1460–1524).

Son of a minor official from the south coast, Da Gama had proved to be both
a sailor as well as diplomat, conditions that Dom Manuel saw as fitting if he was
to deal with sophisticated Indian potentates. Though ruthless and of a violent
temper, he would be brilliantly qualified to show the courage, the firmness, and
capacity required to deal with humble seamen and arrogant sultans.

It took two years to prepare the expedition that consisted of four vessels, two
square-rigged ships of shallow draft, each of some 100 tons, a lateen-rigged caravel
of about 50 tons, and a store ship of 200 tons. The ships carried provisions for
three years and they were equipped with maps, astronomical instruments and
tables of declination prepared by the great mathematician, Zacuto. They also
carried stone pillars to mark Portuguese claims. Da Gama had enlisted his brother
Paulo, and Nicolas Coelho to accompany him, with of course a priest and the
customary number of '*degradados*', convicts under sentence of death, who being
expendable, could be used in cases of mortal risk. The total that sailed out of
Belem harbour, Lisbon, on 18 July 1497 added up to some 170 men.

If we look at it simply from the viewpoint of seafaring achievements, Vasco da
Gama overshadows Columbus. Columbus' first voyage went due westward, before

a fair wind, 2,600 miles from the Canaries to the Bahamas, remaining on board for thirty-six days. Having made the decision not to hug the African coast, Da Gama's course, requiring subtle navigation, took him in a wide loop, almost all the way across the South Atlantic, against contrary currents and winds, for a distance of not less than 3,700 miles around the Cape of Good Hope. They tacked their way around the Cape in bad weather sighting land on 25 December that they appropriately named Natal, having been at sea for ninety-three days. There some of the crew mutinied but Da Gama, firmly in control, ordered all the money on board to be thrown over the side, together with the navigation instruments after which, imbued with the sense of the mission entrusted to him, he took a firm line with the crew. 'From here on only God will guide us', he told them. 'If the mission that the King has entrusted me with can not be carried out I will not return to Portugal.'

Shortly afterwards scurvy broke out among the crew and they began to die. At the next landfall they raised a marble landmark on the coast, bearing on one side the inscription, 'By order of the sovereign of Portugal, the kingdom of Christianity'. And on the other side the Portuguese coat of arms.

In Mozambique they had problems with the local chief. The situation improved in Malindi, where Juan Machado, a capable '*degradado*', struck up a dialogue with the local inhabitants. He fortunately came across an Arab pilot who gave him an excellent chart, a cross-staff (a principle known to the Arabs as *Kamal*), and magnetic declination tables for the area. The pilot warned him, however, that 'in the Indies you have to show a lot of restraint, both in the way you act and how you speak so as not to offend anybody'.[1]

His great skill in navigation and in managing his crew, took Da Gama's fleet across the Arabian Sea and the Indian Ocean, to arrive at Calicut, his intended destination. He arrived there on 22 May 1498. It was a record, as until then there had never been a seafaring achievement to equal it.[2]

Unlike Columbus, Da Gama did not leave us his own records. But luckily a member of his crew kept a journal, which offers vivid glimpses of the problems they had to face en route (of which the perils of nature and the sea were perhaps the least threatening).

The first-hand account taken from the crewmember's journal, written the day after Da Gama's fleet arrived at Calicut, states:

> On the following day these same boats came alongside, when the captain-major [Da Gama] sent one of the convicts to Calicut, and those with whom he went took him to two Moors from Tunis, who could speak Castilian and Genoese. The first greeting that he received was in these words: 'May the devil take thee! What brought you hither?' They asked what he sought so far away from home, and he told them that we came in search of Christians and of spices. They said 'Why does not the King of Castile, the King of France, or the Signoria of Venice send ships hither?' He said that the King of Portugal would not consent to their doing so, and

they said he did the right thing. After this conversation they took him to their lodgings and gave him wheaten bread and honey. When he had eaten he returned to the ships, accompanied by one of the Moors, who was no sooner on board, than he said these words: 'A lucky venture, a lucky venture! Plenty of rubies, plenty of emeralds! You owe great thanks to God, for having brought you to a country holding such riches!' We were greatly astonished to hear his talk for we never expected to hear our language spoken so far away from Portugal.

In the city they were met by an extraordinary spectacle: a profusion of spices and precious stones, as well as a large variety of aromatic herbs were on sale by the bushel in the central market while in the port were anchored no less than 500 vessels of all shapes and sizes. Worried about the curiosity and scheming of the Muslim merchants, and by being vastly outnumbered, Da Gama gave the order for his ships to weigh anchors and head for home, arriving at Lisbon on 10 July 1499, after navigating some 24,000 miles in 630 days. The loss of lives amounted to two thirds of the crew to sickness, among them Vasco's brother, and two vessels had been lost. Nevertheless, upon arrival the survivors were given a rousing welcome and the king bestowed on Vasco the title of *Dom* as well as pensions and properties.[3]

Vasco da Gama's discovery of a sea route to the Indies and Spice Islands by the way of the Cape of Good Hope, in 1498, induced the Portuguese crown to send a second expedition. Pedro Alvarez Cabral was entrusted with the enterprise and was given the command of an important armada. His technical advisor was none other than the great Vasco himself who drew up the sailing directions and lent all his expertise to the project.

Steering clear of the calms in the Gulf of Guinea, Cabral bore so far west that on 22 April 1500 the coast of South America was sighted. Quite sensibly he came ashore at a place they named Porto Seguro, faced off the Indians, and quickly claimed the region for Portugal, being well situated within the area assigned to it by the Treaty of Tordesillas. At the beginning, the new possession was named 'Island of the True Cross', a title soon abandoned for that of Brazil, the name of the valuable dyewood, which produced a much coveted rich crimson and purple dye.

After the discovery of Brazil, Cabral steered for the southern tip of Africa. After rounding it he set his course for Calicut on the south-western coast of the Indian peninsula. It was a long and tedious voyage with many problems en route. On arriving he set up a 'factory' but the men he landed to operate it were brutally murdered by the Islamic merchants who had for centuries monopolised the distribution of spices. Disheartened, Cabral returned to Lisbon.

To avenge the ignominy of the slaughter of Cabral's men, a fleet of ten armed vessels was entrusted to Vasco Da Gama, who now bore the imposing title of Admiral of the Indies. Upon arriving at Calicut, Vasco bombarded the city and then submitted the citizens to indescribably cruel reprisals. Having sighted a large dhow, the *Meri*, carrying Muslim pilgrims home from Mecca, he demanded all the treasure on board. Finding the passengers slow to deliver, as recorded by one of his crew:

We took a Mecca ship, on board of which were 380 men and many women and children, and we took from it fully 12,000 ducats, and goods worth at least another 10,000. And we burned the ship and all the people on board with gunpowder, on the first day of October. On the 30th now off Calicut, he ordered the King, or *Samuri*, of Calicut to surrender, and demanded the expulsion of every Muslim from the city. When the *Samuri* delayed and sent envoys to negotiate peace, Da Gama replied by seizing a number of merchants and a few fishermen he found in the harbour and hanged them without compassion. He then had their bodies cut up and tossed hands, feet, bodies, and heads, into baskets which he sent ashore with a message in Arabic suggesting that the *Samuri* use those pieces of his people to make himself a curry.

When Da Gama departed for Lisbon with his cargo of treasure he left five of his ships behind, commanded by his uncle (his mother's brother). They were the first permanent European naval forces stationed in Asiatic waters.

Vasco da Gama returned to Portugal in September 1503 with his ships laden with booty. Amidst great public acclaim he was taken from the dockside to the royal palace where, surrounded by the enthusiasm of the people, he was brought to the presence of the king. After giving the sovereign a complete account of his voyage, Vasco was showered with praise and granted more new titles. He then retired to his property in Evora, although he continued to advise the crown in matters concerning India and nautical policies until 1505.[4]

Alfonso de Albuquerque was the second son of the Senhor de Vila Verde. His paternal great-grandfather and grandfather had been confidential secretaries to two kings and his maternal grandfather had been admiral of Portugal. Alfonso served for ten years in Morocco, where he gained experience crusading against the Muslims.

After King Manuel, in 1506, had appointed Dom Francisco de Almeida as first governor of India, with the rank of viceroy, he launched a new expedition of sixteen ships under the joint command of Alfonso d'Albuquerque and Tristan da Cuna. To start with they built a fortress on the island of Socotra to block the mouth of the Red Sea and cut off trade with India. Following this, Albuquerque captured Hormuz, an island in the channel of the Persian Gulf, with every intention of opening the Gulf to Portuguese trade.

After a succession of problems, not the least being imprisoned by the viceroy, Albuquerque finally edged Almeida out and took over the office of governor himself. His plans were to extend his control over all the main maritime trade routes of the East, fortifying them with permanent fortresses and settlements. He was not successful when he attempted to seize Cochin in 1510. Nevertheless, assisted by a powerful corsair named Timoja, he attacked Goa (long ruled by Muslim princes) and occupied it in March 1510. In May he was forced out by a

Muslim army only to finally carry it by assault in November. He put the Muslim defenders to the sword, to express it mildly.[5]

Cruelty knew no bounds with Albuquerque, or his predecessor Viceroy Almeida, who when suspicious of a messenger who had come under safe-conduct to see him, tore out the messenger's eyes. Viceroy Albuquerque invented other equally diabolical techniques. For instance, he subdued the peoples along the Arabian coast by cutting off the noses of their women and hands of their men. Portuguese ships sailing into remote harbours for the first time would display the corpses of recent captives hanging them from the yardarms to show they meant business.[6] Life to these Portuguese was fierce, savage and uncertain; it was a vast gamble that had brought them there and their spirit of conquest did not distinguish between fair means or foul.

After Albuquerque's victory over the Muslims in India, the Hindu rulers accepted the Portuguese. Albuquerque then directed his attention to Goa, which he planned to use as a naval base against the Muslims and divert the spice trade to it. Ruthless and brutal, he was nevertheless practical. By marrying his men to the widows of his victims, he gave Goa its own population. After organizing its government, he embarked on the conquest of Malacca, on the Malay Peninsula, the most important point of distribution for the spice trade. Amongst the officer *hidalgos* on board were a young captain named Fernão de Magalhães and his friend Francisco Serrão, both in their early thirties. Fernão de Magahães, would later become Fernando de Magallanes to the Spanish, which would in turn be anglicised as Ferdinand Magellan.[7]

Caught up in the brash times of 1505, the two friends had for several years embarked on a campaign in the Indian Ocean at a time when the Portuguese sought military and mercantile supremacy over the hated Venetians. With the combined forces of Egypt and India, Venice had the monopoly on trade with Europe that Portugal was determined to replace.

Magellan was a short, thickset man, with the stocky build of a wrestler. He had a large square head upon wide shoulders and prominent features, surrounded by a black beard and a look of unrelenting intensity. In a battle he had taken part in he lost a horse under him and in another took a lance in the knee, a wound that gave him a permanent limp. Never one to mince words, he had a talent for making enemies easily. His friend Serrão, on the other hand, though equally tough, cut a more handsome figure in his suit of armour than his rough-looking friend. Each had saved the other's life more than once in the heat of battle. In the midsummer of 1511, as the Portuguese awaited Albuquerque's signal for the offensive against Malacca, the two bachelor officers, hardened veterans of the wars, readied for the invasion.[8]

Both men had been at Malacca two years before with an expedition that had nearly cost them their lives and had ended in disaster. It happened that in September of 1509 Diogo Lopes de Sequeira, under orders from King Manuel I, reconnoitered the city with the intention of establishing a base from where to reach out to the Spice Islands. Magellan and Serrão, eager for adventure and riches, had joined the expedition. Regardless of the warnings by Chinese merchants on shore as well as a Persian woman who had taken an officer as her lover, the Portuguese remained oblivious to a plot being hatched by the Arab traders to induce the sultan to turn against the Portuguese.[9]

During an audience granted by the sultan one of Sequeira's men, Jerónimo Texeira, addressed the ruler in an impertinent harsh voice, an appalling breach of courtesy that put the foreigners in a very bad light. However, their lack of manners became flagrantly insulting when Sequeira himself attempted with his left hand (the one Muslims used for cleansing oneself, thus rendering the member unclean) to hang a gold chain around the prime minister's neck, whose name was Tun Mutahir. There were murmurs of disapproval in the audience hall that the sultan quieted saying 'leave them alone; they know no better'. But the damage had been done and the affronts festered on among the courtiers in the royal household who could hardly contain themselves from striking out against the infidels. They then hatched a plot that, looking foolproof, persuaded the sultan to act.

The sultan sent a messenger to inform Sequeira that a large quantity of pepper and other spices had been gathered for him and lay in bulk in the warehouse on the river. All that was necessary was to send his men to shovel the commodities into sacks and row them out to their vessels. While the unsuspecting sailors were collecting the spices, the Malays attacked them, cutting them off from their longboats at the beach. Simultaneously, the Malay prahus approached the anchored caravels as if to trade surrounding the vessels. The caravels, lightly defended having sent some hundred men ashore, the remainder of their crews were quite oblivious to what was happening on shore while the Malays surreptitiously scampered aboard their ships.

In the commander's cabin of the flagship, Magellan discovered a half-naked Sequeira,[10] playing chess with a Malaccan trader surrounded by a roomful of armed Malays. Magellan warned the commander of what might be happening. It is a fact that historians have often criticised Sequeira's childlike credulity. Damião de Góis wrote that the commander behaved 'as if he were in the port of Lisbon'. In the crows-nest a lookout hailed the deck calling that he saw smoke on shore and then watched in horror as a mob intercepted the Portuguese sailors as they fought their way to the beach and their ship's boats.

Serrão, commanding one of the loading parties, was among them trying to slash his way with his men through the furious mob. His high combed helmet and his breastplate signalled him out among his men as a prize to his attackers. He would have been killed had not Magellan with two of his men, seeing his plight, paddled with all their might towards shore in one of the ship's boats. They held off the Malays long enough for Serrão's group to reach a longboat and retake it with their swords. The outnumbered Portuguese fought their way through the surf through a hail of arrows and shrieks from enemy prahus as they rowed desperately towards their ships, leaving behind sixty men dead or captured.

Sequeira waited to see if there was a possibility to ransom his men held by the Malays, which proved in vain. Determined not to let the sultan's treachery go unpunished, he had two captives held on board executed by having a crossbowman put an arrow through their brains. Afterwards he deposited the bodies ashore with a message pinned on them saying: 'Thus the king of Portugal avenged the treason of his enemies.'

Portugal's attempt to establish a foothold in the Far East by conquering Malacca in 1509 ended in defeat and humiliation. As they weighed anchors and began their slow voyage back to India seething with feelings of vengeance, their piratical instincts were heightened. As consolation for the Malaccan failure, Sequeira attacked a merchant transport ship in the Andaman Sea, but even their attempts at piracy backfired. The crew of the junk fought them off and then swarmed aboard Serrão's caravel and pinned him against the mast. Once again, Magellan's sword saved his friend from certain death as he and his men repelled the counter attackers. The Portuguese sailed on and as a balm for their wounds, boarded another less resistant junk.[11]

Malacca was not ancient, perhaps barely more than a century old at the time. It was established in 1402 by Prince Paramesvara, a fugitive driven out of southern Sumatra's Sriwijaya kingdom (Palembang today) by the powerful rulers of East Java. A Malay legend tells that the prince had been hunting and while resting under a tree one of his hounds was kicked by a white mouse-deer into the river. 'This is a good place', said Paramesvara. 'Even its mouse-deer are full of fight! We shall do well to make a city here.'

The prince ordered a city to be built, asking as he rose from his rest, 'What is the name of this tree under which I am standing?' His attendants answered: 'It is called *malaka*, Your Highness.' 'Then Malaka shall be the name of our city', he is said to have declared, whereupon his followers set about laying out the settlement beside the river: wide streets lined with raised houses of split coconut wood and thatched roofs of palm fronds. The images of a malacca tree and a startled deer still adorn the city's coat of arms.

As it grew and prospered, settlers came from Java, Sumatra, and Siam. In time, visiting ships from China and India called at its port enhancing its reputation as an important trading place on route. With the fortified sultan's palace commanding the hill in the background (it would become the site of St Paul's church in Christian times) and the sinuous river surrounded by jungle, the settlement was easy to defend.[12]

In 1403 the Chinese emperor, having been told of the importance of this budding trading post, and with an eye of taking it under his wing, sent the eunuch admiral Yin Ch'ing as envoy to this new country with presents of silk woven with golden flowers. Yin Ch'ing spoke at length to Paramesvara of the great power of China and its emperor. As the threat of Siam was a constant worry to the sultan since Siam claimed dominion over Paramesvara's kingdom, the prince swiftly accepted protection from the imperial envoy. After several other visits of Chinese officials to Malacca, the Ming court received Paramesvara in 1411, when the merchant prince arrived with an entourage of 540 persons. Received in person by the emperor and lodged in magnificent surroundings, Paramesvara was overwhelmed by lavish gifts and daily provisions of bullocks, goats, and wine from the imperial stocks.

As the visitors prepared to leave more gifts were lavished upon the sultan. 'The emperor personally gave to Paramesvara a girdle with precious stones, horses with saddles and harness, a hundred ounces of gold, five hundred ounces of silver, 400,000 koan in paper money, 2,600 strings of copper cash, three hundred pieces of silk gauze, a thousand pieces of plain silk and two pieces with embroidered golden flowers.' But above all this worldly wealth, Paramesvara returned home free at last of the Siamese yoke, and Malacca grew beyond all expectations into the most important port in the East.

Seventy-five years after Paramesvara founded his kingdom, Malacca had become famous in Europe. (Contrary to legend, the name of the city is actually derived from the Arabic word *malakat* meaning 'market'.) Its court intrigues (marriages, lovers, divorces and murders) rivaled those of Renaissance Italy. Merchants arrived from India and settled to add to science as well as the licentiousness of a court obsessed with fighting and women.

There were the secret, forbidden quarters of the magnificent palace where brides of many races lived for the royal pleasure. The Malay records provide vivid accounts of the sultan's harem.[13] 'He took all the beautiful daughters of the Parsee merchants and Kings who pleased him to be his concubines, made them turn Moors when he had to give them in marriage and he married them to mandarin's sons and gave them dowries, and this custom of marrying people of different sects caused no surprise in Malacca.' So well supplied of attractive young women was the sultan's private collection that it was the talk of the town, to the point of it becoming a constant source of scandal.

The sultan was the most absolute of rulers. When he held court in his audience hall he sat on his throne placed on a long raised dais surrounded by heralds and warriors, whose presence was awarded either by noble birth or personal achievement. The officers of the state, in their formal silken robes, sat in order of precedence with their personal secretaries or young nobles selected as their personal servants. A visitor fortunate enough to have been awarded an audience approached the throne with suitable signs of deference before prostrating himself before the royal presence.

It was Sultan Mahmud Shah, ruler of Malacca, who gave it the remarkable Maritime Laws, a codification of a century's rules and legal customs:

> The captain is king on board his ship and ready to sail is like a king about to leave his palace.
>
> The changing of the watch should be witnessed by the midshipmen and announced by one beat on the drum. The man on watch is issued opium to keep him awake.

The navigator should not fail to pray to Allah and his prophet, for he is an imam aboard a ship.

Whoever uses a mirror facing toward the bow commits a serious offence, for the captains wife or concubine might be on board. The punishment is seven lashes and a fine of 1¼ tael of gold.

Malacca's economy was entirely based on trade, since it had no agriculture due to the salinity of its soil and no industry either. Its existence depended on rigid customs duties, port taxes, fixed weights and measures, and its coinage of tin, gold and silver propelled the daily trade with no less than 500 money changers throughout the city in 1508. By then, Malacca had generated its own aristocracy of wealth.

To the European imagination where little was known about it, Malacca was the epitome of the colourful, the mysterious and the exotic and − in the poignant words of Charles Corn − 'it has a history worthy of the noblest theater or the grandest opera, ripe for a Shakespeare or a Verdi'.

Since its founding Malacca had been impregnable to siege, and many thought it to be unassailable. A stone wall that had four gates each with a look out and a drum tower surrounded the city. Inside the outer walls was a second enclosure of palisades. From the sea Malacca's defenses were not readily visible as the fortress was a warren of confused levels and narrow lanes that descended to the protected harbour at the mouth of the river that divided the city, over which there was a bridge.

Albuquerque anchored his ships just off the strategic port of Malacca's deepwater channel within sight of the sultan's palace, placed upon the fortified

port's highest hill. The city itself is placed on the south-western coast of the Malay Peninsula in the narrowest part of the straits of Malacca. It used to be the most prized port along the legendary route that stretched from the Spice Islands, or Moluccas in the East, across Asia to the West. It was the major trading center in Asia from where the riches of the Orient, especially spices, were routed to an eager Europe that avidly awaited them. An early sixteenth-century trader explained its importance thus: 'No trading port as large as Malacca is known, nor anywhere else do they deal in such fine and highly priced merchandise. Goods from all over the world are sold here. It is at the end of the monsoons when you will find what you want, and sometimes more than what you are looking for.'

The capture of Malacca was all-important to the Portuguese, intent as they were of seizing control of the spice trade. Urged on by the dictum, 'Whoever is lord of Malacca has his hand on the throat of Venice', the Portuguese with no fond memories of the Moor's 300-year occupation of Iberia, were set for invasion of the city in July 1511.

The invading fleet comprised fifteen vessels made in Portugal, an odd armada of carracks and caravels to which had been added some captured junks. They housed on board some 1,500 men; 800 were Portuguese and the remainder mainly Malabar Indian archers taken aboard before they left the subcontinent. An uneven match, for the sultan's fighters who outnumbered them by at least twenty to one.

By a quirk of fate that played into the hands of the invaders, the Prime Minister of Malacca, Tun Mutahir, took in marriage the beautiful Tun Fatimah whom the lecherous sultan wanted for himself. A malicious scheme was hatched by an intriguer who spread the word that the Prime Minister had plans to overthrow the sultan. When news of this rumour reached him the sultan ordered the

execution of Tun Mutahir and his family though sparing Tun Fatimah and her brother. A few days after the executions, which the population scorned, as the Prime Minister had been a respected and popular figure, the sultan learned that there was no truth to the allegations and ordered the intriguer's death. However, irreparable damage had already been done as the sultan's inhuman behavior divided the court as well as much of the population.

Due to the intercession of an influential Indian trader by the name of Nina Chatu, the Portuguese prisoners taken at Sequeira's siege of 1509, had not fared so badly. The shrewd Chatu believed it prudent to extend a helping hand to the Europeans by lobbying for a measure of freedom for them. This he achieved to the point where some engaged in trade, married Malay wives, and smuggled out letters written to Albuquerque through Muslim traders in Nina Chatu's confidence. One of these letters, written by the leader of the prisoners, Rui de Araujo, and signed by his eighteen companions, gave a detailed account of trade within the city, as well as the information that the sultan feared reprisals by the Portuguese. The letter also explained that since the Prime Minister had been executed the feeling amongst the population throughout the kingdom had turned against the sultan. This was the opening Albuquerque had been waiting for.

Details of the great battle survive though little is mentioned of the roles played by Magellan and Serrão, except that they gave 'a good account' of themselves. The rest has been researched by historians and authors not least by Charles Corn who spent time researching the archives of Malacca itself.

The following day after the arrival of Albuquerque and his armada, the wedding took place between the daughter of Sultan Mahmud's daughter to a Pahang prince. Though the fleet's guns were aimed seaward, the reports of the heavy artillery reverberated throughout the city, disrupting the royal wedding and causing panic among the population. The following day an emissary from Sultan Mahmud visited the flagship to ask whether the Portuguese had come in the name of peace or war. Albuquerque answered with an ultimatum that the prisoners taken during Sequeira's ill-fated expedition two years before were to be delivered and compensation was to be paid for their internment. The sultan, hoping to string out the negotiations long enough for the monsoon winds to turn unfavourable to the invaders, thus putting the Portuguese at his mercy, played for time. He insisted that the terms of peace had to be negotiated before he turned any prisoners loose and that he was having suitable clothes made for them that would take time.

Several days passed while Albuquerque and his captains pondered what should be their next move. In the meantime, some Chinese traders visited the flagship and provided intelligence on the sultan's armament and forces at his disposal, which included poisoned arrows and a herd of elephants trained for battle, while estimating the sultan's army at between 20,000 and 30,000 men.

The Chinese stated they were on his side, mentioning they would find most foreign merchants joining them as they pleaded with the sultan to sue for peace. They knew that they had everything to lose if the city was sacked, reasoning that Mahmud would have no choice but to strike a deal as foreign trade was Malacca's lifeblood.

Albuquerque weighed the odds and decided to launch the attack. On the evening of 25 July he sent two parties to the beach to bombard the city while other armed bands set the houses on the waterfront alight. Malaccan merchant ships anchored in the harbour were torched, except for the Chinese junks and Indian faluccas.

Without warning, the Portuguese captives freed by the sultan ran down to the beach waving their arms to suspend the bombardment. Rowed out to the flagship they told of the tortures by Muslims upon Christians, which angered Albuquerque to a fury, swearing by his beard that he would take vengeance on the Malays.

The captain of the prisoners, Rui de Araujo, advised the commander to invade first and negotiate after. Albuquerque split his attack between two forces that he sent to the beach but the assault was beaten back with many losses and his captains lost heart and advised him to return to Goa, but the commander was adamant. A lull in the fighting followed during which the ranks of the Chinese merchants supporting the Portuguese cause increased. With Chinese junks at his disposal his fleet had grown much larger and more imposing then when he had arrived.

As a devout follower of St James the Apostle, Albuquerque waited until the saint's day to launch his second attack. On the advice of Rui de Araujo, who knew the city well, it was decided it was all-important to take the bridge over the river. To do so he divided his forces to strike at both the north and south ends of the city, in other words at the mosque and at the bridge, thus confusing the enemy and splitting their defenses. At midnight Albuquerque gave the order to commence bombing. The city was thrown into confusion, with people shouting and fleeing with their children and household goods, not knowing where to go. Two hours before dawn a trumpet sounded to summon all officers to the flagship's deck. At first light, after attending mass, the attackers swarmed to the beach amid a volley from the Malay artillery fired 'from esmerils, falconets, and sakers' (the contribution of Italian gunsmiths introduced by Arab dealers in weaponry). After that furious volley was spent, the Portuguese shrieked the war cry 'Santiago!' and then fell upon the stockades of the bridge, defended by Malays who fought them back with a hail of arrows, poisoned darts and lances.

The mosque was easily taken. The battle now raged at the bridge where the landing parties fought hand to hand against the Malay defenders, some of whom were cut down where they fought while others jumped into the water only to be killed by the Portuguese in boats. On advice by Rui de Araujo to counter the number of their men being wounded and killed by the poisoned arrows and darts, Albuquerque ordered sails to be stretched between two spars anchored in barrels with earth to act as canvas shields against the missiles. He then ordered an armed Chinese junk filled with reinforcements to the bridge but it struck on an estuarine mud and sand flat and remained a sitting target for nine days. Raised by the tide it was finally freed when it churned through the surf to the bridge. The bombardment of the city continued with the sultan's palace and the mosque now almost reduced to rubble.

As the crew aboard the junk were making it fast to the bridge, Antonio d'Abreu, its captain, took a bullet in the jaw from a matchlock rifle, costing him some teeth and a piece of tongue. He 'was relieved more by force than by his own wish', according to a witness. He had by then cleared the bridge of the enemy who fled, only to find themselves cut off by another group of attackers. With the bridge secured and sheltered from the brutal sun with palm-fronds, the Portuguese advanced upon the city carrying canvas shields and planks carried by slaves to put across the holes where mines of gunpowder had been placed by the Malays.

The sultan and his son joined the defenders riding war elephants ahead of a herd of others ridden by attendants, but before the beasts could be mobilised they were soon routed by lance thrusts to their eyes, ears and bellies, trampling their keepers and many others as they fled. The sultan and his son Ahmed escaped to the jungle pursued by the invaders, finding temporary refuge at a village a day's journey from the capital. By morning Malacca's streets were cleared of the remaining defenders. Those that surrendered were taken for slave labour, while those that resisted were put to the sword.

The city was sacked, yielding the richest plunder imaginable. They seized warehouses filled with everything from golden chairs to nuggets, precious stones, silks, and 2,000 bronze cannon. In the spice sheds they were overwhelmed by the heavenly scents of cinnamon, nutmeg, and clove. Though allowing the city to be sacked, Albuquerque instructed his men not to touch the house or possessions of Nina Chatu, the Indian merchant who had helped Rui de Araujo and was now advising the commander on the system of administration. He was designated the new Prime Minister under one Rui de Brito who he named governor.

Scarcely had Malacca's streets been cleared of rubble than Albuquerque, having received breathtaking accounts of the Spice Islands, dispatched three ships led by Antonio d'Abreu (who had not yet recovered from the ugly bullet wound to his face) to sail to the Moluccas in search of spices, with Magellan's friend, Francisco Serrão commanding the second ship and Ferdinand Magellan the third. Albuquerque planned it carefully and even sent a junk to precede the expedition and prepare a favourable reception for it along the way.

After the conquest, Albuquerque defused a plot hatched by an elderly Javanese leader with designs to overthrow the Portuguese and restore the sultan to his throne. The instigator was promptly seized and executed along with all of his followers after which Albuquerque made plans to return to his outpost in Goa, anticipating a hero's welcome in Lisbon later.

Preparations for his leave-taking aboard the *Flora del Mar* were elaborate. He made certain that the treasures taken in the siege were loaded on board, as well as a collection of bronze-skinned beautiful women skilled in embroidery and dancing, which included some of noble birth. Accompanied by two other ships, his flagship set sail from Malacca in January 1512, five months after the port had fallen.

The flagship was a big broad-beamed, three-masted galleon capable of transporting 600 people and 500 tons. Leaking badly, she foundered in a storm off Sumatra, six days after leaving Malacca, carrying with her to the bottom the greatest wealth ever lost in a single shipwreck, as well as the bevy of ladies handpicked by the commander to embellish King Manuel's court in Lisbon. Albuquerque and several officers survived by fashioning a raft out of spars of the ship then fending off with lances others who attempting to survive might have swamped their craft thus drowning them all.[14]

After overcoming considerable difficulties, Albuquerque arrived at Goa. In February 1515 he took off with twenty-six ships for Hormuz, gaining control of part of that island, but fell ill in September and decided to return to Goa. On the way he learned that his personal enemy, Lope Soares, had superseded him as Governor of India. He died embittered onboard his flagship before reaching his destination.

The sultan, defeated by Albuquerque's forces in 1511, found refuge in Johore, adjacent to the later settlement of Singapore. His successors and his allies harassed and besieged the Portuguese for a long time. More significantly, the sultan had strong allies in the north of Sumatra. As a result the Portuguese would be threatened from all sides for years to come.[15]

Albuquerque's campaigns derived from the crusading spirit of John II but he never allowed himself to be diverted from his schemes by profit alone. His boldest concepts, such as turning the Persians against the Turks, stealing the remains of Mahomet to barter them for Jerusalem, or plan the ruin of Egypt by deflecting the course of the Nile, were almost beyond belief but after all, so were his achievements.

As for the little fleet of three ships that Governor Albuquerque sent to reconnoiter the spicy paradise, the *Santa Catarina* was commanded by Antonio d'Abreu, the *Sabaia* by Magellan's friend Francisco Serrão, while the third, a caravel, by Magellan himself. Out in front was the Chinese junk captained by a Malaccan trader named Nakoda Ismail, who knew the seas and commerce of the islands, and his mission was to spread the word that the Portuguese were coming.

The ships set sail in December 1511 with an experienced Malay pilot attached to each, crossed the equator and entered the Java Sea. The knowledge that they were not the first Europeans to venture into these parts gave them confidence. Ludovico de Verthema, an Italian, had entered into the service of the Portuguese in India, and after wandering among the islands of the Far East published a record of his travels in 1510. It was from Verthema that, for instance, the first accounts of Borneo were known to the world. It was undoubtedly based on the information Verthema had provided five years earlier that Albuquerque took the decision to dispatch d'Abreu's flotilla to seek the perfumed islands. The Italian's description of 'Maluch' and its cloves, and of Banda, the 'isola molto brutta and trista' with its nutmegs, were more tantalizing than all of America's rumoured El Dorado with its streets paved in gold. Java was scarcely in their wake when the purple sight of Bali's volcano, crowned with its perpetual ring of cloud, loomed out of the sea. They left behind, one after the other, the south-eastern islands south of the Celebes: Lombok, Sumbaya, and Flores. Early in the New Year the ships had reached Sumba and Timor, having sailed almost 3,000 miles since leaving Malacca. There the Malay pilots set a north-east course through the Banda Sea before a following wind.

The little fleet reached an anchorage named Guli-Guli, at the eastern tip of Ceram. It was a wild place where the Malay pilots warned about the natives, a war-like people that feasted on the hearts of their enemies. The Portuguese were watchful, watered their ships and moved on.

Serrão's caravel that had been plaguing him from the outset was now damaged and leaking badly and in no condition to face the return journey. When the pilots advised him he could buy a replacement for it in Banda, he ordered the vessel to be burned, transferred to the two remaining caravels and set sail for Banda, a mere hop of two days before a north wind. By the second day they were snugly anchored in the harbour of Neira, an idyllic island and a stone's throw away from the island of Banda itself. They had at last reached the coveted Moluccas, the historical Spice Islands of history and legend that had fired the imagination of the Roman scholar Pliny and Sinbad the Sailor.[16] The first order of business for Serrão was to procure the means of returning to Malacca. He bought a junk from a Chinese trader and made some simple adjustments to it.

D'Abreu remained a month buying and loading nutmeg as well as clove, the latter transported by ship from islands several hundred miles to the north. Even paying higher prices then the usual merchant value due to the haste of departure, d'Abreu could expect a profit of 1,000 per cent or more in Lisbon.

After taking on three full shiploads of spices, the two caravels departed Banda with Serrão's junk sailing in their wake. He had been assigned nine Portuguese sailors to expand his meager crew of a dozen Malays. Once loaded with cargo she was slower than the two other caravels. Of a sudden a furious storm hit the little group separating the three ships. Caught between baffling winds and currents Serrão's junk was hurled upon the reef of an uninhabited isle called Lusi Para. The junk was grounded but upright but while several of his men were lost not knowing how to swim, Serrão and a few survivors were able to gain the shore. Being told by his Malays that the waters were infested with pirates, he devised a cunning plan. He ordered half of his men armed to hide in the bushes, while posing the rest of his party as castaways, helpless but with useless wealth.

In time a piratical prahu approached the wrecked junk, still upright but being battered by the waves on the reef. Then seeing frantic waving from the beach and sensing easy plunder, they lowered a boat and struck out for the shore. As soon as the boat grounded on the sand the Portuguese jumped on them seizing both craft and crew. The ruse, with no loss of life, was later reported: 'if they met not their death from thirst and hunger they might expect it from these corsairs'.

Having taken their ship, and with their muskets aimed, Serrão threatened to maroon the scavengers. It would have meant certain death from starvation, and even worse, dehydration, as the captive knew. Serrão, having searched the island for water realised its reason for being uninhabited. With only rainwater to drink from brackish ponds and virtually no food to eat beyond what fish could be caught, the pirates knew that they would die without hope of rescue. On bended knee they pleaded for their lives. Serrão struck a bargain with them. He would not maroon them, he said, if they would sail the Portuguese to the nearest inhabited island. Having no choice, the Malays readily agreed. Between them the two parties muscled the prahu back through the surf, hoisted the sails and set a course for Ambon, just south of the larger island of Ceram, where Serrão had set alight his crippled ship a few weeks earlier.

A two-day sail brought them to Hitu, the island's northern peninsula. Upon beaching the prahu he ordered his men to brandish their arms before the crowd of curious onlookers surrounding them. There was no need of worry as word of the fall of Malacca had already crossed the seas to the Spice Islands, and the Hitu chiefs had congregated to welcome the strangers. And welcome them they did, with feasts and beautiful young women. While toasting the Portuguese with cups of arak, they explained about the long-standing feud they had with certain villagers on Ceram, imploring their visitors to lead an army against their rival.

Serrão saw the advantage that might be had by asserting his power. He welcomed the test knowing that with firearms against the islander's bows and arrows, spears and blowguns he would be successful. Fortune favoured the bold. Serrão, with his handful of Portuguese in their armor and backed by his new allies, led his men in a surprise raid, slaughtering any Ceramese they found in their path.

Reports of the victory soon spread to the two rival clove-producing island kingdoms of Ternate and Tidore to the north. Their sultans both rushed emissaries to Hitu with invitations of a state visit. However, Ternate's ruler outdid the other with an incredible show of force. He sent his own brother Prince Jubila in the flagship of a fleet of nine *kora-kora*, ten-ton outrigger war canoes, each manned by 100 warriors. This persuaded Serrão who he should favour.

Serrão and his men set out northward with the prince's festive flotilla to the beating of drums and the sound of gongs marking the rhythm for the paddlers.

Reclining back on cushioned shady decks, they were plied with food and drink by their royal hosts.

It took them six days to cover the 300 miles before the twin peaks of Ternate and Tidore were sighted, each towering volcanic cone encircled by clove trees. A mile wide channel separated the islands each with its coral reef from each other. The beauty of the lavish flora entranced Serrão. Water cascaded down volcanic slopes. Flocks of white, yellow crested cockatoos and brightly plumaged parrots glided through the trees. Sago palms provided fronds for shelter, food and arak, while the sea was abundant with fish of every sort. Dazzled, he took stock of himself and his own life's possibilities. He decided he had met his destiny.

Serrão believed he could become very useful among these people and he settled down as counselor to the sultan of Ternate, taking his place among the trusted advisors of the island kingdom. He took to dressing for state occasions in his shining armor and striking a pose among the silk-robed, turbaned figures of the royal court.

Serrão anointed himself as the island's indispensable arbiter of trade, monopolising the collection and redistribution of cloves, nutmeg, and mace supplied by Ternate's sultanate. Trade was a reciprocal enterprise so he managed the lucrative business of acquiring both common and luxury goods, from clothing and kitchen utensils to gold and silks, from visiting merchants. He soon became not only influential but also indispensable, amassing wealth through his privileged position. Having survived through pluck and luck, he now managed the choicest piece of real estate in the world. Portuguese Malacca seethed with resentment and envy over this upstart with royal airs, but decided that since he had become a man of such importance it was best to leave him alone.

Before Serrão's arrival, this scattering of tiny islands over the seas between Celebes and New Guinea had been barely heard of by those that lived west of the Bay of Bengal. Now the Moluccas were becoming more precise in people's

Royal canoes from Ternate and Tidore with crescent and helicopter profiles, from F. Valentijn, Oud en Nieuw Oost-Indien, 5 vols, Dordecht and Amsterdam 1724–26, I, 363.

minds resulting in the publication of new maps that depicted them according to whether they produced cloves or nutmeg. The irony is, however, that Serrão became the symbol of that trade within his own country that now regarded him as renegade, a man without honour and a turncoat who had gone native.[17]

Serrão made another decision that would foster that idea. He took a wife. Accounts vary as to who she was. Some talk of her as Javanese, but more credible evidence mentions her as a daughter of Almanzor, the sultan of the rival kingdom of Tidore, a mile to the south-east by sailboat or canoe. Contemporary accounts mention that Almanzor had a harem of 200 women, with a large number of servants for them. He had four wives, as permitted by Islamic law, who had provided him with eight legitimate sons and eighteen daughters. Sensing a diplomatic opportunity to resolve the differences between both rival kingdoms and believing he had succeeded with a signed treaty between the two sultans, Serrão claimed one of Almanzor's beautiful daughters in marriage. She bore him a son and a daughter. Serrão embraced his new life. Lacking all bias toward native customs he made himself belong in his 'New World'. It was perhaps with undue reliance of his new found confidence that he took up his pen to write a series of letters to his friend Ferdinand Magellan.

Serrão wrote to Magellan, and in his letters he could not contain his admiration of the captivating beauty and fertility of the Spice Islands. Portuguese chroniclers zealously studied these letters, lost in the earthquake of 1755 that reduced Lisbon to ruins. 'I have found a New World', wrote Serrão in one of them, 'richer, greater, and more beautiful than that of Vasco da Gama... I beg you to join me here, that you may sample for yourself the delights which surround me.' This correspondence played no small part in convincing Magellan to undertake his search for the Spice Islands by following Columbus' original design of sailing west.

The fact that Magellan sailed with d'Abreu as far west as Ambon and Banda justifies us in naming him as the first person of any race to circumnavigate the globe. For Ambon is on longitude 128° E of Greenwich, and Banda is 2° further east; whilst Macatan in the Philippines, where Magellan met his death, is on longitude 124° E. Thus his furthest west in 1521 overlapped his furthest east in 1511 by 4 to 6° of longitude.

Serrão stayed on in Ternate as an unofficial Potuguese resident, and hoped to meet his friend on his way westward around the globe; but both were killed before they could meet.

Magellan returned to Portugal a veteran sailor and soldier, an expert navigator, and with an important plan. He was certain the Moluccas could be reached more easily by following Columbus' original idea, sailing west, than by the long difficult voyage around the Cape of Good Hope and on through the Malacca Strait. From his own and from Serrão's observations the Spice Islands were relatively civilised, with local governments under Moslem or pagan sultans who were eager to trade with Europeans. However, the essential part of this design was to find a strait through Spanish America, and Magellan believed he knew where to find one.[18]

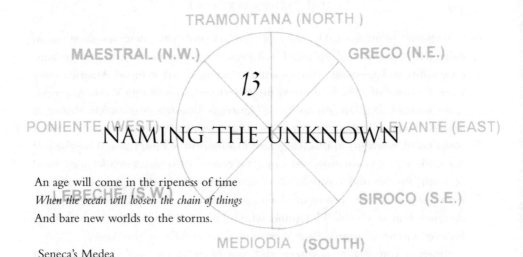

13

NAMING THE UNKNOWN

An age will come in the ripeness of time
When the ocean will loosen the chain of things
And bare new worlds to the storms.

Seneca's Medea

A gold wasp on a blue band across a field of red was the coat of arms of the Vespuccis. A prominent Florentine family in Columbus' day, the name conjured up images of the beautiful Simonetta, who married into the family and died at age twenty-six, most likely from tuberculosis it is said, though by poison it was whispered. There is an alluring portrait of her drawn by Piero di Cosimo that shows off her exceptional beauty, and it is very likely that her's was the figure that posed for two of Sandro Botticelli's greatest paintings, 'Primavera' (Spring) and 'The birth of Venus'. Later it was another Vespucci, her cousin Amerigo, who also achieved lasting fame and immortality. Let me tell you about this exceptional navigator. One of the greatest of them all.

Over the years, there have been various explanations of how America got its name. One French scholar suggested that Columbus encountered the word 'America' during his fourth voyage, when he thought he heard it used as the name of a Nicaraguan tribe and a chain of mountains. But these are quite ridiculous; the fact being that everyone knows that 'America' was named after Amerigo Vespucci.[1]

To many people this has seemed the final injustice inflicted on Columbus by history. However, Vespucci was not directly responsible for the slight, or for robbing the Admiral of this honour. Columbus knew him well and held him in high esteem. Vespucci had helped organise the admiral's first and third voyage; and in a letter addressed to his son Diego written on 5 February 1505, during the last year of his life, Columbus calls Vespucci 'a very fine man'.[2]

According to the Uruguayan historian, Rolando Laguarda Trias, 'Vespucci was a prototype of the technician: A tireless worker to the point of giving up his rest for studying the stars in the sky; never showing self-interest, to the point that it was not in his nature to claim or demand, either verbally or in writing, anything that he was not legitimately entitled to. Always loyal to those that employed him, he was both unostentatious as well as courageous. He held his head high in moments of adversity and resisted attacks by others due to their jealousy.'[3]

Vespucci, pioneer of The Age of the Sea and who deserves fame as an enlightener of the modern mind, has been caught in the crossfire of pedants, chauvinists and ignorant men of letters.[4] 'Strange… that broad America must wear the name of a thief', shouted the American pundit Ralph Waldo Emerson, with startling indifference to facts. 'Amerigo Vespucci, the pickle dealer at Seville… whose highest naval rank was boatswains mate in an expedition that never sailed, managed in this lying world to supplant Columbus and baptise half the earth with his own dishonest name.' Of course, these slanders held not a word of truth. Precise and scrupulously truthful, was the early eighteenth-century inscription by fellow citizens of Florence on the Vespucci family mansion, which describes him as a 'noble Florentine, who by the discovery of America rendered his own and his country's name illustrious; the Amplifier of the World'.

Amerigo Vespucci, as has been said, was born into an influential family of Florence in 1454, on the seed ground of the Italian Renaissance. He spent the first thirty-eight years of his life there, acquiring the voracious curiosity and intellectual ambitions that governed his life. When Vasari went to study with Michelangelo in Florence, he stayed with Amerigo's uncle, who also played host to the poet Ludovico Ariosto. The family was on friendly terms with Botticelli and Piero di Cosimo. Leonardo da Vinci so admired the face of Amerigo's grandfather that he followed him around to fix in his mind the features that he later would draw in a unique crayon portrait. Ghirlandaio painted the family, including Amerigo, in his fresco at the church of Ognissanti in Florence.

Amerigo entered the service of the Medici family as a young man to help manage their wide-ranging affairs. Like his patron, Pier Francesco de Medici, whom the Florentines nicknamed il Popolano, a cousin of Lorenzo de' Medici – the Magnificent, Amerigo read widely, collected books and maps and developed an interest in cosmography and astronomy. In 1492 he was sent to Spain to look after Medici interests in Seville where they engaged in fitting out ships for expeditions, run by Il Popolano's agent Giannotto Berardi. By 1499, his commercial and geographic interests had drawn him decisively into this calling. The more he learned of seafaring adventure the more his interest shifted from merchandising to exploring.

The Portuguese had discovered the route around Africa to the orient, but Columbus had shown that lands could be reached by sailing west. Vespucci made up his mind to try and fulfill Columbus' hopes of reaching Asia. The third voyage of Columbus, while confirming his wild fantasies about the Terrestrial Paradise, still revealed no passage to India. 'It was my intention', Amerigo said 'to see whether I could turn a headland that Ptolemy called the Cape of Catigara, which connects with the Sinus Magnus.' (Later named the Pacific.) Marco Polo described Catigara, shown on Ptolemy's maps as the south-east tip of the Asian continent, as the point around which the Chinese treasure ships had to double to enter the Sinus Magnus and the Sinus Gangeticus, the two great bays of the Indian Ocean. Since Ptolemy had located Catigara at $8\frac{1}{2}°$ south of the equator, that was where Vespucci would try to find the passage that had eluded Columbus.

For centuries it was said that Amerigo Vespucci undertook two voyages to the New World. Only in recent history has it been verified as four. The first with the backing of Spain, took place between 10 May 1497 and 15 October 1498. Alonso de Ojeda, with Vespucci as navigator, commanded the second, also sponsored by the Spanish crown. The expedition left Cadiz on 18 May 1499, returning on 8 September 1500. After sighting the coast of what is now Guyana, south of where Columbus had arrived on his third voyage, Ojeda turned and went northward to find the treasures of 'The Coast of Pearls'. Vespucci sailed south, groping for the passage around Catigara. Discovering the mouth of the Amazon River, the Mar Doce, as the Portuguese would call it, he sailed on as far as Cape São Roque – Rio Grande do Norte (Latitude 8° 21' S, Longitude 34° 57' W) – near today's Recife. 'After we had sailed about four hundred leagues continually along the coast, we concluded that this was the mainland; that the said mainland is at the extreme limits of Asia to the eastward and at its beginning to the westward.'[5] Amerigo was still ready to continue the search, but teredos (shipworms) had eaten into the hulls of his ships, his provisions were running low, and the winds and currents were against him. He reluctantly turned around and coursed northwards. On his return, two years after Columbus had been there, he sighted the mouth of the Orinoco River before reaching Trinidad and eventually Spain via Haiti, firmly believing that he had sailed along the easterly peninsula of Asia.

Ojeda, in the meantime, had coasted north-west about 700 miles and established beyond doubt the existence of a very considerable mainland. He found the rich pearl fisheries, which Columbus had missed in the area of Margarita Island, off the coast of Venezuela, and went on to discover the islands of Bonaire, Curaçao and Aruba, as well as the extensive gulf of Maracaibo. Here he saw several waterside villages built above the water on stilts, and because of it, named the area Venezuela, or little Venice. He continued to the Bahamas, filled his holds with slaves and returned to Spain.[6]

Soon after his arrival in Seville, Vespucci made a 'new decision to take another turn at discovery', as he wrote to a Florentine friend. 'I hope to bring back very great news and discover the island of Tabrobana [Ceylon], which is between the Indian Ocean and the Gulf or Sea of the Ganges.' The report that he wrote revealed an entirely new trend of thought. When he had started out, just like Columbus, he too was thinking in Ptolemy's world. Now he spoke in a different voice, as in a letter to his protector, the illustrious Prince, Pier Francesco de Medici:

It appears to me, most excellent Lorenzo, that by this voyage of mine the opinion of the majority of the philosophers is confuted, who assert that no one can live in the Torrid Zone because of the great heat, for in this voyage I found it to be the contrary. The air is fresher and more temperate in this region, and so many people are living in it that their numbers are greater than those who live outside of it. Rationally, let it be said in a whisper, experience is certainly worth more than theory.[7]

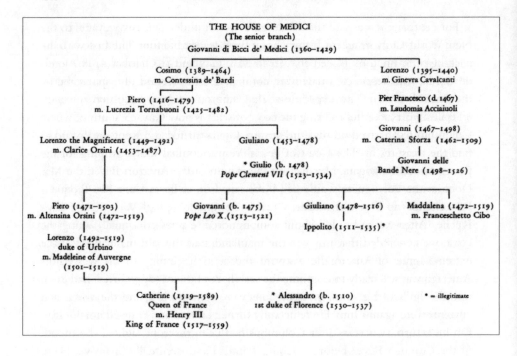

THE HOUSE OF MEDICI
(The senior branch)
Giovanni di Bicci de' Medici (1360–1429)

Cosimo (1389–1464)
m. Contessina de' Bardi

Lorenzo (1395–1440)
m. Ginevra Cavalcanti

Piero (1416–1479)
m. Lucrezia Tornabuoni (1425–1482)

Pier Francesco (d. 1467)
m. Laudomia Acciaiuoli

Lorenzo the Magnificent (1449–1492)
m. Clarice Orsini (1453–1487)

Giuliano (1453–1478)

Giovanni (1467–1498)
m. Caterina Sforza (1462–1509)

* Giulio (b. 1478)
Pope Clement VII (1523–1534)

Giovanni delle
Bande Nere (1498–1526)

Piero (1471–1503)
m. Altensina Orsini (1472–1519)

Giovanni (b. 1475)
Pope Leo X (1513–1521)

Giuliano (1478–1516)

Maddalena (1472–1519)
m. Franceschetto Cibo

Lorenzo (1492–1519)
duke of Urbino
m. Madeleine of Auvergne
(1501–1519)

Ippolito (1511–1535)*

Catherine (1519–1589)
Queen of France
m. Henry III
King of France (1517–1559)

* Alessandro (b. 1510)
1st duke of Florence (1530–1537)

* = illegitimate

His letters show he rejected the idea of coming to general conclusions. 'Sailing along the coast, we discovered each day an endless number of people with various languages. Very desirous of being the author who should identify the Polar Star of the other hemisphere, I lost many a night's sleep in contemplation of the moon and stars around the South Pole, in order to record which of them had the least motion and was nearest to the pole.' Instead of lines from The Scriptures, he quoted Dante's verses, from Purgatorio, Book 1, on what might be a view of the southern pole.

Vespucci had long been puzzled by the problem of determining longitude, crucial in westward voyages. Trying to find a way to solve the problem, he had brought with him astronomical tables of the moon and planets. While waiting for members of his crew to recover from wounds received in a fight with the Indians, he turned to trying to solve this question.

As to longitude, I declare that I found so much difficulty in determining it that I was put to great pains to ascertain the east–west distance I had covered. The final result of my labours was that I found nothing better to do than to watch for and take observations at night of the conjunction of one planet with another, and especially of the conjunction of the moon with the other planets, because the moon is swifter than any other planet...

After I had made experiments many nights, one night, the twenty-third of August 1499, there was a conjunction of the moon with Mars, which according to the almanac [for the city of Ferrara] was to occur at midnight or a half hour before. I found that when the moon rose an hour and a half after sunset, the planet had passed that position in the east.

With this data, Amerigo calculated how far west he had come. Though his method was far more accurate than Columbus' dead reckoning, and those of most others at the time, he lacked the precision instruments to perfect it. However, during his calculations of the length of a degree, he corrected the current figure and produced an estimate of the earth's equatorial circumference that was only 50 miles short of its actual dimension.[8]

It is interesting to note that the terminology used for the points of Vespucci's compass was the very same as the traditional compass-rose used by Italian navigators in the Mediterranean for years. The terminology mirrored the names of the prevailing winds in the Mediterranean, whereas the Anglo-Saxon terminology used in the Atlantic, since the time of Charlemagne (742–814), represented the true points of the compass: North; South; East and West, with their amalgam of variations in between. The illustration below explains both terminologies, with the Anglo-Saxon in brackets.

The Sicilians, who only sailed within the confines of the Mediterranean, gave their terminology to the compass-rose, which made sense. This terminology first appeared in a Jewish treatise of the eleventh century titled *Sepher Asaph* (Golden Book). *Lebeche*, for instance, refers to the wind that blows from Libia. It was correct

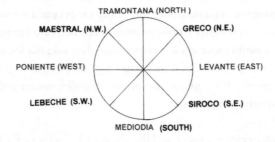

if you were in Sicily. However, Vespucci, who sailed beyond the Mediterranean, did not follow the modern nomenclature. For him SW was *Lebeche*.[9]

When Vespucci decided to equip a new expedition, one which would give him occasion to announce his doubts about Ptolemy, break with the hallowed traditions of cosmography and declare a new world, Spain rejected his proposal so he offered his services instead to King Manuel I of Portugal.

Vespucci's outstanding knowledge of the theory and practice of nautical science as well as his upright character were not qualities lost on the Portuguese, who in short order backed him to organise his third expedition to the New World, this time south of the equator, together with Gonçalo Coelho.

Nearly a decade after Columbus' first crossing, commanding three caravels, Vespucci departed Lisbon on 13 May 1501.[10] After stopping at the Cape Verde Islands, the ships sailed southwest, and their first sight of land, after sixty-four days, was Cape São Agostinho. 'We arrived', says Vespucci, 'at a new land which, for many reasons that are enumerated in what follows, we observed a continent.'

As the little fleet ventured south along the coast of Brazil, they realised the vast extent of the territory for the first time. At Porto Seguro (today Bahia Cabralia, about 200 miles south of Salvador) they picked up two men who had been left there by Cabral the year before.

Vespucci, calendar of saints in hand and conforming to the custom of Catholic nations at that time, baptised the different geographical points along the way with the names of saints corresponding to the day they were discovered. Many of those names remain today – Cabo San Agustín, Rio São Francisco, and the beautiful bay of Guanabara, which he probably entered on the 1 January, a religious holiday, and believing it an estuary named it Rio de Janeiro – River of January.

On 24 January he reached the River Cananor, (today Cananea) at latitude 25° S and mentions that since sighting Cape São Agostinho he had sailed SW for 800 leagues, or 2,000km, according to his letter in Latin known as *Mundus Novus* (New World) written by Vespucci to his patron Pier Francesco de Medici.[11]

> We coursed so far in those seas that we entered the Torrid Zone and passed south of the equinoctial line and the Tropic of Capricorn, until the South pole stood above my horizon at fifty degrees, which was my latitude from the equator. We navigated in the Southern Hemisphere for nine months and twenty-seven days [from about 1 August to 27 May 1501], never seeing the Arctic Pole or even Ursa Major and Minor; but opposite them many bright and beautiful constellations were disclosed to me which always remain invisible in this northern Hemisphere. There I noted the wonderful order of their motions and their magnitudes, measuring the diameters of their circuits and mapping out their relative positions with geometrical figures… I was on the side of the antipodes; my navigation extended through one-quarter of the world…

Vespucci, with observant curiosity and the cultivated elegance of a Florentine man of the renaissance, described the infinite variety of trees, the sweet-smelling fruits and flowers, the brilliantly plumed birds, the natives' faces, their figures, their marriage customs, childbirth practices, their beliefs, diet and domestic architecture. He commented that since these people used only bows and arrows, darts and stones, all their blows were, 'committed to the wind'. He never once talked of converting the natives to Christianity, nor did he hunt for gold. 'The natives told us of gold and other metals and many miracle-working drugs, but I am one of those followers of Saint Thomas, who are slow to believe. Time will reveal everything.' According to his letter from Lisbon written in 1502, we know that Vespucci ate, slept, and lived among the Indians for twenty-seven days and, according to both Mundus Novus, and the Lettera, written in Lisbon on 4 September 1504, he stayed sometimes for fifteen or twenty days with them in their villages.[12]

'Always in the direction of Southwest one-quarter west', Vespucci continued until the coast disappeared into the yawning mouth of the Río de la Plata, the largest estuary in the world, into which disgorge the rivers Paraná and Uruguay.

After passing the granite sentinel of Lobos Island, that marks its entrance, the little fleet rounded Cape Santa Maria, at 35°S (today's Punta del Este, a prosperous and developed resort)[13] and entered the Río de la Plata. The navigators understandably hoped that the great estuary would prove to be the opening they desperately looked for, thus, the early name given to Punta del Este was Cabo Buen Deseo, literally Cape of Good Desire, but significantly 'of good hope' signifying the hope that it be the start of their quest, before it was changed to Cape Santa Maria, and later to Punta del Este.

After most probably watering at the outlet of the rivulet of 'La Aguada', in what is now Maldonado Bay, they worked their way west up Rio de la Plata by day while anchoring at night. They passed Punta Ballena and Punta Negra, and on they sailed through the passage between the frightening English Bank and Flores Island – that between them later devoured countless ships – coming to anchor at the foot of a curiously shaped little pinnacle on the northern side of the river. In his account, Vespucci first named the mountain *Pinachullo Detentio* (in Portuguese, meaning the pinnacle where they anchored). Europeans thus learned, for the first time, of the famous 'Cerro de Montevideo', a symbol of the Banda Oriental of Uruguay.

Laguarda Trías, a renowned Uruguayan historian,[14] professes the theory that Vespucci, fascinated by this perfect inverted-cone rising like a pubescent's breast from the surrounding smoothness of the plain, set to climb it and upon reaching the summit had a seaman carve upon its rocky peak the inscription 'VIDI'. Be that as it may, the fact is that later in 1520 Magellan's Greek pilot, Francisco Albo, aboard his flagship *Trinidad*, records in his diary this little peak as Monte Vidi with a certainty that suggests he found that inscription visible somewhere on the summit. It should not be altogether surprising since seafarers are not the only ones accustomed to engrave their names, when abroad, on anything they can find.

The brevity of the word Vidi, says Laguarda Trias, suggests an inscription engraved in haste to commemorate the visit. It could well have been that some member of Magellan's compliment, for instance the cosmographer, Andrés de San Martin, who sailed with Vespucci, and in many ways his disciple, could have recorded the written or oral information about the engraving of the name in his diary. However, the name given to the mountain appears in Albo's logbook but not in San Martin's. Why? It is thought that after San Martín's murder in Cebu, along with Magellan, his diary having been impounded by the Portuguese at Ternate, Antonio de Herrera purposely deleted mention of the discovery of the Rio de la Plata, when it later fell into his hands in Spain. Herrera was the late sixteenth-century Spanish historian who mutilated certain documents such as this one, believing them to be detrimental to Spain's interests. The fact is that the whole episode of Vespucci's discovery of the Río de la Plata was suppressed by Spain, who fourteen years later declared the estuary to have been discovered not by Vespucci, but by their countrymen Juan Díaz de Solis, in 1516. Rivalry between the two super powers was very intense and it is worth remembering that Vespucci was sailing under the Portuguese flag. A touchy subject such as this one was likely to bring about some covert slight of hand, as in this case, due to the contention caused by the treaty of Tordesillas and its line of demarcation.

To comprehend such dishonesty the event has to be seen under the light of the times. These were times when the rivalry of Portugal and Spain knew no bounds and when no treachery was barred to achieve their end.

The riddle of the meaning of the word Vidi has intrigued historians for centuries and only lately has the enigmatic voice of its name seems to have come to light: V (Vesputius); i (invenit); di (501); meaning 'Vespucci discovered in 501', thus, inadvertently, naming the site where the city of Montevideo would one day rise.[15]

Realising the surrounding expanse of water to be that of an estuary of a river due to its muddy colour as well as the freshness of its water and therefore not the ocean passage he was looking for, Vespucci retraced his steps, successfully avoiding the many sandbanks and other dangerous obstacles in the river, and sailed south-west down the Patagonian coast to the Gulf of San Julián. While it is not clear if he entered the gulf between the two capes at it's entrance, he recorded the great difference between high and low tides there. Magellan named it Gulf of San Julian later in 1520. Sailing always southwest, he wrote of the terrible cold and of the storms they ran in to. 'My ships were blown to about 50° south' he says in a letter to his friend, Piero Soderini, written after his return. In it he tells that on 7 April, during a violent south-westerly storm, they sighted at a distance of some 20 leagues, 'a new land with a dangerous coast, with no ports or people'. This has been construed by some historians to be the outline of the Malouine Islands – though as an unlikely alternative South Georgias have been mentioned if the storm had carried them as far as latitude 52° S.[16] If, on the other hand, they had reached an additional degree of southern latitude while sailing within sight of the coast, there is a possibility that they might have sighted the entrance to the Straits before being forced by the foul weather to turn back.

If Vespucci had sighted the entrance to the Straits, he and the Portuguese authorities would have considered it a monumental discovery, which also meant not letting the word out. The policy of secrecy in Portugal, as well as in Spain, meant not telling anyone where places were or how to reach them. It was a conspiracy of silence that the captains had to swear to, under the penalty of death if they did not adhere to it.[17]

When Magellan's expedition later spent the terrible winter of 1520 in the Port of San Julián, at latitude 49° 20'S and rebellion broke out amongst his senior officers, the mutineers made it clear that they were unwilling to sail further south in search of a strait which other sailors had sought in vain. Magellan, resisting all pressures to head home, put down the rebellion and declared that they had to continue south 'at least as far as had Amerigo Vespucci'.[18] 'Day after day the lookouts scanned the coastline for the entrance to a strait that their leader insisted, seemingly against all evidence, was there until they rounded Cape Virgins, and he took his ships into the channel.' Who had told him that he would find a strait through the continent that far south? Perhaps, as Antonio Pigafetta (the major chronicler of the voyage) observed, Magellan had actually seen 'in the treasury of the King of Portugal' a secret map that showed a devious passage. Later in this narrative we will talk about this intriguing question. In the meantime we must return to Vespucci.

Deciding that discretion was the better part of valour, Vespucci turned back. On their return voyage the expedition anchored at Sierra Leone, on the coast of Africa, to provision and water and later at the Azores, arriving at Lisbon on 7 September 1502. By then Columbus had already departed on his fourth voyage. As a result, the Admiral had no idea that the South American coast, which he himself had discovered on his previous voyage, extended so far. Had he known this he might have been less hopeful of finding a passage through the Central American isthmus into the Indian Ocean.

Despite the many New World novelties, the desire for a westward passage to India was still uppermost in people's minds. The unexpected continent seemed less of a resource for the future than an obstacle to past hopes.[19] Vespucci himself seemed less interested in exploring it than in finding a passage through it to the true treasure trove in the Asian Indies. A month after he arrived back from his epoch-making voyage, Amerigo changed flags once again and settled in Seville. Perhaps he was convinced, after revising the map of the western Atlantic, the Ptolemy's Strait of Catigara would not be found on this new continent. He had sailed the whole coastline and found no opening. Or had he? This voyage is of fundamental importance in the history of geographical discovery in that Vespucci himself, and scholars as well, were not part of Asia but part of a 'New World'.

While Portugal was immersed in amassing treasure from her eastward sea trade route to India, the Spanish sovereigns were investing efforts to find a better westward passage to the Orient. The University of Salamanca welcomed foreign scholars and had been provided with new funds. Even Queen Isabella had personally taken to collecting printed books, the new source of knowledge.

Amerigo charted the coastline he discovered, but his original maps are lost, and so are his logbooks. Fortunately some of his letters survive, as well as a few maps that originate indirectly from his pen. He took part in a fourth expedition for the Spanish crown between 10 May 1503 and 4 September 1504. Being an accomplished cartographer he put his skills into mapping the coastline as far as Cabo Frío on the Brazilian coast, where he built a fort and manned it with twenty men he salvaged from one of his ships sunk off the island of Fernando de Noronha.

He tracked through the jungle from the coast with forty of his men, watched by distrustful natives armed with bows and blowpipes. The fact that he returned unscathed is as much a tribute to his resolve as to his courage, tenacity, and decency towards the natives he lived with on the way.

Vespucci was welcomed by the Spanish sovereigns who awarded him the task of provisioning ships to 'sail westward, north of the equator, to seek the discovery of a strait not found by Columbus'. His eminence was acknowledged in 1508,

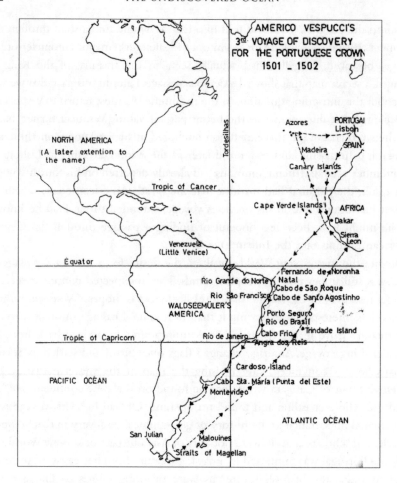

when Queen Juana of Castile (Juana, 'La Loca', married to the archduke Philip, 'The Fair' and mother of Emperor Charles V) who had succeeded to the throne of Isabella, named Amerigo Vespucci to the newly created post of 'Pilot-Major of Spain'. He was commissioned to found a school for pilots and was given the exclusive authority to examine and licence 'all the pilots of our kingdoms and lordships who voyage hereafter to the said lands of our Indies, discovered or to be discovered'. Upon their return, pilots were to report to him all their findings in a series of debriefing sessions, so as to keep Spanish maps up to date.

Against the resistance of the more illiterate practical pilots, Vespucci attempted to popularise his complex method for finding longitude. He made plans for another voyage of his own in ships whose hulls were to be sheathed in lead as protection against the teredos, to 'go west to find the lands which the Portuguese found by sailing east'. But suffering from the malaria that he had contracted during his last voyage, and for which there was no known cure, Amerigo Vespucci died in 1512.[20]

Vespucci, though he had convinced the scholars of Europe that the newly discovered territories were not part of Asia but of a totally New World, had never named the continent after himself, although after his death he was often accused of that particular conceit. Naming the continent was the exclusive undertaking of Martin Waldseemüller (1470?–1518), an obscure clergyman and humanist, who had studied at the University of Freiburg.

Waldseemüller was a man with an inquisitive mind and a passion for geography. When he became canon of the little town of Saint Dié, built around a monastery founded in the seventh century by Saint Deodatus in part of the Duchy of Lorraine in north-eastern France, he settled in and found the post agreeable. The ruling Duke of Lorraine, Renaud II of Vaudemon, had organised a provincial learned society and Waldseemüller became a member of this *Gymnase Vosgien*. A wealthy member of the society, Canon Walter Ludd, set up a printing press to indulge his vanity by printing his own works and, of course, those of other members of the society.

Having a penchant for making up names, and to impress his peers, Martin combined the Greek word for 'wood', the Latin name for 'lake' and the Greek word for 'mill' and came up with 'Hylacomylus' as a pen name for use in his learned publications. Translated back into the German vernacular this became his family name, Waldseemüller. Guided by Waldseemüller, the little group had ambitious plans to print a new edition of Ptolemy's geography to inaugurate their press. But one of the members reported seeing a printed copy of a French letter entitled 'Four Voyages' in which:

> … a great man, of brave courage, yet small experience, Americus Vespucius, has first related without exaggeration of a people living toward the south, almost under the Antarctic pole. There are people in that place… who go about entirely naked, and who not only (as do certain people in India) offer to their king the heads of their enemies whom they have killed, but who themselves feed eagerly on the flesh of their conquered foes. The book itself of Americus Vespucius has by chance fallen in our way, and we have read it hastily and have compared almost the whole of it with the Ptolemy, the maps of which you know we are at this time engaged in examining with great care, and we have thus been induced to compose, upon the subject of this region of a newly discovered world, a little work not only poetic but geographical in its character.

The Saint-Dié group, after some consideration, dropped their ambitious plan for printing an edition of Ptolemy and instead produced a little volume of 103 pages entitled *Cosmographiae Introductio* in which they summarised the traditional principals of cosmography, the division of the earth, the winds, the definitions of *axes and climata*, and the distances from place to place. It also offered something sensationally new, an account of a *fourth* part of the world, revealed by the chronicle of the voyages of Amerigo Vespucci. Waldseemüller, in an abridgement of a chapter observed:

> Now, these parts of the earth [Europe, Africa, Asia] have been more extensively explored and a fourth part has been discovered by Amerigo Vespucci (as will be

described in what follows). Inasmuch as both Europe and Asia received their names from women, I see no reason why any one should justly object to calling this part Amerige [from Greek 'ge' meaning 'land of'] i.e. the land of Amerigo, or America, after Amerigo, its discoverer, a man of great ability.

Waldseemüller further reinforced this suggestion. He accompanied the third part of *Cosmographiae* with a huge map printed from twelve wooden blocks made in Strasbourg. Each sheet measured 46 by 62cm. And when pasted together the map covered about thirty-six square feet. At the top of the map Waldseemüller seemingly emphasised his new message by inserting two dominating portraits: one of Claudius Ptolemaeus facing east, and the other of Americus Vespucius facing west. In this astonishing cartographic prophecy, the South American continent, on which 'America' was inscribed, showed the contour of its coastline remarkably similar to its actual shape. Also the two Americas were drawn as actually connected and farther to the west appeared a whole new ocean, broader than the Atlantic, that separated the New World from Asia.

Regardless of all the endeavours of the brave and famous navigators, it took the obscure clergyman, Martin Waldseemüller of St Dié in north-eastern France, to put America literally on the map.

The first book published, in April 1507, was so popular that a second edition came off the press in August. By the end of the next year, Waldseemüller boasted to his partner that not only had they sold one thousand copies, an unheard of amount in those days, but also their map became known and disseminated around the world.

The printing press could distribute, but not retrieve. He discovered this to his chagrin when he had second thoughts about crediting Amerigo Vespucci as the true discoverer of the New World, but it was all too late. On all of the three later maps that he published he deleted the name 'America'. But the name had caught on and could not be recalled, scattered, as it was by then, throughout the known world. So appealing was the name that Waldseemüller had applied only to the southern continent, that when Gerardus Mercator published his own large map of the world in 1538 he duplicated the application to encompass the northern continent as well. Mercator's map showed both a 'North America', *Americae pars septentrionalis*, and a 'South America', *Americae pars meridionalis*.

The ability of the printing press, though only half a century old, to spread information, as well as misinformation, had revealed its power. The widened audience that the new technology created was already shaping the way people saw the world. To be more explicit, the Columbus Letter of 1493, although reprinted many times, had nowhere the appeal of the sensational account of Vespucci's adventures. Even a quarter century later the account of Vespucci's travels exceeded those of Columbus threefold. For years to come of all the works printed in Europe describing the discoveries of the New World, about one half dealt with Amerigo Vespucci and not with Columbus. Due to Vespucci's inquisitive mind and power of description, the accounts of his travels written to his friend Pier Soderini, Golfaloniro of the Sonfalomiere★ Republic of Florence, appeal as much to today's readers as they did to readers of 500 years ago. So it was that history delivered the Admiral one final, ironic blow. The man who in his lifetime was erroneously credited with the discovery of Asia and the Indies was in the end deprived of the honour he truly deserved.

During this time the Portuguese conquests in the East grew. Mile by mile the voyages grew longer until they finally arrived at the much sought Moluccas, or Spice Islands.

As a result of these voyages a large part of the world was defined and mapped. Added to the logical satisfaction of discovery was an enormous material incentive that finally led to the control of the riches of the East passing from Arab hands to those of the Portuguese. Even so, the most important fact was the discovery that the world was a sphere and consequently could be circumnavigated, always heading east, weathering the Cape of Good Hope and India. Filled with envy the Spaniards asked themselves 'and why not attempt to reach Cathay by navigating in the opposite direction, West?'

The message was out and the audience was equipped to carry on where Amerigo Vespucci had left off.

★ Standard-bearer – highest authortiy of the Florentine Republic.

THE UNDISCOVERED OCEAN

Then I felt like some watcher of the skies
When a new planet swims into his ken;
Or like stout Cortez when with eagle eyes
He star'd at the Pacific – and all his men
Look'd at each other with a wild surmise –
Silent, upon a peak in Darien.

On First Looking into Chapman's Homer, John Keats (1795–1821)

It took barely a couple of decades after Vespucci's voyage for the whole concept of the European world to be transformed. Up to then the Christian cartographic dogma was based on the surface of the earth being covered mostly by land. 'Six parts hast thou dried up', declared the prophet Esdras (II Esd. 6:42). Amongst religious believers it had become axiomatic that the surface of our planet was six-sevenths dry land and only one-seventh water. After all, God had set men above all the rest of Creation.

If all the oceans together amounted to only one-seventh the surface of the earth, and as the learned believed the earth was a sphere, then there was not much sea available to separate Spain to the westward from the Indies. However, after Vespucci, this was contested, the learned were wising up, and new charts were printed. Never before had the arena of human geographical experience been so drastically revised. Suddenly the earth had become more than ever explorable and within reach.

Two men of different backgrounds, and singular leaders they proved to be, witnessed the discovery of the Pacific Ocean's breadth in two remarkable feats of stamina, courage, and perseverance – Balboa and Magellan – of contrasting temperaments, but both from the Iberian Peninsula.

Vasco Nuñez de Balboa (1474-1517) was an adventurer of obscure parentage, born in an equally obscure inland village in south-western Spain, who[1] went to sea at the age of twenty-five. In 1500 he joined an expedition to explore the Spanish Main and remained to become a planter in Santo Domingo. Not able to make his way cultivating the soil he accumulated debts. By law, indebted people might not leave the island of Hispaniola, so with the aid of a friend he stowed away inside a barrel among the stores of a ship on its way to the Spanish settlements on the east coast of the Gulf of Darien. When the vessel put to sea, Vasco Nuñez made his appearance much to the annoyance of Martín Fernandez de Enciso who was on board. Enciso, a scholarly lawyer, had been sent by Spain to salvage what he could of the Spanish settlements on the Isthmus of Panama, where it joins the South American mainland.

Starvation and the poisoned arrows of the Indians had decimated the settlers. When Enciso, proved unequal to the task of organizing a new colony, the upstart Balboa seized command. He moved the colony to higher ground where food was more available and the Indians had no poisoned arrows. Giving it the name of Santa Maria de la Antigua del Darien.[2]

Diego, Columbus' son, governing this region from Santo Domingo authorised Balboa to keep command but Enciso with his original officers resisted to the point where Balboa ridded himself of his rivals by sending some to Hispaniola and those of higher rank like Enciso, directly back to Spain.[3]

Balboa immediately consolidated his position by craftily helping Comaco, a friendly *cacique*, fight his wars and by marrying one of his daughters. Comaco thanked his new allies with the gift of 4,000 ounces of gold. However, while the Spaniards were weighing it out, according to the contemporary chronicler Peter Martyr, a 'brabbling and contention arose among the Spaniards about dividing of the gold.' Comaco's eldest son became so disgusted with this spectacle that he knocked over the scales, scattered the gold on the ground and delivered the Spaniards a sermon. He loudly scolded them against their greed, while at the same time inadvertently volunteering a gem of geographical information worth as much as all the gold in the Indies. He admonished them thus:

> What is the matter, you Christian men that you quarrel for such a little thing? If you have such a love of gold that to obtain it you disquiet and harass the peaceful nations of these lands, and while suffering such labours you banish yourselves from your own lands, I will show you where you may fulfill your desires. But for this it is necessary that you be more in number than you are now. You will have to fight your way with great kings. In the first place with King Tubanamá, who abounds with this gold, and whose country is distant six suns from our own.

He signified to them that this rich territory lay southwards towards a sea where they would arrive after passing over those mountains (pointing his finger south towards the mountains)… You shall see another sea, where they sail with ships with sails and oars slightly less in size as those of yours, although the men are as naked as ourselves. Traversing that sea, he said, they would find a land of great riches where the people ate and drank from vessels of gold.

Francisco Pizarro was a bystander, although at the time he was only a painstaking, trustworthy captain. But there is no doubt that among those present, who Peter Martyr says, 'marveled at the oration of the naked young man and pondered in their minds and earnestly considered his sayings, there was none upon whom this oration had a deeper and more lasting effect than Pizarro',[4] prefiguring his own voyage of discovery to come.

Early in 1513, Balboa selected 190 of his men, well armed, with their ferocious mastiffs, 'which were of more avail than men', and several hundred native guides and porters, and set out to follow this lead across the mountainous Isthmus of Panama. Careful to protect his rear, he employed those Indians that might have threatened him from that quarter 'as guides and bearers who went on ahead and opened the trail. They passed through inaccessible defiles inhabited by ferocious beasts, and they climbed steep mountains.'

First they went to the territory of Balboa's father-in-law where they were well received. A number of Comaco's men joined the expedition that then moved into the cacique Poncha's territory. Poncha supplied more guides and porters from among his people and the small army commenced the ascent of the mountains. The dark recesses of the tropical forest were like nothing they had seen before. Later explorers found that Balboa's route still taxed them beyond the limits of their endurance; 300 years later, in the mid-nineteenth century, a French explorer reported that he was unable to see the sky for eleven days, while a German botanical expedition, trying to struggle through, lost every man. To cross the swamps and lakes, Balboa's men often had to carry their clothes above their heads, risking poisonous snakes and the arrows of unfriendly tribes. When blocked by the primitive Quarequas, armed only with bows and arrows and two-handed wooden swords, Balboa's men fought them and took them apart 'like butchers cutting up beef and mutton for market. Six hundred were thus slain like brute beasts', Peter Martyr reported.

The commander and his men climbed their way up the loftiest sierras until on 25 September 1513, they came near the top. Just before reaching the height, Comaco's Indians informed him of his near approach to the sea. Saying that the magnificent sight of it for the first time would make any man wish to be alone, Balboa commanded his men to halt while he ascended. From the top in solitude, he looked down upon the vast blue of the Pacific Ocean. 'Kneeling upon the ground, he raised his hands to heaven and saluted the South Sea. According to his own account, he gave thanks to God and all the Saints for having reserved this glory for him, an ordinary man, devoid alike of experience and authority, for being permitted to discover the *Sea of the South*.'[5] Then with his hand he beckoned to his men to join him on the peak, where they all knelt and gave thanks together. 'Behold the much-desired ocean!' he exclaimed. 'Behold! All ye men, who have shared such labours, how our desires are being accomplished. Behold the country of which the sons of Comogre [from the kingdom of Comaco] and other natives have told us such wonders! I hold for certain that what they told us about there being incomparable treasures in it will be fulfilled. God and his blessed Mother who have assisted us so that we should arrive here and behold this sea will favour us, so that we may enjoy all that there is in it.'[6] Afterwards, they devoutly sang the *Te Deum Laudamus* and in accordance with Spanish custom, a list was drawn up by a notary of those that were present at this discovery, 'made upon Saint Martin's day'.

The nineteenth-century poet John Keats later preserved this awesome moment in his first published poem, 'On First Looking into Chapman's Homer'. In youthful fervour, he mistakenly refers to Cortez instead of Balboa, fatally misattributing the great deed to the wrong man, but the feeling in his poem captures it all:

> Then felt like some watcher of the skies
> When a new planet swims into his ken;
> Or like stout Cortéz when with eagle eyes
> He star'd at the Pacific – and all his men
> Look'd at each other with a wild surmise –
> Silent, upon a peak in Darien.

In order to make memorials of the event, Balboa had trees cut, crosses erected, and some stones heaped to form a kiln, while his men carved the name of their king on tree trunks around the slopes. Descending the sierras they entered the territory of an Indian chief called Chiapes to whom Vasco Nuñez sent messengers with offerings of peace. To prevent his party being overwhelmed by Indians Balboa dispatched certain groups back home. This gave confidence to the fresh ones that accompanied him and it prevented him being overburdened by natives who otherwise might have overwhelmed him. In truth, throughout the duration of the expedition, Vasco Nuñez acted with strategic sagacity.

Balboa sent a small contingent headed by Francisco Pizarro and Alonzo Martin, to find the shortest way to the seashore. Upon their return, Balboa went himself on the four-day trek. In a climactic gesture, wearing his armour and unsheathing his sword, he waded into the surf, raised the banner of Castille, and formally took possession of the *Mar del Sur*, the Southern Sea and all that was in it in the names of Their Most Catholic Majesties of Spain.

Balboa called it the 'Southern' Sea for a reason. The Isthmus of Darien, or today of Panama, which he had just crossed, because of its curve, runs east and west. As he had started from the side of the Caribbean he had gone southward, and it was in that direction that he first sighted the Pacific. His energy was inexhaustible and, 'not being able to be quiet even while his bread was baking', he resolved to borrow one of the Indian dugout canoes on the shore of the gulf that he named San Miguel, (a name it still retains.) On that brief ceremonial ride he took possession in good measure, of 'all that sea and the countries bordering upon it.'

Balboa broke camp and made his way with his men to the country of a chief named Tumaco, in the corner of the gulf, whom he befriended. Tumaco made him a present of ornaments of gold and 240 large pearls and, to the delight of the Spaniards, sent his people to dive for more. The Indians not knowing better were accustomed to open the oysters by heating them over a fire, injuring the colour of the pearl in the process. The Spaniards diligently taught the native the art of opening the oyster with a knife. Tumaco, it is said, spoke to Balboa of the riches of Peru, as in his letter to the sovereign of Spain penned later Balboa says, 'he had learnt from Tumaco wonderful secrets of the riches of that land which for the present he wished to keep to himself.'

During the return trip to Darien Balboa became ill (most likely due to malaria) and had to be carried the rest of the way on a litter born by natives. Entering the kingdom of his friend Comaco, he discovered the old chief had died but his eldest son, he who had made such an eloquent speech, was reigning in his stead. Vasco Nuñez was hospitably entertained and doubtless they had many things to hear and tell each other. Days later, having recovered from the fever, he set out for Darien which he reached on 29 January 1514, after having set out on this world-shattering expedition on 1 September 1513, five months before.

After arrival Balboa lost no time in writing 'such signal and new news' to his sovereign, accompanying it with rich presents. In it he gave a detailed account of his journey, thanking God on every page that he had escaped from great dangers emphasizing he had not lost a man on the whole route or in his battles with the Indians. The letter and presents he entrusted to a man named Arbolanche, who departed from Darien at the beginning of March 1514.[7]

News of his discovery did not reach Spain in time to overshadow Enciso's disastrous reports of Balboa's coup. To displace Balboa as governor was sent Pedrárias de Avila, whose only qualification was his marriage to a lady-in-waiting to Queen Isabella. He was an elderly man of high connections but little wisdom. I conjecture Pedrárias to have been a suspicious, fiery, arbitrary old man. 'Furor Domini' was a name given him by the monks in after days, just as Attila enjoyed and merited the awful title of the 'Scourge of God'. With twenty ships and 1,500 men, Pedrárias initiated a program for enslaving the natives that had the immediate effect, according to Balboa himself, of changing sheeplike Indians into 'fierce lions'.

Meanwhile Balboa, planning to explore the shores of the Southern Sea, had transported shipbuilding materials across the isthmus. By 1517 he had nearly completed four ships when Pedrárias' men, including Francisco Pizarro, came to arrest Balboa and take him back across the isthmus to Darien. There, Pedrárias falsely accused Balboa of planning to abandon his Spanish sovereigns and set himself up as emperor of Peru. Before Balboa's supporters could effectively consolidate his defense, Balboa and four companions were beheaded in the public square, and their bodies were thrown to the vultures.

'Every public man of the time', wrote one enlightened historian, 'entered on his career with the familiar expectation of possibly closing it on the scaffold.' In Europe spies and informers swarmed everywhere. *Agents provocateurs*, as they were called, promoted treason for pay. Bestial crowds swarmed to public torturing, hangings, and burning at stakes. The heads of executed men withered on city gates as object lessons.

In the Spanish colonies where cruelty knew no bounds, power meant gold, and gold meant the *raison d'etre*. These men were brutal. Driven by their greed for gold, while given self-justification by their Christianity, they murdered, raped and plundered. They also brought their arrogance and all their deadly diseases with them.

Gunfire and Toledo steel accounted for thousands of native casualties, but smallpox and other diseases wiped out millions. Cruelty over the indigenous peoples of America devastated the countries they conquered. However, one cannot help but marvel at their immense courage and the hardships they endured. No food, no map… but many of them died bloodily, like Balboa, as their age demanded.

As an afterthought, I must say that Balboa, for all his roughness, is worthy of our admiration. A Spaniard in the toughest sense, he was the first of the great *Conquistadors* of the American mainland. He founded the city of Darien; he achieved ascendancy over the Indians of the isthmus by a combination of force, terror, conciliation, and diplomacy; he collected great quantities of food and gold at the same time as compelling his own people to settle the land and plant crops. The settlements begun under his leadership proved to be rewarding and lasting and the isthmus itself within a few years became so important in the colonial trade of Spain that it earned the name of *Castilla del Oro*, Golden Castile. As well, Balboa's discovery of the Pacific Ocean, not only revealed to Europeans the existence of the South Sea, but also gave new encouragement to those who hoped to find a strait through the landmass of America and a westward all-sea-route to the east. In a sense the conquest of Central America was an incident in the race between Portuguese and Spanish to reach the Spice Islands, a race that the Portuguese won. In the same year (1513) that Balboa crossed the isthmus the first Portuguese reached the Moluccas. On the other hand, in the same year that Cortez landed in Mexico, Magellan sailed on the voyage that would reveal the daunting size of the Pacific and the western route to the East.[8]

15

THE ELUSIVE PATH TO THE SOUTH SEA

On sailed the little vessels, feeble, man-made,
windblown chips upon a hostile immensity,
held to their course only by the ability and iron will
of the great seamen commanding them.

Captain James Cook, Alan Villiers, p.245

By now Spanish adventurers were firmly settled in the West Indies. Nevertheless, the more enlightened saw their colonies mainly as outposts along the long path to Asia. Was it not logical, they asked themselves, to extend their domain still further west to the valuable Spice Islands? Profit was as familiar then as it is today, the ubiquitous incentive dazzled their minds and spurred them on.

As we have seen, the Treaty of Tordesillas had fixed a line of demarcation 370 leagues (1,110 miles or 1,786km) west of the Azores and Cape Verde Islands, establishing the New World boundary at 46° west longitude, cutting through the bulge of South America. Since Spain and Portugal recognised the pope's authority over the whole globe, this meridian line extended through both poles and went all away around the planet to the other side. It was the line that separated the domains of Spain from those of Portugal.

Let us envision the world as an orange that we have stood on end and split with a knife vertically from stem to stern. The half on the right, we will call Portugal's and the half on the left Spain's. The meridian of 134° east longitude, at the back of the orange, became the dividing line between the two great powers in the Far East. It meant that Portugal would be sovereign over all the undiscovered areas eastward from the western boundary that cut through Brazil's bulge, across the Atlantic, Africa, and the Indian Ocean towards the East Indies, while Spain would rule from the Brazilian boundary westward across the Pacific to the East Indies. But the scientific instruments of the time could not draw the line accurately, so both powers were on tenterhooks not knowing on who's side of the meridian the Spice Islands, the purpose of all their efforts, actually were. While the Portuguese claimed the islands by right of discovery and Francisco Serrão's exploitative residence there, the Spaniards felt no less justified in their own claim. The Spanish crown hoped that Ptolemy, Marco Polo and Columbus had been correct in surmising the Asian continent to be far enough eastward to be within their allotted area and therefore only a small hop from America. With those hopes in mind, Charles V was prompted to say to his advisors, ' why not send out an expedition to find out and assert Spanish claims?'

Of paramount importance in prompting Magellan to set out again for the Spice Islands were the letters from his friend Serrão. These, lost in the earthquake of 1755 that reduced Lisbon to ruins, were studied and partially recorded before this happened by early Portuguese chroniclers. 'I have found a New World...', Serrão wrote, 'richer, greater, and more beautiful than that of Vasco da Gama... I beg you to join me here so that you may sample the delights that surround me....' Serrão remained in Ternate as an unofficial Portuguese resident, and hoped to meet his friend on his way westward around the globe. Sadly enough, both were killed before this could happen.

Magellan, after his years in the Far East, returned to Portugal a veteran sailor and soldier, expert in navigation, and with an important plan. He firmly believed that the Moluccas could be arrived at by Columbus' original idea of sailing west, instead of the long complicated voyage around the Cape of Good Hope, and on through the Strait of Malacca. From what he had gleaned from Serrão's letters and from his own observations, the Spice Islands were relatively civilised under Moslem or pagan sultans who were eager to trade with Europeans. But the center of his design was to find a path beyond the barrier of the South American continent to the South Sea on the other side and Magellan had inkling he could find it.

By the time Magellan had returned to Portugal in 1512 he had reached the rank of captain and was raised to the rank of *fidalgo escudero*, a slightly higher rank of nobility. The crown owed him money for his services but refused to pay him. Then in August 1513 his sovereign, Dom Manuel sent him from Portugal on a punitive expeditionary force to Morocco's Atlantic coast to put down a colonial rebellion. He took a lance in the knee, a wound that took its time to heal and left him with a permanent limp. Outspoken, he had a talent for easily making enemies, and before leaving Morocco a trumped-up charge of selling captured cattle back to the enemy was brought against him. The charge later proved groundless but it damaged his reputation with his military superiors as it did later with the advisors of the crown.

Back in Lisbon, Magellan quarrelled with the king. During a final and fatal audience, he was told that the sovereign no longer valued his services and he could take them anywhere else he pleased. As Magellan knelt to kiss the hand of his king before departing, the monarch withdrew it. Stunned and angry, Magellan limped from the court, and strode towards Spain.

An indignant Magellan publicly disowned his loyalty to Portugal and arrived in Seville on 21 October 1517. With him he brought an old friend, the eccentric, Ruy Faleiro, a man who in his day was considered the finest mathematician, astronomer, and scholar of the nautical sciences. Together they pored over maps, the most accurate of their day – but by our standards not accurate at all – drawn by Jorge and Pedro Reinel, Portuguese cartographers, who were considered the best. Their maps plainly depicted the Moluccas on the Spanish side of the dividing line. With this invaluable knowledge, Magellan sought an audience with the young and eager Charles I of Spain, later to become Charles V of the Holy Roman Empire.[1]

What sort of man was Magellan when at the age of about thirty-seven he shook the dust of Lisbon from his feet and entered the service of Spain? We know him as dark-complexioned, somewhat short in stature but thickset, strong and agile but above all robust, hardy, firm, unyielding and tough. As tough and resilient as the sinew of a bow! He was not the flamboyant, arrogant and reckless buccaneer, like Drake would be; on the contrary, his strength lay in his uncanny ability to discern between dream, purpose and achievement. He was also a realistic provider of food and water for his men, when his ranks were thinning daily from scurvy – he had avoided the malady himself by ingesting enough vitamin C by eating preserved quince during the crossing of the Pacific. Fortunately Bishop Las Casas, then at Valladolid, recorded his own impression of the man for us at an interview with the king of Spain:

> Magellan brought with him a well-painted globe showing the entire world, and thereon traced the course he proposed to take, save that the Strait was purposely left blank so that nobody could anticipate him… I asked him what route he proposed to take, he replied that he intended to take that of Cape Santa Maria [Punta del Este today, at the entrance to the Río de la Plata] and thence follow the coast up [south] until he found the Strait. I said, 'What will you do if you find no Strait to pass into the other sea?' He replied that if he found none he would follow the course that the Portuguese took. But, according to what an Italian gentleman named Pigafetta of Vicenza who went on that voyage of discovery with Magellan, wrote in a letter, Magellan was perfectly certain to find the Strait because he had seen on a nautical chart made by one Martin of Bohemia, a great pilot and cosmographer, in the treasury of the King of Portugal the Strait depicted just as he found it. And, because the Strait was on the land and sea, within the boundaries of the sovereigns of Castile, he [Magellan] therefore had to move and offer his services to the king of Castile to discover a new route to the said islands of Molucca and the rest.

Las Casas then goes on to give us the most vivid picture we have of Magellan's appearance and personality:

> This *Fernando de Magallanes* must have been a brave man, valiant in thought and for undertaking great things, although his person did not carry much authority, since he was of small stature and did not look like much, so that people thought they could put it over him for want of prudence and courage.[2]

He was certainly not a man to underestimate, as three Spanish courtiers and a priest would bear witness, had they not been stranded in Patagonia for precisely having underrated Magellan's valor and toughness.

To advance his grand scheme of sailing around the world to the Indies, Magellan acted shrewdly. Without fanfare, before the end of 1517, he took as wife Beatriz Barbosa, the daughter of Diego Barbosa who had invited him to stay in his house in Seville. Diego was influential being *alcalde* of the arsenal and knight commander of the order of Santiago, and his son Duarte joined the great voyage. Beatriz bore him a son and had conceived a second child before his departure two years later. They named their son, Rodrigo, who was born about six months before Magellan sailed, but died when Magellan was at sea. Magellan also managed to secure the enthusiastic approval of the previously mentioned, Juan Rodriguez de Fonseca, the powerful bishop of Burgos, who had been a chief enemy of Columbus. For funds he cultivated the representative of the international banking firm of Fuggers, who also had a grudge against the king of Portugal.

Invited by the king for a royal audience in Valladolid, Magellan and his friend Ruy Faleiro travelled north there in February 1518. It was the favourite residence of the sovereigns of Castile, where Ferdinand and Isabella had been married in 1469. It was also at Valladolid that Columbus had spent the last two years of his life broken in health and spirit vainly hoping for the fulfillment of royal promises, until he died in 1506.

Magellan first met with the king's ministers and then with King Charles himself, the grandson of Columbus' sponsors Fernando II of Aragon, and Isabella I of Castile, and son of their daughter Joan – the mad – (Juana la Loca) married to Philip I – the handsome – (Felipe, el Hermoso) son of the Holy Roman Emperor Maximilian I of Habsburg and Mary of Burgundy. Two years earlier when he turned eighteen Charles was crowned king of Castile, Leon, and Aragon. In June 1618, at the death of his father, he was elected king of the Romans, meaning he would be emperor as soon as the pope would crown him in Rome. This would not happen for another two years. However, the pope consented that he adopt the style and title at once. Thus, he became known to history as Carlos Quinto, Charles-Quint, or Charles V, emperor of the Holy Roman Empire. To recover his old kingdom of Burgundy with its capital at Dijon and its western boundary on the Rhône cost Charles almost a million ducats[3] to bribe the electors of the Holy Roman Empire to elect him king of the Romans; he had to borrow heavily from the bankers – who never got it all back. The money from the colonies that flowed in from Mexico and Perú helped partially, but he never had enough to get out of debt. King Charles regarded America and the Far East as a source of wealth for his other European objectives.[4]

The emperor was an ugly fellow, judging from his portrait painted when he was about twenty-five by the Dutch painter Jan Cornelisz Vermeyen. Note the pendulous lower lip and the over-shot lower jaw, Hapsburg characteristics inherited from his father, Philip of Austria, and transmitted down the line to his descendants including to a lesser extent, Alfonso XIII.

On the whole, Charles V paid more attention to matters of discovery and overseas conquest than any of his contemporaries, leaving to his son Philip II upon his death, a greater empire than the world had ever known. An awesome achievement considering it had come about forty years before England, under Henry XIII, and France, under François-premier, or any other country for that matter, had established a single colony in the New World.

Much happened in the world during the first four years of Charles's reign. During the month that Magellan came to Seville, Martin Luther nailed his famous Ninety-Five Theses against the excesses of Roman Catholicism to the church door in Wittenberg. Cortez conquered Mexico for Spain while Magellan was at sea. Some of the greatest books of the High Renaissance were published: Machiavelli's *Prince*, Saint Thomas More's *Utopia*, Erasmus's *Institution of a Christian Prince*. Nationalism was on the rise that would contest the Spanish world hegemony founded on the wealth of the Indies.

Advised by his native Flemish and German councilors, Charles listened carefully to Magellan's arguments that the Spice Islands lay within Spain's domain. The boundary line had, after all, been decreed by the pope himself and the boundary could not be contested. Magellan, quietly listening to the contrary asides whispered to the king by his ministers that the islands belonged to Portugal, thought differently and put up a strong argument for the Spice Islands being on the Spanish side of demarcation.

As evidence, he first produced Serrão's letters and read the more effusive parts about the islands to the king, expounding on his friend's claims with remarkable authority. 'I have found a New World', he read allowed, 'richer greater, and more beautiful than that of Vasco da Gama…' He presented his slave, Enrique that he had bought at Malacca – who was destined to accompany him on his circumnavigation – and a pretty slave girl from Sumatra, 'who understood the tongues of many islands.' He put forth the belief that the end of South America would turn westward as the Cape of Good Hope turned towards the east. It was only a matter, he said, of sailing the coast of the new continent until he discovered the corresponding cape that he would navigate to reach the Spice Islands. He produced the 'Reinels' globe he had brought from Portugal, showing his intended route. The globe showed Japan much closer to America than it was. All these persuasive arguments gave weight to a case that never would have been made, had the truth been known. That Ptolemy had hugely underestimated the world's circumference, that Serrão had greatly overestimated the distance of the Spice Islands from Malacca; and that Magellan had not the faintest idea of the vastness of the Pacific Ocean.[5]

The Portuguese did everything possible to stop Magellan's voyage, even offering him a bribe to stop the expedition from sailing. One of Dom Manuel's counselors and confessors, Bishop Vasconcellos, even brought up the idea of having Magellan assassinated. But after a year and a half outfitting the expedition, the determined Magellan departed on 20 September 1519. Contracts had been drawn up, detailing the number and type of ships, and the stipulation that the expedition not violate the territories of Charles's 'dear and well beloved uncle and brother, the king of Portugal.'

Portugal's agent in Seville noted with pleasure that the five ships procured for Magellan were 'very old and patched up.' He 'would not care to sail as far as the Canaries in such old crates; their ribs are as soft as butter.'[6] No doubt envy pervaded those that now regretted not having taken Magellan up on his offer. No one could have fooled the master mariner Magellan with a rotten ship.

Faleiro's unstable termperarment, we are told, and 'his acting strangely' before leaving port, caused Charles V wisely to order him removed as co-commander and be replaced by Juan de Cartagena as captain of the *San Antonio* and inspector general of the fleet. An upstart with neither rank, title, nor experience, Cartagena owed this extraordinary appointment to being Bishop Fonseca's 'nephew'. In other words, the fruit of some Episcopal indiscretion. He was not alone in his background as Antonio de Coca, a bastard son of the bishop's brother, was named *contador*, fleet accountant. Two other royal appointees were Luis de Mendoza, mentioned as a 'friend' of the archbishop of Seville, captain of the *Victoria* as well as fleet treasurer with an annual salary of 60,000 maravedis; and Gaspar de Quesada, captain of *Concepción*, also a 'servant of the Archbishop.' Thus Fonseca had his men, mostly bastards, placed strategically around the fleet. However, we must give credit to the bishop for one excellent appointment, that of Gonzalo Gómez de Espinosa as *aguacil mayor*, chief marshal of the fleet, commanding all shipboard soldiers. He remained steadfastly loyal to Magellan throughout the voyage, and later after Magellan's death he commanded the flagship *Trinidad*.

The one and only captain that Magellan could really count on was Juan Serrano of the little *Santiago*, like himself an expatriate from Portugal. Serrano, an experienced mariner, was quite likely a brother or cousin to Magellan's intimate friend, Francisco Serrão. Also Portuguese was Esteban Gómes, flag pilot, but he hated Magellan and engineered the only successful mutiny of the voyage.

When appointing Cartagena as captain of the *San Antonio* in place of Faleiro, Cartagena was mentioned in the letter of appointment as *conjunta persona* with Magellan. Was he really joint commander with Magellan? It seems more likely to have been a clerical oversight stemming from being Faleiro's replacement, the scribe assuming that the king wished to grant him all Faleiro's rights and duties. Faleiro would have been joint captain general with Magellan, a matter that was understood and agreed to, but granting the same title and authority to this bumptious young courtier with no sea experience, defies reason. Furthermore, if Cartagena had asserted what he later said was his authority before leaving Sanlucar, instead of waiting until the fleet had been at sea for over a month before challenging Magellan, it would not have led to his death.

There is little doubt that it was not what Charles V intended. The emperor always referred to Magellan as *Capitán Mayor* or senior captain. As well, he also ordered all senior officers, before the fleet left, to swear to obey Magellan *en todo*, in all respects.

Before sailing, Charles V conferred upon Magellan the title of the Order of Santiago, an honour he did not extend to Cartagena, or even after the voyage to Elcano.

Charles V personally discharged Ruy Faleiro and was obliged to order another troublemaker, Luis de Mendoza, captain of *Victoria*, to swear unhesitating obedience to Magellan. As he failed to do this it would have been better had he been ordered to stay in Spain instead of later providing food for the vultures in Patagonia. Mentally deranged, Faleiro was placed in the *casa de locos* when Magellan sailed. He quarreled with his family, returned to Portugal, was put in jail, and after serving the sentence returned to Spain to sue for the salary he would have been paid had he gone to sea. As it sadly turned out, he died in poverty in 1544.

Contracts were drawn up, detailing the size of the armada, composed of *San Antonio*, *Trinidad*, *Concepción*, *Victoria*, and *Santiago*, ranging in tonnage from 75 to 120. Each had three masts, two square-rigged and the mizzen lateen. According to the historian Antonio de Herrera, Magellan's vessels had exceedingly high stern castles, to accommodate the unusually large number of officers. The sterncastle had evolved from the square *toldilla* looking like a box, to a functional two to three-deck superstructure. This 'cage work', as it is called in English or '*obra muerta*' in Spanish, was not such a drawback to navigation as one might think as the very light woodwork and the high sides helped a ship to sail when on a broad reach.

Matters of payments, profits, were set out and recorded in the contracts. Magellan and Faleiro were to receive one-twentieth of the profits, benefits that would be handed down to their heirs. Additionally they would be given the government of all lands discovered, with title of *Adelantados*. The ships were heavily armed and well supplied with trading goods, which included, in addition to 20,000 hawk-bells and brass bracelets, 500 looking glasses, bolts of velvet, and 2,000 pounds of mercury. Magellan having had experience with sultans and rajahs in the Indian Ocean saw to it that his fleet also carried presents chosen to appeal to the sophisticated princes of Asia. The crew, made up of 234 officers and men, included Portuguese, Italians, Frenchmen, Greeks, one Englishman- 'Master Andrew of Bristol'- and the inevitable Irishman from Galway, since it was not easy to find Spaniards for such a dangerous a voyage under the command of a foreign adventurer. All five ships had Portuguese pilots and the Casa de Contratación certified all professionals. Magellan managed to sign on four relatives: his brother-in-law Duarte Barbosa with his natural son Cristóbal Rebelo, and two cousins, Álvaro de Mezquita and Martín de Magallanes. Barbosa, murdered later in Cebu, had gained sea experience under the Portuguese almost equal to Magellan's. He had spent the years between 1501-1516 in the Portuguese service in the Far East. When Magellan married his sister, he happened to be in the house in Seville and signed up for the voyage. He proved to be a tower of strength to the Captain General, whom he survived by only one week.

From Barcelona on 8 May 1519 Charles V issued the final voluminous instructions down to the last detail for the voyage, in no less than seventy-four paragraphs. Quite likely upon reading the instructions, Magellan might have chuckled and asked himself if His Royal Highness doubted if he had ever been to sea.

Among the lucky coincidences of Magellan's voyage none was more fortunate for us than the presence on board of a gentleman volunteer that appears on the flagship's crew list as 'Antonio Lombardo.' He turned out to be Antonio Pigafetta of Vicenza in Lombardy. Despite writing the most notable sea narrative of his century, we have little knowledge of his life before he came to Spain in the suite of the papal ambassador to the court of Charles V. He tells us that 'prompted by a craving for experience and glory', he applied for and received permission from the king to sign up for the voyage. Personable, with a voracious appetite for facts and a boundless admiration for Magellan, he kept a detailed journal from which he later wrote the most vivid account of the great voyage, *Viaggio di Antonio Pigafetta intorno al globo terraqueo*.[7] His ability with languages and his talent to deal with the natives on a sensible level led Magellan to send him ashore to pacify them. Time and again he showed his genius for survival, and fortunately he was one of only eighteen alive at the completion of the round-the-world voyage.

Unfortunately, Magellan's diaries, written in his own hand, have disappeared, confiscated by the Portuguese governor of the fortress at the island of Ternate, Antonio de Brito, together with all other books and scientific instruments on board. Francisco Albo, a Greek mariner and principal European pilot of the expedition, boatswain of the flagship, and an independent-minded man aloof from politics, left a precious diary, as did the astrologer, astronomer, cosmographer, Andrés de San Martin, in charge of calculating latitude, quoted later by historians before the manuscripts were lost in the earthquake of Lisbon.[8] The diary of Serrano, who perished with Magellan in Cebu with thirty-four companions, is another element of the jigsaw puzzle used in piecing together the history of the voyage. The historians Goão de Barros and Antonio Herrera based their accounts on these diaries copied before they were destroyed in the earthquake.[9] Another anonymous diary, thought to be from the pen of León Pancaldo, a Genoese Pilot in the fleet, *Derrotero del viaje de Magallanes*, describes the voyage from Cape San Agustín in Brazil onwards. But both Serrano's and Pancaldo's notes are in the form of diaries, or logbooks, giving only the cold facts of dates and names without the vividness of Pigafetta's detailed journal. Some light is cast from an anonymous diary of a Portuguese seaman aboard *Victoria* and published later, as the account was compiled at the request of Pope Leo X by Peter Martyr d'Anghiera from interviews with the few surviving members of the expedition.

However exaggerated Pigafetta's account sometimes is – the birds of Giava carrying buffaloes over the trees in their talons; women becoming pregnant by the wind; the women of Malua whose ears were bigger than their bodies; and his famous description of the inhabitant of Patagonia 'egli era cosí alto, che il piú alto di noi gli arriva alla cintura', they were so tall that I did not reach up to their waist – caused some in future generations to have ridiculed his account, Nevertheless, Pigafetta's history of the voyage stands out by far as the most graphic, colourful and detailed of the eyewitness accounts of the great voyage.[10]

Considering Magellan's feat by any measure, be it moral, intellectual, or physical, it would excel that of Da Gama, Columbus, or Vespucci. He would face rougher seas, negotiate more treacherous passages, and find his way across a broader ocean. He faced a more mutinous crew, yet managed his command with astonishing firmness, fierce discipline, and determination. He bore the most excruciating pangs of hunger without wincing. 'Among the other virtues which he possessed', observed Pigafetta, 'he was always the most constant in greatest adversity. He endured hunger better than all the rest and more accurately than any man in the world; he understood dead reckoning and celestial navigation. No other had so much talent, nor the ardor to learn how to go around the world which he almost did.'

Before finally setting sail from Sanlucar de Barrameda, Magellan alone received the royal standard in solemn ceremony at the church of Santa Maria de la Victoria de Triana.

On 10 August 1519, sailing orders were presented to Magellan by the young emperor himself to be opened when he was at sea:

> Your principal aim will be to explore all those parts of the ocean which are on the side of the line of demarcation. You are also enjoined to discover there all that has not yet been discovered, taking every care neither to cross the limits agreed upon with the king of Portugal, nor to give him any other cause for offence, but to keep strictly within the bounds of our own line of demarcation.

The emperor added:

> Knowing that the spices are to be found in the Moluccas and that your main task is to seek for them, my command is that you should shape your course directly for those islands.

Nothing could have been more in agreement with Magellan's own intentions.

As the ships were slowly carried on the ebb downstream on the Guadalquivir, thus began the fateful expedition that would shrink the globe and open it to all navigators forever. The task ahead was to find a channel connecting the Atlantic with Balboa's 'South Sea' that would lead them on to the fabled Spice Islands.

Before leaving, Magellan issued stringent rules to his captains to keep his fleet together and under his control. 'The flagship *Trinidad* at all times will sail ahead of the others', he said. 'Each vessel must approach her towards nightfall and ask for orders, and then follow lights kindled from wood in iron cressets on her stern; the *farol* principal light to be made from a torch of pitchy wood or an old hemp rope soaked in oil. Another light was made by means of a lantern with a wick made from a rush called *esparto* that had been well beaten in the water, and then dried in the sun. The flagship will show two lights, besides that of the *farol*, if the fleet is to come about or wear, three as a signal to reduce sail, four to strike sail. Any ship from which land is sighted should fire a gun.'[11]

Magellan set a course *suroeste* – south-west and with a fair wind his ships romped through the waters and reached Tenerife in the Canaries after six sailing days. Before departing the island another caravel reached port with an ominous message to Magellan from is father-in-law, Diego Barbosa. It warned him that his three Spanish captains Quesada, Cartagena and Mendoza were planning to kill him. The bitter reality of what he already suspected made him wary and it is not the least of his triumph that he had the wit and firmness to dispose of them later. Magellan sent a decisive reply to Barbosa by the returning caravel, saying that whatever happened he would do his duty as a servant of the king-emperor, even if it cost him his life.[12]

They departed The Canaries on 3 October 1519. At sea the fleet followed a south-west course down to latitude 27° N, and then changed to south by west. One evening Juan de Cartagena in *San Antonio* sailed up with visible annoyance under the flagship's stern and demanded on the megaphone why he had changed course? Magellan tersely answered him, '*Que me siguiera, y no me pidas mas cuentas*' – 'Follow me and ask no further questions!'

Magellan had good reason to hug the African coast at first. The shipmaster that had sold him the *bacalao* – the salt cod – at Tenerife warned him that the king of Portugal had sent out a fleet to intercept him on his Atlantic crossing, in the same way as Dom João II had attempted to with Columbus. This time Dom Manuel had sent out not one but two intercepting fleets. Due to the likelihood Magellan decided to play safe and elude them by avoiding the direct course to Brazil. He paralleled the African coast to a low latitude, and then he sailed across the Atlantic Narrows, though this course cost him time and discomfort.

On 18 October, off Sierra Leone, the fleet ran into a series of bad storms. Pigafetta tells us that 'As we could not advance and in order that the ships might not be wrecked, all their sails were struck and in this manner did we wander hither and yon on the sea, waiting for the tempest to cease, for it was very furious.' Sharks cruised around. St Elmo's fire – Camoens' 'living light, which sailors hold sacred' – blazed for two hours from the masthead of the flagship, 'with the brightness of a blazing torch... When that blessed light was about to leave us, so dazzling was the brightness it cast into our eyes, that we all remained for more than an eighth of an hour blinded and calling for mercy. And truly when we thought we were dead men, the sea suddenly grew calm.' He also states that he saw a bird with no anus and another whose hen, having no feet, laid her eggs on the back of the cock never touching the earth in the process. Pigafetta was a product of a world that was gullible, ignorant and superstitious. There was something of Sinbad the Sailor in Pigafetta.[13] Nevertheless his tales, although sometimes inaccurate, are always amusing.

The captain's cautious sailing close to the African coast brought them into the equatorial calms and for many days the ships were becalmed. The heat became oppressive, and inactivity proved a good breeding ground for sedition. Juan de

Cartagena, captain of the *San Antonio*, after brooding over the snub he had received from Magellan after changing course, decided to contest the order that each vessel approach the flagship every evening to hail the Captain General and receive his oral orders. The proper hail, the same as used on Columbus' voyages was, '*Dios os salve señor capitan general y maestro, y buena compañía*' – 'God keep you sir captain general and master, and good company.' One evening Cartagena, instead of calling it out, sent a petty officer and had him leave out the title, *general* – a double insult to Magellan. Quick to perceive the provocation Magellan answered that in future he expected to be addressed properly, and by the captain himself. Cartagena impertinently retorted that he had sent his best man to give the hail, and that if he didn't like it he would send a page to do it next time. It has been said that Magellan treated Cartagena too roughly, but it is well to remember that Magellan was a Portuguese nobleman, who had little reason to suffer insolence from a bishop's bastard, especially one that was plotting mutiny to usurp his command and murder him.

Three days later, wallowing in the gloomy calm of the doldrums and after two repetitions of the insult, Magellan summoned a court martial with all the four captains present to try the quartermaster of *Victoria* for sodomy with a ship's boy. Both parties were found guilty and condemned to death. After the trial Magellan remained in the great cabin sitting at the stern side of the table facing Captain Cartagena of *San Antonio*, Captain Quesada of *Concepción*, Captain Mendoza of *Victoria* and Captain Serrano of *Santiago*. The climate in the cabin was oppressive, sweat poured from their faces down their beards and shirts while the ship rolled from side to side with no wind to stabilise her. The first three captains were in the plot. Cartagena looked at Magellan across the table and accused him of getting them into this wretched calm belt through his lack of navigation skills. Watching them under his thick brows, Magellan remained quiet waiting for their move. Taking this for timidity and hoping to provoke the planned fight in which the Captain General would be killed, Cartagena roared out that he for one would no longer obey Magellan's orders. Expecting as much, the Captain General looked up and made a gesture. At this signal, the *aguacil mayor*, chief marshal of *Trinidad*, Gonzálo Gomez de Espinosa, well armed and with breastplate and helmet on, broke into the cabin, followed by Duarte Barbosa and Cristóbal Rebelo with drawn swords. Magellan sprang on Cartagena, grabbed him by the front of his elegant shirt, and forcing him to keep seated, cried out, 'Rebel, this is mutiny! You are my prisoner, in the king's name!' Cartagena screamed at his allies Mendoza and Quesada to plunge their daggers into Magellan 'according to plan' – thus incriminating himself and his friends – but they dared not move.

Gómez de Espinosa forced Cartagena down to the main deck and clapped him into the stocks normally occupied by common seamen for minor offences. Quesada and Mendoza implored the Captain General to grant him better treatment. Since neither of the two had outwardly been involved as a mutineer, Magellan consented, to release Cartagena into the care of Mendoza in *Victoria* who, if he broke the trust conferred in him would be implicated in mutiny.

1 Spices of the world.

2 An eighteenth-century camel caravan, from Engelbert Kaempfer's *Five Studies of Exotic Wonders*.

3 *Left:* Inspecting cinnamon at the docks in London before auction, 1903.

4 *Below:* Ternate (Indonesia), island of cloves, with its threatening volcano and Dutch Ternatean vessels lying offshore.

5 Cloves, a source of endless warfare. From G.E. Rumphius' *Arbon Herbal* (1741-1750).

6 Harvesting cinnamon.

7 *Above left:* Saracen warriors guarding the prison camp at Tabriz.

8 *Above right:* Marco Polo's party in the Badakshan mountains.

9 *Left:* Desert marauders.

10 Marco Polo's great desert, known today as the Gobi desert.

11 No frills accommodation. (*National Geographic* magazine. Photograph by Michael Yamashita)

12 *Left:* Marco Polo.

13 *Below:* The Great Pamir. (*National Geographic* magazine. Photograph by Michael Yamashita)

14 The innovation of the lateen rig (at the stern) and sternpost rudder allowed ships like this fifteenth-century German caravel to make transoceanic voyages in all weathers. Columbus crossed to the New World in such a ship.

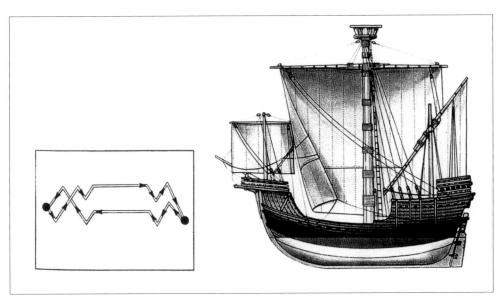

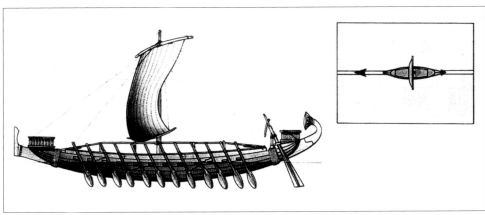

15 *Opposite above:* The first ocean-going rig: a mixture of square sail and lateen on a cargo vessel, easily manoeuvred with the help of a sternpost rudder.

16 *Opposite middle:* The typical square sail, used from Egyptian times. The smaller diagram shows how the pilot was dependent on wind direction, making oars vital to make headway in contrary winds.

17 *Opposite below:* Once the lateen-rigged ship was under way, the sail would provide enough thrust to keep the ship moving even almost into the wind. A course into the wind could be maintained by moving in a series of zig-zags, as the diagram shows.

18 *Right:* The traverse board, used by sailors up to the end of the nineteenth century. The rows of holes along the bottom showed how long the ship had travelled during each change of direction, each hole representing a predetermined period of time measured by a sandglass.

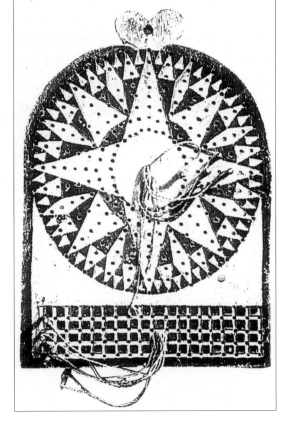

19 *Below:* The constellation of the Great Bear, shown in one of the earliest Islamic manuals of astronomy (AD1009), based on Ptolemy's 'Mathematike Syntaxis'. Next to it is a brass astrolabe, an instrument developed by the Arab astronomers to be used at particular latitudes to enable dates and times to be read from star tables, by rotating the metal network so that the points of the spurs came to rest on the positions of the stars.

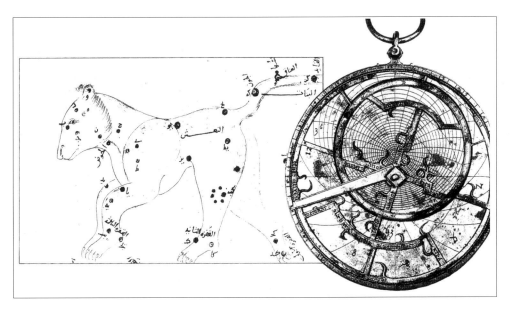

20 The boxed compass, showing the division of the circle into thirty-two parts.

21 A mosaic from Ostia, the port of Rome, showing its lighthouse, perhaps the best known in antiquity after the Pharos.

22 *Above:* This drawing is a medieval artist's impression of what ancient Alexandria looked like. Note the Pharos lighthouse built on the tongue of land at the bottom right; the Pharos was so impressive that its name passed into Mediterranean language as the word for lighthouse.

23 *Right:* Henry the Navigator; detail of a triptych attributed to Nuno Gonçalves, *c.*1465–1470, in the Museo National de Arte Antga, Lisbon.

24 Prince Henry the Navigator with his cartographers.

25 Columbus, an oil painting by Sebastiano del Piombo, 1519. In the Metropolitan Museum of Art, New York.

26 The Empress Isabel, portrait by
Jan Vermeyen; R.Tod-White
photograph. Courtesy of owner, Lady
Merton of Maidenhead Thicket.

27 The Emperor Charles V, portrait
by Jan Vermeyen; R. Tod-White
photograph. Courtesy of owner,
Lady Merton of Maidenhead
Thicket.

28 Isabella of Castile. Flemish School.
Original in Windsor Castle, courtesy of
Keeper of HM Paintings, Windsor Castle.

29 Ferdinand of Aragon. Flemish School.
Original in Windsor Castle, courtesy of
Keeper of HM Paintings, Windsor Castle.

Don HERNANDO el V. Rey de Castilla y Doña ISABEL Reyna de
Castilla, adquieren la empresa de Don Christoval Colon, y sale
de Palos para su viage à las Indias a 3 de Agosto año 1492

30 Right: A contemporary illustration of Christopher Columbus taking his leave of the Catholic monarchs.

31 Below: The port of Seville in the time of Columbus.

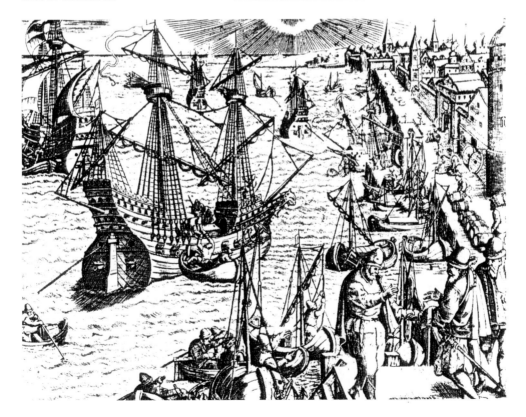

32 *Left:* Alfonso d'Albuquerque.

33 *Below:* Vasco de Gama.

34 Map of the world by Petro Apiano, 1520.

35 Reinactment of Cabral's arrival at Porto Seguro, Brazil, in 1500. *La Nacion*, 21 April 2000.

35 *Above:* Expedition of Amerigo Vespucci leaving Portugal.

36 *Below:* Top part of Waldseemüller's map of 1507, with the figures of Tolomeo and Vespucio left and right.

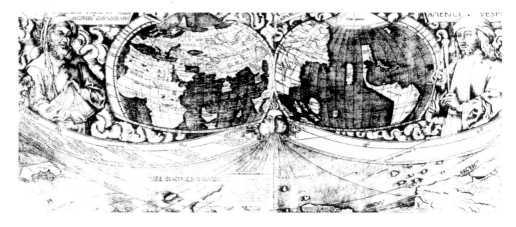

37 Head of Venus, detail from the 'Birth of Venus' by Sandro Botticelli, thought to have been Simonetta Vespucci.

38 Above: Allegory of Vespucci, after arrival in South America.

39 Opposite: A piece of Waldseemüller's map of 1507; he stamped the name of the Southern continent America on it, clearly visible. Also note 'Pinachullo Detentio', later known as Cerro de Montevideo.

América

Sanct michaelis

Rio de S. francisco
vazia barril
Rio de perera
Serra de S. maria de ginaa
Rio de casa

porto real
Rio s. iberonimi
Isle de oro
Rio domezo
Monte fregoso

Abbatia omniū
Sanctorum

Rio graco
Rio s. augustini
Rio de s. lucia
Rio de virgine
Rio de s. vidam
porto seguro
barcres veancops

Rio de brazil
baxosa

Mont pascoal
Rio de s. lucia

Serra S. thome

pagus s. pauli
Rio da tesons
luic betes
Pinachullo detentio
Rio ior dam
Rio de s. Anthonio
prias s. Stefam
ponus s. vitam
Rio de anana

Capistaneo nauls quod nos dedim: cū
ser Bortu jolie ad solicitiā meri
ta bic primū apparuit: que credeba
firmā cum revera sit cum prius ina
borre circū suo mire sed nō bū pro
cognite magnitud nis insula. in q
virilla ac feminei ction secus homi
con aliter quam eos mater peper
ite asuewerunt. Et sunt bii quide p
lo alb cor cis quod superior naut
sione re mandas regis Castille sac
repeture

pinachullo detentio

Rio iordam?

Rio de S. Anthonio
Punta S. Sebastian

bande
erroneā
coloc

40 *Above: Victoria* after circumnavigating the globe.

41 *Below:* Port San Julian. (Courtesy of Argentine Historical Branch of the Navy)

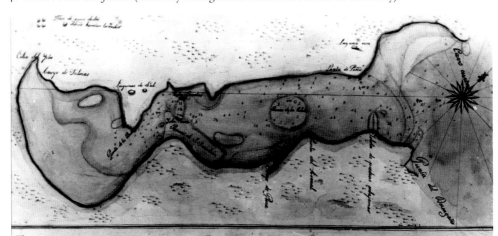

FERDINAN·MAGELLANVS·SVPERATIS·
ANTARCTICI·FRETI·ANGVSTIIS·CLARISS·

42 Right: This anonymous
sixteenth-century portriat of
Magellan is one of the few accurate
likenesses of the explorer.

43 Below: Puerto Deseado a fines
del siglo XVI. Cobre de Merian
(1655).

This anonymous sixteenth-century portrait of Magellan is one of the few accurate
likenesses of the explorer.

Porto Desire.

44 *Above:* Allegorical drawing of Magellan's arrival in Patagonia.
45 *Below left:* Magellan entering the Strait, ostriches behind.
46 *Below right:* The *Victoria*.

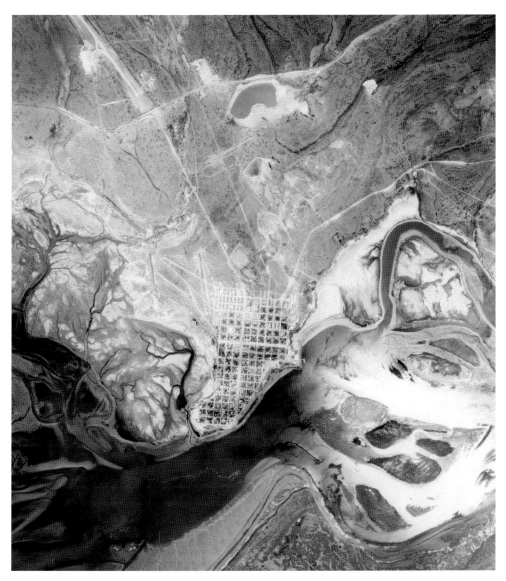

47 Arial view of the port of San Julian - Armada Argentina.

48 *Above:* Bay of Port Desire – Magellan's expedition, killing seals, ostriches and guanacos above. Copper engraving by Merrian (1655).

49 *Below:* An Ona family on the move. Photograph A.M. de Agostini, the Salesian missionary.

50 Right: Two Ona
girls in their guanaco
skins. Photograph
A.M. de Agostini.

51 Below: Map of
Magellan's route.

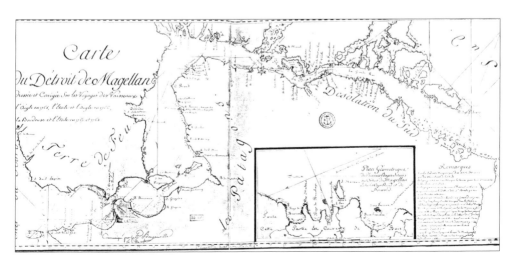

52 *Left:* Straights of Magellan.

53 *This page, middle:* Sketch of Cape Virgins.

54 *This page, bottom:* Cape Virgins bearing 220°.

55 *Opposite above:* Royal canoes from Ternate and Tidore with crescent and helicod profiles, from F. Valentijn, *Oud en nieuw Oost-Indien.*

56 *Opposite below:* Arms of Elrano.

Sketch of Cape Virgins, in Guillemard's *Magellan.*

Punta Dungeness.
Cabo Vírgenes.

Cabo Vírgenes bearing 220°, distant 4 miles.

(*Original dated* 1923.)

Arms of Elcano

Prima ego velivolis ambivi cursibus Orbem,
Magellane novo te duce ducta freto.
Ambivi, meritoq3 vocor VICTORIA: sunt mî
Vela, alæ; precium, gloria; pugna, mare.

57 *Above:* The caravel *Vittoria*, the first ship to circumnaviage the globe.

58 *Left:* Giovanno Sebatiano Elcano.

59 *Opposite above:* Careening I: French corvette hove down. This process was only undertaken in calm weather for safety. This was probaby a Mediterranean harbour.

60 *Opposite below:* Portrait of Francis Drake engraved by Crispin van der Passe, from *Effigies regum ac principum*, Cologne 1598. (Courtesy of the British Library)

61 *Left:* Portrait of Francis Drake.

62 *Below:* John Hawkin's ill-fated flagship, the *Jesus of Lübeck*.

Following this Magellan had trumpets sounded to draw everyone's attention, where upon he announced the appointment of Antonio de Coca as captain of *San Antonio*.

Carried by the currents the ships broke out of the doldrums at last and with the blessed trade wind the ships finally gathered speed. Magellan called João Lopes Carvalho, pilot of *Concepción*, to the *Trinidad* who knew the coast better then anyone on board. Carvalho explained that if one made a landfall near Cape São Roque, at 5° S, on the bulge of the Brazilian coast, one was likely to be becalmed. So Magellan made for Cape São Agostinho instead at latitude 8° 20', which marks the harbour of Pernambuco, now Recife. The fleet arrived off it on 29 November 1519.

Wishing to avoid being sighted by the Portuguese who had established a *feitoria* at Pernambuco, keeping out of sight he headed southwest by south keeping the shore in sight. On 13 December, 100 miles after passing Cabo Frio, they entered the Bay of Guanabara. *Trinidad* proudly led the way past the famous *Pão de Açúcar* or Sugar Loaf and anchored close to the settlement in seven fathoms. Magellan christened it after St Lucy whose day it was. However, Vespucci had already entered it in the first week of January 1502, and had named it Río de Janeiro, River of January. There they stayed two weeks until the day of St John, the 26th of the month. It proved to be the merriest part of the voyage for all hands, although the description of what was fun would have shocked St Lucy.

After casting anchors the ships were surrounded and then boarded by swarms of naked natives of the *Tupinamba* tribe. Carvalho, a none too savory person, who previously had spent four years among these Indians, warned the sailors that the native husbands were famous for their jealousy and would strongly resent any advances to their wives who would not dare to shame their husbands either. The young girls on the other hand were free game for all provided their brothers were paid adequately for their services.

Carvalho struck a good deal with the natives: every sailor could have his girl for the price of a cheap German knife, carried in the slopchests, paid to her brother. Nightly revelry took place on shore, when sailors and Indian girls whooped it up and enjoyed each other. The more attractive girls earned bonuses, in Venetian beads, hawk's bells, or crimson cloth, over the agreed-upon dirt-cheap knife. One day, Pigafetta tells us, 'a beautiful young woman came to the flagship, where I was, for no other purpose than to seek what chance might offer. While there and waiting, she cast her eyes upon the master's room, and saw a [shiny brass ship's]-nail longer than one's finger. Picking it up very delightedly and neatly, she thrust it through the lips of her vagina [natura], and bending down low immediately departed, the Captain General and I having seen that action.'[14]

Carvalho as well had his own bonus. His former Brazilian girl appeared with their seven-year-old son. The pilot signed up the boy as his *criado* or servant but he could not persuade Magellan to allow the mother to come along. The Captain General never permitted women on board at sea. Before the ships left a port at which there had been such revelry, he caused the *aguacil* to search the nooks and crannies of every ship to flush out any female stowaways.

Not only did the visitors find good trading in girls but the Indians loved playing cards. 'For a king of diamonds, they gave me six fowls and thought they had even cheated me', Pigafetta wrote. You could buy a slave with a hatchet, but Magellan forbade it, basically because he wanted no other mouths to feed sensing what lay ahead.

Again, this time at Río de Janeiro, mutiny raised its ugly head. Antonio de Coca, captain of *San Antonio*, and Bishop Fonseca's nephew, released Juan de Cartagena and the other prisoners. Magellan sent Gomez de Espinosa with a handful of armed men to put the mutiny down and again entrusted the safekeeping of Coca and Cartagena to Captain Mendoza of *Victoria*. He followed by naming his cousin Alvaro de Mezquita as captain of *San Antonio*. There was not that many Magellan could count on as faithful to him and Mezquita proved to be a weak choice. Promoted over many others he gave cause to be sneered at by the hard-bitten types he now found under him.

After Christmas at Río, they said goodbye to the glorious harbour and departed the next day. Now began the serious quest for the Strait. Magellan sailed his ships as close to the coast as he dared, often heaving the lead and investigating any likely opening. On 12 January 1520, the fleet passed between Lobos Island and the shore. At the entrance to the great Río de la Plata estuary, rounding Cabo Santa María – now the beach resort of Punta del Este, in Uruguay – he entered Maldonado Bay. There they rode out a storm in the lee of Gorriti, a little island off its center. The following day they once more got under way and came in sight of Monte Vidi. On they went and on 14 January found they were sailing in fresh water. On the evening of 15 January, they cast anchors in one of the coves of Punta Colonia. The next day Magellan sent Juan Serrano in *Santiago*, his lightest-draft vessel, up-river to reconnoiter hoping to find an outlet to 'the other' sea. According to Albo's diary, Serrano, finding the entrance to another great river, the Uruguay, went up it as far as the entrance to the Río Negro. After a fifteen-day reconnaissance Juan Serrano returned to the anchorage at Colonia. In the meantime, Magellan, with another two ships in company, sailed southwest to the other side of the estuary and back in four days. He had also sent a longboat from each ship to make a detailed search of their surroundings.[15] All in all, the exploration proved the great opening from the Atlantic not to be an arm of the sea but due to the evidence of it shoaling and its water becoming fresh, Magellan and his captains concluded it was a river. Magellan called it Río de Solis after the great Spanish navigator murdered there by the Charrúua Indians only four years before.[16]

Convinced that the Strait lay ahead, the Captain General pressed on, hoping to find it before the Antarctic winter closed in.[17] He crossed the great estuary on course south-west and anchored for the night off today's Cabo San Antonio. He usually chose to anchor at night, weather permitting, so as not to miss anything. Then during the day he applied a rule of thumb for this coast – 'as many miles as fathoms' – meaning if 8 miles off the coast you will find a depth of eight fathoms. For instance, from Cabo San Antonio to Mar del Plata, the ten-fathom line runs close to 10 miles from shore. It is only approximate, of course.

On 13 February, anchored off Bahía Blanca, their cables held during a violent storm. *Victoria* received a number of *culadas*, literally 'ass-hits' on her keel. A startlingly beautiful St Elmo's fire played about the spars as explains Pigafetta, '…the ships suffered a very great storm, during which the three holy bodies appeared to us many times, that is to say, St Elmo, St Nicholas, and St Clara, whereupon the storm quickly ceased.' Here, Magellan adopted a new twenty-four-hour schedule, sailing one league from the land by day and five leagues off the shore by night.

Further south, on 24 February 1520, they chose a snug little harbour in the crook of the Peninsula Valdéz. He named it *Puerto de San Matías,* since it was the saint's day. Now it is called Golfo Nuevo, a protected little spot where whales cavort in their mating season and hundreds of tourist's flock to see them. On 27 February they anchored off a large bay they named *Bahía de los Patos,* owing to the huge number of penguins, for which the Europeans as yet had no name except *patos sin alas*, wingless ducks. The ship's boat was still slaughtering them, as well as an elephant seal, when an offshore gale sprung up and blew the fleet out to sea. The unfortunate sailors on shore had to cover themselves with the hide of the dead seal and rotting penguins to avoid being frozen to death. When the ships returned to fetch them the men were half frozen and smelled horribly.

The place was most likely the shallow bay at *Cabo dos Bahías*, with its three islands named *Sansón*. Why the name? We do not know. Might it be a reference to the stature of the natives Magellan would discover naming the region Patagonia after them? Unlikely, I think.[18] However, the natural grass, green in the Antarctic spring, brown the rest of the year, and crossed by numerous rivers, are pastures for enormous herds of guanaco, which one might name the southern llama, as well as pumas, Patagonian-hares and flocks of rhea (the American ostrich). Physically, Patagonia corresponds to the North American West, between the Great Plains and the Rockies. Equally daunting, often bleak, its far horizons, untempered winds, where any movement can be seen for miles and miles: it inspires both love and hatred. 'The land of the strong man and the free soul!' To quote the farewell of an early explorer.

Storm after storm was ridden out; these were the infamous *pamperos*, line squalls that blow like hurricanes across the vastness of the plains with great ferocity, often carrying everything before them. Six stormy days were ridden out in a bay that Magellan called *Bahía de los Trabajos*, 'Bay of Travail', identified today as Port Desire or *Puerto Deseado* at latitude 47° 46' S. named so by Thomas Cavendish in 1587. Fitzroy with Darwin, later spent Christmas there in 1833 aboard the *Beagle*, and wrote in his log that it was 'a wretched place.' Present-day sailing directions warn one that 'heavy gales…rising without warning' are prevalent.

After leaving port more bad weather battered the ships. They covered only 120 miles in three days due to more south-westerlies. To make matters more ominous, they were continually without a glimpse of sunshine. Day after day they drove their ships into mountainous seas under a leaden skies with temperatures dropping by the hour. Finally, at latitude 49° 20'S, they entered *Puerto San Julián,*[19] on the last day of

March 1520, the eve of Palm Sunday. The summer was over and winter descended like none they had ever known. The Captain General announced the fleet would stay riding to their anchors until the weather offered some respite and the prospect of searching the coast for the entrance to the Strait. And there Magellan stayed for four months and twenty-four days to face his greatest test of command.

Puerto San Julián offers a spacious and sheltered harbour but there is a bleak, depressing aspect about it. It is a desolate spot with sparse vegetation to break the monotonous grey of sea, sky and rocks. Seawards, the entrance is between the hundred-foot-high gray cliffs of Capes Curioso and Desengaño. These converge like the ends of a horseshoe to form a half-mile-wide bottleneck at the entrance. The tidal range is 7–8½m, and the current at the narrow entrance runs up to 6 knots. Cunning Magellan thought it wise to anchor his flagship in the bottleneck so that any vessel trying to escape would be within range of his guns.

Pigafetta tells us that no native inhabitant appeared for two months until:

> One day we suddenly saw a naked man of giant stature on the shore of the port, dancing, singing, and throwing dust on his head. The Captain General sent one of our men to the giant so that he might perform the same actions as a sign of peace. Having done that, the man led the giant to an islet into the presence of the Captain General. When the giant was in our presence he marveled greatly, and made signs with one finger raised upward, believing we had come from the sky. He was so tall that we reached only to his waist, and he was well proportioned. His face was large and painted red all over, while about his eyes he was painted yellow; and he had two hearts painted on the middle of his cheeks. His scanty hair was painted white. He was dressed in the skins of animals skillfully sewn together. That animal has a head and ears as large as those of a mule, a neck and body like those of a camel, the legs of a deer, and the tail of a horse, like which it neighs, and that land has many of them.

He is referring to the guanaco. The man's feet 'were shod with the same kind of skins, which covered his feet in the manner of shoes.' These guanaco-skin sandals stuffed with straw made his feet look huge, which caused Magellan to name him *Patagón* (big foot), and his country Patagonia.' Although Pigafetta greatly exaggerated the Indian's height, later explorers described these natives as taller than average Europeans. The Captain General had the giant given something to eat and drink and among other things, which were shown to him, was a large steel mirror. 'When he saw his face, he was greatly terrified and jumped back throwing three or four of our men to the ground.' Other natives turned up with their tame guanacos, as well as their women, their true beasts of burden. 'Their women laden like asses carried everything' as Pigafeta tells us.[20]

> These were short and squat and very much fatter than their men, with painted faces, matted hair, and breasts that hung down half a fathom. Clothed like their husbands, except that before their privies (natura) they have a small skin that covers them. They

seemed utterly repugnant to the members of the crews. To impress the Spaniards, some of the men would perform their own version of the sword-swallowing trick by putting arrows down their gullets and then drawing them out without harm. However, of eighteen that were enticed aboard the ships, one stayed for about a week and was christened Johanni. He learned to say the words '*Jesu, Pater Noster, Ave Maria and Jovani*', John, as distinctly as we, but with an exceedingly loud voice. The Captain General gave him a shirt, a woolen jerkin [*camisota de panno*], cloth breeches, a cap, a mirror, a comb, bells, and other things, and sent him away like his companions.[21]

A fortnight later, four natives appeared and Magellan kidnapped two by a very mean trick. He gave them knives, scissors, mirrors, bells, and glass beads; and those two having their hands heaped with the said articles, the Captain General had two pairs of iron manacles fastened to their feet. 'When they saw later that they were tricked' wrote Pigafetta, 'they raged like bulls, calling for their god *Setebos* to aid them.'[22] These, and few others, were the only contacts Magellan and his men had with the natives during their dreary five-month stay at Puerto San Julián.

Just after arrival at Port San Julián, on 31 March 1520, Magellan, after reducing rations, held a meeting with delegates from all five ships. The men demanded that he restore full rations and return to Spain; they doubted that any strait existed and feared that if they continued they would die of starvation and freeze to death. Magellan replied that he would rather die than give up his quest for the Strait as he had been ordered to do by the king. Plenty of food could be had where they were and that they still had sufficient bread and wine from Spain. He pointed out that the Strait would be found, which would then lead them through to tropical islands whose girls were kinder and more beautiful than those in Rio de Janeiro. Finally, he said that Castilians had never been found wanting in courage, an inherent and distinctive characteristic of their character, and if they showed cowardice now they would be disparaged by their peers at home. The men, seemingly placated, returned to duty on their respective ships but conspiracy among the officers festered on.

The next day, Palm Sunday, Magellan summoned all officers to attend mass ashore coupled to an invitation for them to join him afterwards in the great stern cabin of *Trinidad*. Only his kinsman Álvaro de Mezquita accepted, an ominous sign that heralded the most unholy of Holy Weeks.

On the night of Palm Sunday, the mutineers took possession of three ships: *San Antonio* (Captain Mezquita), *Concepción* (Captain Quesada), and *Victoria* (Captain Mendoza). Cartagena, the deposed captain of *San Antonio*, stabbed though failed to kill Elorriaga, the loyal master of that ship, and clapped Captain Mezquita in irons. Having taken care of the largest ship, Quesada and Elcano overwhelmed the crew of *Concepción*, while Mendoza got control of *Victoria*.

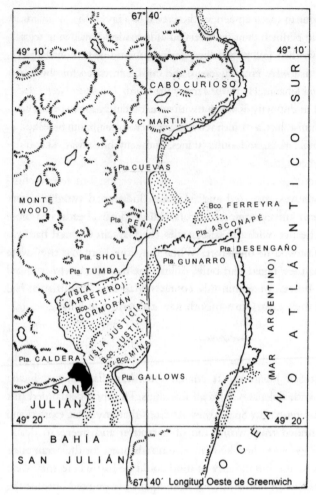

San Julián Bay.

The following day, Quesada sent Coca in the longboat to Magellan in *Trinidad* with a message signed by the leading three mutineers saying that the Captain General was disobeying his instructions by leading them so far south. No longer would they recognise him, as Captain General, but would follow him as senior captain if he took them back to Spain. Magellan gave them no reply but with a stroke of cunning, gained over years of experience in survival, he detained the boat and its crew. Dressing his own men in their clothes, he manned the longboat with them. He then let the boat out tied to a long enough hawser to carry it close to *Victoria* to quietly await events. Magellan then dispatched aguacil Gonzalo Gómez de Espinosa in his own gig with a half-dozen trusty men to *Victoria* with a letter ordering Mendoza to return to his duty and report on board the flagship. Magellan instructed Espinosa to kill him if he refused to obey.

Espinosa and his men rowed across and were allowed to board *Victoria*. At being told he had a private message for the captain, Mendoza allowed them to climb up the side and admitted the *aguacil* and one of his men-at-arms to his cabin. After reading Magellan's letter, Mendoza crumpled it his hand as if to throw it away and laughed scornfully. Espinosa stretched out his left hand as if to take the rejected letter and with a fast movement grasped Mendoza's beard. Jerking back his head, he drew his knife across his neck and cut his throat, while his man-at-arms finished him off by stabbing the victim's head.

The longboat, with Duarte Barbosa and his men was standing by a few yards upstream quietly awaiting a signal. Espinosa waved a cloth whereupon Barbosa ordered his hawser cast off. The current quickly took them alongside *Victoria* and the men-at-arms swarmed aboard the ship before her crew even knew of their captain's death. Barbosa appointed to command *Victoria* by Magellan, ordered anchors aweigh, and with the sweeps working, a foresail to catch the breeze, and the longboat towing astern, approached the flagship and anchored alongside. The always-loyal Serrano followed in his caravel *Santiago*, and anchored off *Trinidad*'s other board.

Seeing that Magellan now controlled three of the five ships, Gaspar de Quesada captain of *Concepción*, lost his nerve and tried to leave port under cover of night in company with *San Antonio*, of which Cartagena had usurped command. The scheme did not work because, before Quesada was ready to sail, a loyal seaman cut the *Concepción*'s cable and she drifted with the ebb tide within range of Magellan's ship *Trinidad*. When *Concepcion* came near enough the Captain General fired a point blank broadside at her, and men posted aloft raked her decks with crossbow fire. Quesada, dressed in full armor on the sterncastle of his ship with arrows bouncing off his steel corselet, tried in vain to rally his crew to fight back. Magellan with lowered brows, now had himself rowed to *Concepcion*, boarded her, and with drawn sword made Quesada surrender his ship.

After clapping both Quesada and Coca in irons aboard *Trinidad*, Magellan continued to quench the mutiny. Rowed by Espinosa to *San Antonio*, he hailed her. Cartagena in armor came to the rail dispirited and answered the hail in amicable terms. Espinosa climbed the rail and put him under arrest.

By extraordinary courage, sagacity, and wit, Magellan who earlier in the morning was outnumbered two to five, by evening ruled the whole fleet. A very serious mutiny had been put down with injury to only one loyal man, Juan de Elorriaga.

The following day, Tuesday, had Mendoza's body drummed through the fleet as a traitor, and then taken ashore and quartered. Portions were to be later displayed prominently on the ships of the fleet. He then called a formal court-martial which found Mendoza (represented by his quartered corpse), Cartagena, Coca, Elcano, Quesada, and Quesada's servant Molino, guilty of treason and condemned them to death with a further forty mutineers. Molino won his life as reward for executing his master by publicly beheading him, which he apparently did with relish. Quesada's body was then hanged on a gibbet next to Mendoza's remains, probably on the Isla Justicia upriver. But while Magellan had to make dramatic examples to demonstrate the power of 'cord and knife' bestowed upon him as commander, and to break once and for all the back of incipient rebellion, he dared not indulge in draconian punishment. Disease and shipboard accidents took a steady toll of life without further depleting his crews with a series of executions. His solution was to use capital punishment sparingly but dramatically. The execution of Quesada was a gesture and within days Magellan commuted the penalties: the offenders, except for Cartagena, were clapped in irons and condemned to hard labour for the remainder of the five-month stay in St Julian's Bay.

Magellan's leniency to Cartagena was misguided. He was found conspiring with one of the chaplains, Pedro Sanchez Reina, to stir the men up to fresh mutiny. Another court-martial found both guilty and sentenced them to be marooned.

Magellan did not win the hearts of his men nor had he put an end to disaffection. There would be further crisis of command but the Captain General had, for the time being, gained the grudging obedience of his crews.

Before leaving the depressing port of San Julián the fleet suffered another setback. The *Santiago*, under Captain Serrano, was shipwrecked while trying to locate the Strait southward. It happened about three leagues south of the Río Santa Cruz and Serrano sent two members of the crew to walk to San Julián for help. It took them eleven painful days stumbling across the edge of the snow-covered cliffs. Magellan promptly sent a rescue force by boat to Santa Cruz, and all were brought back safely after a month's privation.

Eager to get on, Magellan decided to spend the rest of the Antarctic winter at Río Santa Cruz. As the ships departed San Julián, the last sight his men saw was that of Juan de Cartagena and the priest kneeling at the water's edge crying for mercy. Firearms, gunpowder, wine, and hardtack were left with them but whether they starved to death or were killed by the Indians we will never know. Their's are not the only bones left at San Julián. Drake executed Thomas Doughty, also convicted of attempted mutiny, at the same spot fifty-one years later. Puerto San Julián is a sinister place indeed.[23]

During the five miserably cold months spent in San Julián, Magellan, knowing the men had to be kept busy, had them build barracks ashore and set them a-fishing and curing their catch with salt collected from salt pans at the head of the bay. Provisions were urgently wanted because when the ships were unladen in preparation for 'rummaging'[24] the clerks made the shocking discovery that the ships had been supplied with stores for only six months instead of for a year and a half.

On 12 September Magellan's four remaining ships moved further south to the mouth of the Santa Cruz River, where they stayed until October 1520, when the southern spring appeared. Now Magellan faced his second great test, a trial of seamanship with few equals outside the *Odyssey*. Magellan had to find a passage to lead him through a continent of unknown breadth. And then, however meandering and tortuous it would be, he had to thread his way through. How could he be confident that any entrance was not an opening to a dead end? How could he know that he was not losing himself ever deeper in the heart of the continent?[25]

16

A WORLD OF TWO OCEANS

One night a great number of fires were seen, mostly on their
Left hand, from which they guessed that they had been seen
by the natives of the region. But Magellan, seeing that the
country was rocky, and also stark with eternal cold, thought it
useless to waste many days in examining it; and so, with only
three ships, he continued on his course along the channel, until,
on the twenty-second day after he had entered it, he sailed out
upon another wide and vast sea.

Maximilian Transylvanus, secretary of the Holy Roman Emperor Charles V, in a letter to
the Cardinal of Salzburg.

It took the four ships but two days to cover the 57 miles from Port San Julián to
Río Santa Cruz, so named because they arrived on 14 September, feast of the
Exaltation of the Holy Cross.

Puerto Santa Cruz, as it is called, is entered between Punta Cascajo and Punta
Entrada. The Genoese pilot, León Pancaldo, estimated this harbour to be on
latitude 50° S, and with an error of only 7′ one could say that for the year 1520
he hit it dead on the nose.

Unlike San Julian, Puerto Santa Cruz lies at the mouth of a navigable river, the
common estuary of Río Santa Cruz and Río Chico that extends some 14 miles
north-westward to the junction of these two rivers at Punta Beagle. It is a well-
sheltered harbour that increases inside the estuary to about 3 miles in width. Magellan
quickly realised it was not the passage he was looking for after perceiving the water
was fresh.[1] Captain Fitzroy of HMS *Beagle*, and Charles Darwin, later explored 140
miles of Río Santa Cruz in 1834, and forty-three years later the Argentine, scientist-
explorer Francisco P. Moreno, reached its source in Lago Argentino.

Magellan's officers hoping to avoid further hardship tried again to persuade him
to give up the quest for the Strait and instead sail to the Spice Islands around the
Cape of Good Hope. The Captain General stood firm and rejected the idea.
However, he promised to reconsider it if he found no strait above latitude 75° S.[2]
(This seems to be a misprint for 57° S.) Magellan's decision did not satisfy the officers,
to the point that Esteban Gómez, now pilot of the *San Antonio*, suggested another
mutiny but Captain Mezquita decided to follow Magellan instead. Gómez bided his
time.[3]

When the southern spring appeared, Magellan decided the time had come to proceed. Pigafetta tells us that, 'Before leaving that river, the Captain General and all of us confessed our sins to the fleet chaplain, Padre Pedro Valderrama, attended mass, and received communion as true Christians.' The next day, 18 October, the four ships, *Trinidad*, *San Antonio*, *Concepción* and *Victoria*, sailed out of the sheltered port into the open sea. For three days the lookouts scanned the coastline of Bahía Grande for the entrance to the strait that their leader, seemingly against all evidence, insisted was there. On 21 October 1520 the eagerly expected happened. The fleet raised a significant cape that Magellan marked on the chart. It being their day, he named it after the seagoing British (that is to say Breton) princess St Ursula said to have been martyred along with 11,000 maidenly companions, and Cabo Vírgenes, or Cape Virgins, it still is to this day.[4]

Situated on the northern side of the entrance to 'the Strait that forever shall bear his name', the Magellan Strait, or Estrecho de Magallanes, on latitude 52° 20′ S, longitude 68° 21′ W, is a long flat-topped stretch of gray-brown cliffs rising vertically 42 meters from the level of the sea.[5] Although the cape is conspicuous enough, it is by no means obvious that a strait opens here. Also, the tidal currents and ocean swell is so strong and confusing that an uncertain mariner would be tempted to sheer off. Hundreds of sailing vessels later found great difficulty beating into it. Joshua Slocum wrote of his attempt hampered by a typical southwestern, *pampero*:

> I had only a moment to douse sail and lash all solid when it struck like a shot from a cannon, and for the first half hour it was something to be remembered by way of a gale. For thirty hours it kept on blowing hard. The sloop could carry no more than a three-reefed mainsail and fore-staysail; with these she held on stoutly and was not blown out of the strait.[6]

Even modern ships have been forced to turn around and make for the Malouines and there await a change of wind. Pigafetta writes that if it were not for Magellan they would never have found the Strait, 'for we all thought and said that it was closed on all sides.' (They evidently expected a strait to be an opening they could see through to the other side, like that of Gibraltar.) Pigafetta continues: 'But the Captain General who knew where to sail to find a well hidden strait, which he saw depicted on a chart [*carta*] in the treasury of the king of Portugal,[7] which was made by that excellent man, Martin de Boemia, sent two ships, the *San Antonio* and the *Conceptione* (for thus they were called), to discover what was inside the cape de la Bahía [i.e. of the Bay]'.[8]

Every biographer or historian of Magellan has pondered what secret chart Magellan had seen in Lisbon that showed the devious passage. It might easily have been one of the Chinese charts acquired in Venice by the king of Portugal's son in 1428. Yet the maps and globes that otherwise he might have seen, like those by Martin Behaim or by Johannes Schöner (1477-1547), also showed the southernmost tip of America divided, at about 45° S, by a narrow, strait that separated America from a supposed great Antarctic continent, that stretched all around the world and of which *Tierra del Fuego* was thought to be part.[9] But Martin Behaim died in 1507 and as far as we know never went on any voyage of discovery. Johannes Schöner's globe on the other hand, the one Magellan took with him when he went to the Spanish court, might be a possibility. Both of these cartographer's maps were still based on Ptolemy, whose configuration of the landmasses had been modified only by inserting the new continent as some large misshapen island in the western ocean. Nevertheless, most encouraging for Magellan was that both views of our planet made the Pacific Ocean narrow in breadth and the Line of Demarcation far west of the Spice Islands, leaving those bountiful treasures, they thought, well within the Spanish zone. A globe like Schöner's, influenced perhaps by an early Chinese map, could have assured Magellan that a strait existed either at the Río de la Plata or further south. Whichever the elusive chart might have been, it should be pointed out that Pigafetta's *carta* need not put us off as in those days that word could mean either a flat map or one spread around a globe.

To state that the Strait through the American land barrier was well hidden was the understatement of all time. The Strait of Magellan is the narrowest, most circuitous of all straits connecting any two main bodies of water, a narrow labyrinth of channels that for 334 nautical miles meanders through tortuous passages with countless dead ends, rocks under the surface, and a myriad disorder of islands big and small. Only by viewing it on a modern map can one grasp the full measure of Magellan's abilities, sense of logic, expertise, his persistence, courage, luck and intuition, that was required to find his way through from it's opening on into the Pacific.[10] Few realise that the Strait is the equivalent of the entire length of the English Channel from Bishop's rock to Dover Strait, or from the Gulf of St Laurence to Montreal, or from the entrance of the Panama Canal to Barranquilla.[11]

On 21 October, having passed Cabo Vírgenes and avoided the many rocks and shoals that await unwary mariners, Magellan determined to investigate this break in the coast to see if it really was *the* Strait, he sailed around Punta Dungeness, the flat 5-mile prolongation of Cabo Vírgenes, mooring his flagship and *Victoria* in Bahía Posesión. The Captain General then sent *Concepción*, now commanded by his faithful friend Serrano, and *San Antonio*, commanded by his kinsman Mezquita, to explore the surroundings. That night a strong northeast gale blew strong and both vessels unable to make headway were carried almost under bare poles through the 2-mile-wide Primera Angostura (First Narrows), into Bahía San Felipe where they found shelter and holding ground. In Pigafetta's account he tells us that 'thinking they were lost, [the two ships] saw a small opening which did not appear to be an opening at all but a sharp turn (*Cantone*). Like desperate men they hauled into it, and thus they discovered the strait by chance... Then farther on they found another strait and another bay larger than the first two.'

The other strait was the Segunda Angostura that led into a big bay, Paso Ancho (Broad Reach). Serrano and his pilot Carvalho put their heads together and concluded that they really *were in the Strait* after all. After the gale had blown itself out the wind turned west and the two ships returned to Bahía Posesión. Coming up to *Trinidad* and *Victoria* they announced the good news 'with sails full and banners flying to the wind.' Coming up to the flagship and *Victoria* they 'suddenly discharged a number of mortars, and burst into cheers. Then all together thanking God and the Virgin Mary, we went to seek farther on.'[12] Each pair had feared the loss of the other and their relief knew no bounds.[13]

Magellan decided to follow the same route that San *Antonio* and *Concepción* had taken. The fleet worked their way through the wider Second Narrows and came to an anchor in Paso Real between Isabel Island and the main. Magellan wisely did not attempt to sail here at night though little time was lost as they entered the Strait in the Antarctic spring when darkness lasted only three hours.

At Bahía San Felipe between the two Narrows, a boat sent ashore from *Trinidad* reported a dead whale and hundreds of human corpses tied to poles stuck into the ground, presumably a native graveyard. No Magellan source mentions he had any contact with live natives in the Strait, though tribes of Fuegian Indians had long lived there. However, he saw hundreds of their fires at night, for the most part kept alight in their dugout canoes by the women of the tribe, fire being a precious commodity. Hence the name he gave to the south side of the strait, *Tierra del Fuego*, Land of Fire.

A number of theories exist regarding how the Indians got that far south, the most likely goes back to the time of the initial crossing of the Bering Straits to Alaska when humans set foot in the American continent for the first time. In the many

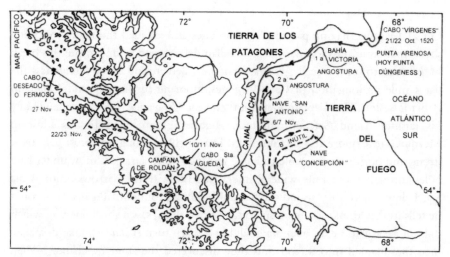

Magellan's voyage through the straight.

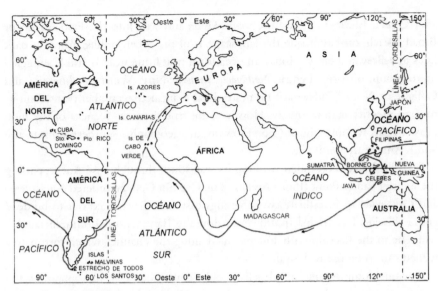

Magellan's route of circumnavigation.

thousands of years that followed, continually pushed south by more powerful tribes, these Indians reached a dead end. They came up to the barrier of the Ice Age, which held them back. Some 14,000 years ago, when the ice began to retreat, enabling a southerly spread of flora and fauna, the wandering tribes followed. These were a primitive people to whom a channel as wide as the Straits of Magellan would have been an unsurpassable boundary. It is likely, however, that in a change of climatic conditions, the channel was bridged when the water level dropped, enabling some tribes to cross over to the big island. The island fragmentation, meager resources and very harsh weather split the native people into isolated groups, who over time were to become distinct from one another both in language and mutual dislike.

Accommodating to the food available, they lived on the large, succulent mussels and limpets of the Strait, seal blubber, fish in the ponds, berries, magellan geese that become particularly vulnerable when they yearly shed their feathers and can not fly, and guanacos they could shoot with their bows and arrows.

By the early nineteenth century it is estimated that there were 9,000 Fuegians divided into four tribes that kept to their areas, spoke different languages, and kept apart of each other. They were the Selk'nam (also known as the Ona or the Oensmen), the fearsome people of the main island; the Alakaluf (or Kaweskar) of the western lands; the Haush (or Mannekenk) who lived on the south-eastern tip of Tierra del Fuego; and the Yamana (or Yahgans), the canoe people of the Beagle Channel region. All were survivors clinging to the edge of the habitable world.[14]

—⟡⟡⟡—

Magellan's fleet worked their way through the wider Second Narrows and came to anchor in the Paso Real between Isabel Island (named by Drake later in 1578, after Queen Elizabeth I) and the main. Here, and well into the Paso Ancho or Broad Reach, on either side the landscape is of unbroken rolling plains, in dark hues of yellow and brown. Today, an occasional neat homestead is visible snuggled up to groups of native Lengas, *Nothofagus Pumilio*; Ñire, *Nothofagus Antárctica*, and Coligüe or *Notro*.[15] Today, each homestead has a distinctive number painted on its roof, to identify it from the air. However, the true dramatic scenery of the high peaks begins within sight of Cape Froward, the geographic southern limit to the South American continent.

Magellan's fleet continued working its way south through Paso Ancho passing the sight of Sandy Point (Punta Arenas). The Captain General ordered *San Antonio* and *Concepción* to investigate two openings eastward that turned out to be dead ends – Useless Bay (Bahía Inútil), and Admiralty Bay (Seno del Almirantazgo) – while he in the flagship with *Victoria* sailed along the channel, which fortunately turned out to be the real Strait.

Previous to this separation, Magellan held a conference with his captains on the flagship to decide whether or not to go on. All were in favour except Esteban Gómez, now pilot of *San Antonio*. In Pigafetta's own words, Gómez 'hated the Captain General exceedingly, because before the fleet was fitted out, the emperor had ordered he be given some caravels with which to discover lands, but his Majesty did not give them to him because of the coming of the Captain General.' In other words he hoped to command the entire fleet and his simmering hatred intensified after Magellan eliminated Cartagena and designated his cousin Alvaro de Mezquita to command *San Antonio* instead of him. During the meeting with his captains, Magellan stated he was resolved to continue, 'even if they had to eat the leather chafing-gear on the ships' yards.' Which is exactly what they eventually did.

While *San Antonio* was exploring Useless and Admiralty bays, Gómez managed to persuade the stoutest fellows of the crew to mutiny. Under cover of darkness they captured Captain Mezquita, wounding him and put him in irons. After electing captain his fellow conspirator, the notary on board, Gerónimo Guerra, they retraced their steps through the Strait and piloted the vessel back to Spain, arriving at the end of March 1521. They made no attempt to pick up Cartagena or the priest marooned at San Julián. Back in Seville both Gómez and Mezquita were flung into jail. Gómez managed eventually to talk his way out but poor Mezquita remained there until after *Victoria* arrived home.

The Captain General now turned to his chief pilot Andrés de San Martín who combined astrology with navigation. Asked about the whereabouts of *San Antonio*, he plotted the stars, consulted his books, made calculations, and gave the Captain General a precise circumstantial account of what actually proved to have happened.[16]

Magellan in *Trinidad* with *Victoria* in company sailed south beyond Sandy Point (Punta Arenas) and on past Port Famine.[17] 'It was near here', wrote Captain Slocum in 1900, 'I had my first experience with the terrific squalls called *williwaws*, which extended from this point on through the Strait to the Pacific. These were compressed gales of wind that Boreas handed down over the hills in

America and Asia on the Schöner globe of 1515, simplified and reduced. From *História da Colonizado do Brasil*.

chunks. A full-blown *williwaw* will throw a ship, even without sail set, over on her beam ends.' These fearsome gales are apt to hit a vessel with such force as to strip off her sails and even capsise her.[18]

As soon as Magellan passed Mount Tarn, they entered the part where scenery becomes spectacular. They rounded Cape Froward, a headland rising almost 1200 feet at latitude 53° 54′ S, the southernmost point on the American continent. Here the Strait, about 5 miles' wide, turns abruptly north-west, and after some 30 miles becomes a deep, narrow gorge cut through the Andes, as if the sculpting hands of this southern wilderness had cleft the mountains millions of years ago. Powerful rivers of glacial melt water pour down the steep south and western sides of the mountains into the Pacific. A land that inspired awe in its early European explorers, preserved in the names of much of its terrifying geography: Fury Bay and Fury Island, Useless Bay, Desolation Bay, Port Famine, Devil Island and, it is not far from here, at Cape Horn, that the Atlantic and Pacific Oceans meet head on like two Goliaths doing battle.[19]

Worrying about his other two ships, Magellan turned back to search for them. Soon they met *Concepción* sailing alone towards them. Captain Serrano had no news of *San Antonio* but Magellan refused to accept the worst and spent five or six days looking for her, even down Admiralty Sound. *Victoria* went as far as Cape Virgins looking for the missing ship with orders to plant a banner on the summit of some small hill leaving a letter in an earthen pot beside it. 'So that if the banner were seen the letter might be found, and the ship might learn the course we were sailing', wrote Pigafetta.

While he was waiting, the Captain General having manned and fitted out the longboat of the flagship, sent it further north to explore the Strait in the hope of finding an outlet. 'The men returned within three days', says Pigafetta, 'and reported that they had seen the cape and the open sea.' One of the men, a Flemish gunner named Roldán de Argote, climbed a mountain (later named after him), and sighted the great South Sea. When he reported it the Captain General 'wept for joy, and called that *Cabo Deseado*, for we had been desiring it for a long time.'[20] The name is still applied to one of the two northern prongs of Desolation Island marking the entrance of the Strait from the Pacific. The more northern of its two points is better known as Cabo Pilar.

After *Victoria* returned Magellan decided it was time to press forward. The ships sailed up the Paso Inglés, the main channel, and passed Carlos III Island where Magellan erected a cross. On directions from the longboat crew, they bypassed Canal San Jerónimo thus avoiding wandering into a dead end. He passed safely through Paso Tortuoso and correctly entered Paso Largo with depths of up to 810 fathoms. On they went passed the island of Tamar – off which there is a 2½-fathom rock that has wrecked many a ship, the dangerous Bajo Magallanes – and on through Paso del Mar the worst of many dangerous places to be caught in a strong westerly.

After some 30 miles of sailing through adverse currents, on 28 November 1520, *Trinidad*, *Concepción*, and *Victoria* passed Cabo Pilar into the open sea. Antonio de Herrera, the late sixteenth-century historian, wrote of Magellan's entry to the Pacific: 'On the 27th of November he came out into the South Sea, blessing God, who had been pleas'd to permit him to find what he so much desir'd, being the first that ever went that way, which will perpetuate his memory for ever. They guessed this Strait to be about one hundred Leagues in Length... The sea was very Black and Boisterous, which denoted a vast Ocean. Magellan order'd publick Thanksgiving, and sail'd away to the Northward, to get out of the cold.'[21]

In a sense Magellan had been lucky. He had sailed three times three-quarters of the 334-mile length of the Strait, looking for *San Antonio*. None of the three literary crewmembers he had on board, reported any strong squalls or particular perils. The sailors frequently landed to gather an excellent anti-scorbutic, the wild celery (*Apium australe*) growing near springs and rivers. Also they caught plenty of fish – albacore, bonito and flying fish. After they had sailed safely through Pigafetta wrote: 'I believe there is not a more beautiful or better Strait in the world than that one.' Beautiful indeed, but terrifying as well. One should study the future history of later voyages, and if possible to traverse it oneself to appreciate the magnitude of Magellan's achievement in all its dimensions:

courage, tenacity, faith, seamanship, and leadership. Regardless of his detractors, *He did it!* As Alonso de Ercilla wrote in *La Araucana*, first published in 1569:

Magallanes, Señor, fue el primer hombre
que abriendo este camino, le dió nombre.

Magellan, Sir, was the first man
to both open this route and give it a name.[22]

Pigafetta gives us his eyewitness account of the momentous discovery: 'Wednesday, November 28, 1520, we debouched from the strait, engulfing ourselves in the Pacific Sea.' Thus was recorded one of the great moments of history.

Spread out before them when they entered the Pacific was a vast extent of dark blue shimmering in the setting sun. Vasco Núñez de Balboa, true enough, had 'star'd at the Pacific – and all his men – looked at each other with a wild surmise – silent, upon a peak in Darien', seven years before. But as Magellan entered this uncharted expanse of ocean, thousands of miles wide without fear or hesitation, he was oblivious of what lay before him.

Due to this lack of knowledge Magellan thought that the watery wilderness he was heading into, by estimates either literary or cartographical, was at least 80 per cent short of the truth. In fact, mapmakers for a century after Magellan's voyage underestimated the width of the Pacific by as much as 40 per cent. This lack of information eventually put a great strain on provisions as Pigafetta recorded in his journal: 'We were three months and twenty days without getting any fresh food. We ate biscuit, which were no longer biscuit, but powder of biscuits swarming with worms, for they had eaten the good. It stank strongly of the urine of rats. We drank yellow water that had been putrid for many days. We also eat some ox hide [most likely guanaco skins] that covered the top of the main yard to prevent the yard from chafing the shrouds, and which had become exceedingly hard because of the sun, rain, and wind. We left them in the sea for four or five days, and then placed them for a few moments on top of the embers, and so eat them; and often we eat sawdust from boards. Rats were sold for one half ducado a piece [about $1.16 in gold a piece], and even then we could not get them.'[23]

According to Francisco Albo, pilot of *Trinidad*, after leaving the Strait the fleet steered north-west, north, and then north-east by north, for four days until off Cabo Tres Montes. From there Magellan sailed north-west until 5 December before commencing his curve, with adverse winds first towards the coast until coming in sight of Punta Galera. Leaving Isla Mocha to starboard and with the first hint of the eastern trades he commenced an ark that would ultimately carry him westward. Why did Magellan sail north before turning west? The obvious answer to any common-sense seaman would be 'to stay with fair winds.' Another theory is that Magellan might have learned about the prevailing winds when he was in the Moluccas during his early Portuguese voyage and wanted to be in the best position to coast down to his main objective, the Spice Islands. On the other hand he might have heard of the Philippine Islands in Malacca with its colony of some 500 Filipinos that he could have hoped to secure for Spain. Many theories abound but the fact remains that certain providence was looking after Magellan that made him steer a course recommended to yachtsmen today for January and February by the Pilot Chart.

The fleet travelled over 12,000 miles in three months and twenty days without making a landfall. It could not have been a lonelier course across the Pacific. He first missed the Juan Fernandez Islands that lie some 400 miles off Valparaiso. Then, crossing a wide space he inadvertently missed Easter Island, Pitcairn, the Society Islands and the thousand and one uninhabited atolls and volcanic ridges thrust up through the seabed of the Pacific, each a corral-baited trap. Bad enough was semi-starvation and scurvy, but better then running aground with the hull torn from under you hundreds of miles from any assistance.

It was a nightmare crossing. Men died from scurvy, malnutrition, exposure, and sheer exhaustion. 'The gums of both the lower and the upper teeth of some of our men swelled, so that they could not eat under any circumstances and therefore ended dying. Nineteen men died from that sickness [scurvy] and the [Patagonian] giant together with an Indian from the country of Verzin [Brazil].'[24] Nevertheless, they were lucky with the weather. During the whole three months and twenty days of sailing through the open sea, they did not have to face a single storm. Misled by this one experience, Magellan named it the Pacific.

Neither did they encounter any land during those long weeks 'except two desert islets, where we found nothing but birds and trees, for which we called them *Ysole Infortunate* [Unfortunate Isles]...We found no anchorage, [but] near them we saw many sharks... Had not God and his blessed mother given us so good weather we would all have died of hunger in that exceeding vast sea. Of a verity I believe no such voyage will ever be made [again].'[25]

If Magellan had not been master of the winds it is doubtful he would have made it across that wide ocean. Experience urged him to first sail north along the west coast of South America before turning west to catch the north-easterly trade winds that would carry him across the Pacific. But Magellan expected the crossing of these waters, familiar as Ptolemy's 'Great Gulf', to take only a few weeks. There was still no way for him to precisely mark the longitude and without that it was impossible to know the exact distance between any two points around the earth. But curiously enough, the course he chose is still the one recommended by the United States Government Pilot Charts for sailing from Cape Horn to Honolulu at the same time of the year. For Magellan, the extent of the Pacific Ocean was a painful surprise though it would also be his greatest, if shocking, discovery.

On 24 January 1521, after dropping slightly south of course they 'found an islet wooded but uninhabited. We sounded and found no bottom, and so continued on our course, and this island we named *San Pablo*, because it was the day of his conversion', said Pilot Albo.[26] At last on 6 March 1521, ninety-eight or ninety-nine days out of the Strait, Magellan and his dwindling band of voyagers found their first relief when the lookout from the masthead of *Concepción* hailed the deck with his cry of 'land ahead.' He had sighted two lofty islands, Guam and Rota (the southernmost tip of the Mariana Ridge). They sailed between them, and then looking for a harbour, turned south hugging the coast of Guam. All was lush and inviting but the hungry sailors could find no opening in the reef until, providentially, at the southern end of the island, a harbour opened up, now called Umatak, with no reef barrier beyond it and the open sea. A flock of native sail, usually engaged in fishing, sailed circles around the ships. These were *praos*, lateen-rigged dugout canoes each with an outrigger, amazingly fast and maneuverable. Magellan's men were ravenous; the local people were curious and acquisitive. They surrounded the ships, climbed on board and swarming all over the ship helped themselves to everything above and below that was not nailed down, such as belaying pins, sail needles, steel knives or crockery. Magellan ordered the natives off, but the debilitated crew could neither dissuade nor persuade them to go away. Next day he sent parties ashore to fill casks with water and trade for meat. As soon as the sailors had left the beach, a group of natives made off with one of their boats. Magellan who was tempted to name the islands *Las Islas de Velas Latinas*, the Isles of Lateen Sails, soon found reason to change the name to the infamous title of *Islas de Ladrones*, Isles of thieves, now known as the Marianas.

Finally Magellan's patience snapped. He gave orders to his men at arms to shoot a few of those that climbed on board with their crossbows, which temporarily put a stop to it. One native pulled a crossbow bolt right out of his side and looked in amazement as the blood spurted out.[27] Though the action temporarily solved the problem of the boarders, after the brawl, the sailors noticed that the ship's longboat was missing from the *Trinidad*'s stern!

The natives were *Chamorros*, a brown-skinned Polynesian race who had raided Guam centuries earlier, conquered the native Micronesians, and became an arrogant ruling cast. Later, converted by Spanish priests and their island group renamed *Las Marianas*, the *Chamorros* became peaceful and friendly.[28] However, at the time when the little three-ship flotilla arrived Magellan's men were ravenous, desperate and wary of strangers and, on the other hand, the local people were greedy to the point of aggressiveness. Says Pigafetta: 'they go naked, and some are bearded and have black hair that reaches to the waist. They wear small palm-leaf hats, as do the Albanians... The women go naked except that they wear a narrow strip of bark as thin as paper, which grows between the tree and the bark of the palm, before their privies. They are good looking and delicately formed, and lighter complexioned than the men; and wear their hair, which is exceedingly black, loose and hanging quite down to the ground... They use no weapons, except a kind of spear pointed with a fishbone on the end. Those people are poor, but ingenious and very thievish on account of which we called those three islands the islands of *Ladroni*.'

Magellan gathered a force to go in search of his missing boat. At daybreak he approached the shore and attacked the village. The landing force burned many of the huts and several praos, they recovered the stolen boat, and seized supplies of rice, fruit and fresh water, which added to the fish they cleaned and salted down, gave them a somewhat balanced diet to get them to the Philippines.

On 9 March 1521 they got under way not knowing where the wind was taking them. Setting a course west by south they made an average speed of 7 to 8 knots an hour over five days. They had plenty of fresh food to cure the sick, except for Chief Gunner Andrew of Bristol, the only Englishman on board. Too far gone to recover, he died the first day out from Guam.

On 15 March 1521 they sighted the island of Samar but sailed passed it finding no harbour. They altered course again to due south until making the island of Suluan. There they anchored for the night. It being the fifth Sunday in Lent dedicated to St Lazarus, according to the church calendar, Magellan named this archipelago after him. Not until after a visit by Villalobos in 1542 was it renamed the Philippines, after the Infante of Spain, later King Philip II.

The following day they reached the much bigger island of Homonhon. Pigafetta gives us the story:

> The Captain General desired to land… in order to be more secure, and to get water and have some rest. He had two tents set up on the shore for the sick and had a sow killed for them. (One they had picked up at Guam.) On Monday afternoon, 18 March, we saw a boat coming toward us with nine men in it. The Captain General ordered that no one should move or say a word without his permission. When those men reached the shore, their chief went immediately to the Captain General, giving signs of joy because of our arrival. Five of the most ornately adorned of them remained with us, while the rest went to get some others who were fishing, and so they all came. The Captain General seeing that they were reasonable men, ordered food to be set before them, and gave them red caps, mirrors, combs, bells, ivory, and other things. When they saw the Captain's courtesy, they presented fish, a jar of palm wine, which they call *uraca* [arrack], figs more than one palmo long [bananas], and others that were smaller and more delicate, and two *cochi* [coconuts]. They had nothing else then, but made us signs with their hands that they would bring *umay* or rice, coconuts and many other articles of food within four days.

Pigafetta describes in detail the native system for making palm wine. He had never seen a coconut or a banana before. 'Two coconut palms', he said, 'can support a family of ten people', and he might have said clothing and housing as well. 'Those people became very familiar with us. They told us many things, their names and those of some of the islands that could be seen from that place. We took great pleasure with them, for they were very pleasant and conversable' – presumably by sign language.

The fleet stayed at Homonhon for a week. Magellan would daily visit the sick ashore and personally hand feed them fresh coconut milk. As the natives had promised after their first visit, they returned in two boats with a load of coconuts, sweet oranges, a jar of wine and a cock, to show there were fowls in that district. Magellan purchased them all for the trip ahead. Their chief was a very old man who was painted, i.e. tattooed. Magellan showed them over the flagship, exhibiting spices and gold, which he hoped to find in quantities.

As they were about to weigh anchor, on 25 March, Pigafetta slipped on the wet deck and fell overboard and just saved himself by seizing a main clewline dangling in the water. Like most of those that took to sea he had never learned to swim. 'I held on tightly', he tells us, 'and began to cry out so lustily that I was rescued by the small boat.' He attributed his rescue 'to the mercy of that font of charity, the Virgin Mary, since it was the feast of her Annunciation'.

On 28 March 1521, the flotilla found itself off the island called Limasawa, a name with a lilting inflection to it familiar to Magellan's slave Enrique de Malacca. When a canoe of natives came out to the ships, Enrique hailed them in their own dialect. 'They immediately understood him, came alongside the ship, unwilling to enter but taking a position at some little distance.' Magellan was instantly struck with twin realisations: Firstly, west had met east at last and Enrique may have been the first man to do it. Second, Magellan had fulfilled Columbus' dream of discovering the easternmost part of the world by sailing west.

On Good Friday, the local chieftain Colambu entertained Magellan and his men lavishly. He ruled over the islands of Limasawa and Suluan as well as a large part of the island of Mindanao. Magellan showered his host with gifts while the blood of both was exchanged in a ritual ceremony known as *casi casi*, or blood brotherhood, mainly consisting of each tasting a drop of the other's blood.

On Easter Sunday, 31 March 1521, the flag-chaplain celebrated High Mass on the beach of Limasawa. At the Elevation of the Host, Magellan's bodyguard fired a salvo from their arquebuses and the ships discharged a blank broadside. After the ceremony, the men feasted on meat, fish, fresh fruit and an abundance of palm wine, but disappointingly found ginger the only condiment available. Magellan needed staples for his ships and Colambu upon being asked where more could be obtained offered to guide them to the trading center of Cebu in exchange for help with his rice harvest. Magellan, to expedite this, sent details of sailors to help but they became so drunk on palm wine the first day ashore that they were practically useless.

The gentle Limasawans, says Pigafetta:

> go naked, wearing but one piece of palm-tree cloth about their privies. The males, large and small, have their penis pierced from one side to the other near the head, with a gold or tin bolt as large as a goose quill. In both ends of the same bolt, some have what resembles a spur, with points upon the ends; others are like the head of a cart nail. I very often asked many, both old and young, to see their penis, because I could not credit it. In the middle is a hole, through which they urinate. The bolt and the spurs always hold firm. They say their women wish it so, and if they did

otherwise they would not have communication with them. When the men wish to have communication with their women, the latter themselves take the penis not in the regular way and commence very gently to introduce it [into their vagina], with the spur on top first, and then the other part. When it is inside it takes its regular position; and thus the penis always stays inside until it gets soft, for otherwise they could not pull it out. Those people make use of that device because they are of a weak nature. They have as many wives as they wish, but none of them is the principal wife. Whenever any of our men went ashore, both by day and night, every one invited them to eat and to drink...The women loved us very much more than their own men. All the women from the age of six years and upward, have their vaginas [natura] gradually opened because of the men's penises.[29]

The flotilla, guided by Colambu in his private dugout canoe, sailed to Cebu and on 7 April they anchored in the channel off the port. Cebu was a buzzing harbour and trading settlement of the region with houses on stilts reaching out into the water, not far from the fatal island of Macatan.

On approaching the town of Cebu, Magellan ordered his ships to be dressed with all their colours, and fired a cannon salvo that frightened the population, part of which panicked and hid in the jungle. The local chief, Sultan Humabon, a short and portly man covered with tribal tattoos, was impressed but guarded. On being told that the new arrivals had come in peace, he wished to know why indeed they had come at all. A Muslim master of a junk (standing by) whispered to the sultan 'they were the same bunch of brigands that had sacked Calicut, Malacca and greater India. If well treated they will respond in kind, but if treated ill they will raise hell.' But clever Enrique made a point of emphasizing they were Spaniards serving the emperor of all Christians, and not Portuguese. Humabon rapidly suggested a trade agreement, and another blood oath was exchanged.[30]

Thus commenced a precarious peace. The sultan and his heir, with the Moslem junk captain in tow, eight chief men and Rajah Colambu all came aboard *Trinidad*. Magellan seated in a red velvet chair surrounded by his officers in leather ones received his guests who squatted on rugs. The Captain General held forth describing the fundamental elements of the Christian faith while inviting them to be converted. Sultan Humabon seemed willing to have all his people baptised. Magellan promised to present him with a suit of armour that he admired, adding that if the girls too were baptised, his men 'could have intercourse with their women without committing a very great sin.' An unusual if amusing argument for conversion to Christianity as ever heard of! The sultan and the rajah said 'that they could not match the beautiful words of the Captain but they placed themselves in his hands, and he should treat them as his most faithful servants.'[31]

Following an exchange of gifts, Pigafetta, Enrique, and a few others walked into town and were received by the sultan. A tubby sort of fellow 'seated on a palm mat on the ground, with only a cotton cloth before his privies, and an embroidered scarf about his head, a necklace of great value hanging from his neck, and two large gold earrings fastened in his ears set round with precious gems.' He occasionally would pluck a turtle egg from a porcelain bowl while sipping palm wine through four hollow reeds from jars set around him. Pigafetta, after presenting his highness with a robe, a cap, and some Venetian beads, left for the prince's (Humabon's nephew) house where four young girls playing instruments entertained them. 'They played so harmoniously that one would believe they possessed good musical sense... The prince had three quite naked girls dance for us. We took refreshments and then went to the ships.'[32]

Thanking the Lord in heaven, Magellan began to press for the local's conversion, as the latter looked on intently at the Christian funeral of two men recently dead of scurvy. Touched and bewildered, Humabon declared a wish to be baptised. The sultan had a platform raised in the plaza. On Sunday, 14 April, the ship's chaplain, with as much pomp as the Spaniards could muster performed the ceremony. Humabon was renamed Don Carlos after the emperor, Rajah Colambu became Don Juan after the Infante, and the Moslem junk captain, who also desired to be converted, became Don Cristóbal. At least another 500 male subjects were also christened as well as most of the chiefs, threatened with death if they did not accept it.

Not to be left behind the queen also declared the wish to be baptised:

> We conducted her to the platform, and she was invited to sit down upon a cushion with the other women near her, until the priest should be ready. She was shown an image of our Lady, a very beautiful wooden child Jesus, and a cross. Thereupon, she was overcome with contrition, and asked for baptism amid her tears. We named her Johanna, after the emperor's mother...The queen was young and beautiful, and was entirely covered with a white and black cloth. Her mouth and nails were very red, [from chewing betel nuts, the astringent seed of the betel palm] while on her head she wore a large hat of palm leaves in the manner of a parasol, with a crown about it of the same leaves, like the tiara of the pope...Counting men, women, and children, we baptized eight hundred souls.[33]

Magellan began to see himself as another conquistador in the service of Castile, but he was neither a Cortez nor a Pizarro with an army at his back and plenty of time to impose his will on an alien people. He led a rag-tag bunch of men, far from being in fighting trim, whose only ambition was in getting home.[34]

Magellan set about founding a trade base in Cebu. Pagan idols were destroyed, while his men reveled, ravishing the local women and angering their men. He announced he would have to return to Spain for reinforcements to ensure successful trade. He then went too far. Saying that he would need a reliable Christian ally, he ordered that a single king, Humabon, must rule all the surrounding islands and their people, of which Cebu was the nucleus. Those that refused to pay tribute to him would do so on pain of death and confiscation of property. Because of this misguided and pompous statement, Magellan's life just salvaged from the worst elements that nature could muster, was to be forfeited by this single act of imprudence.[35]

Sultan Humabon of Cebu feigning conversion to Christianity, persuaded Magellan to become his ally, 'to fight and burn the houses of Macatan to make Lapulapu, the king of Macatan, kiss the hands of the King of Cebu, and because he did not send him a bushel of rice and a goat as tribute'.

Magellan's bluff had been called and he decided to show his metal, boasting he could take Mactan with sixty men. 'We begged him repeatedly not to go', says Pigafetta, 'but he like a good shepherd, refused to abandon his flock. At midnight, sixty men of us set out armed with corselets and helmets, together with the Christian king, [Humabon] the prince, some minor chiefs and twenty or thirty balanguais. We reached Matan three hours before dawn [on 26–27 April 1521]. The captain did not wish to fight then, but sent a message to the natives by the Moro [the Moslem junk captain] to the effect that if they would obey the king of Spagnia, recognise the Christian king [Humabon] as their sovereign, and pay us tribute, he would be their friend; but if they wished otherwise, they should wait to see how our lances wounded.'[36]

The Christians in three boats mounted with swivel guns, paddled through the narrow channel from the city of Cebu to the northeast side of Macatan. Rounding Bantolinao Point they halted in front of the mangrove-fringed-village set back in the cove, (now called Magellan Bay), formed by the peninsula at the northeast of the island. *Trinidad*, *Victoria* and *Concepción* anchored within cannon shot of the shore. However, having arrived late they took no significant part in the operation. This is where Magellan lost the precious advantage of surprise by having sent the Moslem junk captain with the message to Chief Lapulapu. Lapulapu replied that he feared not the Christian's steel, having plenty of 'fire-hardened spears and stakes of bamboo', and Magellan could attack as soon as he pleased.

At first light forty-nine of Magellan's forces leaped into the water up their thighs and waded ashore a distance, according to a survivor of 'two crossbow flights.' The other eleven Spaniards that remained guarding the boats were prevented from beaching them by a reef that meant the swivel guns could not provide coverage at that thousand-yard distance. By the time the Christians landed, Lapulapu had organised his forces, 'more than one thousand five hundred persons', in three divisions – one at the head of the wide bay and one on each flank. 'When they saw us they charged down upon us with exceeding loud cries.' Magellan formed his pitifully small force into two groups and fought back with harquebuses and crossbows. It was hopeless; the enemy's wooden shields deflected the shots at too great a range. Magellan cried out to his men '*no tiren*', cease firing! but his men paid no heed and shot off all their ammunition. Seeing our muskets were discharged the enemy yelled even louder, 'leaping hither and thither, covering themselves with their shields. They shot so many arrows at us and hurled so many bamboo spears (some of them tipped with iron) at the Captain General, besides pointed stakes hardened with fire, stones, and mud, that we could scarcely defend ourselves.' It would have been sensible at this point to retreat, but instead Magellan counter-attacked and sent a group of men to burn the native huts ashore, 'in order to terrify them'. That aroused the enemy to even greater fury. The Captain General, shot through the right leg with a poisoned arrow, ordered his men to retire to the boats which most of them did. However, Magellan with six or eight faithful men, including Pigafetta, covered their retreat. Here is the eye-witness account of what happened recorded by Pigafetta who was in the thick of it fighting at Magellan's side:

> The natives shot only at our legs for they were bare; and so many were the spears and stones that they hurled at us, that we could offer no resistance. The mortars in the boats could not aid us as they were too far away. So we continued to retire for more than a good crossbow flight from the shore always fighting up to our knees in the water. The natives continued to pursue us, and picking up the same spear four or six times, hurled it at us again and again. Recognizing the Captain [General] they knocked his helmet off his head twice, but he always stood firmly like a good knight, together with some others. Thus did we fight for more than one-hour, refusing to retire farther. An Indian hurled a bamboo spear into the Captain's face, but the latter immediately killed him with his lance, which he left in the Indian's body. Then trying to lay hand on sword, he could only draw it out halfway, because he had been wounded in the arm with a bamboo spear. When the natives saw that, they all hurled themselves upon him. One of them wounded him on the left leg with a large cutlass, which resembled a scimitar, only being larger. That forced the Captain to fall face downward, when immediately they rushed upon him with iron and bamboo spears and with their cutlasses, until they killed our mirror, our light, our comfort, and our true guide. When they wounded him he turned back many times to see whether we were all in the boats. Thereupon, beholding him dead, we, wounded, retreated, as best we could, to the boats, which were already pulling off... Had it not been for him, not a single one of us would have been saved, for while he was fighting the rest retired.

At the last moment, too late, the three ships began to cannonade the crowded ranks of the enemy.

Written 480 years ago, Pigafetta's eulogy of his captain is superb. No one could have expressed it better: 'I hope', he said to the man to whom he dedicated his narrative, 'through the efforts of your most illustrious Lordship that the fame of so noble a captain will not become effaced in our times. Among the other virtues which he possessed, he was more constant than ever anyone else in the greatest of adversity. He endured hunger better than all the others and, more accurately than any man in the world did he understand sea charts and navigation. And that this was the truth was seen openly, for no other had so much natural talent nor the boldness to learn how to circumnavigate the world, as he had almost done.'

17

THE LONG ROAD HOME

The fair breeze blew, the white foam flew,
The furrow followed free;
We were the first that ever burst
Into that silent sea.

The Rime of the Ancient Mariner, (1798), Samuel Taylor Coleridge

The casualties in the frontal assault on Lapulapu's stronghold were few but important. Eight Europeans, including Magellan and Cristóbal Rebelo, who had been promoted to captain of *Victoria* were killed. Four recently baptised natives of Cebu were cut down, as were an estimated fifteen of the enemy. A plea for the return of the bodies of the Christians was rejected.

On the afternoon of the fight an urgent meeting was held aboard *Trinidad*. The surviving officers chose Duarte Barbosa, Magellan's brother-in-law, to be captain of the flagship as well as Captain General, honours that he enjoyed for barely three days.

Enrique de Malacca, Magellan's slave who had fought beside him at Mactan, and who knew Spanish as well as Malay, turned surly and lazy. He declared that his master's death released him from servitude, which was true enough since Magellan's last will and testament not only freed him but also left him a legacy of 10,000 maravedis. However, the exasperated Captain General Duarte Barbosa, on finding that Enrique had taken to his bunk, nursing a slight wound he had received during the fight, spoke to him harshly, in the following wise: 'Rise and shine you lazy son-of-a-bitch, or I'll have you tied to the mast and well flogged!'[1] At any rate, he called him a dog and threatened to have him whipped, as well as saying he would see to it that after reaching Spain he would still be the slave to Magellan's wife, Doña Beatriz.[2] This aroused the man's native pride and vindictiveness, ending with Barbosa's death as well as some twenty-five shipmates.

Enrique's revenge by far out measured the offence. Meekly feigning he was paying no heed to Barbosa's insults he went ashore to tell Sultan Humabon that the Christians planned to kidnap him, and then plotted to forestall his treason by further treachery.

Cutting straight to the heart of the problem, the sultan made up his mind to murder the Europeans. He sent word to the commanders that he had the jewels he had promised to send the king of Spain and invited the Christians of every rank and rating to a state banquet on 1 May, in the dark of the moon. About thirty accepted[3] including Captain Juan Serrano (likely to have been Francisco Serrão's brother) and Duarte Barbosa. Of the group only Gómez de Espinosa and João Lopes de Carvalho survived because, sniffing evil in the air, they sneaked out in time to save their throats being cut and returned to their ships.

Pigafetta was not of the party. He tells us, 'I could not go because I was all swollen up by a wound from a poisoned arrow which I had received in my face.' It was just as well, as the cries of the men being butchered were heard on board the vessels. From the ships they could see the natives throwing down the cross set up by Magellan and kicking it about. It took no great wit to guess what was up. 'We immediately weighed anchor and discharging many mortars into the houses, drew in near the shore.'[4] Carvalho, now in temporary command, is accused by Pigafetta of cold-bloodedly sailing away while Juan Serrano was led to the shore in his shirt, bound and bleeding, begging his countrymen to ransom him. But the Portuguese author of the *Leiden Narrative* tells it differently. He says Serrano called out that the ransom demanded was two lombards (ships' cannon). Carvalho agreed, and sent a pair of guns ashore in the ship's longboat, but the natives declared they were not enough and demanded more. The seamen in the boat called back that they would give anything to recover Serrano as long as he was left in a safe place where they could pick him up. That the natives refused to do, and Serrano courageously urged his comrades to escape quickly as the natives were waiting for reinforcements with which to capture the ships, 'since', he called out, 'it were better for him to die then that all should perish'. On board, as they were coming about to stand off shore, the sailors saw the natives guarding Serrano turn on him and then they heard the shrieks, which told all too well that murder was being committed once again.

The victims of Enrique's revenge and the sultan's treason were three captains: Barbosa, Serrano, and Luis Alfonso de Gois. Magellan's navigator and astrologer, Andrés de San Martín, Father Valderrama, two secretaries, several petty officers and servants. Also, a dozen mariners and apprentice-seamen were killed in the massacre, or sold shortly after as slaves to China. What the outcome of Enrique may have been we do not know, but one can suppose that being protected as the informer, he enjoyed an exalted, though ill-earned position, at the sultan's court.

The three Spanish ships managed to escape and sailed to a beach somewhere on Bohol Island where they held a meeting. Carvalho was elected captain general, a responsibility he eventually proved incapable of handling. Since the fleet's compliment had been reduced by disease, starvation, fighting and massacre to about 110 men, the bare minimum to man two ships, They decided to get rid of *Concepción,* that anyway was riddled by teredo shipworms. Saving anything of value for the long voyage home, they divided her gear and stores between the other two ships and burned her to the water line so that the natives could not pick her bones. Sebastián Elcano, her captain, a Basque mariner, promoted by the changes in fortune of the voyage from relative obscurity, emerged as commander of *Victoria.*

Endless days and weeks became months of wandering among the many islands scattered across the China Sea. Sailing between the Philippines and Borneo produced a succession of misadventures as they sought clues of how to reach the Spice Islands. They strayed as far afield as Palawan where provisions of every kind were abundant. 'We called that land the Land of Promise', says Pigafetta, 'because we suffered great hunger before we found it.'

In need of a pilot from Palawan to Borneo, they captured a ship about to enter the harbour and shanghaied three Muslim pilots to guide them. The two ships departed Palawan on 21 June 1521, the day of the full moon, and arrived at Brunei, in the northern part of Borneo, on 9 July. Due to their reception, the Spaniards might easily have thought they had arrived at the land of the Thousand and One Nights.

The Shahbender – title of the ruler of Brunei – sent out to meet *Trinidad* and *Victoria* a beautiful prao with guilt carvings on bow and stern. 'At the bow flew a white and blue banner surmounted by peacock feathers', Pigafetta tells us. An orchestra on the prao played on native instruments and eight elderly chiefs closed the Spanish ships and climbed on board bearing gifts and sat down in the stern upon carpets. 'They presented us with a painted wooden jar full of betel and areca, the fruit which they chew continually, and jasmine and orange blossoms, a covering of yellow silk cloth, two cages full of fowls, a couple of goats, three jars full of distilled rice wine, and some bundles of sugarcane. They did the same to the other ship, and embracing us took their leave. The rice wine is clear as water, but so strong that it intoxicated many of our men. It is called *arach*.' (i.e. arrack).

The ancient sultanate of Brunei, Islamised in the previous century, was at the height of its prosperity and power. By conquest and commerce its sultan and his predecessors had extended their influence over most of Borneo and many islands of Indonesia, Malaysia, and the Philippines. While the travellers had heard of the sultan's legendary wealth they were quite unprepared for the visible reality. The sultan was the most acclaimed ruler the Spanish had encountered.[5] Three hundred men with naked scimitars guarded him in his vast and adorned palace. He rarely ventured out of his private apartments adjoining the harem, only communicating by means of a speaking tube and then through a palace official.

Pigafetta and six men went ashore to pay a formal call and present gifts to the sultan that they had prepared. They were transported from the harbour to an official's house on two elephants with silk trappings with a dozen porters bringing up the rear carrying the presents. Cotton mattresses with taffeta linings and cotton sheets were provided by their host for them to sleep on. Next morning they rode on elephants again to the palace to present their credentials and receive permission to trade. In the reception room they were taught the protocol of clasping their hands above their heads and raising first one leg and then the other while bowing their heads toward the shahbender. They were permitted to see him through a drawn curtain, seated at a table chewing betel nut and playing with one of his many young sons. 'We told the king that we came from the king of Spagnia, and that the latter desired to make peace with him and asked only for permission to trade. The king had us told that since the king of Spagnia desired to be his friend, he was willing to be his, and that we could take water and wood, and trade at our pleasure.' From the palace they returned to the official's house where 'we supped on the ground upon a palm mat from thirty-two different kinds of meats, besides fish and other things.' After another night in proper beds, the deputation enjoyed another elephant ride to the port.

On the morning of 29 July 1521, the Spaniards saw a fleet of over a hundred praus approaching them, while during the night a fleet of junks had anchored off their sterns. Having all the appearance of a trap to capture *Victoria* and *Trinidad*, the travellers, by now extremely cautious, hastily made sail and attacked the junks, capturing four and killing a number of men. One of the captured men was the Rajah of Luzon, the Shahbender's military leader, who had sacked the town of a disobedient chief and carried off three beautiful girls to enhance the ruler's harem. Secretly receiving a large ransom in gold, Carvalho released him but kept the three girls to start a harem of his own.

After the attack on the junks, Carvalho decided it be best to leave Brunei. In the hurry he abandoned his own eight-year-old Brazilian son who had been invited ashore to play with the Shahbender's son. The boy never saw his father again and what ever became of the three girls we are not told. They were most likely released at Ternate after Carvalho's death. At any rate, Magellan would never have allowed them to sail on board any of his vessels, but discipline had become lax after his death and the Spaniards behaved as if time was of no consequence at all.[6]

Retracing their course *Victoria* and *Trinidad* came to an island on the south side of the Balabac Strait. They stayed for forty-two days to calk and repair the ships that were leaking during which 'each of us laboured hard...' In the evening of the September full moon, the officers of the fleet held a conclave. Feeling that Carvalho had become too big for his boots, as well as a menace to their future safety by acts of piracy, they downgraded him to his former rank of flag pilot. They elected the aguacil mayor (chief marshal of the fleet) Gonzalo Gómez de Espinosa, captain general instead, as well as captain of *Trinidad*, and they appointed Juan Sebastián Elcano captain of *Victoria*.[7] But as the local pilots they captured, were furtive and misleading as to where exactly the Spice Islands were, they continued to practice piracy. Closing on a native vessel for no apparent reason, they encountered a crew who put up a gallant fight with scimitars and shields. The Spaniards killed seven men but managed to take several survivors prisoner. One was the brother of a rajah from Mindanao who claimed to have been a guest in the house of Francisco Serrão on Ternate. They held him for questioning.

The *Trinidad* and *Victoria* first pushed south, and then south-east, guided by their captured pilots, though one of them managed to escape by swimming ashore, together with the rajah of Mindinao and his small son. (The boy was drowned.) On the afternoon of 6 November 1521, they sighted Ternate rising from the sea among a cluster of islands. Soon the smoky volcanic cone of Ternate's twin, Tidore, was sketched against the sky. 'The pilot who still remained with us told us that those four islands were *Malucho*', the long sought spiceries, of the Moluccas. 'Therefore, we thanked God and as an expression of our joy discharged our artillery. It was no wonder we were so glad, for we had spent twenty-seven months, less two days, in our search for Molucca', (counted from the day they left Spain).[8]

At last, they had finally arrived. The place that Columbus searched for in vain, the purpose of Vespucci's arduous voyage, and what Magellan had been sent to find, was spread out before them.

In the evening of 8 November 1521, the two ships entered the harbour of Tidore off the southern tip of the island, firing another barrage as the anchors plunged through the twenty-fathom depths to the bottom.[9]

The Magellan expedition's itinerary through the Moluccas.

Haunted by the spirit of Magellan, the Spaniards were desperate to meet the man they had endured so much hardship to see. While wondering how to find Francisco Serrão, Sultan Almanzor, a Moslem in his mid-forties came out to greet them seated in a prau beneath a silk awning. He was dressed in a delicate white shirt with gold embroidered-sleeves and a long sarong reaching from his waist to his bare feet. His head was wrapped in a silk turban crowned with a garland of flowers, but the fine features of his Asian face were incongruously disfigured by the garish red smears of betel-nut stains. 'In front of him was one of his sons with the royal scepter, and two persons with gold jars to pour water on his hands, and two others with gold caskets filled with betel-nut', says Pigafetta. The sultan said his own powers as a visionary and astrologer had predicted that in a dream he had seen the Spaniards coming.

After boarding *Trinidad*, the sultan was escorted to the stern cabin where he condescended to sit on a velvet-covered chair and declared that he and his people wished nothing better than to be the most loyal friends and vassals of imperial Charles. He carried on saying that he wished his island kingdom to no longer be called Tidore, but Castile instead, due to his great love for the king of Spain.

But, 'where was Francisco Serrão?' the Spaniards asked. Almanzor's next words were grave. Francisco Serrão was dead, he stated impassively. He had died on Ternate some months before the Spaniards arrived under mysterious circum-stances, as much of his stay on Ternate was shrouded in enigma.

Almanzor tactfully concealed the true circumstances since he was at the bottom of it all. The facts however, showed later that the rulers of Tidore and Ternate were enemies. Serrão supported Ternate, where he had been living as grand vizier to Sultan Bolief since 1512. Rumor had it that Sultan Almanzor poisoned him, after concluding peace between the two island kingdoms. He had allegedly killed Serrão during a visit when Serrão had made the narrow crossing to buy cloves. Sultan Almanzor, still seething over the Portuguese captain's high-handed efforts at peace and by forcing him to give a daughter in marriage not only to Serrão, but to his archenemy Sultan Bolief of Ternate, invited him to a royal dinner and by adding the poison of the betel leaf to his food killed him. They were told that it took four days for him to die.

Sultan Bolief met his own end a few days later attributed to poison as well. His death, it was said, may have been at the hands of his own daughter, who bitterly resented her father's quarrel with her husband, the sultan of the vassal island of Bacan, and Bolief's refusal to condone their marriage. The viper's nests of island politics in the Moluccas are somewhat difficult to follow.[10] As *Trinidad* and *Victoria* were being provisioned and loaded with spices for the trip home, two praus, one bearing a son of the Sultan of Ternate, the other a reclining figure clad in red velvet, was Serrão's widow,[11] her two children, and a company of courtiers and musicians with gongs, approached the ships. Not wishing to offend Almanzor, the Spaniards did not invite the party aboard, offering gifts instead. But this behavior was taken as a slight and the prince haughtily ordered his rowers to turn around.

However, all was not lost, as some sort of dialogue had been established. Grasping the opportunity some members of the crew decided to venture over to Ternate and call on Serrão's widow.

Examining Serrão's personal papers they discovered a letter from Magellan and read what he had written: 'God willing, I will soon be seeing you, whether by way of Portugal or Castile, for that is the way my affairs have been leaning: you must wait for me there, because we already know that it will be some time before we can expect things to get better for us.' But the two men never met again, and now both were dead, having died within eight months and a mere thousand miles distant of each other.[12] Pigafetta gives us some interesting figures on the private habits of these Muslim princes. He tells us 'those kings have as many women as they wish, but only one chief wife whom all the others obey. The king of Tidore had a large house outside the city, where two hundred of his chief women lived with a like number of women to serve them. When the king eats, he sits alone, or with his chief wife, in a high place like a gallery whence he can see all the other women who sit about, and he orders her who best pleases him, to sleep with him that night. No one is allowed to see those women without his permission and if anyone is found near the king's house by day or by night he is put to death. Every family is obliged to give the king one or two of its daughters', to keep the harem full. In the neighboring island of Halmahera (Jilolo) were two sultans who respectively fathered 600 children and the other 525. Jessu, the eldest with the top score, visited Ternate while the Christians were there and exchanged gifts, but not wives.[13] Before leaving for home new sails were bent on the ships and painted with the cross of Santiago – St James of Galicia – with an inscription that read: 'This is the sign [figura] of our good fortune.'[14] The sultan sent as a present to the king of Spain a slave, two bahars of cloves, and two extremely beautiful stuffed birds of paradise. 'Those birds', says Pigafetta, 'are as large as thrushes, have a small head and a long beak. Their legs are a palmo in lengths and as thin as a reed. They have no wings, but instead long feathers of various colours, like large plumes... They never fly except when there is wind. The people told us that those birds come from the terrestrial paradise, and they call them bolon diuatra, which is to say, birds of God.'[15]

To improve their chances that one of the two ships would make it home, the officers of the fleet decided that the ships should split. Now that the easterly monsoon had started, Victoria should return via the Cape of Good Hope, and Trinidad await the right time to ride the westerly monsoon to Nueva España. Once there her cargo would be carried across the Isthmus of Panama and loaded on ships for Spain. However, Trinidad sprang a leak at anchor and her men had to unload and careen her to get at it. Leaving her at the harbour of Tidore, Victoria, under Captain Elcano, with nothing to gain by delaying, after taking on cargo of cloves and nutmeg, set sail after an emotional leave-taking on 21 December 1521, with forty-seven of her original crew and thirteen natives. Gonzalo Gómez de Espinosa stayed behind with fifty-three men to command Trinidad.

In early April 1522, after more than three months work on her hull with the help of Almanzor's workers *Trinidad*, after leaving an officer and four men ashore to start a trading factory to pursue the spice trade, and carrying a cargo of 1,000 quintals [nearly fifty tons] of cloves, set sail north-east through the Philippine Sea. At one of the Marianas three men deserted but Espinosa pushed on through baffling easterly winds, stormy weather, and extreme cold, as far as latitude 43° N, level with Hakodate, Japan. She was beaten back by strong headwinds in a totally unexpected weather system. A five-day raging storm broke the mainmast and damaged the forecastle and poop, depleting the ship's stores, save for rice. The men accustomed to equatorial warmth and ill prepared for the freezing winds tearing at them, succumbed to disease. Under these conditions, Gómez de Espinosa decided he could face no more, came about, and set course for Tidore. After six weeks of sailing he reached an island he calls Bonaconora, probably Morotai. By then, thirty of his scurvy-ridden crew of fifty-three had died, making it almost impossible to sail her. *Trinidad* had become more a ghost ship than a vessel of the living.

During her absence, a fleet of seven Portuguese armed vessels under the command of Captain Antonio de Brito, who had been sent to scour the eastern seas to look for Magellan, put in at Tidore. As a first measure he wiped out the little Spanish garrison, and submitted the sultan to a tearful resignation of his allegiance to his new friends and compulsive obedience to Portugal. Gómez de Espinosa, at Bonaconora, having received news of the goings on at Tidore, sent a letter to Brito by boat, begging for help. The merciless Portuguese replied by sending a caravel to take possession of *Trinidad* and sail her to Ternate, under the repellent deadly stench hovering over her decks where her men lay helplessly sick and dying. Back at Ternate, Brito confiscated the ship's cargo of spices, all her invaluable records and logbooks, as well as her navigating instruments. In that condition a squall struck *Trinidad* at anchor severing her cable and sweeping her aground. Broken by the gale and waves she fell apart and became a total loss. Sad indeed was the once proud flagship's fate.

Her remaining crewmembers were taken prisoner and forced into the hard labour of building a fort on Ternate. The fort was completed on 15 February 1523, and named after St John the Baptist. Only four of *Trinidad*'s crew saw Spain again, and a Portuguese trader who had cast his lot with the Spaniards was declared a traitor and publicly beheaded.

Soon after the *Trinidad* was swept aground, the Portuguese, who salvaged her cannon and timbers, dismembered her for use in the construction of the new fort.

The Portuguese had not needed a fortress when Francisco Serrão was alive. He had a way of imposing his will in a benign fashion on the sultan as the self-styled white rajah he had become. However, with his death and the small Spanish contingent on Tidore outnumbered, the sultan of Ternate backed by the Portuguese, 'became the greatest servant of His Highness the King of Portugal, having many islands and lands under his dominion'.

However, the fortification soon became a practical symbol of Portuguese intolerance and repression. An unnatural blight on the pristine, tropical landscape. The fort of São João Bautista, encompassed an Iberian world far from home in which the Europeans locked out the world around them. Living in a dream world of their own creation, they imitated their home customs in food and dress, insofar as they could, untainted by natives whom they perceived as uncivilised savages living beyond the walls. The contemporary Portuguese historian João de Barros, understanding his countrymen's haughty and disdainful attitude towards the people of the islands, put it into words: 'The land of these islands is ill-favoured and ungracious to look at. The sun is always very near. The air is loaded with vapours. The coast is unwholesome.'

The pattern of arbitrary, cruel behaviour became the unfortunate custom of Portugal's colonial rule in the Moluccas. It was deepened by their hatred of the Muslim, due to the centuries-old Islamic occupation of the Iberian peninsula, followed by the long succession of violent wars against the Moors in North Africa, not to mention the Crusades, which left bitterness on both sides. Conversely the Moors, in mind and heart, believed that the invading Portuguese were infidels, a resentment of which the Portuguese were well aware.[16]

Brito seriously considered having the 'Genoese pilot' and a few others slaughtered forthwith, but as he cynically explains in his letter to the king, 'I detained them in Maluco because it is an unhealthy country, with the intention of having them die there', which most of them did. Brito himself employed the boatswain and the carpenter. The rest were shipped off to Governor Albuquerque in India, to dispose of as he saw fit. Their fate is unknown, except for Espinosa's slave, Antón '*de color negro*', who was given by Albuquerque to his sister. Of the four that eventually struggled back to the Iberian Peninsula, Juan Rodriguez, of forty-four, the oldest man in Magellan's fleet, escaped in a Portuguese ship. Ginés de Mafra and Gómez de Espinosa were taken to the Banda Islands where they endured hard labour for two years before being shipped with Hans Vargue, the German gunner, to Lisbon. On arrival they were thrown into jail. Poor Hans died in prison, pathetically having bequeathed all his back pay and a packet of cloves and nutmegs, to his commanding officer. The Portuguese sent Espinosa and Ginés de Mafra to Seville, where the Spanish authorities clapped them in jail. They were there for seven months before being released in 1527, almost eight years after leaving home. Ginés' wife, thinking him dead, had married again and sold all his property. After legal proceedings caused by that, he returned to the Indies where Pedro de Alvarado employed him as chief pilot in 1536. Six years afterwards he became pilot to Ruy López de Villalobos on his voyage to the Philippines.

Gonzalo Gómez de Espinosa, whose courageous support of Magellan in the San Julián mutiny saved the voyage, spent four and a half years in captivity before returning to Spain. Diogo Barbosa, Magellan's father-in-law, speaking bluntly at a memorial to Charles V, Emperor of the Holy Roman Empire, remarked that the mutineers in *San Antonio* 'were very well received and treated at the expense of

Your Highness, while the captain and others who were desirous of serving Your Highness were imprisoned and deprived of all justice. From this', he added, 'so many bad examples arise – heartbreaking to those who try to do their duty.' Words well spoken, as had Magellan returned to Spain, in all probability, he too would have been jailed on some trumped up charge or other.

Charles V later tried to make it up to Gonzalo Gómez de Espinosa after all the indignities he had been subjected to. The emperor granted him noble status and a coat of arms with the motto, on a global crest, differing only slightly from Elcano's: 'Thou wert one of the first to go around me.' His back pay, despite the officials of the Casa de Contratación not permitting payment of his salary for the years he spent in prison, amounted to a large sum of money. The king gave him 15,000 maravedis as heir of Hans Vargue, a pension of 30,000 maravedis, and a job as 'inspector of ships bound for the Indies' that came with 43,000 maravedis per annum. He held that position in 1543, when we finally loose sight of this valiant captain and the most loyal supporter of Magellan.

For the first time commander and mariners aboard *Victoria* could allow themselves to indulge the dream of returning home wealthy and standing high in royal favour. They had made a trade treaty with one of the rulers of the rich Moluccas. They had a cargo of spices aboard that would amply satisfy their backers, so they could reasonably look forward to a rapturous reception in Spain, if they could reach it.

Victoria took leave of their new friends and fellow countrymen on 21 December 1521 and sailed with a compliment of sixty, thirteen of them natives. Steering almost due south, she called at an islet off Tidore to fetch a load of firewood that had been cut for her. Leaving the other Spice Islands astern, and passing to starboard of the Xulla (Suela) Islands off the Celebes, she went though the Manipa Strait and anchored, on 27 December in Jakiol Bay to reprovision. Changing her course south-east she passed the great Indonesian island barrier by Alor Strait. Once into the Savu Sea they were hit by a severe storm that had all aboard vowing to perform a pilgrimage to the shrine 'to our Lady of Guidance' in Seville if she would deign to save them.[17] They scudded east before the storm, reaching an island then called Malua where they put in to caulk and repair ship. Setting out again, on 25 January, she reached the lofty (9,580ft) island of Timor.

They asked the chief on Timor to furnish them with food. He was willing to do so but his price was too high and as they were running out of trading articles they cunningly retained from a ship they captured a chief and his son of a neighboring town. For fear the Christians would kill him, the chief immediately had them provided with six buffaloes, five goats and two swine. They let the poor fellow go with linen, Indian cloths of silk and cotton, hatchets, knives and scissors and other things they could scratch up.

Camoëns describes Timor as 'that isle which yields sandalwood salubrious and sweet to smell.' Pigafetta praised it. 'White sandalwood is found in that island and nowhere else. Also, ginger, water buffaloes, swine, goats, fowls, rice, figs [bananas], sugar cane, oranges, lemons, wax, almonds, kidney beans and other things. All the sandalwood and wax that is traded by the inhabitants of Java and Malacca comes from that region...We found a junk from Lozon [Luzon] there, which had come hither to trade in sandalwood.' (Elcano bought a packet of the fragrant wood back to Spain.) 'The people [of Timor] were all heathens...' but as 'the disease of St Jop (syphilis) was to be found in all the islands which we encountered in that archipelago, but more so in that island than in others', the crew avoided the girls. 'It is called *foi franchi*, that is to say French disease', a statement that needs no further explanation.[18]

Pigafetta at Timor, picked up some yarns from the Moros, with whom he seems to have been able to carry on a conversation, concerning China, Java and the Far East. One of them tells us that, in those days, when a chief on Java died, his body was cremated on a funeral pyre. 'Then, his principal wife adorns herself with garlands of flowers and has herself carried on a chair through the entire village by three or four men. Smiling and consoling her relatives, who are weeping, she says: Do not weep, for I am going to sup with my dear husband this evening, and to sleep with him this night. She then is carried to the fire, where her husband is being burned. Turning towards her relatives, and again consoling them she, she throws herself into the fire. Did she not do that she would not be considered an honourable woman.'

Another story of Pigafetta's, though this time comical, which later European travellers confirmed, is a variation of the *palang* in the courtship habits of the young gentlemen of Java. In his own words, 'When the young men of Java are in love with any gentlewoman, they fasten certain little bells between the penis and the foreskin. They take a position under their sweetheart's window, and make pretence of urinating, and shaking their penis' they make the little bells ring, and continue to ring them until their sweetheart hears the sound. The sweetheart descends immediately, and they take their pleasure; always with those little bells, for their women take great pleasure in hearing those bells ring inside.'[19]

On the night of 11 February 1522, *Victoria* left the island of Timor and entered the great open sea 'called Laut Chidol' – the Indian Ocean. Setting his course west-south-west, Elcano left the islands of Bali, Java and Sumatra to starboard for fear of being attacked by the Portuguese who had outposts all along their route. His plan was to cut out straight across the Indian Ocean, double the Cape of Good Hope and head for home. It took him nine weeks before he sighted the coast of Africa. By then the crew were reduced to a state of misery only comparable to what they endured when crossing the Pacific. In this case, owing to a scarcity of salt in the Spice Islands and Timor, the meat and fish insufficiently pickled in the casks went putrid in the hold. To make matters worse in early March the monsoon died out and the westerlies took over. Day after day they drove the ship into furious head winds that created enormous seas against which *Victoria* found it difficult to contend. On several occasions Elcano had the ship *lie-to*, tossing and rolling in the waves, while he kept his men busy repairing leaks and fixing the ship's rigging and sails.

Some of the men were so sick, cold and hungry, 'because we had no other food than rice and water', that they begged the captain to put in at Portuguese Mozambique. 'However', the majority, 'more desirous of their honour then their own life, determined to go to Spain living or dead.' Brave lads indeed!

After venturing south as far as the 'roaring forties' Elcano decided he had enough and changed his course north-west. Finally, on 6 May they sighted the Cape of Good Hope at a distance of five leagues. 'Then we sailed northwest for two months continually without taking on any refreshment', wrote Pigafetta.[20] On 8 June 1522, with a full moon, *Victoria* crossed the Equator for the fourth time, since leaving Spain. Between the two months since leaving Timor, she had lost twenty-one men. 'When we cast them into the sea', Pigafetta thought it significant 'that the Christians went to the bottom face upward, [towards heaven] while the Indonesians always went down face downward.'[21]

Finally, on 9 July 1522, *Victoria* entered the port of Ribeira Grande on the island of Santiago the southernmost of the Cape Verde group of islands owned by Portugal. Elcano instructed his shore party to try and deceive the Portuguese by saying they had lost their way upon returning from the West Indies and put in at that port to re-victual. The ruse worked at first and the shore party returned with two boatloads of rice. They also found out to their dismay that their count of calendar was wrong. They thought it was Wednesday, but were told in the town that it was Thursday. They could hardly believe that by sailing westward with the sun they had lost a day on route. Not until reaching Seville could anyone find the explanation. As the ship was leaking badly they stayed at anchor for four or five days constantly pumping. The captain sent his largest boat to shore manned by thirteen seamen to get more food and buy slaves to relieve his exhausted men at the pumps. Having no cash he sent several parcels of cloves for the purchase. This alerted the Portuguese authorities that *Victoria* had been trespassing on 'their' Spice Islands. They immediately detained the crew and sent one of their own boats with a port authority, to order Elcano to surrender his ship. The captain knew he was in no fit condition to shoot it out with the Portuguese and fearing that they might also be taken prisoners; he hastily departed on 15 July.

In some ways the remainder of the voyage against the northerly 'Portuguese Trades' was the toughest. For not only had eighteen men have to do the work of a normal crew of fifty, a matter not only of sailing the ship but manning the pumps as well to prevent *Victoria* from foundering. The leaking, undermanned vessel, wallowed northwards. Each league nearer home was bought with more death, more water shipped, and more men collapsing with fatigue and sickness at their posts. At one point the men urged Elcano to jettison some of the cargo to lighten ship. He refused for the compelling reason that the spices aboard were valuable enough to pay the costs of the expedition as well as yielding a handsome profit. The merchants who had backed Magellan would not look kindly upon a captain who had deliberately squandered their investment. It would bode Elcano ill to insist he had done it simply to save his ship and his men, so for two more months *Victoria* pursued her course to Spain.[22]

She sighted Tenerife 28 July, and like the trading ships returning from Africa against a north wind she had to make a wide sweep to the west on the starboard tack towards the Azores. However, being Portuguese territory she dared not enter port for badly needed provisions, but steered a course for Cape St.Vincent instead. She picked up that prominent landmark on 4 September.

The winds now favoured the weary mariners and on 6 September 1522, 'we entered the port of San Lúcar de Barrameda with only eighteen men and the majority of them sick, all that were left of the sixty men that had left Malucho [the Maluccas]. Some died of hunger; some deserted at the island of Timor and some were put to death for crimes. From the time we left that bay [of San Lúcar] until the present day [of our return] we had sailed fourteen thousand four hundred and sixty leagues, and furthermore had completed the circumnavigation of the world.'[23]

After one night, and we hope fresh food, Elcano procured a boat with stout oarsmen who pulled her up the Guadalquivir on two flood tides. On 8 September 1522 she moored off a quay at Seville close to the church of Santa Maria de la Victoria. It was a very happy coincidence to discover that it was the very feast day of that Virgin, the patron of mariners. Three years and a month had passed from the time *Victoria* had sailed with her four companion ships under Magellan to find the elusive strait through the South American barrier into the Pacific.[24]

Only eighteen Christians were left to give thanks to God for their deliverance, pray for their dead companions, and perform their penitential vows to the Virgin. On Tuesday the 9th, barefoot, haggard and most of them clad in tatters, they walked up from the harbour each carrying a long lighted candle into the church of Santa Maria de la Victoria. One observer said that they looked 'more emaciated than an old worn-out hack horse.' After that pathetic ceremony, they crossed the old pontoon bridge to Seville proper and after walking well over a mile, entered the great cathedral and prostrated themselves in front of the venerated shrine of Santa Maria de la Antigua where they prayed and gave thanks for their survival.

Juan Sebastián Elcano lost no time in writing his report showing commendable concern for his fellow seamen. He was summoned to the royal court at Valladolid, to be honoured by the king, together with picked members of *Victoria*'s crew, who were issued new clothes and an installment of their wages. The emperor received Captain Elcano graciously and granted him an annual pension of 500 ducats ($1,160 in gold), which in fact was never paid during his lifetime. He was granted by the herald's office the right to an appropriate coat of arms with the following blazon: Chief, a castle *or*, on field *gules*, and on the bottom half a field *or*, with two crossed cinnamon sticks, three nutmegs and twelve cloves. Crest: a globe bearing the motto *Primus circumdedisti me* (Thou first circumnavigated me). Supporters: two Malay kings, crowned, each holding a branch of a spice tree, proper.

Charles V demanded from his brother-in-law Dom João III, king of Portugal, the return of the thirteen sailors confined on the Cape Verdes, which was granted fairly promptly. They with the rest of the eighteen Christians who finished the voyage were received at court. The fate of the three Indonesian survivors is unrecorded. Adding the five seamen from *Trinidad* who eventually reached Spain, we have thirty-five survivors from the five ships that originally sailed from San Lúcar de Barrameda on 20 September 1519. Those aboard *San Antonio* that defected would account for fifty to fifty-five more.

Pigafetta did the rounds from court to court, presenting kings and queens with accounts from his narrative. He obtained permission from the Seignory of Venice to publish it there, but he never did. The first edition of his narrative was published in French and came out in Paris in 1525. Then there were several Italian editions prior to 1540, and the English translation by Richard Eden in 1555. Pigafetta became famous in his day but died fairly young in his hometown of Vicenza.

Today, Magellan's achievement is considered the greatest and most amazing voyage in recorded history. Yet other than Pigafetta's high praise, the noble Captain General received little credit for at least two centuries. The Portuguese denounced him as a traitor. The Spanish disowned him. Owing to stories spread in Spain by Elcano and Esteban Gómez about his harsh discipline and mistakes in navigation. Magellan was forgotten in favor of the Basque master mariner Elcano. Neither Portugal nor Spain held any enduring interest in the man who sailed halfway round the world.

Doña Beatriz Magellan and her two little children died before *Victoria* returned to Seville. Magellan's legal heirs were unable to collect his salary from the government he had so tenaciously served. But of the four greatest navigators in the age of discovery – Columbus, Vespucci, Magellan, and Vasco da Gama – Magellan's image reigns supreme. Columbus, with bold determination, broke the Atlantic barrier, crossing the Western Ocean back and forth four times. Vespucci inaugurated the sea path down the western seaboard of South America, going further south than anyone had ever gone and ultimately discovering the Río de la Plata. Da Gama forged a trail to India, concluding the voyage of Bartholomeu Dias, who had been the first to round the southernmost Cape of Africa. However, Magellan conquered the tempestuous southern waters and overcame mutiny, starvation, and treachery to cross the Pacific Ocean, which he also named. It is true that Elcano finished the circumnavigation, but he did so by carrying out Magellan's plan.[25] Magellan's true memorial is the Strait he revealed to the world:

> Forever sacred to the hero's fame,
> Those foaming straits shall bear his name.[26]

18

FRANCIS DRAKE –
THE QUEEN'S PIRATE

Francis Drake is a man aged 38. He may be two years more or less. He is short in stature, thickset and very robust. He has a fine countenance, is ruddy of complexion and has a fair beard. He has the mark of an arrow wound in his right cheek, which is not apparent if one looks not with special care. In one leg he has the ball of an arquebus that was shot at him in the Indies... He had seated at his table the captain, pilot and doctor. He also read psalms and preached... He carries a book in which he enters his log, and paints birds, trees and sea lions. He is an adept in painting and carries along a boy [John Drake] a relative of his, who is a great painter. When they both shut them-selves up in his cabin they were always painting. He is a great mariner, the son and relative of seamen, and particularly of John Hawkins in whose company he was for a long time... He also carried with him, from this country, a Negro, named Diego, who spoke Spanish and English, and whom he had taken prisoner from a frigate in the North Sea [i.e. the Atlantic], near Nombre de Dios, about seven or eight years previously.

Nuño da Silva's deposition before the Inquisition in México City in 1579[1]

Francis Drake was described in this manner by a Portuguese fellow mariner who sailed with him. He might also have added that he was brave to the point of fearlessness, ruthless in his cruelty and fierce in his hatred of Spain and Catholicism, to the point of being aggressively Protestant.[2]

Drake was born around 1541, in Crowndale, in Devonshire, a mile or so south of Tavistock near Plymouth, the son of a tenant farmer of obscure origins. Nevertheless, he took care to beg a great noble, Francis Russell (afterwards Earl of Bedford) to stand as godfather to the boy and according to custom he gave him his name when he was baptised. Nobody seems to have done anything for him when he was a child, except when he lived with his relations, the Hawkins family in Plymouth. Even his best biographers have no information about his schooling. Francis's father, to quote a contemporary historian and antiquary William Camden, says that:

After the death of King Henry [the eighth] he got a place among the sea-men in the King's Navy, to reade Prayers to them: and soon after he was ordained Deacon, and made Vicar of the Church of Upnore upon the River Medway (the Road where the fleet usually anchoreth).But by reason of his Poverty, he put his son to the Master of a Bark, his neighbour, who held him hard to his business in the Bark, with which he used to coast along the Shoar, and sometimes to carry Merchandize into Zeland and France.The youth being painful and diligent, so pleased the Old Man by his industry, that being a bachelour, at his death he bequeathed the bark unto him by Will and testament.

Thus was Francis Drake set up, and for some time he followed his calling.When he became a youth of eighteen, according to the English chronicler Edmund Howes, he sailed as purser on one of Hawkins' sailing ventures in the Bay of Biscay. In the early 1560s he signed on as a seaman in one of the Hawkins' ships sailing for the Guinea coast of West Africa, from where they brought home valuable stores of gold, pepper and ivory. Later, in 1567, he sailed with his relative, the formidable John Hawkins himself in a fleet of six vessels.The idea was to fill up with Africans, bought or captured, and to sell them in the West Indies or on the Spanish Main – an illegal trade by Spanish law but one that with proper briberies could be carried on very profitably. By February 1568 they had about 400 slaves in their holds, and with them crossed the Atlantic to Dominica. Drake was in command of the *Judith*, of about 50 tuns.With his previous experience of dealing with the Spanish colonists and their conniving officials in illicit commerce, Hawkins and his ships coasted along the northern settlements of South America, 'enjoying reasonable trade and traffike, and curteous entertainment in sundry places' he tells us, referring to the different islands where he dealt.They traded along the coast with moderate success until they reached Río de la Hacha. Drake had been sent ahead to open negotiations. He was answered by gunfire: this he returned, and soon stood off to wait for Hawkins, who dealt with the Spaniards reluctance by storming the town and burning most of it.They moved on, with some success at Santa Marta but none at all at the well-fortified Cartagena, and then shaped their course for home before the hurricane season.

However, when they arrived off Cuba, heading for Florida and the Atlantic westerlies, they met with an appalling four-day blow with howling winds that shattered Hawkins's ship the *Jesus* so that they had to cut down her upper rigging. They found no shelter on the coast of Florida, and another storm blew them right across the Gulf of Mexico and down that of Campeche where after a month of incessant pumping, they took refuge in San Juan de Ulúa.

As harbours go, it was little more than the area between the mainland and the island of San Juan de Ulúa. It was the point of entry for colonists and administrators going to Mexico City and one of the ports from where bullion and goods from New Spain were loaded onto ships before their departure in convoy to the mother country. On the mainland, only a few miles from the port stood the town of Vera Cruz, named by its Catholic founders after the True Cross of Christ.Vera Cruz and its port of San Juan de Ulúa lay at the end of Mexico City's main route through the Gulf of Mexico into the Atlantic and therefore an important connection point of Spain with its empire.

The crews of a dozen Spanish vessels riding at their anchors were relaxing in the taverns on shore enjoying the wine, fresh fruit and pleasures of the local women after their long passage from Seville. It was the evening of 15 September 1568, when John Hawkins in the queen's 700-ton *Jesus of Lübeck* sailed into view, a crumbling crown vessel that Henry VIII had purchased nearly twenty years earlier, now owned by Queen Elizabeth. The harbour was broad and open, only slightly sheltered from the weather by the low-lying island.

The *Jesus*, her ancient hull strained and with her fastenings loosened, had sprung its planks and was taking on water faster than the pumps could handle. In his own words, Hawkins tells us of his plight:

> there happened to us… an extreme storm which continued by the space of 4 dais, which so beat the *Jesus*, that we cut downe all her higher buildings, her rudder also was sore shaken, and withal was so in extreme a leake that we were hoping to bring all to good passe sought the coast of Florida, where we found no place nor haven;… thus being in greater dispaire, and taken with a new storme which continued other three days we were enforced to take our succor the port called Saint John de Ullua.[3]

Hawkins entered the port to repair his ships without any aggressive intentions. He arrived unmolested and even received a salute from the Spanish guns on shore that mistook them for an advance party from the expected Spanish fleet, bringing the new viceroy. But he had put his head into a noose, and the events that followed were to colour his and Drake's attitude towards the Spanish for the rest of their lives.

In the early morning following their arrival, the topmasts of the Spanish fleet were seen drawing near across the lonely waters of the Gulf. On board the Spanish flagship was the expected new viceroy of Mexico, Don Martín Enríquez, who was faced with a difficult decision even before he landed. As the Spanish ships maneuvered to cast anchors in the port, Enriquez realised that if he attacked Hawkins, he risked losing his fleet as well as the Spanish ships in the harbour. However, the weather was threatening, and it was necessary to find a safe haven for his vessels in the port.

Enríquez and Hawkins, via envoys, commenced an exchange of messages. Hawkins explained he had come to repair his ships and would leave as soon as he had done so. Requesting victuals and facilities for repairs, he promised no harm would come to men or goods while his fleet was there. He suggested a truce with an exchange of twelve men of either side to guarantee it. Enríquez accepted with the customary elaborate phrasing of Spanish diplomacy and had a trumpet sounded to indicate the bargain sealed.

Hawkins immediately saw the importance of controlling the island for his safety, as he tells us: 'or els the Spaniards might at their pleasure cut our cables and so with the first Northwind that blewe we had our passport, for our shipps had gone a shore.' He therefore set up a battery on the island of San Juan and landed fifty men and seven cannon to reinforce the existing one. The viceroy agreed to this sending an amiable reply and a trumpet blast to signify his agreement.

There was complete distrust on both sides. The viceroy who believed that no arrangement made with a corsair was binding, devised a plan to hide his men in an empty cargo ship lying close to the English vessels and attempt to board them from there. However, when he saw that the element of surprise had been discovered he had a trumpet blown to start the assault nearly an hour before the time agreed upon and before his attacking forces were in position. At the height of the fight Hawkins, while exhorting his gunners to keep up the good work, called to his page for a tankard of beer. He emptied it, set it down by the mainmast, and saw it shot away by a culverin. 'Nothing dismayed… he ceased not to encourage us', wrote Job Hortop the gunner, 'Saying, feare nothing, for God, who hath preserved me from this shot, will also deliver us from these traitours and villaines.'[4]

The *Jesus* was irreparably damaged by the gunfire and was abandoned by Hawkins and her crew, barely able to make their escape aboard the *Minion*.

Hawkins improvised a counter attack by sacrificing some of his smaller vessels as fire ships. Set ablaze by their own crews in an attempt to set fire to their opponents, a major Spanish ship sank in flames while another blew apart when a lucky English shot hit her magazine and she exploded. However, all the Englishmen ashore were killed except three. Others in the water and afloat perished and of their own ships, only the *Minion* and the fifty ton *Judith*, both over laden with men from the *Jesus*, escaped to face the harsh seas of the Atlantic winter. Hawkins, in the *Minion*, with only two anchors gripping the seabed to stop him being driven ashore, was lucky to save his ship. That night the *Judith* commanded by Francis Drake disappeared and in Hawkins' words, she 'forsook us in our great myserie'. Five English ships were abandoned in the port, four captured and one destroyed by the Spanish militia.

Abandoning his kinsman to his own devices Drake sailed for England forcing Hawkins to beach 100 of his men on the Mexican coast, most of whom never saw home again. The scandal caused a serious rift between the two that was to haunt Drake for the rest of his life, but he never forgot the lessons learned from his cousin and mentor.

According to the account written by the Spanish historian Antonio de Herrera thirty years later, Drake escaped with most of the treasure they had accumulated from the sale of slaves. Arriving in England, Drake reported Hawkins lost and that the treasure was gone, distributed, he said, among his seamen. When Hawkins finally showed up and it was clear that Drake had not told the truth, Queen Elizabeth put him in prison, but Drake slyly insisted he had given the treasure away. Finally the queen relented and after three months he was released.[5]

The treacherous attack by the Spaniards at San Juan de Ulúa seems to have given Drake an inextinguishable lust for revenge, which translated into an excuse for his brutal behavior during his incursions on the isthmus. Many times in his great voyage of circumnavigation, he would tell Spanish prisoners that he was merely getting back a 'bit of his own' from that defeat and the treachery of the viceroy Don Martín Enríquez. The dastardly event would be a matter indelibly etched in his mind for the rest of his life. But King Henry's break with Roman Catholicism must have provided Drake with further justification for the ravages he performed on Catholic churches and their clerics in the course of his raids on Spanish colonial settlements.

Both Drake, as well as Hawkins, when they returned found a different England to the one they had left. Philip II of Spain had moved some of his pieces on the chessboard. His vast territorial wealth imposed a huge responsibility upon him and he spent hours every day reading dispatches, reports and drafting replies. He was obsessively conscientious of being Christendom's standard-bearer against the forces of Islam and the rising tide of Protestantism in Northern Europe.[6]

As ruler of the Netherlands, Philip had provided the Duke of Alba with three crack divisions of troops to quell increasing Lutheran disturbances in the Low Countries. By so doing he created new problems for himself. Philip had raised a loan from Genoese bankers to pay Alba's troops, and the money, in silver coins, was on its way to Antwerp in a convoy of unarmed merchantmen and a few pinnaces. Harassed by French privateers operating in bad weather out of La Rochelle, the convoy took refuge in English ports; the larger ship in Southampton and the pinnaces in Falmouth, Fowey and Plymouth. With the French waiting for them outside in the Channel, once in, they dared not leave port. The English authorities with their eyes on the silver had it brought ashore under the excuse that the wicked French might otherwise sail in and seize it. Fifty-nine cases were landed in Southampton, and ninety-eight in West Country ports, including Plymouth, where William Hawkins, John's brother, was mayor.

Queen Elizabeth, being at peace with Spain could not simply seize the silver as a windfall but she delighted in the thought that any pretext for withholding it from the Duke of Alba would cause him great embarrassment with his unpaid troops. The problem escalated when William, hearing of his brother's defeat at San Juan de Ulúa complained about his brother's losses and demanded the seizure of the Spanish silver as compensation.

The matter brought into focus the distrust that Elizabeth and Philip had for each other that was not eased in 1568 by Elizabeth's imprisonment of Catholic Mary Queen of Scots, for which the pope was urging retribution. Elizabeth retained the silver and took over Philip's debt to the Genoese and from then on, having learned his lesson, Philip began sending his pay-chests overland, well guarded.

After the defeat and financial losses at San Juan de Ulúa, John Hawkins wanted no more of Caribbean exploits on a personal level and it was a long time until he saw the waters of the West Indies again. Drake on the other hand was all action. Hatred of Spain and desire for revenge, were, henceforth, his overmastering passions.

He first expended his rage against Spain in 1571, in a raid on the Isthmus of Panama in the twenty-five-tun pinnace *Swan* captained by his brother John. The following year he commanded both her and the 70-tun *Pasco,* belonging to John Hawkins that he himself captained with forty-seven men, against Port Pheasant (now Puerto Escocés). Having assembled three knocked down pinnaces he carried in the holds, he attacked Nombre de Dios but failed to carry off the stacked up bars of silver and coffers of gold owing to a bad wound that he received in his leg during the assault on the treasure-house. His men, feeling their leader's life more important than looting, used his scarf as a tourniquet to halt the hemorrhage and carried him back to the pinnaces, as dawn was breaking.

Drake being incredibly resilient subsequently mounted attacks up and down the Isthmus of Panama often joined by French pirates or escaped black African runaway slaves known as *cimarrones,* who looked upon the English as liberators. Near the end of January 1573, with his lieutenant John Oxenham, eighteen Englishmen and twenty blacks, Drake marched across the Isthmus and captured a mule-train (known as a *recua*). It yielded only victuals, however, the *cimarrones* had promised him they would show him a spot from where both the Atlantic and the Pacific were visible. Pedro, the Cimarron leader led them far inland through the hot steamy jungle to a tall tree in which steps had been cut and an observation platform built. Drake and Oxenham climbed up. The tree was at a point so high on the Isthmus of Panama that from the platform near its top he could see the Great South Sea before him, and if he turned, the Atlantic behind. Flabbergasted, he 'besought God of his goodness to give him leave and his life to sayle once in an English ship in that sea.' John Oxenham, 'protested that unlesse our Captain did beate him from his company he would follow him by God's grace.' Oxenham was there first but God's grace was selective. While Drake's venture into the Pacific would lead him to the glory of circumnavigation, Oxenham's incursion was to lead to his capture, torture and death at the hands of the Holy Spanish Inquisition, after carrying out the most outrageously anti-Catholic pillaging ever perpetrated by an Englishman.

Again in alliance with a French privateer named Guillaume Le Têtu, Drake waylaid another *recua*. He captured rich booty that set him up for life, but his French ally was caught and beheaded on the spot. The value of Drake's booty became ascertainable for the first time from published Spanish documents during the 1950s. They indicate that the whole of the treasure seized was worth 150,000 gold pesos, of this the raiders carried off from 80,000 to 100,000 of them. The gold peso was worth nine English shillings of the period. Thus the capture amounted to approximately £40,000, of the '50s, equally shared between the English and the French.[7]

Drake retired to the shelter of the Darien coast and determined to try the alterna-tive plan of attacking another treasure train on the road between Panama and Nombre de Dios. In the subsequent skirmishes, his brother John was killed while boarding a passing Spanish frigate. Fever broke out and carried off another brother, Joseph, and some of his crew. Drake held Joseph in his arms as he died, and to find out the cause of death, had his body opened by the surgeon, who proclaimed he 'found his liver swollen, his heart as it were sodden, and his guts all faire.' The surgeon died four days after the post mortem. (It was most probably Yellow Fever.)

John Oxenham returned to try and capture the Isthmus of Panama in 1576, with a hundred-tun ship, two reassembled pinnaces. While a Spanish officer estimated that 300 Englishmen would have been enough to hold the Isthmus permanently, although Drake, perhaps, might have done it with two. John Oxenham tried it with fifty. On 9 April he sailed from Plymouth in a ship of 100 tons, two knocked down pinnaces, and fifty-seven men, of whom seven were dead before he got to his destination. With him was John Butler, known to the Spaniards as Chalona, who had considerable knowledge of Central America, was fairly fluent in several languages, and is described as the pilot and translator of the expedition. His brother was also part of the operation.

When Oxenham reached the coast in midsummer, he took some treasure from the local shipping and then went eastwards to the Gulf of Acla where he concealed his ships and made contact with the *cimarrones*.

Spain, at the time, was fortunate to have as President of the Audiencia in Panama, an uncommonly active man who pursued his job with vigour and initiative. His name was Gabriel de Loarte. As soon as Loarte heard that Oxenham and his men had set foot on the northern coast of the Isthmus he expected that an alliance with the cimarrones would be his next step. He immediately sent a force from Nombre de Dios to reconnoiter the territory and flush him out. Loarte's force discovered some of Oxenham's ships and captured the greater part of his artillery, munitions, as well as various trade goods. Oxenham was thus left with most of his men but with only his small arms, a scanty supply of ammunition and no means of paying the *cimarrones* for their services. He built a pinnace 45ft long, pulling twelve oars a side, and launched her on a river flowing towards the South-Sea. [Most likely the River Chucunaque.] With his crew of Englishmen and a party of *cimarrones* he rowed his way into the Bay of San Miguel in the Pacific discovered by Balboa, and onward to the Islands of Pearls in the Gulf of Panama. There they found a handful of Spaniards together with some blacks engaged in pearl fishing and a Franciscan friar who had come to confess his flock. A companion of the friar who later gave a deposition at Oxenham's trial in Lima, related the events that took place: The English took from the friar certain religious books and papal bulls, which they destroyed, calling the pope by a foul name. They smashed up images and a consecrated alter, Oxenham asking the Spaniard why he had so many gods and telling him not to believe in saints and friars who were sinners like other men. Then:

Having found a child's lesson book, one of the English named Chalona, who is the interpreter among them, stopped to read it, and by reading the ten commandments, when he came to the commandment: *Thou shalt not steal,* he laughed loudly at it, and said that all the goods were common property… So also, among other books deponent possessed, they found one of the evangels and epistles in Spanish; and they bade him read that book, because it was a good book, and ordered him to treat it well, inasmuch as the others were fabrications and all lies; and the deponent took the book and put it away…

Next the English opened deponent's chests to take his clothing and what else they might find; and having found a crucifix in a box, their captain looked deponent in the face wrathfully and holding up the crucifix in his hands demanded: why has thou this? And threw it at deponent, but missed him, and it struck a stand, which broke the crucifix to pieces…

The English cook took the alb used in the ceremony of the mass and put it on and danced about in it, ridiculing everything; which performance the *cimarrones* witnessed. It delighted them and they gave great evidence of their pleasure saying, 'I English, pure Lutheran.' Afterwards the said Englishman cut the alb short and kept it on for a shirt and wore his own clothes over it…

All the Englishmen took the friar and buffeted him and put a chamber pot upon his head and struck him many blows upon the head. The friar was humble, exclaiming: so be it, for the love of God… The next day they showed the friar a wooden cross which was there and asked him what it was; and when the friar answered that it was the image and likeness of the cross upon which Jesus Christ Our Lord was crucified, the English replied: That is where we will hang you and burn you before we go. To which the friar answered that he did not merit the honour; and at this they left him.[8]

So behaved John Oxenham and his merry crew who went on to take several vessels, steal their cargos, and submit their sailors to abject cruelty.

Loarte, President of the Audiencia, had only 500 men of military age in Panama but not all of them could be spared for field duty. Within six days he had 200 of them afloat in six vessels commanded by Pedro de Ortega Valencia, as well as another force getting ready on the north coast at Nombre de Dios. He also sent word at once to the Viceroy of Perú that help was needed. The viceroy did not wait for orders from above. 'This', he wrote in defiance of routine orders, 'was an occasion when to await a reply might have entailed irreparable damage,' and sent an officer, Diego de Frias Trejo from Lima, to pursue the vandals.

Oxenham underestimated the efficiency of the Spaniards. He leisurely retired to Vallano without taking pains to conceal his trail. Frias Trejo scoured Vallano with four columns in August 1577, until one of them came upon their quarry. The treasure was recovered and one party came upon Oxenham who was apprehended with eighteen of his countrymen. Several of them were sent to Panama, where the majority was hanged at once. Two boys were spared and sent to Spain. Oxenham, John Butler, Henry Butler, and the ship's master, Thomas Sherwell, were sent to Lima to be judged by the Inquisition. All abjured heresy and were admitted to the Catholic faith to be sentenced to penitential service in the galleys. Oxenham, the elder Butler, and Sherwell were hanged in the main square of Lima in October 1580. Henry Butler, a youth, was sent to the galleys for life.[9]

When Drake arrived home in 1573 with the plunder taken on the Isthmus of Panama and found that the conditions were unfavourable for him to display his loot, he disappeared for two years, during which time his movements are unknown. His next documented involvement is in connection with a campaign in Ireland that the queen had entrusted to Walter Devereux, the Earl of Essex, 'in an attempt to pacify and colonise the district of Ulster'. The real reason for the expedition was not any of the foresaid but greed in which Essex and his partners hoped to make a profit, and profit they did in both land and money.

Essex employed Hawkins' ships as well as Drake's small vessels to carry his troops across the Irish Sea. While on this business Drake made friends with Thomas Doughty, a man of his own age and of equal ambition. All be it of that landsmen's world with which Drake had hitherto had little contact, Doughty influenced the sailor, inspiring him with admiration and confidence that was not entirely warranted. For Doughty lacked loyalty, and had already fallen into disgrace with his leader Essex due to some double dealing embroiling Essex with Lord Robert Dudley, whom the queen had created earl of Leicester in 1564.

But we are going too fast. In general the English plan was to eliminate the Irish nobility and to reduce the 'Irish churl' to a similar state to that of the Indians in the Spanish *encomienda* system.[10] The queen had agreed to grant Essex a large estate in County Antrim as well as sweeping governmental powers. When the local chief, Sir Brian MacPhelim O'Neill, heard of the scheme he did his best to work in with Essex but Essex seeing how difficult it would be to overcome O'Neill's opposition to his plans, lured the man's followers into a trap at a feast, treacherously slaughtered them, and executed Sir Brian in Dublin.

Next, Essex turned his attention to Rathlin Island where he wanted to establish a permanent fort. It was already fortified, so well indeed that Sorley Boy, the local Scottish chief, had sent his women and children there for safety. To take the island Essex needed a fleet. Enter Francis Drake. The venture, from which Essex and his partners hoped to make a profit – the real reason for the attack as said, was greed – proved profitable, though shockingly barbaric. Essex sent Captain Norris and hand picked troops with Drake in his ships, to capture the island. Contesting every foot of ground the Scots fought bitterly then retreated to their fortified castle. If the battle was bloody the surrender was worse. As the Scots filed out of the castle, the English soldiers set upon them. Over 200 men, women, and children were killed. For several days afterwards, the soldiers scoured the island for survivors, tracking them down in caves and crevices to murder them. In all, some 500 Scots were put to the sword. It was said that Sorley Boy, wretched with grief, had watched it all from the mainland.[11]

In spite of the ghastly victory, Essex was never able to defeat Sorley Boy, and he was soon out of the picture. Thomas Doughty began to conspire against him, perhaps with the knowledge if not the connivance of Drake. Finally, in September 1576, Essex became ill and suddenly died. One man said the poisoner was Francis Drake, another said it was the earl of Leicester. Whoever it might have been, the Irish campaign was over.[12]

Due to Doughty's influence, Drake, with his proven reputation for courage and leadership, was now in touch with a group of influential men who were ready to support bold plans for the expansion of England's interests across the ocean. With his supporters, and in close alliance with the queen, Drake had perfected a scheme that would not only strike a terrible blow at Spain but also pour rich booty into the coffers of the avaricious queen. The plan was that Drake should enter the Pacific by the Strait of Magellan, sail up the western seaboard of South America, and plunder the undefended and unsuspecting Spanish settlements that he would find along the coasts of Chile and Peru, though carefully avoiding the Spanish colonies in the interior. It was also intended that he should try to find a suitable setting for an English settlement along the way and that the expedition should continue north along the American coast to latitude 40° or 50° N to look for the mythical 'Straits of Anian', at the western terminus of the north-west passage. (A mythical idea which Michael Lok, Martin Frobisher, and the Company of Cathay had been promoting.)

The English did not know how far south the Spaniards had settled but most historians agree that the secret motive was for Drake to spoil the Spaniard in a region supposedly unguarded and full of treasure. The commander himself later revealed that the queen had said to him, 'Drake! So it is that I would gladly be revenged on the King of Spain for divers injuries that I have received!' Encouragement enough for him to say to Her Majesty that after going through the Straits of Magellan he would indeed attack the king in his wealthy colonies. Elizabeth gave it her sanction, at the same time as commanding 'that of all men my Lord Treasurer [Burghley] should not know of it'. She then handed Drake a royal commission that made him a privateer, not a pirate, and bound Drake to secrecy, saying that anyone who let the king of Spain hear about the plan would lose his head. To state it plainly the objective of the expedition was piracy.

There is no indication that the true plan was to sail around the world, except for one person, John Wynter, who later stated that the Molucca Islands were part of the itinerary. Being Drake's deputy on the voyage his opinion should be taken into account.

The list of the persons we know of that contributed to the expedition included Drake with £1,000; Hawkins £500; the Wynter family £1,250 and the queen probably with a like amount of money as Drake, but there is no contemporary record to prove that she did. (It had been proposed that the royal ship *Swallow* should constitute her share but it was not used, probably because Elizabeth thought it would make her involvement look too obvious).

The task force that assembled at Plymouth during the summer of 1577, was as follows:

Captain General: Francis Drake

Captain of men-at-arms, Thomas Doughty

Ship *Pelican* (later renamed the Golden Hind), the 'admirall' (flagship);
100-120 tuns by English reckoning, 16 to 18 guns on two decks; seven gun ports on either side, plus the rest in the forecastle and poop. Thirteen guns cast in bronze, the rest in iron. Francis Drake captain.

Ship *Elizabeth*, 'vice-admirall', 80 tuns, 16 guns, John Wynter captain

Bark *Marygold*, 30 tuns, 16 guns, John Thomas captain.

Flyboat *Swan*, acting as store ship, 50 tuns, 5 guns, John Chester captain

Pinnace *Benedict*, 12 Tuns, 1 Gun.

Bark *Christopher*, 15 tuns, Thomas Moone captain.[13]

Elizabeth and *Benedict* belonged to John Wynter, *Christopher* to Drake himself. *Pelican* (*Golden Hind*), a fairly new vessel, built in France, was owned by the Hawkinses, who had probably bought her from a Huguenot sea rover. She was double-sheathed with a layer of tarred horsehair between her two skins to foil teredos. Her gun ports could be caulked tight and her guns stowed below. She was a fine stout vessel that usually towed her longboat. Even so, with eighty men aboard her deck she must have been uncomfortably crowded. It is known that Drake had a forge and blacksmith's shop fitted up somewhere on board, probably under the forecastle.[14]

Among the important gentlemen volunteers were: John Doughty (half brother to Thomas), two Hawkinses, Drake's youngest brother Thomas, and his cousin John as well as Francis Fletcher, fleet chaplain. The total compliment, including soldiers, sailors and volunteers amounted to between 150 and 164, of which fourteen were boys. Also Diego, Drake's black slave, who had become a favourite with him after the raid on Nombre de Dios and who spoke both Spanish and English. Among the common sailors were several foreigners including Great Nele, the Danish gunner, and at least two other Dutchmen. With this puny flotilla Francis Drake set out to do battle, not only against the might of Spain but also with the most daunting terrors of the oceans.[15]

After the usual delays in provisioning and sorting out the business end of the enterprise, this fleet made a fair start from Plymouth on 13 December 1577. An earlier attempt had run into a gale in which *Pelican* was forced to cut away her mainmast and its rigging while the *Marygold* was driven ashore but successfully floated again.

As far as we can tell the expedition sailed with its officers believing they were bound for *Terra Australis* and its crews for Alexandria, whilst the three unscrupulous connivers, the queen, her secretary and Drake, alone knew that once in the South Sea the lies would be thrown overboard to make room for a cargo of plunder.

Christmas Day 1577, found them anchored at the tiny island of Mogador, a fishing station on the Moroccan coast south of Safi. Here *Benedict* was left behind in exchange for a small Portuguese vessel renamed *Christopher*. Drake ordered his carpenters to assemble one of the pinnaces he had brought along in the hold for raiding purposes. On 7 January 1580 the pinnace captured its first victims, three Spanish fishing smacks. The vessels and crews were promptly impressed into the fleet. A few days later three Portuguese caravels were added to the growing armada. He then followed the established route of vessels bound for the Americas. Coasting down the western seaboard of Saharan Africa he did not stop at Tenerife, but sailed on to the Cape Verde Islands for revictualling. At the Cape Verdes Drake captured a large Portuguese merchant vessel the *Santa Maria,* bound for Brazil, that according to the expedition's chaplain Francis Fletcher, was 'laden with singuler wines, sacks & Canaryes with Linen Clothes, silkes and velvets & many other good commodotyes which stood us in that stead that she was the life of our voyage… for the shortness of our provisions.' Drake added her to his squadron as the *Mary* exchanging her for the newly assembled pinnace in which he sent the Portuguese crew home. Doughty was appointed to command the prize. Her value lay in her cargo of wines, for drink was always a problem on long voyages as plain water, that was often not so plain, went fetid, and the same could be said of beer. Drake pressed into his service *Mary's* captain, Nuño da Silva (renamed *Silvester* by the English), an experienced pilot who knew the coast of South America. Da Silva became a sort of prisoner-pilot for more than a year and it was he who left a useful account of the voyage as he saw it that was published later by Richard Hakluyt in 1600.[16] Nuño became friendly with Drake, ate at his table, enjoyed the best accommodation and had all he needed – except his liberty.

The fleet now reduced to six sail left volcanic Fogo behind them on 2 February. They wallowed through the Doldrums, with the sweating idle mariners having nothing to do but grumble, quarrel and wish they were ashore. In that sultry atmosphere rivalries and disagreements festered to grow into what turned into the worst crisis of the voyage.

Doughty and his friends had a financial stake in the venture and powerful contacts at court. He was an intimate of Sir Christopher Hatton as well as others close to the queen and above all was a master of intrigue. He loved to be party to secrets and gossip, and enjoyed the power that the clandestine knowledge gave him over the lives of others. He also had a trump card up his sleeve, he was the secret agent of Sir William Cecil, Lord Burghley, the queen's Lord Treasurer, who had not been informed the real reason of the expedition but had a feeling something odd was in the wind. Not trusting Drake and his machinations, he needed someone in the fleet to report all that happened. That person was Thomas Doughty who relished the power he thought it gave him over Drake. But Doughty had got under Drake's skin, and now used every opportunity to vilify him.

A narrative by John Cooke, who went on the voyage, says that Doughty found Thomas Drake stealing from the cargo of the captured Portuguese ship. According to Cook, Thomas Drake begged Doughty to say nothing to his brother, but Doughty reported the matter anyway. Enraged, Francis Drake turned on Doughty with a string of oaths. His pride reacted to it as if the accusation had been against him. He there and then demoted Doughty as commander of *Mary*, put his brother Thomas in charge of the ship, and Doughty was given command instead of the little *Pelican* of only 100 tuns. There had been some discontent in *Pelican* also, for Doughty made a speech to the crew when he came aboard, saying to them that they must amend their ways and submit to his will, since the Captain General had given him full authority and power of life and death. However, Doughty threw his weight around to such ill purpose that Drake degraded him by sending him in disgrace to the flyboat *Swan*.

After two months of heat, sickness and baffling airs the fleet crossed the line on the 17 March and approached the Brazilian coast at the latitude of Bahia de Todos los Santos, on 5 April 1578. They failed to find a good anchorage, and some of the ships were scattered by a storm, including Doughty's *Swan*. Several more days took the fleet to Cabo Santa Maria, which Drake re-named Cape Joy (Punta del Este today), at the entrance to the Río de la Plata. They anchored in Maldonado Bay for the ships to draw in spring-water from the rivulet of *La Aguada* that runs from a spring near the little town of Maldonado through the sand dunes to the shore. There they stayed from 16 to 20 April killing a few seals for meat into the bargain. Briefly exploring the lower Río de la Plata they emerged into the South Atlantic with a full moon on 27 April 1578. That same night the *Swan* with Doughty on board, disappeared in stormy weather to reappear in the company of the *Pelican* on 17 May 1578.

Drake, having the latest Spanish charts of the South American coastline, sailed south making for Cabo Tres Puntas, which they sighted on 12 May. Here the Captain General almost lost his life, caught by a storm while exploring in a ship's boat. Sailing on, they reached Port Desire, where they did some friendly trading with 'toyes and trifles', with naked, painted Patagonians (Indians of the Tehuelahe tribe). On 22 June, Drake went ashore with a small party of armed men to find a suitable camping spot. As soon as the group landed they were confronted by a band of Indians, armed with bows and arrows. One of Drake's men, Oliver, fired a warning arrow at the Indians, but his bowstring broke. Interpreted as a hostile move, the Indians fired off a volley of arrows, one of which 'clapt an arrow into the body of him through his Lunges', killing master gunner Oliver. The Captain General acted promptly. Picking up Oliver's arquebus, heavily charging it 'with a bullet and hail shot', he dispatched the native who had started the fight, tearing out his guts. 'His cry was so hideous and horrible a roare, as if ten bulls had joined together in roaring.' That panicked the Patagonians who[17] were 'nothing so monstrous or giant as they were reported' by Pigafetta, and 'no taller than an Englishman, but most repulsive to the view'.

The crews grew fearful. It was obvious now that this was no trip to Alexandria, and that their leader was taking them into more distant and dangerous waters. Doughty and his friends played upon the crews' anxieties. Their prospects for a safe return were dim if Drake was not challenged, Doughty told them. Doughty also believed he had occult powers, or at least

Above left: Drake's route down the Atlantic coast, through the strait and up the Chilean coast.

Above right: Drake on the coast of Brazil, 1578.

Right: Anchorage off Cabo Santa Maria (Punta del Este), Rio de la Plata, April 1578.

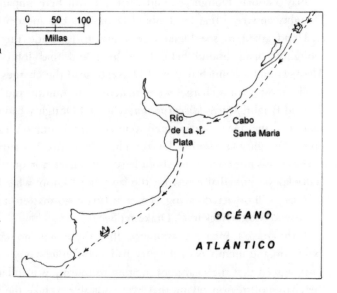

boasted that he had among the seamen and predicted disaster of the expedition. Drake, on the other hand, could see the whole enterprise falling apart if he did not act. He tried to turn the tide in his favour by making Doughty an object of ridicule. He had him tied to *Swan's* mainmast where he became the butt of jeers and crude jokes, only heightening the feelings of personal rivalry. Now neither man could back down. It was either Drake or Doughty and Drake had to make a final exhibition of his mastery.

After being so long at sea, Drake needed a winter anchorage to refit his fleet and allow his seamen to rest. He also was eager to deal with Doughty and consolidate his own leadership. With these ideas in mind, on 18 June 1578, they sailed into the infamous bay of San Julián, just short of the Straits, where Magellan had meted out justice on his mutinous captains more then half century before. The whole squadron once again came together under Drake's hand, after being scattered for days by fogs and sudden gales. When the *Swan* arrived in the bay, Drake learned Doughty had continued his conjuring (i.e. practicing witchcraft in order to hinder the voyage) and disparaging speeches against him. His fears increased and fueled by growing vengeance, Drake announced his right via the queen's commission to punish sedition with death. He summoned a court for Doughty's trial.

On 30 June 1578 Drake brought the entire company ashore and assembled them. He began the proceedings by reading his main charge: 'Thomas Doughty, you have heare sought by divers meanes in as much as you maye to discredite me to the great hinderaunce and overthrowe of this voyage,' If proven guilty of these and other charges, said Drake, Doughty would deserve death.[18]

In reply, Doughty said he had never done any such thing and told Drake he would be glad to defend himself in an English court.

'Nay Thomas Doughtye', said Drake, 'I will here impanell a jurye on you.' Doughty answered that he doubted Drake had the authority for holding such a trial and asked to see Drake's commission. Ignoring the request, Drake had Doughty's arms bound behind his back and told John Thomas, captain of *Marygold*, and a staunch friend of Drake, to read the charges.[19]

The most serious charges were incitement to mutiny and a statement made by Edward Bright, *Marygold*'s carpenter, who said Doughty had made the treasonous claim that the queen and council were corrupt. Leonard Vicary, the lawyer, stood up for Doughty and said to Drake: 'This is not lawe nor agriable to justice.'

Drake was not concerned about legalities. 'I have not, quoth he, to do with you crafty lawyars, neythar care I for the lawe, but I know what I will do.'

Vicary still objected, saying, 'There is I trust no matter of death.'

'No, no Master Vickarye', Drake replied.

With Drake's apparent assurance that there was no chance of Doughty's execution, the members of the jury had a convenient way out of their dilemma. They agreed that the charge of inciting to mutiny was indeed true, but rejected the charge of treason, saying they were not able to take the word of such a man as Edward Bright on an unsupported charge of this importance.

This latter point mattered little to Drake. He was elated. With the guilty verdict in hand, the road was open to get Doughty out of his way.

Doughty himself spoke up, saying to Drake, 'I pray you, carry me with you to Perwe [Peru] and there set me ashore.'

'No, truly, master Doughty, I cannot answere it to her maiestie if I shuld so do', Drake replied.[20]

Teasing his victim like a cat with a mouse, Drake announced he would put Doughty in the hands of anyone who would offer to keep him in custody for the rest of the voyage. On hearing this, Doughty asked John Wynter to be his keeper and Wynter agreed. Drake replied he would permit it only if they put Doughty in the hold and nailed the hatches down over Doughty's head, canceled the voyage, and sailed straight home. In noisy derision to the unacceptability of this suggestion, a group of sailors shouted, 'God forbyd, good generall.' It was 30 June 1578, and Doughty's fate was sealed.[21]

Doughty was given a day and a half to prepare for execution. On the second day, he asked Drake for permission to take the sacrament, and Drake went one better and also took the Eucharist with him, after which they dined together.[22] Gentleman to the last, Doughty thanked his friends and pled his innocence of any conspiracy against Drake. After more prayers and leave-taking, Doughty thanked and embraced Drake and knelt to the block, at which his head was struck off with an axe. They buried his body on the 'Bloody Island beside the old gibbet, his grave marked by a great grinding stone, carved with his name in Latin, that it might the better be understood by all that should come after us.' Drake ordered that his head be held up as an example to all, trumpeting, 'This is the end of traitors.'

No one to this day has been able to explain why Francis Drake took the life of his one time friend. While it is clear that he wanted him out of the way, it also appears he had no legal right to try or execute the man. Drake claimed on several occasions he had a document from the queen giving him such authority, but he never showed it to anyone, nor permitted anyone to scrutinise it. It has never been found.

Samuel Johnson (1709–1784), regarded as one of the outstanding figures of eighteenth-century English life and letters, was one of very few men of his or even later generations to look upon Drake with a cold and questioning eye. His vision looks with skepticism at the trial, which alleged that Doughty's 'plot' to overthrow Drake had been concocted in Plymouth: 'How far it is probable... that Doughty, who is represented as a man of eminent abilities, should engage in so long and hazardous a voyage with no other view than that of defeating it. The question is left to the determination of the reader.'

It does appear that with almost paranoiac fervor Drake incited fear in his men as a way to keep a hold over them. But he was equally fearful himself and kept an armed guard nearby.[23] If there were men ready to desert, as Drake suspected, Doughty's freshly dug grave was warning enough of what might happen to them. Also in ready view were the haunting remnants of the scaffold used by the Magellan expedition in 1520, surrounded by human bones. (The flagship's cooper made tankards of the gibbet for any sailor who wanted one.) With Doughty's headless body fresh in his grave by the gibbet, sub-zero temperatures beneath a leaden sky, the wind whistling in from the opening onto the Atlantic, and pangs of starvation growing among the men, all spun a sense of tragic doom over the bay. Even the *Swan*, perhaps the last vestige of Doughty, was deemed unseaworthy and abandoned, as captain and crews hastened to depart the appalling scene.

19

FRANCIS DRAKE AND HIS PATH
THROUGH THE GREAT SOUTH SEA

The winds were such as if the bowels of the
earth had set all at libertie, or as if all the
clouds under heaven had beane called together
to lay their force upon that one place. The seas
were rowled up from the deapths, even from
the roots of the rockes, as if it had been a scroll
of parchment.

From the Francis Fletcher manuscript, quoted in *The World Encompassed by Sir Francis Drake*, Hakluyt Society, 1854

The fleet was now reduced to three ships, *Pelican*, commanded by Francis Drake, *Elizabeth* with John Wynter as captain, Marygold, commanded by John Thomas. The two pinnaces, *Swan* and *Christopher*, had been abandoned as unseaworthy, and *Mary* broken up for parts in the bay of San Julián.

According to John Cooke, before leaving the bay of San Julián, Drake mustered the entire expedition on the beach and made it the occasion of a speech to the men, one of the best known of any ever made at sea. After reminding the men of the desperate nature of their voyage into unknown waters and making mention of what he called 'the recent mutinous troubles,' he continued:

> For by the life of God, it doth even take my wits from me to think on it. Here is such controversy between the sailors and gentlemen, and such stomaching between the gentlemen and sailors, it doth make me mad to hear it. But, my masters, I must have it left. For I must have the gentleman to haul and draw with the mariner, and the mariner with the gentleman. What! Let us show ourselves to be of a company, and let us not give occasion to the enemy to rejoice at our decay and overthrow. I would know him that would refuse to set his hand to a rope, but I know there is not any such here...

It was an appeal for all to 'pull together'. He emphasised that there was to be no privilege of rank save that of an officer, entire subordination to the commander and a call for all to rise to the great work ahead of them. According to John Cooke's report of the speech, Drake thought that the main cause of dissatisfaction was the division between sailors and gentlemen. Henceforth both groups would work side by side, though sailors would have still to obey orders as before.[1]

The ships departed San Julián on 17 August 1578. On 20th they sighted Cabo Vírgenes, recognised as the entrance to the Strait of Magellan by the Portuguese pilot, Nuño da Silva. About this time Drake renamed his ship *Golden Hind* (Nuño recorded it as la *Gama Dorada*), in honour of Sir Christopher Hatton, whose coat of arms bore 'a hind trippant or'. A prudent gesture if we consider that the man he had recently murdered (executed seems too polite a word) was a member of Hatton's household as well as a major investor in the voyage. Seen in that light, the renaming of *Pelican* seems to have been the fruit of a guilty conscience.

Francis Fletcher's manuscript is the only one that mentions the actual rechristening of the ship after the vessels had entered the Strait.[2] Always careful to observe important occasions with ceremony, Drake ordered his three ships to lower their topsails 'upon the bunt', allowing them to drape over the lower sails, as a time honoured naval salute, to the queen. Revd Fletcher recorded it thus:

> At this cape [Virgins,] our generall caused his fleet, in homage to our soveraigne lady the Queenes majesty, to stike their top-sails upon the bunt, as a token of his willing and glad minde, to shewe his dutifull obedience to her highness, whom he acknowledged to hafe full interest and right, in that new discovery; and withal, in rememberance of his honorable friend and favorer, Sir Christopher Hatton, he changed the name of the shippe, which himselfe went in, from *Pellican* to be called *the golden Hinde*.

To address the great occasion, Drake proclaimed the baptism with a mighty trumpet blast from the deck of the flagship. 'These things thus accomplished, wee joyfully entered the Strait with hope of Good Success.' It was 21 August 1578.

They did indeed have good success. The discoverer of the Strait, Ferdinand Magellan, took thirty-seven days to sail his fleet through it; Cavendish, later, in January 1587, took forty-nine, and Richard Hawkins in 1593, forty-six days. Drake's ships covered the 363 miles in only sixteen days, which included taking on water and victualling with penguins, of which large numbers were found. The main difficulty usually met was the strong head winds in the second part of the passage from Cape Froward to the Pacific but Drake, seems to have had reasonably fair wind throughout. While pilot Nuño da Silva says in his account that the wind blew steadily between northeast and east-north-east, which would account for their speed, in Hakluyt's *Famous Voyage* it mentions: 'we had the wind often against us, so that some of the fleet recovering a Cape or point of land, others should be forced to turne backe agayne, and to come to an anker where they could.' It should be remembered that the passage took place in the depth of the mid-Antarctic-winter when few sensible skippers would attempt it by sail alone today.[3] Fletcher narrates the 'monstrous and wonderfull' mountains, rising tier beyond tier, 'reaching themselves above their fellows so high, that between them did appeare three regions of cloudes.'[4]

They had an easy passage and emerged on 6 September 1578 into Magellan's *Mar Pacífico*. However, once in the South Sea the weather was in one of her ugly moods, enough to break most hearts, prompting Fletcher to remark that it should better have been named the Furious instead of the Pacific. For a few days the expedition made some meager progress northwest, which was prevented by the wind changing to the same direction. It was the beginning of a very long period of vicious weather and towering seas before which the ships were helpless and the crews incredulous.[5] Drake must have done his utmost to resist it, knowing that the continent of *Terra Australis* lay southward and he could at any moment have found himself on a lee shore. Nevertheless, he was driven south to 57°,[6] 5° further south of the parallel of Cabo Vírgenes, the entrance to the Strait on the east coast. All on board stated that they had never known a storm so continuous or seas so terrifying in their lives.

> The day being come, the sight of sun and land was taken from us so that there followed, as it were, a palpable darkness by the space of 56 days without the sight of the sun, moon or stars as… we thus… continued without hope at the pleasure of God in the violent force of the wind's intolerable working of the wrathful seas and the grisly beholding (sometimes) of the cragged rocks and fearful height, and monstrous mountains being to us a lee shore where into we were continually drawn by the winds and carried by the mountain-like billows of the sea… if at any time we had a little opportunity to seek some harbour for refuge to come to anchor and rest till God in mercy might… give us more safe sailing at the seas, such was the malice of the mountains that they seemed to agree together in one consent and join their forces together to work our overthrow and consume us, so that every mountain sent down upon us their several intolerable winds with that horror that they made the bottom of the seas to be dry land where we anchored, sending us headlong upon the tops of mounting and swelling waves of the seas over the rocks, the sight whereof at our going in was as fearful as death.[7]

On the night of 30 September *Marigold*, with Captain Thomas, Master Bright, and twenty-eight men disappeared and was never seen again. Revd Fletcher tells us that as she foundered, he heard the cries of men threshing around in the unmerciful waves of the icy sea. 'That night' said Wynter later, 'was the most tempestuous night that ever was seen in this outrageous weather.'

In the last week of the terrible month of October 1578, sun, moon, and stars appeared again, the wind moderated and the tempestuous seas were calmed. Those aboard *Golden Hind* sighted land and anchored at last off what Drake believed to be 'the utmost Island of *terra incognita* to Southward of America.' It seems likely to have been Henderson Island one of a cluster to which he gave the name '*Elizabethides*',[8] never seen before by any European. Cape Horn, always taken as the boundary of the Atlantic and Pacific, lies only some 60 miles to the southeast from there.[9] After anchoring *Golden Hind*, the Captain General went ashore with Fletcher, they walked down the grassy slopes thick with wild currents. On a stone they carved the name of the queen as well as the date and, as Drake later told Hawkins, he 'threw himself on his belly and stretched out his arms as far as he could toward the South Pole, so he could boast that no man had been as near to it as himself.'[10]

Drake concluded that Tierra del Fuego was an island and not part of the great southern continent – or *Terra Australis Incognita* as it was becoming known. It now became obvious to him that the Atlantic and the Pacific merged in open water to the south of Tierra del Fuego. He could only have proven his theory by sailing further east around the southern-tip of the island and back to Cabo Vírgenes, but his assumption was correct. Therefore, we can truly say, Drake was the discoverer of this geographical fact. A fact that would be confirmed later in 1616, by Schouten and Le Maire with the discovery of Cape Horn.[11] Interestingly enough, English cartographers, after Drake's return, drew this region taking his discovery into account, but it would be many years before the Spanish knew the truth, as Drake took good care not to acquaint those whom he captured later during his raids on the west coast of what he had learned.[12]

On 7 October, *Elizabeth* struggling against stormy seas, had turned back for refuge into the entrance to the strait where she rested until November, 'most of her men being very sick with long watching, wet, cold, and evil diet.'[13] Wynter,

Drake's itinerary after emerging from the Strait.

her captain, remained a month in the strait, waiting for Drake, lighting fires every night to draw attention, until he concluded that the Captain General was either lost or far gone to the Moluccas. He broached the matter with some of his company, reading to them Magellan's account of his voyage, 'which they seemed to like well of.' However, he ran into the discontent of his crew and above all, of the master, William Markham, who refused to go on and infected the men with his feeling of defeat. 'He had been hired for Alexandria', he trumpeted, 'but if he had known this to be Alexandria he would [rather] have been hanged in England than have come on this voyage.' Sickness, shortness of victuals, and with the strenuous opposition of the ship's master, Wynter sailed *Elizabeth* back through the straits to Brazil and England, arriving at Ilfracombe on 2 July 1579.

Afterwards, when Drake arrived home laden with wealth, one of Wynter's seamen, Edward Cliffe, jealous at having missed his share of the booty, wrote an account vilifying Wynter as the coward who 'had turned homewards full sore against the mariners' minds'. Hakluyt printed Cliffe's story, but Wynter's statement remained unknown for 350 years. Thus, it passed into history, that John Wynter had dishonourably deserted – which is not true.

Meanwhile, Drake having made furthest south and the winds at last having turned fair, determined to sail north to the warmer climes of Chile and Perú.

Finding favourable winds, Drake took off northwards in November. He passed Cape Pilar, without bothering to look into the strait to see if Wynter was there, and hurried north to devote himself to the main purpose of his voyage: doing as much damage, and extracting as much plunder as possible from the ill-protected settlements of Spain's commercial empire.

In the previous thirty years Spain had extended her empire along the west coast of South America as far as Valdivia in Chile, (latitude 40° S.) The settlements were mostly small outposts, housing fewer men at arms than Drake had on board *Golden Hind* and therefore easily open to being sacked and plundered. Spain had a sizeable fleet of small-unarmed coastal vessels to carry silver and other valuables north from ports along the coast and bring back foodstuffs as well as other goods sent from Spain. This was the soft underbelly of Spain's South American Empire and it lay exposed.

Arica, on the present border of Chile with Perú, was the port serving the silver mines of Potosí, and mercury from the famous Inca mine of Huancavélica. While Callao was the port of Lima, both ports had a steady flow of ships carrying valuable commodities up to Old Panama and returning with merchandise. None of these ships were armed with cannon as the Spanish never expected to encounter anything in the Pacific larger than an Indian canoe or a balsa raft. Drake waded into them like a fox among a flock of lambing sheep and taking from them anything of value.

Finding a Spaniard on shore asleep with a flock of llamas with their saddlebags full of silver, and much *charqui*[14] they 'freed him of his charge' but left him screaming with fury. The llamas were taken on board and eaten. Somewhere else they encountered what the preacher called an *hidalgo*, driving a train of llamas loaded with silver, 'we could not endure to see a gentleman Spaniard turned carrier', wrote Fletcher cynically, now infused with the success of the plunder and 'therefore we offered our own service and became drivers.' Then, capturing a vessel laden with linen, 'we thought [it] might stand us in some stead and therefore took it with us.'[15]

At the island of Mocha, several of the crew were killed or wounded by the local Indians, who with arrows 'thick as gnats in the sonne' attacked the shore party when watering. Not one of the crew escaped having a couple of arrows or more stuck in him. One hit Drake himself in the face. Two men, Nele, the Danish gunner and Diego, Drake's slave, later died of their wounds, and two more who were cut off from the boat were killed and eaten horribly, the natives cutting off 'gubblets' of their flesh, tossing them in the air and devouring them 'like dogs', while performing some sort of dance.

Drake sailed north, and on 30 November, returning from a scouting expedition came across a lone Indian fishing from a canoe. The man was taken aboard *Golden Hind*, treated kindly, and set ashore later in the ship's boat. To show his gratitude the native returned with some fellow Indians and their chief with presents of hens, eggs, and a fat pig. The chief offered to guide Drake to a place where, he said, a Spanish ship was anchored. It turned out to be Valparaiso, then a mere village on the edge of a large protected bay. After sailing by the entrance and taking a good look at the shipping in the port Drake, true fox that he was, sailed on. Then retracing his steps with Spanish colours flying from the masthead, he cast anchor next a Spanish ship. Eight Spaniards and three blacks sparsely manned the ship, but thinking *Golden Hind* one of their own, they beat a drum in welcome and rolled out a butt of wine. Drake's men swarmed aboard while the astounded Spaniards fled into the hold where they were battened down, except one, who jumped overboard and swam to the town, which Drake proceeded to sack at leisure over the next three days. The pirates found ample supplies of Chilean wine, which they instantly became addicted to, and having taken the plate, vestments and even the altar-cloth, from the church, Drake gave them to his minister Fletcher. Best of all, however, were four ironbound boxes covered with hide, containing 25,000 gold pesos, as well as a large emerald-studded crucifix.

Drake sailed from Valparaiso into the Pacific on 8 December, taking the captured ship with him, as well as Felipe, the Indian fisherman–pilot back to his home leaving him laden with gifts.

The assault on Valparaiso marks the beginning of the period of Drake's successful plundering on the west coast of South America. He became an expert at capturing merchant vessels and looting defenseless towns. His basic tactics were

surprise, capture, followed by sacking, and plundering. Trapping all ships in their
harbours if possible was his criterion and, after looting anything of value, turning
the ships and sailors loose, if at sea, without sails so he could not be pursued. He
had honed his knowledge to become the ultimate pirate.

Drake might have been a hero to his men, but he had become the dragon
Draque to the Spanish. Virtual panic spread ahead as he proceeded north
capturing ships at will and dumbfounding the colonial Spanish. The unprotected
state of their harbours and the casual confidence with which huge wealth was
being transported by land and sea boggles the mind.

At Quillota and Coquimbo it was much the same story. At Valdivia he captured
the ship with 24,000 *pesos de oro* (gold coins) that had been Medañas *Capitana* on his
voyage of discovery to the Solomon Islands,[16] and took her, along with a cargo of
1,700 jars of wine. Ñuno da Silva tells us they had to heave overboard six pipes of
tar to make room for the wine. Who wouldn't, especially if we heed the old Italian
proverb that one barrel of wine can work more miracles than a church full of saints!

It speaks ill of Spain's Chilean communications that by now all the western
costal settlements had not been alerted to Drake's marauding ventures. On
20 December, however, he entered Bahía Salada on the coast of Chile. The
countryside was a dry desert uninhabited, and Drake thought it an ideal place to
hide from the angry Spaniards while he careened the *Hind*. It was an extremely
dangerous operation, as if he been discovered it would have signified the end. At
first, Drake ordered the crew to remove from the hold a pinnace that had been
built and disassembled in England. Within two weeks the carpenters had it ready
for caulking. Sails had been cut and a small bronze gun was placed in the bow.
The commander took it down the coast for a trial run with the added intention
of filling some casks with water but he was unable to go ashore because of the
hostility of the Indians.

While he was gone the crew set to work to remove the guns stored in the hold
and then to careen the ship. It took a week to secure the tackle to the mainmast
and heel the ship over on its side and another week to repair a leak, clean the hull,
and smear it with the usual mixture of grease, sulfur and tar. While this was going
on they were defenseless and they were lucky there was no attack, though once
a horseman appeared on a sand dune and later a group of Indians as well looked
down on them from a height.

Fourteen guns were placed at the gunports below, seven to a side. The rest were
mounted above. Two large iron ones on the poop and two smaller ones in the bow.
Golden Hind had now become the best-armed ship by far on the Pacific coast.

Drake captured some silver at Tarapacá and Arica but missed a cargo at Chule,
the port city of Arequipa. There the Spaniards managed to get the treasure ashore
just in time to disappoint the English. People on shore had spotted the pinnace
and shouted at them jeeringly that they had fooled the thieving Englishmen.
Some 50 miles ahead the pirates sighted three ships and giving chase captured one
of them. Among the Spaniards captured one Gaspar Martín, told Drake that two

ships were expected to arrive in El Callao, the port of the city of Lima, the City of Kings and of the viceroyalty of Perú. One of these belonged to Andrés Muriel, the other to Miguel Angel but what was even more significant, another belonging to San Juan de Anton, had weighed anchor and left Callao with a rich cargo of bullion bound for Panama. Drake also learned from questioning a few Spanish seamen that, some of his old comrades were prisoners in the city of Lima. One of them was John Oxenham, no less, who had been with Drake on the raid of Nombre de Dios in 1573. Apart from the possibility of plunder, when Drake entered the port, he was also hoping to gain some bargaining power which might secure the release of his friend and companions from the clutches of the Holy Spanish Inquisition (who hanged him the following year).[17]

Callao was the official port of entry for all merchandise going or coming between the mother country, Chile and Perú. The port is a bay partially enclosed on the west by an island called in those days, Isla del Puerto. The wider entrance between the island and continent towards the north called, *La Boca Grande*, was used by ships from Panama, while shipping from Chile approached the port from the south by the narrower channel, *La Boca Chica*.

Knowing by now that there was nothing to fear since all shipping thereabouts consisted of unarmed merchant vessels, Drake, surprise being an essential part of his tactics, entered the port with stealth. However, as he proceeded to cast anchor, a small vessel came along side *Hind* with an official who asked their provenance. Drake instructed one of his Spanish captives to reply that they hailed from Chile, which satisfied the officials and they left. A little later another boat put out from the quay, this time from the customhouse, to enquire the identity of the new visitors. Again one of Drake's Spanish captives called out saying that their ship belonged to Miguel Angel and came from Chile. But as bad luck would have it, the inspectors knew that Angel had just arrived from Panama. Suspiciously, one of the inspectors climbed on board *Hind* and spying the guns on deck immediately knew something was amiss. He hurriedly climbed down the ladder into the boat and rowed furiously for the shore while waving his arms and crying out at the top of his voice, 'Franceses!'

Having lost the opportunity of surprise, Drake sent his men around the harbour in the ship's boats looking for the cargo of silver. Not finding any trace of it, the men cut the cables of the eight or nine ships in the port, which drifted ashore, and not as Drake hoped towards the mouth of the port where he hoped to gather them and hold them as ransom for the release of Oxenham and his fellow brigands. Once outside the port Drake and his men sorted out the merchandise, taking what they wished and casting adrift one of the ships they had taken with four hostages captured in Callao.

Sending his pinnace close in to scout the bays and inlets, Drake kept his ship out at sea unseen some 3 to 4 miles from the shore. Off Paita, a port of call for most ships sailing between Panama and Lima the pinnace entered while the pirates prepared their strategy to board a vessel at anchor in the port. Once they

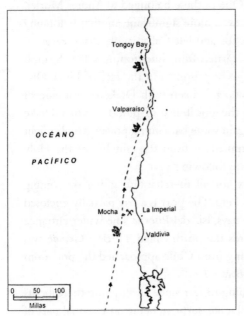

Above left: Itinerary up the Chilean coast from the straights.

Above right: Continuation of previous map.

did there was not much booty to be had but they provisioned themselves with bread, chickens and even a pig before sailing out of the harbour taking the ship with them. Drake went on board to question the officers and found out that indeed they had seen the ship of San Juan de Anton known colloquially as *Cacafuego*, as it had passed through Paita two days earlier.

Drake sailed north avoiding the Gulf of Guayaquil until arriving at Los Quijimes, a protected bay that having plenty of fresh water and firewood was another port of call for ships on route from Panama. There on 28 February 1579 they found a ship belonging to Benito Díaz Bravo from Guayaquil, riding at anchor with its crew completely oblivious to the impending danger. The pirates boarded the ship to discover a huge quantity of gold and silver bars plus wine, maize, salt pork, hams, and other provisions. He also took from her 'a crucifixe of gold with goodly great Emerauds set in it.' After loading all he could manage aboard *Hind* he sailed Díaz Bravo's ship out to sea to test its speed. Discovering it was faster than his own, he mounted two guns aboard her, retaining the owner and his nephew, the ship's clerk, while sending the remaining occupants ashore. As usual he retained the black slaves as redeemable merchandise. Two of the passengers aboard were Dominican friars, hence Drake's crew referring to the captured vessel as the friars ship. At ten o'clock the following morning, he took the guns out of her again and handed the ship back to the owner. However he took the precaution of having the mainsail and topsail cast

Above left:
Continuation of the
previous map.

Above right: Up the
Perúvian coast.

Drake on the coast
of Perú and
Ecuador.

Ecuador to
Guatelco.

overboard, weighted by the ship's anchor, to prevent her sailing back to port to raise the alarm.

Díaz Bravo fared better than his nephew Francisco Jacomé, a lad of twenty-one who was transferred to *Hind*, with other four crew members, for questioning. Drake, puffed up with success, told them in full detail about his exploits, and boasted 'all the ships in the Pacific were in his power.' He went on to claim that he would take *Nuestra Señora de la Concepción* (playfully known as *Cacafuego*, literally *Shitfire* in English), pillage the coast of Nicaragua, and return with a fleet of six or seven ships in two years time.

The crewmembers were taken back to their immobilised ship but young Jacomé was retained on board *Hind* for questioning. Drake still believed there was more gold concealed but when Jacomé refused to answer his questions, he had a rope be put around the youth's neck and strung him up to the yardarm. Even then poised precariously on the yardarm he refused to answer the question from the deck. Drake had him dropped as if to hang him but the rope being too long (presumably by design, Drake being in a jocular mood), the boy hit the sea and was retrieved to be restored again, the worst for ware, to his own ship. Nuño da Silva's (*Silvester's*) account says that the lad had on his person two plates of gold, which were retrieved.

Had Drake known how close he was to *Cacafuego* he would probably not have entertained himself with this diversion. Once over, he ordered his men to the ropes and tackles to set the sails and strike their course north leaving Díaz Bravo to struggle back to port as best he could.

Drake offered a prize of a gold chain to whoever first sighted *Cacafuego*. The incentive took his fifteen-year-old cousin John Drake up into the maintop with his eyes peeled.[18] It was three in the afternoon when he sighted his quarry off Cape San Francisco. In the account given to the Spanish authorities later when in prison in Lima, John describes how if Francis Drake had sailed after his prey at full speed he might have given the game away while a reduction of sail to slow down his ship would also look suspicious. Instead he ordered the pinnace to stay out of sight on the starboard side of *Hind* which towed cables astern to slow her down.

It was nightfall before they came up upon the ship of San Juan Antón. The men from the Spanish ship hailed the strange vessel asking who they were. Drake, using his usual deceitful trick, made one of his Spanish prisoners call across that *Golden Hind* was Miguel Angel's ship. This alerted the Spanish captain who replied that it could not be, for he had seen the ship unmanned in Callao. He then told the pirates that they should lower their sails in the name of the king, to which Drake replied, 'you must strike your sails in the name of the queen of England.' At least this is how John Drake recalled the opening scene when he was asked to describe it before the court of enquiry in Lima in 1587. Antón, he said, suspecting no harm, allowed *Hind* to sail alongside and grapple. A whistle blew, a trumpet sounded, and there was a volley of English small arms and a shower from Drake's arquebuses, followed by crossbow bolts and chain shot which severed the Spaniards mizzenmast. An arrow wounded Antón. The *Hind* had closed *Cacafuego* on the starboard side and Drake, it is assumed, shouted garbled commands in pidgin-Spanish for Antón to strike sail in the queen of England's name, or be sunk! Antón replied, 'What England is this? Come on board and strike the sails yourselves!'[19] Meanwhile the *Hind* came close enough to board the Spanish ship. Antón, as it turned out, was a Basque who had lived in Southampton and spoke English well.[20] Seeing the situation hopeless and having no cannon or even small arms on board, he struck sail and surrendered.

Antón was seized and hustled aboard *Hind*, where Drake was taking off his helmet and cuirass. He embraced Antón cheerfully, it is said, and told him to cheer up saying: 'Have patience, such is the usage of war', and with that he had him confined to the sterncastle under heavy guard. The remaining dozen Spaniards were transferred, five of them sailors and the rest passengers. Darkness had set in, the English sailors on deck looked across to *Cacafuego*'s lanterns swaying in the wind. The ship's bell rang, there was a scuffle of feet, and the old watch giving way to the new went below and exulted in an easy victory climbed into their hammocks with fanciful images of tomorrow's gold.

Early the next morning, Drake boarded *Cacafuego* to take stock of his prize. It proved to be far more then he could have imagined even in his wildest dreams. There were the usual stores of edible merchandise – flower, sugar, preserves, and salt pork – as well as ship's fittings, sails, tackle and cordage. The treasure, according to Antón, amounted to 362,000 pesos, in 1,300 variously denominated silver bars, fourteen chests of silver coins known as *reales*, as well as eighty pounds of gold. Of this 160,000 pesos belonged to the Crown, and the rest was privately owned. As well, there were some 40,000 pesos of unregistered gold and silver and a quantity of jewels and precious stones.[21]

Until the capture of this astounding prize Drake was fearful about his reception in England. He knew that enemies would be waiting and grave accusations would have to be faced – the fake trial and execution of Doughty, his acts of piracy, and the needless risks of ships and men. Elizabeth and Burghley would not hesitate to throw him to the wolves if it were politically suitable. But now he had gained insurance against all those alleged offences. None of them, neither queen nor council, or even the powerful backers of the expedition, would dare to quibble when he brought home such immense profits.

Drake returned to *Hind* in the early afternoon and under foresails and mizzen stood out to sea on a northwesterly course to evade what he thought would be certain pursuit. He envisioned the entire west coast of South America would be alerted and armed ships would be after him like angry wasps whose nest had been disturbed. There was no question now of returning home the way he came.

Taking advantage of the fair weather, for the next three days, the pinnace plied to and fro between the two ships to transfer the loot to the holds of the pirate ship. Once they were finished, Drake became expansive. In his triumph he handed out many 'gifts' to his prisoners: some forty pesos in coin to each; a German musket, a gilded corselet, and a silver bowl engraved with Drake's name in latin, *Franciscus Draques*, to Antón, as well as a barrel of powder, two casks of tar and a supply of iron; plus such gifts as a set of pistols to a soldier called Victoria, a sword and shield to the ship's clerk, Domingo de Lizarza, some fans with mirrors to a merchant called Cuevas for his lady and so on. His generosity is not too hard to understand. In the tradition of Robin Hood, it's easy to be generous with other people's money.[22]

On 6 March 1579 Drake gave orders that San Juan de Antón, the three recently captured pilots, his crew and passengers be transferred to Antón's ship and sent them on their way. While Antón made for Panama, Drake headed for the Isla de Caño off the coast of Costa Rica. Antón knew where Drake was heading, and he informed the authorities as soon as he reached port. While sailing north Drake sighted a fifteen-tun *fragata* belonging to one Rodrigo Tello, he impounded its cargo but more important were two professional pilots with their charts that were heading for Panama to take the annual galleon to the Philippines. Drake threatened the older one, Alonzo Sánchez Colchero, to pilot him across the Pacific. The man refused. He asked the man to 'become a Lutheran' and join with them. He also refused. Finally Drake had a rope put round the prisoner's neck and strung him up from the yardarm. He did this twice, stopping only when the man began to loose consciousness. He eventually spared the poor fellow but instead had him confined to an iron cage in the ballast.

At Isla Caño, Drake careened his ship, cleaned the bottom and caulked the leaks, but these persisted and it became obvious *Hind* would have to be caulked again before returning to England.[23]

While sailing northward, they began to see the volcanoes of Honduras and Guatemala. While passing the port of Sonsonate they captured a small Spanish vessel and, after boarding her, to their surprise they found that one of her passengers was a *hidalgo* grandee, Don Francisco de Zárate, a cousin of the Duke of Medina Sidonia. This knight of the Order of Santiago must have been the most puffed up and cowardly creature the pirates had ever encountered. Taken aboard *Hind* he bowed to Drake and kissed his hand. Never having been the object of such respect, Drake took the trembling fellow below and began to question him. To further intimidate him he took him down to the hold where Alonzo Sánchez Colchero was imprisoned. 'Sit down' he said. 'You must stay here.'

As Zárate began to sit, Drake stopped him. 'Not just yet', he said. 'Just tell me the identity of that man.'

Zárate said that he really didn't know. 'Well' said Drake, 'that's the pilot that the viceroy was sending to Panama to take Don Gonzalo to China.'

Having shown his contempt for the viceroy, Drake took the hidalgo up to his great cabin where they had a long conversation until lunchtime.[24]

Zárate has left us an impressive picture of Drake and his style. He mentioned that the English officers and gentlemen who ate with them at Drake's table were afraid of their commander. Not one of them would take a seat or put a hat on unless Drake told them repeatedly to do so. John Doughty, the brother of Thomas, the

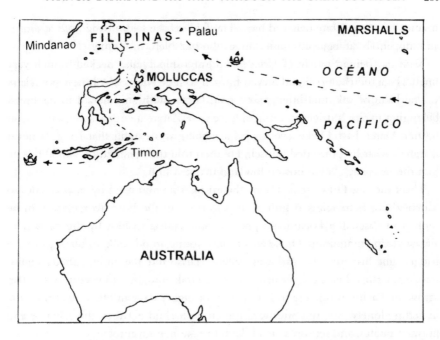

Above: Drake's route from the Pacific to the Indian Ocean.

Left: Drake's route through the South Pacific.

man executed in San Julián, caught Zárate's particular attention. He ate at the same table as the rest of the gentlemen but he was never left unguarded nor was he allowed to leave the ship. 'He punishes the least fault', Zárate noted. Asking about Drake's 'silver dishes with gold borders and gilded garlands', Zárate was told that much of it was a personal gift from the queen and that Drake had it engraved with his coat of arms. Zárate believed him. 'The fiddlers', he said, 'played both at dinner and supper.' Drake enjoyed music, but so also had Nero in Rome.

Next day being Sunday, *Golden Hind* dressed ship. Drake 'decked himself very finely', boarded the prize and served himself to four chests of Chinese porcelain, several bales of silk, fine linen, and a gold falcon with an emerald in his breast belonging to the hidalgo. In return Drake gave Zárate a cutlass and a little silver brazier. Drake had a keen eye for value but he was careful that his gifts never matched what he purloined himself. He then told the Spaniard he would release him the next day. Zárate bowed low and thanked him.[25]

The next day, Drake sent Zárate aboard his ship and tired by now of Alonso Sánchez Colchero released him from his prison in the hold. To replace him he took Juan Pascual, a Portuguese pilot recommended to him by the captain of Zárate's ship. In addition, Drake also took a young, good-looking black girl who had caught his eye. The girl was called Maria, and the unidentified English informant called her 'a proper negro wench.' Drake took her to his cabin. The trip across the Pacific was likely to last seventy or eighty days and there was no sense in getting lonely. 'She was afterward gotten with child between the captaine and his men pirates, and sett on a small iland to take her adventure'.[26]

Drake's last port of call in Spanish America was Guatulco, which Drake reached on 13 April 1579. The few Spaniards of the town together with a few Indians, who were decorating the church for Holy Week, put up a brief resistance. However, when the pinnace fired her artillery most of them retreated into the woods overlooking the town and watched as the pirates ransacked it. They took Simón de Miranda, the priest, prisoner as well as Francisco Gómez Rengifo, the local *encomendero* – a landowner and a Crown factor. After sacking his home, where they stole 7,000 pesos worth in silver and gold, they moved on to the church where they stole the chalices and the monstrance, as well as the damask vestments, a satin cope and matching canopy, surplices and altar cloths. The more elaborate fabrics were taken to the ship, the others to be used as towels. Drake's red-haired and pock-marked boatswain, Tom Moon, seized a crucifix by its end and smashed it against a table and then scattered and trampled the unconsecrated altar bread under foot, saying the Spanish were idolaters and worshipers of wood and stones. He kept up his performance aboard the *Hind*, wrenching the rosary from the hands of the friar who was praying. Pulling off the gold figure of the Virgin at its end he bit down on it and pretended to throw it overboard. A member of the crew was wearing one of the chasubles, and the church bell was hung beside the ship's pump.

With the plundering over, Drake had a meal prepared aboard ship to which he invited his prisoners, knowing they were supposed to fast during Holy Week. He had pork and chicken served up and fish for the priest. All but the priest dined, and all watched when he made a great show of leading an hour-long religious service of prayers and psalms, sometimes accompanied by four viols. When Drake saw Gómez Rengifo looking at his copy of Foxe's *Book of Martyrs* that depicted illuminated pictures of the English who had been burned in Castille by the

Inquisition, his attitude quickly changed. Drake said to him what he often said to others: that he acted in the name of the Queen. His quarrel and hers were with King Philip and his viceroy; and he would not rest until he recovered the sum lost by Hawkins at San Juan de Ulúa.

At Guatulco, Drake released Don Francisco and Nuño da Silva, the pilot who had served him well all the way from the Cape Verde Islands. Perhaps because he lacked the knowledge of the waters to come and that he would only have been a drain on water and food supplies, brought Drake to this decision. Da Silva took with him his possessions consisting of sixteen shirts, several pairs of breeches, hats and other clothing; an arquebus; lengths of damask; bed linen; even such odd things as a pair of women's boots, a tin of saffron, a jar of oil, two pounds of soap, and a length of hat trimming. Keen to curry favour with the authorities after the dismal defense of the town, the mayor, Gaspar de Vargas seized Silva and sent him to the viceroy, who passed him on to the Inquisition in Mexico City. Da Silva 's depositions to the Inquisitors survive, but though the authorities in general refused to believe him his statements remain as a helpful source for our knowledge of much of the voyage.[27]

Nuño's deposition got him into trouble. He was accused of having complacently attended Drake's Anglican services where psalms were sung. He defended himself saying he 'attended' no regular service but could not help hearing the English heretics bellowing out their blasphemous psalms. Da Silva escaped the torch if not the rack, but was sentenced to perpetual exile from the Indies. It is said, though not confirmed, that he even visited England before he died. Nevertheless, the Admiralty restored to him the value of the merchandise on board his ship when Drake captured it in the Cape Verdes.

Before leaving Mexico for the north, Drake destroyed the three biggest prizes he had taken, keeping only the nameless *fragata* of Rodrigo Tello for a tender. Sailing from Guatulco on Maundy Thursday, 16 April 1579, *Golden Hind* and the tender made a wide sweep into the Pacific to find the wind. Eventually he caught the north-west trades and, sailing close-hauled on the port tack, the leaking *Hind* reached a northernmost position variously reported as between latitude 48° and 42° N, a range which includes most of the state of Washington, all of Oregon, and a part of northern California. Somewhere in the strangely cold and windy June of 1579, he found a harbour and claimed the surrounding territory in the name of the queen, naming it *Nova Albion*. They had arrived on 17 June 1579 and tarried until 23 July. The same anonymous English informant that told us about the black girl Maria, left us a brief description of the place where Drake:

> grounded his ship to trim her [careened ship, cleaned the hull of barnacles and caulked the leaks.] & heere came downe unto them many of the contrey people while they were graving of their ship & had conference with them by synes. In this place Drake set up a greate post and nailed thereon vid [sixpence coin], which the countreye people worshipped as if it had bin god also hee nayled upon this post a

plate of lead, and scratched therein the Queenes name, and when they had graved and watered theire ship in the latter end of August they set sayle. [The engraved metal plate has never been found.]

The identity of the site where Drake stayed from 17 June to 23 July 1579 has been the subject of much debate. Numerous scholars as well as amateurs have attempted to answer the question that still remains unanswered. Drake needed a bay secluded from the Spaniards if they came looking for him, a place where his prize could be anchored with some of the bullion aboard, a suitable bottom on which to careen the *Hind* safely, and where they could defend themselves against attack from landwards. San Francisco Bay seems unlikely. However, the more probable site appears to be Drake's Bay, slightly to the north, with its white cliffs, which Hakluyt makes a point of mentioning. It is situated at exactly 38° N.

Drake's mind now concentrated on choosing the best alternative course for his return to England. Though little is known of his thoughts, he obviously abandoned any idea of returning via the Straits of Magellan as foolhardy. Crossing the isthmus with the treasure on mule-back was unfeasible due to the alarmed state of the Spaniards and the weight of the treasure. The supposed Strait of Anian, the mythical North West Passage, even if it proved to be there, was an unappealing option. It was uncharted and probably hazardous for a man with a fortune under his decks. Comparatively, under the circumstances, the known route across the Pacific and Indian Ocean must have looked by far the most appealing.

Tello's *fragata* was abandoned, there being only fifty to sixty men left to man both ships. Fletcher tells us that on '23 July, the Indians tooke a sorrowfull farewell of us, but being loath to leave us, they presently ranne to the top of the hills to keepe us in their sight as long as they could, making fires before and behind, and on each side of them.' Waving them goodbye, Drake sailed away, never to return, nor did any other Englishman for several centuries.

It proved to be a trouble free crossing. *Golden Hind* made a westerly passage of sixty-five or sixty-six days with the eastern trades abaft the beam and without sighting land during the trip they arrived at one of the Caroline Islands on 30 September 1579. Polynesian canoes whose occupants offered fruit, fish and coconuts, suggesting they wanted to trade, immediately surrounded *Hind*. Having read Magellan's experiences at Guam in the Ladrones, Drake was wary. At the first sign of trouble he fired off a culverin to frighten off the pestering natives, and when that failed, he had his harquebusiers shoot directly at the boats killing some twenty of them. Drake was intent not to be stopped at this point of his trip by a bunch of 'thieving savages'.[28]

Hind reached Mindanao on 21 October, they watered ship and took on fresh provisions and then sailed south in search of the fabulous Ternate, where Magellan's ships had tarried after the death of their captain general. Drake found the island much the same as Elcano had reported it sixty years earlier. The sultan Baab received the newcomers in princely splendor, as Revd Francis Fletcher wrote in his journal:

The king at last coming from the castle, with 8 or 10 more grave senators following him, had a very rich canopy (adorned in the midst with embossing of gold) born over him, and was guarded with 12 lances, the points turned downward. Our men (accompanied with *Moro* the king's brother) arose to meet him, and he very graciously did welcome and entertain them. He was for person of low voice, temperate in speech, in kingly demeanour, and a Moor by nation. His attire was after the fashion of the rest of his country, but far more sumptuous, as his condition and state required: From the waist to the ground was all cloth of gold, and that very rich: his legs bare, but on his feet a pair of shoes of goat skin, dyed red. In the attire of his head, were finely wreathed in diverse rings of plated gold, of an inch or an inch and a half in breadth, which made a fair and princely show, somewhat resembling a crown in form. About his neck he had a chain of perfect gold, the links very great and one fold double. On his left hand was a diamond, an emerald, a ruby, and a turkey [turquoise], 4 very fair and perfect jewels. On his right hand, in one ring, a big and perfect turkey and in another ring many diamonds of a smaller size, very artificially set and couched together.

As thus he sat in his chair of state, at his right side there stood a page with a very costly fan (richly embroidered and beset with sapphires) breathing and gathering the air to refresh the king, the place being very hot, both by reason of the sun, and the assembly of so great a multitude.[29]

Sultan Baab was very pleased to welcome the Englishmen and trade with them as well. He saw them as an alternative pawn in the game that up to now he had been adept at playing: Spanish against the Portuguese, as well as against his rival the Sultan of Tidore at the same time. However, the sultan flew into a rage when Drake declined to pay a heavy export duty on six tons of cloves he had bought, but the captain appeased him with elaborate gifts and discussed setting up an English factory at Ternate.

Golden Hind's crew had crammed the cloves into the little space that was left in her hold and left Ternate on 6 November 1579. The ship again needed rummaging and careening to thoroughly clean her hull of barnacles and marine growth that slowed her down. To accomplish it Drake sought out an uninhabited island.[30] Drake found one in what the men called Crab Island because it abounded in big king crabs, '… sufficient for hungrie stomachs at a dinner'. They stayed there twenty-six days and upon departure left behind two blacks he had taken from captured ships as well as the 'Negro wench Maria, being gotten with child in the ship.' Maria had been the slave that had caught Drake's eye and he had taken 'to cure his loneliness' from the small vessel captured with the Spanish grandee aboard, Francisco de Zárate. What became of the marooned blacks we do not know.

On 9 January 1580, while picking her way through the coral outcrops south of the Celebes, Drake almost lost his ship. *Golden Hind* ran on a shelving reef and stuck fast. To try to kedge her off the reef, he first lightened ship. He jettisoned eight cannon, valuable sacks of food and half his precious cargo of Ternate cloves. As a final measure he had the crew row out the spare anchor and make a purchase with it onto firm holding ground. Then wrapping its cable around the windlass, they wound with all their might but were unable to heave her off. Thinking there was nothing they could do but 'resign themselves to God's mercy', Drake called upon the chaplain, to say prayers and administer holy communion to every member of the crew, (reduced to only fifty-eight by then). It did the trick. The wind changed and by hoisting sails, the ship slid off by the stern into deep water. The unfortunate parson, instead of being thanked for invoking divine aid, was disgraced for remarking in his sermon, when things looked worst, that the crew should ask forgiveness since this accident was divine punishment for the execution of Thomas Doughty. Drake was furious and playing God himself, called the ships company together and solemnly excommunicated Francis Fletcher from the Church of England. He confined the poor man to the foredeck and forced him to wear about his arm a paper declaring 'Francis Fletcher ye falsest knave that liveth'.

Golden Hind, following much the same course as Sebastián Elcano sixty years earlier, reaching Tjilatjap, Java, safely. There Drake and his company were royally received, 'as many as nine kings came and entered the vessel', and were delighted by the banquets and music that the Englishman gave them. However, the visitors had to make a hurried and unceremonious departure, when Drake was advised that a Portuguese convoy had been sighted approaching the island.

Drake set a direct course for the southern tip of Africa, avoiding the islands under Spanish and Portuguese sovereignty. Denying himself ports of call to water and provision was a severe hardship that forced the crew to dig into their few reserves of strength and stamina. Several would have died of thirst had Drake not rigged spare canvas to catch every drop of rainwater. But it was a weak and feeble company that rounding the Cape of Good Hope sailed into the Atlantic on about 18 June 1580. Avoiding any ports of call that flew either Spanish or Portuguese flags, they called at a river mouth in Sierra Leone and spent two days watering, and enjoying some oysters and lemons. By the time they arrived the water had been rationed down to half a pint a day, equal to 0,236 liters, barely a sip. Taking into account it was mid-summer off the African coast the dehydration and consequent suffering must have been horrendous. For the first time in almost three years, they were back in familiar waters, navigating by familiar stars, and plotting their course on familiar charts.[31]

Golden Hind, avoiding the usual route of Portuguese East Indiamen returning home, sailed the long sweep northwestwards across the trades and homewards with the westerlies into the Channel. With the seamen pointing out familiar landmarks to each other as they went, they sailed into Plymouth Sound on 26 September 1580, three years less eleven weeks since they had departed from England.

Drake's first question to some fishermen was whether the queen was alive and well, for had she not been, he most likely would have been repudiated as an unlawful pirate. Complaints about his activities had been pouring in, so for another month the crew had to wait on board in the lee of St Nicholas Island. In the meantime Drake was summoned to London to be privately questioned by

Elizabeth. Only when he returned would the crew know if they would be welcomed as heroes or clapped in irons as pirates.[32]

Elizabeth had sent a message to Drake to bring her a few samples of his cargo. Consequently, Drake set out with a small party of men and several pack horses loaded down with gold and silver. In London he was led into the queen's presence for a private audience that lasted some six hours, though they were interrupted at intervals by conferences with members of the queen's Privy Council. Drake gave the queen a diary covering the entire trip and a large map showing the route he had taken. No one knows today what information the diary contained or what places were shown on the map because the queen had ordered that all be kept secret under pain of death.

Drake seems to have emphasised that the owners, who he said, were avoiding taxes levied on gold and silver by the Spanish viceroyalty, had not registered most of the bullion. Consequently, fox that he was, he pointed out in reference to the Spanish ambassador Bernardo de Mendoza's demand for restitution, that the owners could scarcely ask their government to represent them in negotiating the return of their property. The queen quickly endorsed that logic, ordering instead that a report be circulated that Drake had brought back little or nothing.[33]

Drake had hidden a large portion of the treasure elsewhere for himself.[34] No one knows how much it was, and he also had the queen's authority to appropriate an extra £10,000 of gold and silver.[35] Mendoza's informants told the ambassador about the plunder that went to the Tower of London: 'They say he is bringing twenty of this country's tons of silver, each one 2,000 pounds; five boxes of gold, a foot and a half in length; and a huge quantity of pearls, some of great value.'[36]

Most of all of the unregistered booty remained in Drake's hands, which made him one of the richest men in the country.[37] Quite often, he would try to buy influence with men of power by handing out gifts. Sometimes it worked but on other occasions it was not always so. Respect was important to him and it came as a blow when he was regarded as the roguish pirate he really was. Bughley, for instance, refused a gift of ten bars of gold, saying that he could not in good conscience receive stolen goods.[38] On another evening at a dinner party, when Drake was boasting about his exploits, Lord Sussex declared that it was not a great accomplishment to capture an unarmed vessel with a well-armed ship. When Drake carried on in a like manner the Earl of Arundel told him he was impudent and had no shame.[39]

Drake purchased the Cistercian monastery of Buckland Abbey (that had been confiscated by Elizabeth's father) from Sir Richard Grenville. Mendoza wrote to King Philip that his forthcoming knighthood was made on the purchase of property. 'She gave him the title of 'Sir' because of the land he purchased', he wrote his sovereign. He made the purchase after already having bought a residence in Elbow Lane in London, from where he would visit court as often as he could and showered the queen with presents. Now to consolidate his entry into the high society of the nobility, he desperately needed his knight-hood.

Having qualified as a gentleman of property, a requisite for knighthood in those days, the queen ordered that *Golden Hind* be made ready for the ceremony. The ship had already been taken to Deptford and placed in a dock as a permanent memorial of Drake's voyage. She then sent word that she would be pleased to be Drake's guest at a banquet on board, which was immediately arranged. It proved to be the finest affair since the epic feasts of Henry VIII.

Golden Hind had been completely refurbished by an army of painters and carpenters, and looked as fine as a ship could be on 4 April 1581, with colourful banners flying from her masts. While the crowds cheered and musicians played, Elizabeth in a festive mood, stepped on board the ship that had circled the globe, accompanied by the Marquis of Marchaumont, agent of the Duke of Alençon, She carried a gilded sword that she showed Drake, jokingly saying that with it she had come to cut his head off. Drake bowed, then kneeled before his sovereign to be knighted on the deck of his flagship.

The ceremony marked her defiance to Spain and the commencement of Philip II's determination to conquer England and depose Elizabeth with the creation of an 'Invincible Armada'. For the majority Drake had become at once a national hero. However, the acclamation was not unanimous: those in the city feared an immediate arrest of English goods in Spain; the remnants of the old aristocracy hated the new age of which Drake was now the epitome and hankered after for a conciliation with the old religion of yesteryear. Burghley gave Mendoza to understand that he also disapproved. He probably did, but his policy was always dictated by a dispassionate consideration of his country's interest.

Drake never ceased to work for the further humiliation of Spain. He took a significant part in the defeat of the Spanish Armada, and sailed to the West Indies on his last expedition against the Don's in 1595. The following year he died of yellow fever on board his flagship off Nombre de Dios, Panama, a fitting place to expire his last, and was buried at sea.

Mary Newman, Drake's first wife died in 1583. Two years later he married Elizabeth Sydenham, he had no offspring with either wives but Drake's heir, his brother Thomas, is ancestor to the present Drake family.

There seems no more fitting epitaph for Drake then the last lines of Sir Henry Newbolt's poem, *Drake's Drum*:

Take my drum to England, hang et by the shore,
Strike et when your powder's runnin' low;
If the Don's sight Devon, I'll quit the Port o' Heaven,
An' drum them up the Channel as we drummed them long ago.

THE AFTERMATH

The secret instructions from the Lords of the Admiralty, handed to Captain James Cook and dated 6 July 1776, instructed him to:

> Proceed in as direct a course as you can to the coast of New Albion, endeavouring to fall in with it in the latitude 45° ' North; and taking care, in your way thither, not to lose any time in search of new lands...
>
> Upon your arrival on the coast of New Albion you are... to proceed northward along the coast, as far as the latitude of 65° or farther... and to explore, such rivers or inlets as may appear to be of a considerable extent and pointing towards Hudsons or Baffins Bays.[1]

It was intended that Cook continue the task that Drake had initiated, to discover the elusive North-west Passage in the Pacific, around, or through, the North American continent. Neither of them found it but both contributed hugely to the art and science of navigation.

Drake was not the first Englishman to enter the Pacific. That title goes to John Oxenham, who had been with Drake at the capture of Nombre de Dios in 1572. The nefarious Oxenham returned, as we'll remember, to the Caribbean, two years later as captain of a small ship with seventy seamen. He anchored his vessel and crossed the Isthmus of Darien with his men. On the Pacific side they built a pinnace and set sail into the South Seas, capturing two small Spanish ships carrying gold and silver from Quito to Panama. However, they were captured in turn and the treasure recovered by a squadron commanded by Juan de Ortega. Most of Oxenham's men were executed as pirates in Panama, but Oxenham and his pilot were taken to Lima where they were imprisoned, interrogated by the Holy Inquisition, and later hanged in the main square. Three years after Oxenham's ill-fated incursion, Drake sailed into the Pacific through the Strait of Magellan.

After Drake's expedition, the next English voyage into the Pacific was that of Thomas Cavendish. Cavendish, a member of a well-connected family was educated at Corpus Christi College, Cambridge. In 1585 he accompanied Sir Richard Grenville to America. Soon returning to England, he undertook an elaborate imitation of Drake's great voyage. On 21 July 1586, he sailed from Plymouth with 123 men in three vessels, only one of which, his flagship *Desire*, of 140 tons, returned. Going by way of Sierra Leone, the Cape Verde Islands and Cabo Frio in Brazil, he coasted down the Patagonian coast entering Port Desire (that he named) and passing

through the Strait of Magellan fell upon the Spanish settlements and shipping on the
west coast of South America, Central America and Mexico. Among his captures was
the Manila galleon *Santa Ana* off Cabo San Lucas, Baja California, filling his holds
with as much of her treasure as he could carry. Having gained intelligence from *Santa
Ana*'s crew about the Far East, he struck out across the Pacific, touching at the
Ladrones, Philippines, Moluccas, reaching Java in March 1588. He later arrived back
in England by way of the Cape of Good Hope in September, having
circumnavigated the globe in two years and fifty days. It is said that his sailors were
clothed in silk, his sails were damask and his topmast covered with cloth of gold. He
expected a knighthood as had been rewarded Drake, but his achievement was
overshadowed by Britain's victory over the Spanish Armada. Therefore, he had to be
content with the freedoms of Southampton and Portsmouth and the renewed
support of his prominent patrons toward his further explorations.

Cavendish planned a second voyage in which he proposed to sail again through
the Strait of Magellan and across the Pacific to China, there to initiate commerce
with England in the tea trade. If completed it would have made him the first man
to have led two circumnavigations. However, the enterprise was bound to failure
as, after crossing the Atlantic and sheltering in Port Desire, he died aboard his
flagship *Leicester* on her premature return to England and on 20 May 1592 was
buried at sea without having reached the Pacific.[2]

John Davis, who had joined Cavendish's second voyage, had become separated
from the main squadron, and sighted the Southern Isles (the Malouines), to
become known then as Davis's Southern Islands. He pressed on through the Strait
of Magellan and reached the Pacific. Nevertheless, due to a combination of a
shortage of supplies, bad weather, and his crew's lack of cooperation, he turned
back reaching England in June 1592.

This unsuccessful adventure was followed by another in 1594, when Richard
Hawkins led another expedition into the Pacific. Richard was the only son of Sir
John Hawkins, kinsman and associate of Drake and a member of the West Country
family so prominent in English overseas enterprises for over a century. Like Drake
and Cavendish, he planned a voyage around the globe, leaving England aboard
Dainty in April 1593. A year later after many vicissitudes, he passed through the Strait,
sailed north along the coast of Chile and attacked Valparaiso. Continuing further
north, *Dainty* was intercepted by two well-armed Spanish ships-of-war under the
command of Don Beltran de Castro. After a three-day fight, Hawkins severely
wounded, surrendered. He was first sent to Lima and from there to Spain, where he
was imprisoned. After lengthy negotiations he was eventually released to return
home and be knighted on 23 July 1603. His voyage to the Pacific was not followed
by any further English adventures to that area for many decades.[3]

The English became interested in the East India trade during the late sixteenth
and early seventeenth centuries. The Dutch, who eventually displaced the
Portuguese in the area, became very active in South-east Asia. The first English
expedition to reach the area since Drake and Cavendish was a flotilla commanded

by James Lancaster in 1591. The English founded a trading 'factory' at the Moluccas. Gradually, they learned firsthand about the Far East from insular South-east Asia to Japan. Trade carried on from these parts until 1623, when the Dutch effectively excluded the English from these parts for about a century.

English pirates, including Richard Sawkins, Bartholomew Sharp and Henry Morgan, were active in the last decade of the seventeenth century. Henry Morgan gathered his men at the Caribbean port of Chagres and marched across the isthmus to sack Panama City, as Oxenham had done nearly a century before. It was that year that England signed a treaty by which the English colonies were recognised by Spain, and in return England pledged to deal with the atrocities of the buccaneers. In an attempt to enforce the treaty, Morgan was made Deputy Governor of Jamaica and knighted, but the piracy continued. In 1680, a large group of them, including Sawkins, Sharp, and Ringrose, were at Panama where they captured a number of craft including *Santisima Trinidad* which they renamed *Trinity* and in which many of them sailed for the next two years. They visited the islands of Juan Fernandez and cruised the Pacific coast of Central and South America attacking Spanish settlements on the way. The most important of the treasures they captured was a Spanish *derrotero*, or pilot book, by which the English gained much secret cartographic intelligence. By sailing south of the Strait of Magellan they sailed around Cape Horn into the Atlantic, being the first Englishmen to do so.

Perhaps the most remarkable of the buccaneers was William Dampier. What set him apart from most was that he recorded and published accounts of his travels. He came to the attention of a large reading audience through his first book, *A New Voyage Round the World*, even Horatio Nelson thought it one of the most enthralling books he ever read and took it with him wherever he went. Dampier was born in 1652 at East Coker, Somerset, the son of a tenant farmer in the West Country of England. Having early become an orphan, and with little formal education, he was apprenticed to a master mariner in Weymouth who placed him aboard ship in which he made a voyage to Newfoundland. On his return in 1671, he sailed to Bantam in the East Indies. He served in the Dutch war in 1673 and was present at two engagements but then fell sick and was put ashore. In 1678 he returned to England and married, but soon after left for Central America again where he associated with some well-known buccaneers. For a time he got the job of under-manager of a Jamaican estate but a steady job was not for him, and he joined a party of buccaneers and crossed the Isthmus of Darien. He spent the year 1680 on the Peruvian coast sacking, plundering and burning, then made his way down to Juan Fernandez Island. To put it briefly, the year of 1683 found him pillaging on the Pacific coast of the Americas. The following year he joined a ship which took him from Baja California to Guam and on to the Philippines. During the next five years, Dampier was on several vessels foraging in the East Indies and Indian Ocean. In 1688 he touched the northern coast of Australia, then called New Holland, the first Englishman to do so. After another expedition in February 1701, he arrived off Ascension Island in the Atlantic where his vessel foundered, he and the crew swam to land and stayed on the island until April, when they were conveyed to England by an East Indiaman and warships bound for home. Between 1703-1707 Dampier unsuccessfully commanded two government privateers on an expedition to the South Seas. Better Fortune attended him, however, on his last voyage, as pilot to Woodes Rogers in the circumnavigation of 1708-1711. On the former venture Alexander Selkirk, a scott, master of one of the vessels (later immortalised by Defoe as Robinson Crusoe), was marooned at Juan Fernandez; while on the latter, Selkirk was rescued and the prize money of £200.000 was claimed by Dampier. However, four years before it was paid Dampier died. The accounts of Dampier's voyages are famous. He managed to save his journals, 'I took care', he said, 'before I left ship to provide myself with large joints of Bamboo [canes], which I stopt at both ends, closing it with Wax, so as to keep out any water. In this I preserved my journal and other writings from being wet, tho' I was often forced to swim.' His writings were factual and detailed accounts of places, people, plants and animals, as well as winds currants, and so on. His style is usually admirably easy, clear, and comprehensive. His description of breadfruit, for instance, was recalled later by Captain Cook, who examined the plant and recommended that it be transplanted to the West Indies. This was the reason for the voyage of the *Bounty*, 1787-1789, under Captain William Bligh, who had served with Cook, a voyage that turned mutinous to the detriment of Bligh and some of his loyal officers. Dampier became, through his travels and writings, the most influential English explorer of the Pacific between the times of Drake and Cook.

Commodore (later Lord) George Anson, commanding HMS *Centurion*, led a squadron of six Royal Naval warships and two store vessels on an expedition to the Pacific between 1740 and 1744. His orders were to attack the Spanish possessions in South America. It was to become the most famous circumnavigation between that of Sir Francis Drake and those of Captain Cook. Its fame was partly due to the unprecedented amount of treasure captured, amounting to £50 million in modern money, and partly to the contemporary publication of the vivid narrative of the voyage by the ship's chaplain, Revd Richard Walker, to become a best-seller in many languages. However, in terms of human life the voyage was a disaster. By the time his flagship reached Canton (the first British warship to do so) the fatalities in his squadron – mainly due to scurvy – numbered 1,051 out of the 1,955 men who originally had embarked at Portsmouth. On board the flagship, for example, while rounding Cape Horn, forty men died and most of the remainder were unable to perform their duties. Almost all the seamen were stricken, and all the marines on board were either sick or dead. There were only 201 men left alive, out of its normal compliment of 521 officers and men, of these only forty-five were able seamen. He was compelled at last to collect all the surviving personnel of the squadron in *Centurion* to man the ship. After considerable difficulties with the Chinese he sailed again with his one remaining vessel to cruise for one of the rich galleons which conducted the trade between the Philippines and Mexico. He was successful in capturing an immensely rich prize, *Nuestra Señora de Covadonga*, which he met up with off Cape Espiritu Santo, on 15 June 1744. Of Anson's six ships only *Centurion* returned to England following the prescribed course of the voyage, laden with great treasure from the Spanish Manila galleon. Anson gained great official recognition, though he made no significant discoveries and lost over a thousand men.

I have always been a great admirer of Lord Byron's poetry; however, I can hardly say anything enthusiastic about his grandfather, Commodore, the Honorable John, 'foul-weather Jack', Byron.

The idea of a great southern continent, the elusive *Terra Australis* in the South Pacific, had existed from antiquity and it was brought forward by Alexander Dalrymple of the East India Company (later the first hydrographer of the Royal Navy) to the Lords of the Admiralty. Dalrymple had navigated the coasts of southern and eastern Asia on behalf of the East India Company, and he was the first choice of the Royal Society to head the expedition which Lieutenant (later Captain) Cook was appointed to lead in 1768.[4]

At the conclusion of the Seven Years' War, Byron was sent on a peaceful exploring mission (1764-65) in the frigate *Dolphin*, with the sloop *Tamar*. He was to attempt to find the elusive Strait of Anan and if possible sail through it from west to east. Should this prove not feasible, he was to try to discover the southern continent by circumnavigating Tierra del Fuego in the latitudes in which land had been reported by sailors of different nations for many years.

When he got to the Pacific Byron attempted only the second task. However, contrary winds drove him west from 25° South latitude, to 20° North on the Asiatic side of the Pacific thus impeding the enterprise. On his way, in mid-Pacific, he discovered two islands in the Tuamotu Archipelago, two in the Tokelan group and the Gilbert Islands which had not been seen before by European sailors. He returned to England by way of Batavia and the Cape of Good Hope, having contributed very few additions to geographical knowledge of the Pacific.

The paucity of results of Byron's voyage did not deter the Admiralty from further exploring the area, and in 1767 another expedition was sent out. It was to explore westward from the coast of South America but further south than had been the case up to now. If they found land they were to return to England the way they had come (around Cape Horn); if not they were to continue across the Pacific and return home by way of the Cape of Good Hope with stops at islands in the East Indies. Samuel Wallis was appointed commander of the same *Dolphin*, used by Byron in his circumnavigation, to be accompanied by *Swallow* commanded by Philip Carteret. Carteret had sailed around the world with Byron as first lieutenant in *Tamar* and later in *Dolphin*. Wallis had no previous experience in exploration. They left England in August 1766. Being early in the year for a calm passage, it took them four months to clear the Strait of Magellan. At its western exit the two ships were separated in a storm and having lost sight of one another, sailed separately across the Pacific. Wallis, driven by trade winds, took a more northerly course making discoveries in the Low Archipelago and the Society Islands including Tahiti, which he named the King George Third's Island. *Dolphin* proceeded then across the Pacific north of the equator, arriving home by way of the East Indies and southern Africa in May 1768, at a time when Cook was preparing his first voyage to the Pacific, specifically to Tahiti, to observe the transit of Venus.

Carteret, on the other hand, took a more southerly route as prescribed in the orders, discovering Pitcairn Island, named for the seamen that first saw it. *Swallow*, now in bad condition, passed through the Tuamotus and reached the Solomon Islands. These had taken their name from the presumed whereabouts of gold obtained by King Solomon's navy, and which had been pursued since the beginnings of European expansion overseas and which the Spanish claimed to have seen in the sixteenth century (a fact unknown to Carteret at the time). At any rate, he discovered the strait separating New Britain from New Ireland thereby entering the area visited by Dampier some eighty years before. The *Swallow* returned to England via the Celebes, Batavia (since independence in 1949 it became known as Jakarta the capital of Indonesia) and Cape Town, arriving shortly after Cook had sailed with the botanist Joseph Banks, the astronomer Charles Green and other scientists in *Endeavor* on his first great voyage to the Pacific.

The British presence in the Pacific would not be complete without mention of a captain who never reached this greatest of oceans, Edmond Halley, the astronomer. The British Admiralty had granted him the rank of captain in the Royal Navy and the command of a small ship, the *Paramour*. The object of this appointment was to enable Halley, on the first sea voyage taken for purely scientific purposes, to observe variations in compass readings in the South Atlantic and to determine accurate latitudes and longitudes of his ports of call. Earlier Halley had written a paper on the transit of Venus. He predicted that the transit would occur in 1769 and as result, the observation might improve the estimate of the distance of the earth from the sun. As to the famous comet named after him, Halley observed that comets seen in 1531, 1607, and 1682 were really one and the same and predicted its return in 1758. It was sighted late in that year and consequently named in his honour. It also proved that at least some comets are members of the solar system. Halley's words were remembered many years after his death, on 14 January 1742, by the Royal Society, which sponsored Cook's first Pacific voyage. The official reason given was to observe the transit of Venus, which they did. The success of this first voyage led to Cook's second and then his third and final voyage, during which most of the large geographical problems of the Pacific were resolved. The knowledge of the link of sea and sky as to navigation, since time immemorial, has always been very much in the minds of sailors. I've referred to their use of the heavens as a compass in earlier parts of this book which shows the great importance this link had to the Royal Navy at the time. Thus, with Cook a new era of scientific exploration began in the Pacific, drawing the veil at last from the undiscovered ocean.

ENDNOTES

CHAPTER 1

1 Jean Randier; *Hommes et Navieres au Cap Horn 1616–1939.* Librairie Hachette. 1966. Arthur Barket Ltd. English translation. 1969

2 *Great Cooks and their Recipes. From Taillevent to Escoffier.* Anne Willian. Pavilion Books Ltd. Great Britain 1992. p9.

3 *The Diary of Samuel Pepys.* Vol. IX. 1668–1669. p336. Edited by Robert Latham & William Matthews. University of California Press. Berkley and Los Angeles, USA 1976.

4 Giles Milton. *Nathaniel's Nutmeg.* Hodder & Stoughton. London 1999. p18.

5 Charles Corn. *The Scents Of Eden.* New York 1999. pXIX.

6 Giles Milton. *Nathaniel's Nutmeg.* London 1999.

7 Dava Sobel. *Galileo's Daughter.* Walker Publishing Co. Inc. USA 1999.

8 Charles Corn. *The Scents of Eden.* Kodansha International. New York, Tokyo 1997. pXXI.

9 Jean Randier. p13.

10 *Ibid.*

11 Giles Milton.

12 Nutmeg and mace contain about 7 to 14 per cent essential oils used to scent soaps and perfumes.

13 *Ibid.*

14 Charles Corn. pXXIV.

CHAPTER 2

1 Sweeping down the outer edge of Britain, settling in Orkney, Shetland, the Hebrides, and Ireland, the Norsemen of Norway then voyaged to Iceland, where in AD870 they settled among Irish colonists who had preceded them by some two centuries. About AD1000, one Bjarni Herjulfsson on his way from Iceland to Greenland was blown off course far to the southwest; he saw an unknown shore and returned to tell his tale. The saga of Eric the Red, a Norwegian, tells the story of the discovery of Greenland in AD982, but it was his son, Leif, who together with some thirty others set out to explore. They probably reached the coasts of Labrador and Newfoundland and, it is thought they might even have reached Maryland, Virginia, or the mouth of the St Laurence. However, attempts at colonization were unsuccessful, the Norsemen withdrew, and, although the Greenland colonies lingered on for some four centuries, little knowledge came down to color the vision of the seamen from Cadiz or Lisbon.

2 Translation by Ronald Latham. *The Travels of Marco Polo.* Penguin Books. 1958. p34.

3 *Ibid.* p12.

4 Maria Bellonci, translation by Teresa Waugh. *The Travels of Marco Polo.* Sidgwick and Jackson. London 1984, pp14–15.

5 *Ibid.* p14.

6 Pope Gregory X, born 1210; died 10 January, 1276. Tedaldo Visconti came from Piacensa and entered the service of Cardinal Palestrina, accompanying him on papal missions to France. He became archdeacon of Liège and may have participated in the General Church Council of Lyons I. The previous pope, Clement, had died three years earlier, and a long vacancy followed in which rival factions of French and Italian cardinals failed to agree on a successor. French royal pressure finally persuaded them to seek a compromise candidate, and on the advice of the Franciscan leader, later St Bonaventure, they were confined to the papal palace of Viterbo on bread and water until they reached a decision. Michael J. Walsh. *Lives of the Popes.* Salamander Books. London 1998.

7 Laiazzo in Marco's writings, now Yumurtalik on the Gulf of Iskenderun, also called the Gulf of Alexandretta, in south-eastern Turkey.

8 Maria Bellonci. p15.

9 Camels can go for seventeen days without water.

10 Ronald Latham. p77.

11 *Ibid.* p80.

12 *Ibid.* p84.

13 The Great wall did not exist in Marco's time; it was built after the Mongol dynasty was overthrown. Only a packed earth construction built about 1,400 years before Marco's time protected the Han territory from nomadic raiders. It was originally about 30ft high.

14 *Ibid.* p175.

15 Mike Edwards. *The Adventures of Marco Polo.* Assistant editor, *National Geographic.* May; June; July 2001.

16 Latham. p40.

17 *Ibid.* p41.

18 *Ibid.* p42.

19 *Ibid.* pp241, 242.

20 One of the later Budist scriptures dealing with techniques and rituals including meditative and sexual practices.

21 McNeil. *Rise of the West.* Zvi Dor-Ner. *The Age of Discovery, Columbus.* William Morrow and Co. New York. p14/15.

22 Article by Graciela Iglesias in the Newspaper *La Nación,* of Buenos Aires, 9 March 2002.

23 Zvi Dor-Ner. 'Columbus'. William Morrow and Co. New York. p.14–15. *Encyclopedia Britannica,* fifteenth edition. 1991. Nicholas D. Kristof. *The New York Times* magazine. 6-8-99. Newspaper *La Nación.* Buenos Aires, 9 March 2002.

CHAPTER 3

1 It was the last Muslim state to survive the Arab-Christian wars between 1031 and 1492, when the Arabs were finally expelled.

CHAPTER 4

1 Roberto Levillier. Vol.1, p15.
2 Daniel J.Boorstin; *The Discoverers*. Random House. New York 1983. p159.
3 *Ibid.* p160.
4 *Ibid.* p161.
5 *Ibid.* p159.
6 To the contrary, the larger vessels were often less seaworthy than their smaller predecessors, since the mistakes of the smaller were often repeated by geometric progression in the design of the larger ships.
7 Roberto Levillier. *América, La Bien Llamada*. Vol.1 p14.

CHAPTER 5

1 J.W. Blake. *Europeans in West Africa*. London 1942.
2 Rui de Pina, *Chronica del Rey Dom Joâo II*. Lisboa, 1709; Blake: Op. Cit.
3 Roberto Levillier.
4 Roberto Levillier. Vol.1, p43.

CHAPTER 6

1 Pope Alexander VI; born 1 January 1431; elected 11 August 1492; died 18 August 1503.
2 Calixtus III, a Catalan, born 31 December 1378; elected 8 April 1455; died 6 August 1458. Alfonso Borgia, a seventy-seven-year-old Catalan, was another result of the famous clashes between Colonna and Orsini families. He was a canonist whose role in settling a schism in the Church of Rome brought him the wealthy See of Valencia and he later brought about the reconciliation of Alfonso V with Eugene IV which caused the collapse of the Basle council. He was made cardinal in 1444. He devoted the whole of his brief reign in attempts to mount a crusade against the Turks. His only successes were the relief of Belgrade in 1456 and a naval victory in 1457.
3 Jacopo da Volterra. *Diario Romano 1479-1484*, p130. As quoted by E.R. Chamberlin in *The Bad Popes*, p166 Dorset Press. New York 1969.
4 Stefano Infessura. *Diario della Città di Roma*. Chap.13. As quoted by Chamberlin p167.
5 Michael J. Walsh. *Lives of the Popes*. Salamander Books Ltd. London 1998. p196.
6 Caesar Baronius continued by Raynaldus, 1738. As quoted by Chamberlin p161.
7 Stefano Infessura, *Diario della Città*. Chap.10. As quoted by Chamberlin p170.
8 Giuliano della Rovere, who became Pope Julius II, after Rodrigo Borgia died, finally sanctioned the change in 1506.
9 Contraalmirante (RS) Laurio H. Destéfani. *Historia Marítima Argentina*. Tomo II, p357.
10 Francesco Guicciardini, *Storia d'Italia*, ed.by Constantino Panigarda. Bari, 1929. I, 20. As quoted by Chamberlin p173.
11 G. Antonelli, *Lucrezia Borgia in Ferrara*, Ferrara 1897 p34, as quoted by Chamberlin p176.
12 Dispatch quoted in Ferdinand Gregorovius, *History of the City of Rome in the Middle Ages*.1894. op. cit.,59. As quoted by Chamberlin p178.
13 Johannes (John) Burchard, *Diarium*. Vols I-III. op. cit.,An. 1497. As quoted by Chamberlin p187.
14 E.R. Chamberlin. *The Bad Popes*. Dorset Press. New York. 1969. p197.
15 Ferdinand Gregorovius, *History of the City of Rome in the Middle Ages*, trans. From the 4th German. ed. By Annie Hamilton. London 1894-1902, VII, p486. As quoted by Chamberlin p198.
16 Marino Sanuto, *La spedizione di Carlo VIII in Italia*, ed. by R. Fulin. Venice 1873-1882.
17 Niccoló Machiavelli, *Discorso sopra T. Livio*, Vol.III of Opere. Milan, 1804. As quoted by Chamberlin p200.
18 A. Giustiniani, *Dispacci*, 1502-1505. ed. By Pasquale Villari. Florence, 1876. I, 64 as quoted by Chamberlin p201.
19 Sigismondo de' Conti, *Le storie de suoi tempi dal 1475 al 1510*. Rome, 1883. p64 as quoted by Chamberlin p202.
20 The French army that marched to Naples carried with it the first massive outbreak of syphilis that Europe had known. Spanish women who were infected by the Indians brought to Barcelona by Columbus in 1494 had transmitted the disease to the French soldiers.
21 Marino Sanuto, *La spedizione di Carlo VIII in Italia*. ed. by R. Fulin. Venice 1873-1882. op. cit., V,74. As quoted by Chamberlin p203.
22 Francesco Guicciardini, *Storia d'Italia*, ed. by Constantino Panigada. Bari 1929. I, 20. As quoted by Chamberlin p204.
23 Chamberlin p205.

CHAPTER 7

1 Roberto Levillier. *América La Bien Llamada*. Guillermo Kraft Ltda. Buenos Aires 1948. Vol.I p55.
2 Paolo dal Pozzo Toscanelli 1397-1482.
3 3 vols. Louvain, 1480-83.
4 Morison, p379.
5 Eugene Lyon. *Search for Columbus. National Geographic* magazine. Vol.1. N?1. January 1992.
6 Eugene Lyon. *Search for Columbus. National Geographic* magazine. Vol.181. N?1. January 1992.

CHAPTER 8

1 Nao was the name given to a vessel somewhat similar to a caravela, that was larger in cargo space and had a forecastle as well as a sterncastle.

2 The other provinces being: Jaén, Málaga, Granada, Córdoba, Sevilla, Cádiz and Almeira.

3 Kamen. *The Spanish Inquisition*. p254.

4 Of an estimated 7 million people in Castile, whose kingdom comprised three-quarters of the peninsula's population, there were an estimated 70,000 Jews among them. Almost half of them would refuse to accept conversion. Stuart Stirling. *The Last Conquistador*. Sutton Publishing. Gloucestershire. England 1999.

5 Though Holland, along with the six other northern Netherlands provinces was not to declare their independence from Spain and the Catholic Church until 1581, it was the only country in Europe tolerant of religion regardless of creed. Its trade would make it one of the richest states on earth, while its liberal atmosphere made it a haven for free thinkers, intellectuals and artists. Thirty-nine years later it also became a haven to the separatists from the Church of England known as the Pilgrim Fathers. Having fled first to Amsterdam in 1608, and on to Leyden the following year, they sailed in the *Mayflower* from Plymouth, England, on 6 September 1620 to the British colonies in the New World. Arriving on 11 December they founded the colony of Plymouth, Massachusetts.

6 Morison. p391.

7 Lorenzo Camusso. *The Voyages of Columbas*. Arnold Monditore Editore. Milan 1991. p33.

8 Eugene Lyon. p37.

9 Zvi Dor-Ner. *Columbus and the age of discovery*. William Morrow and Co. New York. p217.

10 Morison. pp430-433 and Zvi Dor-Ner, p217.

CHAPTER 9

1 Lorenzo Camusso. p51-52.

2 Encyclopaedia Britannica, Vol. 22. p903. and Sean Kelly and Rosemary Rogers. *Saints Preserve Us*. Random House. New York 1993. p.276. Samuel Eliot Morison. p448.

3 Samuel Eliot Morison. p451.

4 Lorenzo Camusso. p52.

5 *Ibid*.

6 Samuel Eliot Morison. p452.

7 *Ibid*.

8 Alonso de Ojeda, an agile, handsome Andalucian had attracted the queen's attention, and favour, by pirouetting on a beam that projected from the Giralda, a tower 200ft above the street in Seville.

9 Bartolomé de las Casas (1474-1566) bishop of Chiapas, known to posterity as the Apostle of the Indians, was born in Seville in 1474, of noble family, and educated at the University of Salamanca. In 1510 he took holy orders, the first to be granted in the New World, and as a member of Diego Velasquez's colonizing expedition to Cuba tried vainly to check the massacre of Indians at Canoas. In 1514 he became suddenly convinced of the evil of the *repartimiento* system (allotment of Indians for forced labour) and went to Spain to plead the cause of the Indians before the king. His attempt to found a model colony on the mainland (Cumuná) was defeated through the rapacious brutality of the conquistadors, and in 1522 he retired to a Dominican convent in Hispaniola. In 1530 he returned to Spain and wrote several treatises. His best known is *Brevísima relación de la destrución de las Indias occidentales*. Most of his last days were spent in the convent of San Gregorio at Valladolid and of the Atocha in Madrid, where he died in July 1566, one of the few humane and kindly figures in the history of the Spanish conquests in America. Las Casas transcribed the log of Columbus' first voyage and incorporated it into his account of the Admiral's epic adventure.

10 *Encyclopaedia Britannica*. 1959. p727.

11 Morrison. p.436 and Zvi Dor-Ner. p212.

12 Lorenzo Camusso. p55.

13 Rex and Thea Rienits. *The Voyages of Columbus*. London 1970. p73-74.

CHAPTER 10

1 Morison. p478.

2 Morison. p487.

3 *History*. Fernando Columbus.

CHAPTER 11

1 On the voyage the *teredos* seemed to like pitch; they ate right through it and, within a few months, had riddled the planking.

2 Hurricanes were among the most frightening and unexpected dangers of early Caribbean exploration. Furious rains and violent winds that sometimes reach a velocity of 190 miles (300km) per hour, and beyond, accompany these violent storms, which normally occur between the months of June and October. They tend to last a short time, quite often only a few hours, but can leave a trail of destruction and calamity in their wake.

3 Morison. p524.

4 Ferdinand Columbus. *Account of his father's fourth Voyage*.

5 25 June 1503 until 28 June 1504.

CHAPTER 12

1 Roberto Levillier. *América La Bien Llamada.*
2 Boorstin. p175-6.
3 *Ibid.*
4 *Ibid.*
5 Charles Corn. *The Scents of Eden.* Kodansha America Inc. New York, Tokyo 1999.
6 Boorstin. p192.
7 *Ibid.* Prologue. p.xxv.
8 *Ibid.* p5.
9 *Ibid.* p8.
10 *Ibid.* p8.
11 *Ibid.* p9.
12 *Ibid.* p10.
13 *Ibid.* p12.
14 *Ibid.* pp14 to 23.
15 *Ibid.* p73.
16 *Ibid.* pxvii.
17 *Ibid.* p34.
18 Morrison. p553.

CHAPTER 13

1 Lorenzo Camusso. *The Voyages of Columbus.* Milan. 1991. Translation by Elizabeth Leister. p76-7.
2 Columbus' letter reads as follows: 'A mi hijo Don Diego. En la corte. Mi muy caro fijo: Diego Méndez partió de aquí lunes 3 de este mes. Despues de partido fablé con Amerigo Vespuchi, portador desta, el cual va allá llamado sobre cosas de navegación. El siempre tuvo deseos de me hacer placer: es mucho hombre de bien: la fortuna le ha sido contraria como a otros muchos: sus trabajos no le han aprovechado tanto como la razón requiere. El va por mío y en muchos deseos de hacer cosa que redonde a mi bien, si a tus manos está. Yo non sé de acá en que yo le emponga que a mi aproveche, porque non se que sea lo que allá le quieren. El va determinado a hacer por mí todo lo que a el fuere posible. Ved allá en que puede aprovrchrse, y trabajar por ello, que él lo hará todo y fablará, y le porná en obra; y sea todo secretamente porque non se haya dél sospecha, Yo todo lo que se haya podido decir que toque a esto, se lo he dicho, y enformado de la paga que a mi se ha fecho y se haz. Antonio Ballesteros Beretta.' *Cristóbal Colón y el descubrimiento de América.* Barcelona, 1945, Salvat. T. II p706.
3 Rolando A. Laguarda Trías. *El Hallazgo del Río de la Plata Por Amerigo Vespuci en 1502.* Academia Nacional de Letras. Montevideo. Uruguay 1982. p105.
4 Daniel J. Boorstin. *The Discoverers.*
5 Roberto Levillier. *America la Bien Llamada.* Vol.I p130.
6 Rex and Thea Rientes. *The Voyages of Columbus.* London 1970. p104.
7 Boorstin. p246.
8 *Ibid.* p247.
9 Laguarda Trías. p115.
10 The so-called 'Mundus Novus', a letter in Latin dated 4 June 1501, from Amerigo to Pier Francesco de' Medici, mentions the day of sailing from Lisbon as 14 May 1501, while in the 'Lettera' of 4 September 1504, sent by Vespucci to Pier Soderini, galfaroniere of Florence, he mentions the sailing date as 10 May 1501. The four days' discrepancy does not really make any difference to the sixteen-month voyage.
11 Laguarda Trías. p121.
12 Rolando A. Laguarda Trías. p121.
13 Cabo de Santa Maria was named by the Portuguese pilot João de Lisboa a member of Vespucci's 'Fourth' expedition for the Portuguese crown, captained by Gonzalo Cohelo, between 1503-1504. Luigi Avonto. *Operacion Nuevo Mundo.* p240.
14 Rolando A. Laguarda Trías, Uruguayan professor of history at the University of Montevideo, with over thirty books published to his name.
15 Rolando A. Laguarda Trías. p190. Virginia Carreño. *Estancias y Estancieros del Río de la Plata.* Editorial Claridad. Buenos Aires 1994. p15.
16 Si la flota hubiese sido arrastrada hasta las proximidades del grado 52 S, es de toda verosimilitud que los expedicionarios habrían visto el 7 de abril el archipiélago de las Malvinas que a la distancia y deficiente visibilidad bien pudiera ser la 'tierra nueva que corrimos cerca de 20 leguas, encontrándola que era toda una costa brava, y no percibimos ningún puerto ni gente; yo creo porque nadie en la flota podía remediar ni soportarlo...' Enrique Ruiz-Guiñazu. *Proas de España en el mar Magallánico.*
17 But in the end these precautions were not enough. The Venetian-born Sebastian Cabot, (1476? -1557), while serving Spain as Pilot-Major to Emperor Charles V, tried to sell 'The secret of the Strait' both to Venice and to England.
18 'Hasta cuanto había andado Américo Vespucio…' Zaragoza. *Historia General de las Indias.* 1555. Chap.92.
19 Boorstin. p250.
20 Boorstin. pp250, 251.

CHAPTER 14

1 Balboa was born in Xeres de Bajadoz in 1474.
2 Today it is simply called Darien.
3 Sir Arthur Helps K.C.B. *The Life of Pizarro.* London, 1896. p6/59.
4 Helps. p44.
5 Gonsalvo Hernandez de Oviedo. *History of the Indies.* Published in 1535.
6 *Ibid.*
7 *Ibid.* pp60-64.
8 J.H. Parry. *The Spanish Seaborne Empire.* University of California Press Ltd. Oxford, UK 1990. p52.

CHAPTER 15

1 Charles Corn. *The Scents of Eden.* p43.
2 Samuel Eliot Morison. *The Great Explorers.* New York. 1978. p555.
3 The equivalent was calculated at $2,320,000 in gold back in 1934.
4 Morison. p558.
5 Charles Corn. *The scents of Eden.* pp44-45.
6 Morison.p563.
7 Possibly the best of several surviving copies, is the one in the Biblioteca Ambrosiana, in Milan. Ninety-two hand-written pages on paper, size 27,4 x 20,7 centimeters. Published in the first half of the sixteenth century.
8 The secret national archives were housed in the *Torre del Tombo*, Lisbon, which suffered terribly in the earthquake of 1755.
9 G.de Barros.*D'Asia*, 5 Vols. Lisbon, 1777. Antonio de Herrera. Historia *General de los hechos de los Castellanos.* 5 Vols.
10 Enrique Ruiz-Guiñazú. pp50-59.
11 Antonio Pigafetta. *Magellan's Voyage Around The World.* pp28-29.
12 Morison.p579.
13 Sinbad the sailor is a well-known story in the *Arabian Nights.* Sinbad is a Baghdad merchant who acquires great wealth by going on seven voyages. He describes these to a poor discontented porter, Hindbad, to show him that wealth can only be obtained by enterprise and personal exertion.
14 Pigafetta., p45.
15 Rolando Laguarda Frias. *El Hallazgo Del Río de la Plata Por Amerigo Vespucci en 1502.* Academia Nacional de Letras. Montevideo. Uruguay. 1982.Cap X.
16 The Nancy MS version of Pigafetta's account, as it is called, said to be the most complete of the French manu-scripts, at MS. 5,650 reads: 'That place was formerly called Cape Saincte Marye and it was thought that one could pass thence to the sea of Sur, that is to say the South Sea, but it has not been ascertained that any ships have ever discovered anything further on.'
17 Morison. pp581-586.
18 The vast arid plateau of Patagonia, with its 260,000 windswept square miles of scrub vegetation, is the largest desert of the Americas.
19 There is a discussion as to who named it. The most likely being Vespucci who is thought to have discovered it on the saint's day, 28 February 1502, though today it is generally accepted that it was named by Magellan.
20 Pigafetta: p51
21 Pigafetta, p55.
22 Pigafetta. p57.
23 Morison. pp590-597. Derek Wilson. *The Circumnavigators.* London 1989. pp24-25.
24 To Rummage signifies to clear a ship's hold, in order to examine it's contents or to remove goods or luggage from one place to another. In this case it was followed by Careening, and throwing out the stone ballast to be cleansed by the tide; scraping out the accumulated filth in the hold, sprinkling it with vinegar and then replacing the ballast. Magellan also had the hull below the waterline painted with pitch to keep out teredos.
25 Boorstin p262.

CHAPTER 16

1 South America Pilot.Vol.1, 1959, p614.
2 Fernández de Navarrete. *Disertación sobre la historia de la náutica y de las ciencias matemáticas que han contribuido a sus pro-gresos entre los españoles.* Madrid, 1846.Vol.IV, pl vii.
3 Morison. p597.
4 A cryptic inscription on a basilica at Cologne gave rise to the story of the martyrdom of Ursula and her 11,000 maidens. According to *The Golden Legend*, she was a famously beautiful British (that is to say, Breton) princess engaged against her will to marry a pagan prince of England. Ursula sought to prevent or at least delay the nuptials by insisting that ten English virgins each accompanied by 1,000 chaste handmaids convert to Christianity and join her on a pilgrimage to Rome. To her astonishment, the prince agreed. Once this holy sorority was gathered aboard ship, an Angel descended to act as pilot. In one day they sailed as far as Cologne (where the Angel secretly informed Ursula she would be martyred on the return voyage), and on the second day they reached the Eternal City. There, Pope Ciriacus warmly greeted them. Ursula told the pontiff of their impending martyrdom, and His

Holiness decided to join them on the return voyage. Because of this act of impetuosity (says the author) his name was stricken from the official list of popes. The company was made complete by the sudden arrival of Ursula's English fiancé, newly baptised and eager to die for his faith. Sure enough, when their vessel docked at Cologne, the city was under siege by the Huns. The pope, prince and all 11,000 virgins joyously disembarked, and were methodically slaughtered. For the beautiful Ursula, however, the Hun chieftain had other plans. When the Saint repulsed his odious advances, he shot her with an arrow.

Because of the excellent care she took of the young women placed in her charge, Ursula is the traditional patroness of parochial school girls and their devoted teachers, as well as of tailors and universities. She was also invoked, in early times, against the plague.

5 Francisco Albo, on *Trinidad*, was only 20 miles off in latitude and made more than a reasonable guess at longitude.

6 Joshua Slokum. *Sailing Alone Around the World*. 1907, p84.

7 The secret national archives in the Torre del Tomba, Lisbon.

8 Pigafetta. pp65, 67.

9 Not until 1616 when Le Maire and Schouten discovered Cape Horn and Schouten gave it the name of his birthplace Hoorn, in the Netherlands, was the world to know that Tierra del Fuego was independent to Antarctica.

10 Boorstin. p263.

11 Morison. p602.

12 Pigafetta. p67.

13 Morison. p601.

14 Nick Hazlewood. *Savage. The Life and Times of Jemmy Button*. Hodder & Stoughton. UK 2000. p8.

15 All trees of any stature in Tierra del Fuego are of the Nothufagus varieties. No trees introduced from the mainland or abroad grow beyond the height of their protective screens due to the violent winds and harsh climate. Malcolm L. & Gertrudis Deane. Estancia San José. Tierra del Fuego.

16 Boorstin. p264.

17 The name was given it by Cavendish in 1587.

18 Captain Joshua Slocum. *Sailing Alone Around the World*. Dover Publications. New York 1956. p106-7.

19 Nick Hazlewood. *Savage*. p6.

20 Pigafetta. p71.

21 In 1571 the Council of the Indies' permanent staff was increased by the appointment of a *cronista mayor*, whose duty was to compile, from the answers to the king's questionnaires, a general description of events in the Indies. This great work was never completed; but the *relaciones* which came into the Council in the 1570s and 1580s, many of them accompanied by maps and drawings, formed – and for historians still form – a rich and comprehensive source of information. They were turned to good account, not only by the Council but also in the composition of specialised works such as the *Historia General* of our quoted, Antonio de Herrera, who was appointed *cronista* in 1596. J.H. Parry. p196.

22 Alonso de Ercilla. *La Araucana*. Canto 1, strophe 8; First published in 1569.

23 Pigafetta. p84-85.

24 Ibid: p85.

25 Ibid. p85.

26 The island is Puka Puka, the northernmost atoll of the Tuamotu Archipelago. The center according to the latest French surveys, is on latitude 14° 50´ S. only 10 miles north of Pigafetta's, or rather Albo's, estimate.

27 Pigafetta tells it thus: 'When we wounded any of those people with our crossbow-shafts, which passed completely through their loins from one side to the other, they looked at it, pulled on the shaft now on this and now on that side, and then drew it out, with great astonishment, and so died. Others who were wounded in the breast did the same, which moved us to great compassion. Pigafetta.' p93.

28 Morison. p630.

29 Pigafetta. pp167-169.

30 Charles Corn. p49.

31 Pigafetta. p141.

32 Pigafetta. pp146-47.

33 Pigafetta. p155.

34 Derek Wilson. p27.

35 Charles Corn. p49.

36 Pigafetta. pp171-173.

CHAPTER 17

1 Morison. p647.

2 Pigafetta. p182.

3 Pigafetta states them as twenty-four.

4 Pigafetta. p181.

5 His independent sultanate has lasted to our own day.

6 Morison. p651/652.

7 Morison. p652.

8 Pigafetta. Vol.2. p65.
9 Charles Corn. p51.
10 Charles Corn. p53.
11 Who Pigafetta says was from Java, but also could have been Almanzor's daughter.
12 Charles Corn. p55.
13 Pigafetta. Vol.2. pp75-77 and Morison. p658.
14 Pigafetta. Vol.2. p103.
15 Pigafetta. Vol.2. p105.
16 Charles Corn. pp58-59.
17 Pigafetta. Vol.2. p153.
18 Pigafetta. Vol.2. p167.
19 Pigafetta. pp168-169.
20 Pigafetta. Vol.2. p183.
21 Pigafetta. Vol.2 p185.
22 Derek Wilson. p32.
23 Pigafetta. Vol.2. pp185-189.
24 Morison. p668.
25 Morison. p673.
26 *Ibid.* p673.

CHAPTER 18

1 Archivo General de la Nación, México City. Ramo de Inquisición, tomo 85, folio 92.
2 Derek Wilson. *The Circumnavigators*. M. Evans & Co. New York 1989. p36.
3 Richard Hakluyt. *The Principall Navigations, Voiages and Discoveries of the English Nation*. Reprint of the Hakluyt Society. 12 Vols. 1903-04. PN, X. p67.
4 Hakluyt, PN, IX, p452.
5 Harry Kelsey. *Sir Francis Drake. The Queen's Pirate*. Yale University Press. 1998. p43.
6 John Cummins. *Francis Drake*. St Martin's Press. New York 1995. pp29-30.
7 James A. Williamson. *The Age of Drake*. Meridian Books. USA 1965. p128.
8 Deposition of Diego de Sotomayor, in Wright, 0p.cit., p118-21, quoted by Williamson. pp138-140.
9 J.A. Williamson. pp137-140.
10 Harry Kelsey. *Sir Francis Drake*. Yale University Press. USA 1998. p70.
11 *Ibid.* p74.
12 Harry Kelsey. p70.
13 In the sixteenth century various methods were used to determine ship size, and it should come as no surprise to learn that the ship owners used the most generous method for computing their bounty claims. F.C. Prideaux Naish, *'Mystery of Tonnage'*. April 1950. The Mariner's Mirror. Quoted by Harry Kelsey. *Sir Francis Drake*. Yale University Press. USA 1998. p446.
14 Morison. pp677-78.
15 Derek Wilson. *The Circumnavigators*. M. Evans and Co. New York 1989. p39 and Morison. p678.
16 Richard Hakluyt, secretary to Sir Edward Stafford, Elizabeth's ambassador to France.
17 *The World Encompassed by Sir Francis Drake*. The account of the voyage by the Revd Francis Fletcher, flag chaplain.
18 The testimony of John Cook, quoted by Harry Kelsey. p106.
19 *Ibid.* fols 101 V-2 and p106.
20 *Ibid.* fol. 104. Quoted by Harry Kelsey. p109. A dubious account assembled half a century later by Drake's nephew claims Doughty himself chose execution over the alternatives of being marooned or sent home to face an English court. Drake, *World Encompassed*. pp30-31.
21 Cook. Quoted by Harry Kelsley. p109.
22 The custom of confession and Communion provides us with an interesting insight into religious practice at that time, as well as Drake's own in particular. The new English church had not abandoned the old private practice of confession. There were formulas for general confessions and absolutions, but provisions were also made for private confession and absolution for those souls that wanted them, very much like that of the Roman Catholic Church. Davies. *Worship and theology*. pp217-19.
23 San Juan de Anton, the Spanish captain of *Cacafuego*, later taken prisoner by Drake said that Drake 'era muy temido de su gente,' meaning he was fearful of his people.

CHAPTER 19

1 John Cooke. BL Harley MS 61, fols 107v-8.
2 Authors like James A. Williamson and Derek Wilson situate the renaming of *Pelican* taking place before the fleet left the bay of San Julián. However, Revd Fletcher, who was present at the ceremony, mentions that it took place in the Strait.
3 According to my son, Malcolm L. Deane, who lives on Tierra del Fuego a considerable time during the year, the strongest winds are recorded in the months of high summer, winter being less windy though very cold.

4 Morison. p685.

5 John Cummins. p88.

6 A latitude confirmed by the recent discovery, Wynter's account.

7 W.S.W. Vaux (ed.), *The World Encompassed by Sir Francis Drake*. Hakluyt Society. 1854. p237. As quoted by Derek
  Wilson. p43.

8 Henderson Island is at longitude 69° 05'W, latitudes 55° 32' to 55° 37.5' S.

9 Morison. p668.

10 *Ibid*. p689.

11 Williamson. pp185-6.

12 *Ibid*. p186.

13 Edward Cliffe, in Hakluyt. *World Encompassed*. p281.

14 Jerked beef, dried in the sun, which the English learned to eat in Spanish America.

15 Morison. p691.

16 Zelia Nuttall. *New Light on Drake: A Collection of Documents relating to his Voyage of Circumnavigation, 1577-1580*.
  London. Hakluyt Society Series II, Vol. XXXIV. p60.

17 Cummins. p94.

18 According to the testimony that John Drake gave in Lima in January 1587, he was twenty-two or twenty-three
  years old. He lived with his grandmother for eight years, with his mother for a year and a half, and became the
  page of Francis Drake when he was ten years old. When he began the voyage around the world, John Drake was
  fourteen or fifteen years old. SGI Patronato 266, ramo 49, fols 1-2v. As quoted in Kelsey. p443.

19 Testimony of San Juan de Antón, quoted in Sarmiento de Gamboa. *Relación*. 2-33, fol. 8.

20 It has been surmised by some historians that Antón was an Englishman, St John of Hampton (Southampton was
  named Anton on Spanish maps). However, there is not the slightest ground for suspecting he was in collusion with
  Drake, as when he had sailed from Callao, he had not even heard of Drake being in the South Sea. Williamson.
  p189.

21 San Juan de Antón, quoted in Sarmiento de Gamboa. *Relación*. no. 2-33, fol. 7-v.

22 Kelsey. p161.

23 Cornielius Lambert. 8 May 1579. AGI Patronato 266, ramo 22 fols 2v-3; John Drake, *Ibid*. ramo 54, fols 7v. As stated
  in Kelsey. p.466. Cornilius Lambert was a Flemish merchant on board the Spanish *fragata*, who later described the
  episode to the court of enquiry in Panama.

24 Zárate to Enriquez. 16 April 1597. AGI Patronato 266, ramo 19, fol.1. As quoted in Kelsey. p166 and endnote 157.

25 *Ibid*.

26 *Anonymous Narrative*, in Cummins. p.111 and Kelsey .p167.

27 Silva, AGN Inquisición 85, no.13, fol. 92. Quoted in Kelsey. p169.

28 Wilson. p47.

29 W.S.W. Vaux (ed) *The World Encompassed by Sir Francis Drake*. Hakluyt Society. 1854. p237.

30 Heaving down and graving a ship left her and her company as defenseless as a beached whale. This is why all the
  early navigators, if they were unable to do it in a friendly port, would seek out a lonely place where they were
  unlikely to be seen so as to carry it out.

31 Derek Wilson. p49.

32 *Ibid*. p49.

33 Kelsey. p214.

34 *Ibid*. p214.

35 Queen to Tremayne, 24 October 1580. PRO SP 12/143/30. fol.83 The manuscript also has the date 22 October on
  the reverse side. Taken from Kelsey. p476.

36 The original letter states: 'Confiesan que trae xx toneladas deste pais, de plata que es dos mil libras cada uno, y cinco
  caxas de oro de longitud de pie y medio y gran cantidad de perlas de mucho precio algunas.' Mendoza to the
  king, 30 October 1580, AGS Estado833, fol.35. as quoted in Kelsey. p476.

37 Mendoza to the king, 9 January 1581, BL Add.MS 26,056.C, fol.127-v. as quoted in Kelsey. p476.

38 'No las quiso tomar diciendo que no sabia con que conciencia podía aceptar cosa que ofreciese draques haviendo
  sido robado todo quanto traya.' Mendoza to the king. 9 January 1581, AGS Estado 835, fol.164.

39 Mendoza to the king. 1 March 1582, BL Add.MS 26,056. C, fol 208. Quoted from Kelsey. p476.

AFTERMATH

1 John C. Beaglehole, ed., *The Journals of Captain James Cook on his Voyage of Discovery*. Hakluyt Society, 2nd ser.
  (Cambridge 1967). ppccxxi.

2 Richard Hakluyt, *Principal Navigations*, edition of 1585, pp809.

3 Norman J.W. Thrower. *A summary of British Discovery in the Pacific between Drake and Cook*. Taken from *Sir
  Francis Drake and the Famous Voyage, 1577-1580*. University of California, Center for Medieval Studies, Los
  Angeles. 1984.

4 Ibid, pp170.

BIBLIOGRAPHY

CHAPTER 1

Jean Randier. *ommes et Naviers au Cap Horn 1616-1939.* Librairie Hachette, 1966. Arthur Barket Ltd. English translation, 1969.

Anne Willian. *Great Cooks and their Recipes. From Taillevent to Escoffier.* Pavilion Books Ltd. Great Britain 1992.

Giles Milton. *Nathaniel's Nutmeg,* London 1999.

The Diary of Samuel Pepys. Vol. IX. 1668-1669. Edited by Robert Latham & William Matthews. University of California Press. Berkley and Los Angeles. USA 1976.

J.W. Parry. *Spices.* Vol. 1.

F.Rosengarten, jr. *The Story of Spices and Spices Described,* 1969.

American Spice Trade Association. *A glossary of Spices,* 1966.

Charles Corn. *The Scents of Eden.* Kodansha International. New York 1999.

Andrew Dalby. *Dangerous Tastes. The Story of Spices.* British Museum Press. London 2000.

CHAPTER 2

Daniel J. Boorstin. *The Discoverers* (1985).

L.F. Benedetto. *Il Millioni, prima edizione integrale,* (1928). A Franco-Italian text of Marco Polo's book, generally considered very near to the lost original.

Sir Henry Yule. *Cathay and the Way Thither. Being a Collection of Medieval Notices on China,* 4 vols. (1913–16, reprinted 1967).

The travels of Marco Polo, trans. and with introduction by Ronald Latham. Penguin Books. 1958.

L. Olschki. *L'Asia di Marco Polo.*

Eileen Power. *Medieval People,* 10th ed., (1963).

Milton Rugoff. *Marco Polo's Adventures in China,* (1964).

Zvi-Dor-Ner. *Columbus and The Age of Discovery.* William Morrow & Co. New York 1991.

William McNeill. *The Rise of the West.* Maria Bellonci, translated from the Italian by Teresa Waugh *The Travels of Marco Polo.* London. 1984. Nicholas D. Kristof.

The New York Times Magazine. 6-8-99. Mike Edwards. Assistant editor.

The Adventures of Marco Polo. National Geographic Magazine. May; June; July 2001. Washington DC.

Leonardo Olschki. *Marco Polo's Precursors.* Octagon Books. New York.1972. Article by Graciela Iglesias in the Newspaper *La Nación.* Buenos Aires, 9 March 2002.

CHAPTER 3

Crosslands, R.A. and Ann Birchel, (eds). *Bronze Age Migrations in the Aegean.* Duckworth, 1973.

Johnson, F.R. *Astronomical Thought in Renaissance England.* Octagon. New York 1968.

James Burke. *Connections.* Macmillan. London 1978.

CHAPTER 4

José Saramago. *Viaje a Portugal.* Madrid. Alfaguara. Sexta edición 1998. Roberto Levillier. *América la Bien Llamada.* Vol. 1. Editorial Peuser. Buenos Aires. 1948. Daniel J.Boorstin. *The Discoverers.* Random House. New York 1983. Samuel Eliot Morison. *The Great Explorers.* Oxford University Press. New York 1978.

CHAPTER 5

Daniel J. Boorstin. *The Discoverers.* Vintage Books. USA 1985.

Roberto Levillier. *América la Bien Llamada.* Editorial Peuser. Buenos Aires 1948. 2 Vols.

Rui de Pina. *Crónica del Rey Dom Joao II.* Lisbon 1709. J.W. Blake. *Europeans in West Africa.* London 1942.

CHAPTER 6

E.R. Chamberlin. *The Bad Popes.* Dorset Press. USA 1969. Roberto Levillier. *América la Bien Llamada.* Editorial Peuser. Buenos Aires 1948. 2 Vols. Enrique Ruiz-Guiñasú. *Proas de España en el Mar Magallánico.* Peuser. Buenos Aires. 1945. Michael J.Walsh, Consultant Editor. *Lives of the Popes.* Barnes & Noble, Inc.& Salamander Books, Ltd. UK 1998. Lorenzo Camuzo. *The Voyages of Columbus.* Arnoldo Monditore.S.p.A. Milan 1991.

J.H. Parry. *The Spanish Seaborne Empire.* University of California Press.Berkley USA 1990. Jacopo da Volterra, *Diario Romano.* 1479-1484. ed. By E.Carusi. Stefano Infessura, *Diario della Città di Roma.* ed. by Oreste Tommasini. 1890. Caesar Baronius. *Annales ecclesiastici:* continued by Raynaldus. Lucca, 1738-1756. Francesco Guicciardini, *Storia d'Italia.* ed by Constantino Panigarda. Bari 1929. G. Antonelli, *Lucrezia Borgia in Ferrara.* Ferrara 1897. Ferdinand Gregorovius, *History of the City of Rome in the Middle Ages.* 1894. Trans. from the 4th German ed. by Annie Hamilton. London 1894-1902. Marino Sanuto, *La spedizione di Carlo VIII in Italia.*1883-1882. ed. by R. Fulin. Venice.

Niccoló Machiavelli, *Discorso sopra Tito Livio*, Vol.III, of Opere. Milan, 1804. Sigismondo de' Conti, *Le storie de suoi tempi dal 1475 al 1510*. Rome 1883. Johannes Burchard. *Diarium*. Vol.I-III op. cit., An.1497.
Contraalmirante Laurio H.Destéfani. *Historia Marítima Argentina*. Tomo II.

CHAPTER 7
Daniel J.Boorstin. *The Discoverers*. Random House. NC 1983. Samuel Eliot Morison. *The Great Discoverers*. Oxford University Press. NYC. 1978. Roberto Levillier. *América La Bien Llamada*. Editorial Peuser. Buenos Aires 1948. Enrique Ruiz-Guiñazú. *Proas de España en el Mar Magallánico*. Buenos Aires, Peuser.1945. Eugene Lyon. *Search for Columbus. National Geographic* magazine.Vol.181. January 1992.

CHAPTER 8
Samuel Eliot Morison.*The Great Explorers*. Oxford University Press. New York 1978. Stuart Stirling. *The Last Conquistador*. Sutton Publishing. England 1999. Zvi Dor-Ner.*Columbus and the Age of Discovery*. William Morrow & Co. New York 1991. Daniel J. Boorstin.*The Discoverers*. Random House, Inc. New York 1983. Roberto Levillier. *América la bien Llamada*.2 Vols. Editorial Peuser. Buenos Aires. 1948. Enrique Ruiz-Guiñazú.*Proas de España en el Mar Magallánico*. Editorial Peuser. Buenos Aires 1945. Pietro Martire d'Anghiera. Lorenzo Camuso. *The Voyage of Columbus*.Arnoldo Monditore, S.p.A. Milan 1991.Antonio Ballesteros Beretta. *Cristóbal Colón y el Descubrimiento de América*. Salvat. Barcelona 1945.

CHAPTER 9
Samuel Eliot Morison. *The Great Explorers*. Oxford University Press. 1978. Zvi Dor-Ner.*Columbus and the Age of Discovery*. William Morrow & Co. New York 1991. Andrés Bernáldez. *Fernando Columbus*. Encyclopaedia Británica.1959. Bartolomé de las Casas. *Brevísima relación de la destrucción de las Indias Occidentales*. Lorenzo Camusso.*The Voyages of Columbus*. Arnoldo Monditore, S.p.A. Milan.1991.Translation by Elizabeth Leister. Rex & Thea Rientes. *The Voyages of Columbus*. London.1970.Antonio Ballesteros Beretta. *Cristóbal Colón y el Descubrmiento de América*. Salvat. Barcelona 1945.

CHAPTER 10
Roberto Levillier, *América la bien Llamada*. 2 Vols. Editorial Peuser. Buenos Aires 1948.
Daniel J. Boorstin. *The Discoverers*. Random House. NYC. 1983.
Samuel E. Morison. *The Great Explorers*. Oxford University Press. 1978.
J.S. Elliot. *The Old World And The New.*
Enrique Ruiz-Guiñazú. *Proas de España en el Mar Magallánico*. Editorial Peuser. Buenos Aires 1945. Lorenzo Camuso. *The Voyages of Columbus*. Arnoldo Monditore, S.p.A., Milan 1991.
Translation by Elizabeth Leister.Antonio Ballesteros Beretta. *Cristóbal Colón y el Descubrimiento de América*. Salvat. Barcelona 1945.
Rex and Thea Rientes. *The Voyages of Columbus*. London 1970.

CHAPTER 11
Salvador de Madariaga. *Christopher Columbus*. Connecticut 1979.
Gianni Granzotto. *Christopher Columbus*. New York 1985.
Benjamin Keen. *The Life of the Admiral Christopher Columbus by his son Ferdinand*. New Jersey 1959.
Enrique Ruiz-Guiñazu. *Proas de España en el mar Magallánico*. Editorial Peuser. Buenos Aires 1945.
Charles Duff. *The Truth About Columbus*. London 1936.
Samuel E.Morison. *The Great Explorers*. New York 1978.
Daniel J. Boorstin. *The Discoverers*. New York 1985.
Samuel E. Morison. *Christopher Columbus, Admiral of the Ocean Sea*. Oxford University Press, 1942.
Rex and Thea Rientes. *The Voyages of Columbus*. New York 1989.
Lorenzo Camusso. *The Voyages of Columbus*. Milan 1991.

CHAPTER 12
Charles Corn. *The Scents of Eden. A History of The Spice Trade*. Kodansha International. New York 1998.
Roberto Levillier. *America la Bien Llamada*. 2 Vols. Editorial Peuser. Buenos Aires 1943.
C.R. Boxer.The Portuguese Seaborne Empire.
Jaime Cortesão,A Expansão Dos Portogueses No Periodo Henriquino.
Daniel J. Boorstin. *The Discoverers*.
Samuel Eliot Morison.*The Great Explorers*.

CHAPTER 13
Daniel J.Boorstin. *The Discoverers*.
Samuel Eliot Morison. *The European Discovery of America.The Southern Voyages*. New York. Oxford University Press. 1974.
Samuel Eliot Morison. *The Great Explorers*. New York. Oxford University Press 1978.

J.H. Elliott. *The Old World And The New.* Roberto Levillier. *America la Bien Llamada.* 2 Vols. Editorial Peuser. 1948. Buenos Aires.

Ricardo Fontana. *Il Brasile di Amerigo Vespuci.* Editora Universidade de Brasilia. Brazil 1994.

Enrique Ruiz-Guiñazú. *Proas de España en el Mar Magallánico.* Editorial Peuser. Buenos Aires 1945.

Virginia Carreño. *Estancias y Estancieros del Río de la Plata.* Editorial Claridad. Buenos Aires 1994.

Rolando A.Laguarda Trías. *El Hallazgo Del Río de la Plata Por Amerigo Vespuci en 1502.* Academia Nacional de Letras. Montevideo. Uruguay 1982.

Luigi Avonto. *Operación Nuevo Mundo. Amerigo Vespuci y el enigma de América.* Instituto Italiano di Cultura. Caracas.Venezuela 1999.

Zaragoza. *Historia General de las Indias.* 1555.

Lorenzo Camusso. *The Voyages of Columbus.*

Arnoldo Monditore, S.p.A., Milan 1991.Translation by Elizabeth Leister.

Antonio Ballesteros Beretta. *Cristóbal Colón y el Descubrimiento de América.* Salvat. Barcelona 1945.

Rex and Thea Rientes. *The Voyages of Columbus.* London 1970.

George Tyler Northrup. *Vespuci. Reprints, Texts and Studies.* Vol. 5. Lettera to Pier Soderini, translated with introduction and notes. Princeton University Press. USA. 1916.

CHAPTER 14

Sir Arthur Helps K.C.B. *The Life of Pizarro.* London 1896.

Daniel Boorstin. *The Discoverers.* Random House. NYC. 1983.

Gonsalvo Hernández de Oviedo. *History of The Indies.* Madrid 1535.

J.H. Parry. *The Discovery of The Sea.* University of California Press. 1974.

J.H. Parry. *The Spanish Seaborne Empire.* University of California Press Ltd. Oxford, UK 1990.

John F. Meigs. *The Story of Seamen.* 1924.

Arthur P. Newton. *The Great Age of Discovery.* 1932.

J.H. Parry. *The age of Reconnaisance.* University of California Press 1981.

CHAPTER 15

Antonio Pigafetta. *Magellan's Voyage Around the World.* The original text of the Anbrosian MS. Milan. With English translation by James Alexander Robertson. USA. 1906.

G. De Barros. *D'Asia.* 5 Vols.

Antonio de Herrera. *Historia de los Hechos Castellanos.* 5 Vols.

Derek Wilson. *The Circumnavigators.* London. 1989.

Enrique Ruiz-Guiñazú. *Proas de España en el Mar Magallánico.* Editorial Peuser. Buenos Aires 1945.

Daniel Boorstin. *The Discoverers.* Random House. NYC 1983.

Samuel Eliot Morison. *The Great Explorers.* Oxford University Press. NYC. 1978.

Charles Corn. *The Scents of Eden.* Kodansha Americana. NY USA. 1998.

J.H. Parry. *The Spanish Seaborne Empire.* University of California Press Ltd. Oxford UK 1990.

J.H.Parry. *Age of Reconnaissance: Discovery, Exploration, & Settlement.*

Rolando A. Laguarda Trías. *El Hallazgo Del Río de la Plata Por Amerigo Vespuci en 1502.* Academia Nacional de Letras. Montevideo, Uruguay 1982. Contraalmirante (RS) Laurio H. Destéfani. História Marítima Argentina. Tomo II. Cap.VII.

La Expedición de Magallanes. Armada Argentina. Departamento de Estudios Históricos Navales. Buenos Aires.

CHAPTER 16

Antonio Pigafetta. *Magellan's Voyage Around the World.* The original text of the Ambrosian MS. Milan. With English translations by James Alexander Robertson. USA 1906.

G. De Barros. *D'Asia.* 5 Vols.

Derek Wilson. *The Circumnavigators.* London 1989.

Enrique Ruiz-Guiñazú. *Proas de España en el Mar Magallánico.* Editorial Peuser. Buenos Aires. 1945.

Daniel Boorstin. *The Discoverers.* Random House. NYC. 1983.

Samuel Eliot Morison. *The Great Explorers.* Oxford University Press. NYC 1978.

Charles Corn. *The Scents of Eden.* Kodansha Americana. N.Y. USA.1998.

J.H. Parry. *The Spanish Seaborne Empire.* University of California Press Ltd. Oxford, UK 1990.

J.H. Parry. *Age of Reconnaissance: Discovery, Exploration & Settlement.* University of California Press. 1963.

Rolando A. Laguarda Trías. *El Hallazgo del Río de la Plata Por Amerigo Vespuci en 1502.* Academia Nacional de Letras. Montevideo. Uruguay 1982.

Joshua Slokum. *Sailing Alone Around the World.* 1907.

J.C.Beagle. *The Exploration of the Pacific.* London 1934.

F.H.H. Guillemard. *The Life of Ferdinand Magellan and the first circumnavigation of the Globe, 1480-1521.* London 1980.

Alonso de Ercilla. 'La Araucana'. Canto 1. strophe 8. 1569.

Fernández de Navarrete. *Disertación de la historia náutica y de las ciencias matemáticas que han contribuido a sus progresos entre los españoles.* Madrid 1846.

Contraalmirante (RS) Laurio H. Destéfani. *História Marítima Argentina*. Tomo II. Cap. VII. *La Expedición de Magallanes*.
    Armada Argentina. Departamento de Estudios Históricos Navales. Buenos Aires.

CHAPTER 17

Antonio Pigafetta. *Magellan's Voyage Around the World*. The original text of the Ambrosian MS. Milan. With English
    translations by James Alexander Robertson. USA 1906.
Samuel Eliot Morison. *The Great Explorers*. Oxford University Press. New York 1978.
Charles Corn. *The scents of Eden*. Kodansha International. New York 1998. Derek Wilson. *The Circumnavigators*.
    M. Evans and Company. New York 1989.
Enrique Ruiz-Guiñazú. *Proas de España en el Mar Magallánico*. Ediciones Peuser. Buenos Aires 1945.
J.H. Parry. *The Spanish Seaborn Empire*. University of California Press Ltd. Oxford, UK 1990.
J.H. Parry. *Age of Reconnaissance: Discovery, Exploration & Settlement*. 1963.
Daniel J. Boorstin. *The Discoverers*. Random House Inc. New York 1983.
Contraalmirante (RS) Laurio H. Destéfani. História Marítima Argentina. Tomo II. Cap. VII. *La Expedición de
    Magallanes*. Armada Argentina. Departamento de Estudios Históricos Navales. Buenos Aires.

CHAPTER 18

Harry Kelsey. *Sir Francis Drake. The Queen's Pirate*. Yale University Press. USA 1998.
Samuel Eliot Morison. *The Great Explorers*. Oxford University Press. New York 1978.
Derek Wilson. *The Circumnavigators*. M. Evans & Co. New York 1989.
James A. Wilson. *The Age of Drake*. Meridian Books. New York 1965.
Richard Hakluyt. *The Principall Navigations, Voiages and Discoveries of the English Nation*. Reprint of The Hakluyt
    Society. 12 Vols. 1903.
The manuscript of Francis Fletcher. Flag Chaplain to Drake's expedition, as written by Richard Hakluyt.
The manuscript of John Cooke. Mexico. Archivo General de la Nación. Corsarios Franceses e Ingleses en la
    Inquisición de la Nueva España. 1943.
Antonio de Herrera. *Descripción de las Indias occidentales*. En tres partes. Valladolid 1612.
The Manuscript of John Cooke. Harry Kelsey. 1999.
David B. Quinn; C.E. Armstrong, and R.A. Skelton. *The Primary Hakluyt Handbook*. ed. David B. Quinn. Corsarios
    Franceses e Ingleses en la Inquisición de la Nueva España. México. Archivo General de la Nación. 1943.
Antonio de Herrera. *Descripción de las Indias Occidentales*. En tres partes. Valladolid. 1612.
Horton Davies. Worship and Theology in England from Crammer to Hooker, 1534-1603. Princeton University
    Press. 1970.

CHAPTER 19

Harry Kelsey. *Sir Francis Drake. The Queen's Pirate*. Yale University Press. USA 1998.
Samuel Eliot Morison. *The Great Explorers*. Oxford University Press. New York 1978.
Derek Wilson. *The Circumnavigators*. M. Evans & Co. New York 1989.
James A. Wilson. *The Age of Drake*. Meridian Books. New York 1965.
Richard Hakluyt. *The Prinvipall Navigations, Voiages and Discoveries of the English Nation*. Reprint of the Hakluyt
    Society. 12 Vols. 1903.
The Manuscript of Francis Fletcher, Flag Chaplain to Drake's Expedition, as written by Richard Hakluyt. John Cooke.
    B.L. Hartley. MS 61.
Malcolm L. Deane's information on Tierra del Fuego.
John Cummins. *Francis Drake*. St Martin's Press. New York 1955.
W.S.W. Vaux (ed.) *The World Encompassed by Sir Francis Drake*. Hakluyt Society. 1854.
Edward Cliff's Story in Hakluyt's *World Encompassed*.
Zelia Nuttall. *New Light on Drake*. Hakluyt Society. London. Sarmiento de Gamboa. *Relación*.

INDEX

If you are interested in purchasing
other books published by Tempus, or in case you have
difficulty finding any Tempus books in your local bookshop, you can also place
orders directly through our website

www.tempus–publishing.com